THE TRAGEDY *of* BENEDICT ARNOLD

ALSO BY JOYCE LEE MALCOLM

Peter's War: A New England Slave Boy and the American Revolution

Guns and Violence: The English Experience

The Struggle for Sovereignty: Seventeenth-Century English Political Tracts, 2 vols.

To Keep and Bear Arms: The Origins of an Anglo-American Right

Caesar's Due: Loyalty and King Charles, 1642-1646

The Scene of the Battle, 1775

THE TRAGEDY *of* BENEDICT ARNOLD

★ ★ ★

An American Life

JOYCE LEE MALCOLM

PEGASUS BOOKS

NEW YORK LONDON

THE TRAGEDY OF BENEDICT ARNOLD

Pegasus Books, Ltd.
148 W 37th Street, 13th Floor
New York, NY 10018

First Pegasus Books cloth edition May 2018

Interior design by Maria Fernandez

ISBN: 978-1-68177-737-5

10 9 8 7 6 5 4 3 2 1

Printed in the United States of America

Distributed by W. W. Norton & Company, Inc.

To My Children
Mark, Lisa Arienne and George
With Love

Honor is like an island.
Steep and without shore:
They who once leave,
Can never return.

—Nicholas Boileau cited as a reminder by
Capt. Johann Ewald, *Diary of the American War*, May 17, 1781

CONTENTS

INTRODUCTION   xi

ONE: THE PRICE OF HONOR   1

TWO: GREAT EXPECTATIONS   11

THREE: DESCENT   22

FOUR: THE FORTUNES OF WAR   29

FIVE: TAKING CHARGE   41

SIX: SMOOTH AND CHOPPY WATERS   47

SEVEN: LOVE, MARRIAGE, DUELS, AND HONOR   61

EIGHT: "MY COUNTRY CALLED"   74

NINE: THE RACE TO SEIZE FORTS   84

TEN: BURIED IN THE PUBLIC CALAMITY   99

ELEVEN: HONOR IN A "DIREFUL HOWLING WILDERNESS"   116

TWELVE: A FIERCE ATTACK, A WINTER SIEGE   129

THIRTEEN: DEFENDING THE LAKES   146

FOURTEEN: DON'T TREAD ON ME   162

FIFTEEN: "BESMIRCHED HONOR" 175

SIXTEEN: SAVAGE WARFARE 185

SEVENTEEN: DEFENDING NEW YORK, AGAIN 202

EIGHTEEN: THE FATAL BLOW 216

NINETEEN: THE WAGES OF VICTORY 226

TWENTY: THE EYE OF THE STORM 241

TWENTY-ONE: THE COURT-MARTIAL 261

TWENTY-TWO: BECOMING GUSTAVUS MONK 277

TWENTY-THREE: TREASON 301

TWENTY-FOUR: BRIDGES BURNED 314

TWENTY-FIVE: AFTERWORD 339

FINAL THOUGHTS 355

ACKNOWLEDGMENTS 361

ENDNOTES 363

INDEX 397

INTRODUCTION

". . . I have suffered, in seeing the fair fabric of reputation, which I have been with so much danger and toil raising since the present war, undermined by those, whose posterity (as well as themselves) will feel the blessed effects of my efforts. . ."

—Benedict Arnold, summation at
his court-martial, January 1780

"Treason! Treason! Black as hell—That a man so high on the list of fame should be guilty as Arnold, must be attributed not only to original sin, but actual transgression. . . . We were all astonishment, each peeping at his next neighbor to see if any treason was hanging about him: nay, we even descended to a critical examination of ourselves . . ."

—Adjutant General Colonel Alexander Scammell,
eight days after Arnold's flight

Two centuries after Benedict Arnold's death the most infamous man in American history remains a two-dimensional caricature in the minds of most Americans: wicked, self-serving, and greedy. Numerous books have now cast his young wife Peggy as equally evil, an Eve tempting her husband into treason. Yet Arnold repeatedly risked his life and sacrificed his fortune for the patriot cause. As for Peggy, the charges against her are based on flimsy evidence contradicted by her own actions, by eyewitness accounts, and by the historical record. Replacing the cardboard cutouts that pass for historical portraits of Arnold and Peggy with a more authentic picture makes their actions, if still culpable in Arnold's case, at least more understandable; exonerates Peggy; and exposes the bitter animosities within the patriot party. It also helps us make sense of the wild fury that greeted Arnold's betrayal, bringing us closer to the people and frightfulness of that time. That task is the aim of this book.

Arnold was a national hero before he abandoned the patriot cause, and no wonder. He has been reckoned the most brilliant officer on either side of the Revolutionary War. He had that rare ability to inspire men to follow him into the face of death, even when, as at the decisive battle of Saratoga, he was stripped of military command. J. W. Fortescue, author of a classic study of the British army, described Arnold as possessing "all the gifts of a great commander. To boundless energy and enterprise he united quick insight into a situation, sound strategic instinct, audacity of movement, wealth of resource, a swift and unerring eye in action, great personal daring, and true magic of leadership."[1]

He was courageous, resourceful, and, like most men of his time and rank, keenly jealous of his personal honor. When he joined the British side he forfeited that honor forever. Americans greeted the news of his betrayal with outrage, burning him in effigy, while the British never fully trusted him. His was a tragic fall from fame to infamy. We are left wondering why Arnold abandoned the cause for which he sacrificed his health and wealth, and why—when so many others did the same, or prudently kept in contact with the British, or simply abandoned the patriot cause—Arnold's treason has been branded singularly egregious. Contrary to prevailing myths numerous prominent Americans remained neutral, profiteered on the war, preferred the comparative safety of politics to the battlefield, or returned to their families and businesses when their commissions in the Continental Army proved dangerous and thankless. Yet Arnold alone bears the mark of Cain.

Are these questions worth answering? Isn't it enough to know that whatever else he accomplished, the man was a traitor? In the early nineteenth century when Lewis Burd Walker, a descendant of Arnold's second wife, approached publishers about writing a book about Arnold, he was assured no one would want to read about the traitor. Americans enjoy reading about the patriots of the founding era, as an ever growing library of books about them attests. Despite publishers rejecting Walker's proposal, some books have also been written about "the traitor." These and other studies that do grapple with why he committed treason and why his actions were deemed so egregious have arrived at various answers.

Arnold's contemporaries and earliest biographers insisted that he was a vicious individual—period. Jared Sparks, later president of Harvard, set the tone for this wholesale blackening of Arnold's entire life. Sparks finds no tale of Arnold's sinfulness as a child too bizarre to be believed. His *The Life and Treason of Benedict Arnold*, published in 1835, informed readers that one of Benedict Arnold's "earliest amusements" was to snatch baby birds from their nests in order "to maim and mangle" them "in sight of the old ones, that he might be diverted by their cries."[2] This naughty boy also enjoyed strewing broken glass in a nearby schoolyard so the children "would cut their feet in coming from the school." For Sparks, only the timely death of Arnold's devout mother relieved her "from the anguish of witnessing her son's career of ambition without virtue, of glory tarnished with crime, and of depravity ending in infamy and ruin."[3] Here was a thoroughly bad child destined to mature into a very bad man. Arnold's military achievements had already been dismissed by his personal enemies as merely self-serving, reckless bravado.

Charles Royster, in *A Revolutionary People at War*, writes that Arnold's contemporaries "saw more than a criminal in Arnold—they saw a freak."[4] "They did not try hard to devise new ways to thwart potential traitors," because "there could be only one Arnold and when his country talked about him, that is what they said—over and over, in exhaustive detail and fervent imagery—there could be only one Arnold."[5]

This indictment begs the question why Arnold had behaved so heroically and generously. Was the dishonorable treatment he received over and over again from Congress and his rivals mere slights any right-thinking man should have ignored? Or were his attackers, especially those in Congress, anxious to diminish a popular general, frightened Arnold might copy Oliver Cromwell and seize power? Why the focus on Arnold's supposed flaws anyway? Several later authors have presented a more balanced account, and I am greatly indebted to their work.[6] Isaac Newton Arnold—a distant relation—published *The Life of Benedict Arnold; His Patriotism and His Treason* in 1880. He hoped, "The time may come . . . when there will mingle with his condemnation that infinite pity . . . that a nature so heroic and with a record so brilliant, should have been driven, by a sense of bitter wrong and the violence of his passions, to a crime so inexcusable."[7] More than a century later, in 1990, Willard Sterne Randall's massive biography, *Benedict Arnold: Patriot and Traitor* appeared. Seven years afterward James Kirby Martin produced an equally massive biography, *Benedict Arnold: Revolutionary Hero: An American Warrior Reconsidered*, that unfortunately ends without covering Arnold's growing defection, the influence, if any, of his young wife Margaret Shippen, his treason, and its aftermath. Dave R. Palmer pairs Arnold's life with that of Washington in *George Washington and Benedict Arnold: A Tale of Two Patriots*, as does Nathaniel Philbrick in *Valiant Ambition: George Washington, Benedict Arnold, and the Fate of the American Revolution*. Apart from Philbrick none of these authors had the advantage of Russell M. Lea's invaluable collection of Arnold's war correspondence published in 2008, or knew of the cache of Arnold's papers recently discovered in Quebec. None has reevaluated the role of his wife in the treason.

No less than seven recent books focus on the supposed wicked machinations of his beautiful young wife, Margaret Shippen.[8] This trend began in 1941 when Carl Van Doren, in his *Secret History of the American Revolution*, claimed to have found convincing evidence she was an active promoter of his defection, overturning the long-held belief in her innocence. The daughter of a distinguished, neutral Philadelphia family is now viewed as having inveigled her husband into joining the British cause. Peggy is now nearly as infamous as her husband. However, my reexamination of Van Doren's evidence, along with research into Peggy's behavior, presents a compelling case for her innocence. Good story as these new books tell, they have damned an innocent woman. As George Washington, Alexander Hamilton, Peggy's family, those who knew her believed, she was not guilty.

A book about Arnold's life and times is well worth bringing to a wider public because the story it tells is so illuminating. It provides a keener understanding of a talented and flawed man and the meaning of loyalty in the revolutionary context, but it also exposes the bitter tensions within the revolutionary cause and the impact of what was a civil war on the lives of ordinary people. Beyond its historical value Arnold's story is a thrilling one. *The Tragedy of Benedict Arnold* casts a wide net, treating Arnold's personal and public life and the lively cast of characters that peopled his world. The goal is to recover, as far as possible, both the man and his time, and to improve our understanding of both. The aim is not to condone Arnold but to understand why a man who had risked everything for the patriot cause took that desperate decision to turn against it, earning not the success he hoped for, but lasting opprobrium.

The book opens at the battle of Saratoga. Arnold, stripped of command by General Horatio Gates, bursts from his tent and leads the successful charge against the British but is grievously wounded. He is carried from the field, and General Gates, who never set foot on it during the fighting, takes credit for the spectacular victory. When Arnold returns home after a painful hospital stay the narrative then turns to Arnold's childhood. That once happy period ended abruptly when his father's business, and with it Benedict's expectations, collapsed. Benedict was withdrawn from his boarding school and returned home to suffer the humiliation of an indebted and increasingly drunken father. He was apprenticed to kindly relatives and managed to restore his personal and family standing. But this background sets the stage for his lifelong struggle for honor and respect. The sense of shame the family suffered in the confines of a small Connecticut town and the eighteenth-century concept of personal honor would become a crucial facet of the young man's life.

The biography deals with Arnold's personal and professional life, the looming political crisis, and Arnold's extraordinary military adventures—his storming of Ticonderoga, his harrowing trek through the wilderness of Maine to attack Canada, his amazing naval battle with ships he built against a powerful British fleet on Lake Champlain that saved New York, his relief of Fort Stanwix in 1777, his crucial leadership at Saratoga. These successes took place amid the unremitting attacks of personal enemies and the suspicion congressmen had of their own army officers, fearful one might become another Cromwell. To prevent this, Congress micromanaged the army and court-martialed officers on the slightest pretext. As a protégé of Washington and General Schuyler, and a popular hero, Arnold was attacked by those hostile to his patrons.

The Tragedy of Benedict Arnold tracks Arnold's growing dismay and disaffection. As commander of Philadelphia he coped with the constant complaints of the radical Pennsylvania government and Congress's neglect and disrespect. These culminated in his court-martial and conviction in the bitter winter of 1779. Finally, the book recounts Arnold's approach to the British, the unfolding of his plot, the capture and execution of the much-admired spymaster, John André, and Arnold's subsequent treatment by the British commanders. The sad fortunes of his lovely wife Peggy are detailed as she seeks to remain with her family in Philadelphia but is ordered to join her husband in exile by the Pennsylvania government.

The book follows Arnold and Peggy's life after his flight. The British immediately tested Arnold's conversion to their cause by sending him with a small troop of British and German soldiers on forays first into Virginia, home of his devoted friend and commander, George Washington, and then into Connecticut, his home state. The frustrating final years of Arnold and Peggy's life in England and Canada, and final thoughts, conclude the book.

Why has Arnold's treason been treated so particularly viciously? Perhaps his contemporaries' singling him out for the harshest opprobrium is not surprising. Once the revolution's heroic general defected, it served the interest of the patriot party and everyone whose devotion was somewhat suspect to distinguish Arnold from his former colleagues and from all those who remained quietly ambivalent. If Arnold was uniquely wicked everyone else was exonerated. Eliot Cohen, in *Conquered into Liberty*, suggests an explanation for this insistence on Arnold the villain:

> The demonization of Arnold served a rhetorical purpose
> in a new United States struggling to establish its identity,
> and perhaps in a post–Civil War United States struggling
> to recover its unity. But the price . . . is unwarrantable and
> unjustly to forget or exculpate, the circumstances and
> individuals that drove him to betray his country, and to
> reduce a tragic figure to a mere caricature.[9]

To understand this complex man it is necessary to examine his personal and public life and the people who shared his time and place. It is necessary to pierce the memoirs of those contemporaries and historians who viewed Arnold through the lens of his defection and betrayal and instead see events as they happened.

Various aspects of the cultural world of late eighteenth-century America deserve attention and explanation in advance. For Arnold and most men of that era personal honor and reputation was of preeminent importance. This was particularly true for men born into the upper class but perhaps even more for those, like Arnold, aspiring to regain that status. Insults or slights to one's honor or to the reputation of loved ones demanded to be challenged, even at the risk of death. Failure to do so likely meant disgrace. The Arnold family had been a leading family in the early history of Rhode Island. Arnold's immediate family's fortunes, so promising in his youth, suffered a catastrophic downturn as his father's business collapsed and the senior Arnold became a public drunkard and debtor. When Benedict was abruptly recalled from the boarding school that was preparing him for entrance to Yale University, and enrolled as an apothecary apprentice, he dedicated himself to restoring his family's social and economic status, and along with it his personal self-esteem and honor. This was an uphill struggle in a small Connecticut town whose residents kept a watchful eye on each other. Further, despite the opportunity America offered immigrants, class bigotry crossed the Atlantic with the settlers. America's elite college-educated professionals and landowners often looked down on merchants, even successful ones.

Arnold's problems with Congress were to some extent a reflection of the long-standing British prejudice against the military profession, especially professional armies. William Blackstone, in his bestseller, *Commentaries on the Laws of England*, published just before the American Revolution, insisted, "in a land of liberty it is extremely dangerous to make a distinct order of the profession of arms."[10] Blackstone counseled Englishmen to look upon professional soldiers "as temporary excrescences bred out of the distemper of the State, and not as any part of the permanent and perpetual laws of the Kingdom."[11] The citizen militia, by contrast, was considered honorable, virtuous, and safe, or as the American Second Amendment would put it, "the necessary security of a free state." Arnold started out in the Connecticut militia but joined the newly formed Continental Army and remained there. Patriots like John Adams had no patience with the slights America's army officers felt when passed over for promotion. He famously likened them to monkeys scrambling after nuts. Yet Adams and other politicians, members of Congress and state assemblies, were equally, if not more, jealous of their prerogatives. Congress micromanaged its army, fearful of the possibility it might produce a popular general who would seize power and send the delegates packing. Thus the endless second guessing by those Fortescue labeled "the lawyers and praters at Philadelphia," hauling before a court-martial any officer who abandoned a fort or fell victim to an ambush.[12] Although Congress failed to pay Arnold and his men for years on end, the delegates insisted he account for every penny advanced for a campaign. George Washington had enormous patience with such meddling, but Arnold lacked the commander's diplomatic gift. On the contrary, his brusque manner with militia officers he felt were behaving in a cowardly or undisciplined fashion earned him a growing list of tenacious enemies.

The patriots themselves were divided politically between moderates and radicals. This division became so bitter it led to a shootout in Philadelphia between moderates such as James Wilson and the militia of the state's radical Executive Council. Even Lafayette was dismayed at factions within the Continental Congress, writing Washington, "There are open dissentions in Congress; parties who hate one another as much as the common enemy."[13] Once exposed the ugliness and division buried beneath the surface of the patriot side gives a different cast to Arnold's experience and to our sense of the war.

This book begins just as Arnold receives a grievous wound to his leg as he is leading the decisive assault on the British lines at the battle of Saratoga. A large force of British and German soldiers,

Canadians, and Indians under General John Burgoyne had advanced from Canada in 1777, part of an elaborate plan to conquer New York State. Washington had sent Arnold north to bolster the forces trying to stop the British army. On the day of the crucial battle Arnold had been confined to his tent by his angry commander, General Gates. Unwilling to be a bystander at so critical a time he galloped onto the battlefield to the cheers of the men. Without any official command, Arnold led them to victory, grievously wounded in the process. The narrative then goes back to his childhood and chapter by chapter follows the dramatic triumphs and bitter frustrations of his life. The final chapters trace his decision to abandon the American cause, his discovery and flight, and the tragedy this brought upon him and his entire family.

Arnold's is a life worth retelling. It has been more than ten years since Martin's incomplete biography was published. It is time to put Arnold's life and tragedy in a more complete and nuanced context, one accessible to a larger audience. How else can we understand the sole memorial to Arnold's contribution to the American cause, a stone carving of a boot, erected in 1887 at the Saratoga battle site? It is the only American war memorial that does not bear the name of its honoree, instead symbolizing Arnold's leg, shattered leading the American army to victory at Saratoga. The dedication on the back of the marker reads:

> In memory of the most brilliant soldier of the Continental Army who was Desperately wounded on this spot the sally port of BURGOYNES GREAT WESTERN REDOUBT 7th October, 1777 winning for his countrymen the Decisive battle of the American Revolution and for himself the rank of Major General.

THE TRAGEDY *of* BENEDICT ARNOLD

ONE

The Price of Honor

*". . . if the conflict at Saratoga was one of the great battles
which have influenced the fate of nations; if this was the
decisive contest of the Revolution; if it was fought by Arnold,
and his blood contributed to the victory, should he not have
the credit, so dearly earned? Give all honor to Schuyler; give
to Morgan, Stark, Dearborn, and others, all praise as brave
partisans, but let history be just and truthful, and record that
Benedict Arnold was the hero of the campaign of 1777, and
of the battles of Saratoga."*

—Isaac Newton Arnold,
The Life of Benedict Arnold

As Benedict Arnold and his horse fell, Captain Dearborn
called out, asking where Arnold had been hit. "In the same
leg," Arnold answered, "I wish it had been my heart."[1] It
was late afternoon on October 7, 1777 at Bemis Heights, the second

1

and final battle of Saratoga. The American forces were fighting desperately to stop General John Burgoyne's troops from breaking through and moving south to take the city of Albany, on their way to separating New York from New England. The British were just as desperate, their dwindling force needing a victory before winter. After hours of fierce fighting Arnold discovered the British sally point, the spot where their lines opened for retreating soldiers, the point where the British army was most vulnerable. He immediately rallied the men and led a furious charge at it. The German defenders panicked, turning to take one final volley. One bullet hit Arnold's splendid, dark horse, killing the powerful animal. Arnold was a superb rider. Other horses had been shot under him in other battles, in some battles two horses had been shot. As this horse fell though, a musket ball struck Arnold's left leg shattering the bone just above the knee. It was the same leg injured a year earlier during the unsuccessful assault on Quebec. Arnold shouted to his men as he fell, "Rush on, my brave boys, rush on.!"[2] And rush on they did, streaming through the British embankment. The day would be theirs.

Arnold waved off the first officers who rushed to help him. A surgeon glancing at his injury feared his leg might need to be amputated.[3] Arnold would listen to "no such d—d nonsense," insisting "if that was all the surgeon had to say, the men should lift him upon his horse, and he would see the action through." It was a wounded Hessian soldier who had managed to lift himself up and shoot Arnold. John Redman, an American private, had seen Arnold fall and rushed to bayonet the German. But Arnold shouted to Redman from the ground where he lay helpless and in pain, "Don't hurt him, he did but his duty, he is a fine fellow."[4] Major John Armstrong, whom Gates had sent to intercept Arnold caught up with him now to return him to headquarters. Arnold would have none of it. In the end it was the men of Asa Bray's Connecticut militia company, proud the fighting general was one of their own, who placed him gently on a litter and carried their bleeding hero to the field hospital. Afterward he had endured the three-day trip down the Hudson River to Albany fifty miles away, where the military hospital was already overflowing with injured and dying men of both armies.

While Arnold lay in excruciating pain in the military hospital in Albany, General Horatio Gates, who had never set foot on the battlefield that day, was negotiating the terms of surrender and taking credit for the victory. Gates was jealous and vindictive, especially since Arnold was the hero of the battle at Freeman's Farm in September, the first phase of what was to be the battle of Saratoga. Gates had stripped Arnold of his command and, when Arnold decided to yield to the entreaties of other officers and men and remain in the camp, Gates confined him to his tent. But even without any command Arnold could not remain idle while the men were fighting and had galloped off to join them. It was Gates who chose to remain in his tent that day.

Benedict Arnold was just thirty-six. He was solidly built. As an old soldier who served with him at Bemis Heights put it, "there wasn't any waste timber in him."[5] His complexion was ruddy from outdoor living since childhood, his height middling, his hair dark, his eyes gray. "Dark Eagle," an Indian guide had dubbed him during the harrowing trek through the Maine wilderness to Quebec. Before the war he was a successful Connecticut merchant, captaining his own ships in the Atlantic trade. Much of his fortune was now gone, spent on the patriot cause or ruined by the war. The merchant turned soldier had turned out to be a military genius: brave, inspiring, insightful, driven as were so many men of his generation, with the quest for honor and jealous of personal reputation. His exploits had made him one of the revolutionary army's best-known heroes, a legend. The troops loved him. "He was our fighting general," that old soldier explained, "and a bloody fellow he was. He didn't care for nothing; he'd ride right in. It was 'Come on boys'—'twasn't 'Go, boys'. He was as brave a man as ever lived."[6] Arnold was brusque though, and dogged by a growing

and tenacious string of enemies who accused him of being reckless, greedy, self-serving, and dishonest. The greater his fame, the
greater their determination to destroy his reputation. The long
agonizing months in the military hospital in Albany gave him
ample time to reflect on where all his courage and zeal for the
patriot cause had brought him.

Albany with its three hundred houses was 160 miles north of New
York City.[7] Some one thousand sick and wounded men were crowded
into the city. The substantial military hospital there, built during the
French and Indian War, could accommodate five hundred patients in
forty wards. The old Dutch church and several private homes were
also turned into hospitals.[8] The injured foreign soldiers were under
the care and management of their own surgeons. Dr. James Thacher,
a surgeon with the American army at Albany, was present at some
of the more serious operations and praised the English surgeons for
their skill and dexterity. However, he found some of the German
doctors "the most uncouth and clumsy operators I ever witnessed,
and appear to be destitute of all sympathy and tenderness toward
the suffering patient."[9] Like military doctors before and since, Dr.
Thacher found the long hours and terrible wounds "a fine field for
professional improvement. Amputating limbs, trepanning fractured
skulls, and dressing the most formidable wounds, have familiar-
ized my mind to scenes of woe." Still Dr. Thacher had a kind heart.
"A military hospital," he judged, "peculiarly calculated to afford
examples for profitable contemplation and to interest our sympathy
and commiseration." Dr. Thacher described the grim atmosphere
in that hospital where Arnold languished month after weary month.
The hospital made for odd bedfellows. Arnold was placed next to
British Major John Dyke Acland, whose troops had battled the Continentals so obstinately on Bemis Heights.[10]

The surgeons wanted to amputate Arnold's leg. That was a
sensible precaution. A badly wounded limb could putrefy, get
gangrenous, and result in death. But if his leg were amputated

above the knee Arnold would be a cripple for the rest of his life. He was a widower with three young sons. His wife had died two years earlier, while he was away on duty. What sort of future would he or they have now? Better death than such a life. Better to have been hit in the heart, as he told Captain Dearborn, than live in that helpless condition. He was still a young man and had always been physically active. So he chose to endure the pain of a slow recovery—splinters of bone could not be removed—with its risk of death but hope for healing. He was not a patient patient, however. After spending a night watching "the celebrated General Arnold," Dr. Thacher found him "very peevish, and impatient under his misfortunes, and required all my attention during the night," though the good doctor confessed he managed to slip away for an hour to write a letter to a friend.[11] General Lincoln was also a patient in the Albany hospital. He was second in command at Saratoga but, like Gates, was not on the field where the battle took place that last day. Lincoln was an able commander though, and more diplomatic than Arnold. Gates had assigned him to lead the right wing on October 7, but the action was on the left and center. He received a wound to his right leg in a skirmish the following day.

By December 20 Thacher cheerfully noted that the wounded soldiers committed to his care in October "have all recovered" and he had received "a generous and handsome present" from Dr. Potts the surgeon-general for his good work. The hospital was now so quiet he obtained a forty-day furlough to visit friends in New England.[12] Yet when Dr. J. Brown, another army surgeon, visited the hospital the day before Christmas, both Arnold and Lincoln were still there. Dr. Brown found General Lincoln "in a fair way of recovery" behaving as "the patient Christian."[13] "Not so the gallant General Arnold," he wrote, "for his wound, though less dangerous in the beginning than Lincoln's, is not in so fair a way of healing. He abuses us for a set of ignorant pretenders."[14] They were not pretenders, of course, but with the skills they had they could not make him whole.

The formal surrender of the British army took place on October 17, ten days after the battle. General Burgoyne had little option. His army was surrounded. His retreat had been cut off. Winter was coming on and he was short of provisions. His ranks were devastated by the loss of too many officers and men, with no hope of reinforcements. During four hours of fighting, more than one third of the British troops involved were wounded, killed, or taken prisoner.[15] Roger Lamb, a private in the British army wrote,: "Few actions have been characterized by more obstinancy in attack or defence." Burgoyne's 62nd regiment that began fighting with 350 men by early evening had only four or five officers and sixty soldiers who were still effective. One artillery detachment had its captain and thirty-six of its forty-eight men killed or wounded.[16] At first Gates demanded unconditional surrender.[17] When that was rejected he abruptly switched tactics, agreeing to unusually generous terms for fear that General Clinton might bring a British army from New York to rescue Burgoyne. According to the agreed upon terms the British troops were to march out of their camp with the full honors of war, laying down their weapons under the supervision of their own officers. Their army would then be given safe conduct to Boston where a British fleet would be allowed to return them to England, terms that Congress ultimately would not carry out.

For the British regulars honorable terms could not disguise the sadness and humiliation of the occasion. Barely 3,500 of Burgoyne's men remained, the remnant of the seven thousand man force that had left Canada.[18] "About 10 o'clock we marched out," Lieutenant Digby wrote, "with drums beating and the honors of war, but the drums seemed to have lost their former inspiring sounds, and though we beat the Grenadiers march, which not long before was so animating, yet then it seemed by its last feeble efforts as if almost ashamed to be heard on such an occasion."[19] Near to tears himself, Digby was struck by the demeanor of the ragtag American troops that lined the field: "I shall never forget the appearance of the troops on our marching past them. [A] dead silence universally reigned through their numerous columns and even then they seemed struck with our situation and dare scarce life up their eyes to view British troops in such a situation. I must say their decent behavior during the time (to us so greatly fallen) merited the utmost commendation and praise."[20]

Gates had given his young adjutant, Major James Wilkinson, the honor of reporting the wonderful victory directly to Congress. Protocol demanded Gates report it to Washington instead, but he deeply resented the commander in chief and, helped by supporters in Congress, had been agitating to replace him. Bypassing Washington was an act of insubordination. Washington learned of the triumph of his northern army informally from another officer. Wilkinson was in no hurry to deliver the exciting news to Congress and took fifteen days to reach them, stopping along the way to do a little courting. Congress overlooked his cavalier behavior in its jubilation over the victory and, somewhat reluctantly rewarded Wilkinson with a lieutenant colonelcy as Gates had asked, thereby bypassing many experienced field officers of higher rank, needlessly upsetting many good men.[21] Congress was also intent upon honoring Horatio Gates, the triumphant general. On November 4 delegates voted that a gold medal should be struck in his honor stamped HORATIO GATES, DUCI STRENUO, COMITIA AMERICANA: The American Congress to Horatio Gates, the gallant leader.

All the undeserved tribute lavished on Gates simply added to Arnold's misery. Congress had still not even given him the seniority he deserved when it promoted five junior officers, including Lincoln, ahead of him earlier that year. When an adjustment was suggested the supporters of Gates, who ignored or denigrated Arnold's key part in the battles of Saratoga, objected to the restitution of his seniority. Members of Congress would only gradually learn the truth. Nonetheless, since Arnold was grievously wounded there was sympathy for him. On November 29 the delegates, when adjusting other men's ranks, finally agreed to issue a commission to restore

the "rank & precedence" Arnold sought.[22] The commission itself
and attached message written by Henry Laurens, president of the
Congress, was very grudging. It never mentioned Arnold's spectacular deeds on the battlefields and other outstanding service.
Laurens merely wrote politely, "Permit me to assure you sir I
respect your character as a citizen and soldier of the United States
of America, that I rejoice at your recovery from the dangerous
wounds which you lately received in the defense of your country,
that I wish you perfect health and a continued succession of
honor."[23] Not only was his leadership and valor never mentioned
but there was something in Laurens's personal note that implied
that he was speaking for himself, not the delegates. On January
20 Washington wrote from Valley Forge with Arnold's commission, apologizing for his tardiness. Whatever the aspersions on
his character by others, the commander clearly held Arnold in
the highest esteem and understood who the actual hero of Saratoga was. "May I venture to ask whether you are upon your legs
again," Washington inquired, "and if you are not, may I flatter
myself you will be soon? There is none, who wishes more sincerely for this event, than I do or who will receive the information
with more pleasure. I shall expect a favorable account upon this
subject, and as soon as your situation will permit, I request that
you will repair to this Army, it being my earnest wish to have
your services in the ensuing campaign."[24]

Arnold had endured the indignity of having been passed over for
promotion by five men junior to him, none of whom had been so
distinguished, putting the cause ahead of his pride. He had endured
other aspersions on his honor for the same reason. Benjamin
Lincoln, however, who as one of these five officers now junior to
Arnold, was so upset that Arnold was to get seniority over him,
he apparently considered resigning in protest. Washington soothed
Lincoln's feelings, honoring both Arnold and Lincoln with handsome gifts of epaulets and sword knots sent to him by an admiring
French gentleman.

By late February Lincoln was able to travel. On February 23, helped by his son, he arrived at his family home at Hingham, Massachusetts.[25] Arnold would spend that winter in Albany, still unable to walk. By late winter or early spring he finally left the hospital, still grievously disabled. Passing through Kinderhook, New York on his way home to Connecticut, a doorpost of the house he was to stay in had to be removed to permit his litter to enter.[26] He was carried on to Middletown, Connecticut receiving a grand reception. He spent several weeks at Middletown, only a day's journey from New Haven, resting and recuperating at the home of his old friend, Comfort Sage. Sage was, like Arnold, a successful merchant and served as a lieutenant colonel in the Connecticut militia. While there Arnold learned to walk on crutches. He and Sage discussed various financial opportunities to help replenish his depleted fortune and Arnold became part owner of a privateer. Finally, on May 4, he reached New Haven and his own home where his dear sister, Hannah, and young sons awaited him.[27] An enthusiastic crowd turned out to welcome him back—military officers, militia members, local dignitaries, friends, and neighbors. He was home for the first time in just over a year.

As the long days in the hospital had stretched into weeks and then months of pain, impatience, and frustration, Arnold couldn't shake from his mind the triumphs and turmoils of his life, his pursuit of honor, and the growing numbers of his detractors. He had become a hero to many Americans in and out of the military but an enemy to others. He was generally disliked by Congress, where soldiers, especially popular ones unwilling to spend time courting the delegates, were regarded with suspicion. Because he was held in high esteem by Washington and General Schuyler, their enemies regarded him as an enemy. His every daring and heroic deed was branded by his detractors as sheer recklessness, bravado, self-aggrandizement. Congressmen sitting comfortably through endless meetings, insisting on approving every promotion, questioning the patriotism of any officer who suffered a defeat, doling out niggling funds to the troops, and leaving them in wretched condition, demanded he account for any perceived financial irregularity. These men who never saw a battlefield during the war for independence set themselves up to judge him, who had risked his life time after time, and generously gave of his fortune to help the cause. He was tired of it all, all the personal animosities, all the carping, the constant pain. His whole life seemed to have led up to that moment on Bemis Heights, stripped of all command but commanding the love and loyalty of the men in the decisive battle of the Revolution. Had that musket ball pierced his heart rather than his leg, bringing death at the moment of his greatest triumph, he would have died one of America's greatest heroes. He wanted to lay down his life for honor and the patriot cause. Having lost his chance to die for the cause, could he live for it in this reduced state, seeing Gates honored for his work, bedeviled by men determined to vilify him? How to maintain dignity and respect in these circumstances?

TWO

Great Expectations

A rnold, looking back later, was painfully aware it was a single-minded drive for honor and respect which shaped his entire life that brought him to a court-martial table. But what more worthy passion could a man have? Had not the men who signed the Declaration of Independence famously pledged to each other "our lives, our fortunes, and our sacred honor."[1] Honor was sacred. Particularly in a country of self-made men, honor mattered deeply because a man's stature and reputation were in his own hands. Birth of course helped, class and education helped, and the Arnold family was blessed with illustrious beginnings in the New World and again at the time of Arnold's birth. But the boundless possibilities, the great expectations for the boy's future, were sadly squandered by the father who had bestowed them. By Benedict's twelfth birthday his family's honor and reputation were gone, sunk in shame and public humiliation. The responsibility to restore his own and his family's honor had fallen to him and him alone. If there

11

had been no great expectations to begin with, if they had not been dashed so cruelly, everything might have been different. He might have borne with more patience this loss of respect. Honor might have mattered less.

Benedict's great-great grandfather, the first American Benedict Arnold, sailed from England to the Massachusetts Bay Colony with his family in 1636, not long after the arrival of its first planters. The Arnolds settled in the little port village of Hingham south of Boston. Within a year they were off again following the upstart Roger Williams into the wilderness and helping him found his new, more tolerant colony of Rhode Island. That first Benedict Arnold was an extraordinary man. He succeeded Roger Williams as president of the infant colony then went on to serve several terms as its governor. He was as enterprising as he was public-spirited—a successful farmer and shrewd merchant, reputed to be the richest man in the colony.[2] What a model of honor, probity, and reputation for a boy to ponder and hope to emulate.

The problem was that as a thoughtful parent, Governor Arnold abandoned the English pattern of primogeniture and divided his property among his five sons. That pattern continued for several generations. The inevitable result was that the early fortune was dissipated and succeeding generations were left to fend for themselves with uneven success. Benedict's own father, another Benedict, and his father's younger brother Oliver had no great expectations at all. They were two younger sons in a family of six children. Their older brother, Caleb, seems to have inherited their father's 140-acre farm.[3] Their legacy was to be apprenticed as coopers, a useful trade but one offering a limited future.

Growing up, Benedict's own father was held up as a model for him. Captain Arnold had been poor in property, but blessed with the

Arnold family's courage, charm, intelligence, and sound business instincts. About 1730 he and his brother Oliver left their home in Providence, Rhode Island, heading west and settling in the town of Norwich in eastern Connecticut. While a more modest community than Providence, Norwich was a good choice. It was a thriving inland port of some five thousand residents. The town comprised six villages occupying the narrow and beautiful valley of the Yantic and Shetucket rivers that flowed south and east joining the Thames River estuary south of the town. With this location Norwich was perfectly placed for both seafaring and inland trade. It was a center of shipbuilding. Local captains sailed the Atlantic bringing back goods that could be easily transported and sold to farmers and townsmen in inland communities. Norwich's own fine stands of woodland were interspersed with family farms that managed to yield decent crops from rather indifferent soil. The town was also the land of the famed Mohegan Indians, still much in evidence in the eighteenth century. Its waterfront's wharves and warehouses were bustling as ships docked, loaded or unloaded cargo, and sailed off. In contrast the town's central square seemed quietly sedate, with its timeless symbols of provincial life. There stood a courthouse with jail conveniently nearby, several taverns, a churchyard, and an array of businesses backed by some fine meadows. Norwich's many better homes, some with river views, were typical of the time, with their large central chimneys, spacious rooms, and unpainted wooden exteriors. Their interiors were being increasingly furnished with European luxuries, the fruits of the town's shipping trade.

The young cooper found work in Norwich with Absolom King, a prosperous merchant and captain. Like many enterprising merchants in Norwich at that time, King sailed his own ships to ports in Europe and the Caribbean. On the way back from a voyage to Ireland in September 1732, he died at sea, leaving his lovely wife Hannah to mourn him.[4] Hannah was a young woman of twenty-five, of "good exterior and estimable qualities." She belonged to the large Waterman family and was related to the Lathrops, one of the oldest and wealthiest Norwich families.[5] The cooper courted the widow and on November 8, 1733, just over a year after King's death, Benedict's parents were wed.[6] At a stroke Benedict's father's fortunes changed. While his brother Oliver remained a cooper the rest of his life, Benedict's father gave up the craft and took over the King business and property. The landsman turned into an able seaman. With great panache he followed in Absolom King's footsteps and took to the sea, sailing north to Canada, south along the American coast as far as the Caribbean, and across the sea to England buying and selling cargoes. With the profits he built a fine, large house for his growing family with a shop next door where the goods purchased on his journeys were sold. In addition to his thriving business and frequent travels, Arnold's father emulated that first Rhode Island Benedict Arnold by devoting himself to community work. He served as a collector, a selectman, a constable, and a militia captain. He became known as Captain Arnold.

Five years after their marriage Hannah and Benedict had their first child, a son who, as custom dictated, was named after his father. Sadly their first little Benedict died less than a year later when a wave of diphtheria, a fearsome child killer, swept through the area.[7] Two years later, on January 3, 1741, a frigid winter day, a second son was born.[8] They also named him Benedict and, probably fearing he too might die young, hurried their tiny infant off in the wintry cold to Norwich's First Congregational Church for the Reverend Benjamin Lord to baptize. The congregation of family, friends, and neighbors prayed for the baby and welcomed him into the faith. Another year and baby Hannah, Benedict's dear sister, was born. Then came Mary and another son, Absolom King, named for Hannah's first husband. Last, in 1749 when Benedict was eight, baby Elizabeth was born. Little Absolom died when he was only two and a half, leaving Benedict his parents' only son.

The joy and hopefulness of his childhood made its sad and sudden close hard for that only son. Benedict's mother and father were devoted parents. It was a privileged and carefree time, full of grand possibilities. The boy had forests to explore. Mohegan Indians lived nearby. And the woods still harbored some exciting wildlife. Most of the wolves and even foxes had been exterminated but Norwich had an impressive number of bothersome snakes, particularly rattlesnakes and black snakes. The town was keen to eradicate them. Bounties were offered for bringing in a rattle or other proof a snake had been killed. Just before Benedict's birth the bounty for killing snakes was raised to 10 shillings a head, although the snake killer was obliged to take an oath that he or she went out for no other purpose than to destroy snakes. Some Norwich women availed themselves of the opportunity to earn money this way. Tales of their prowess abounded. One year the Widow Woodworth was paid a bounty for twenty-three snakes and the Widow Smith for nine.[9]

Benedict's childhood also had all the trappings of colonial civility. He lived in one of the finest houses in the town, staffed with servants and slaves. He was surrounded by a loving, prosperous, and prominent family. During the summers when Benedict was old enough his father took him on some of his voyages. Together they shared the excitement of Atlantic crossings and visiting ports from Canada to the Caribbean. It was a wonderful introduction to the sea and to his father's business. But his father had other aims for his son.

Captain Arnold had never had the opportunity for more than a rudimentary education. Hannah was well educated for a woman of the time but women did not attend college or go into the professions. Both parents were determined to give their son the best schooling available, one that would open doors to future opportunities. Britain's American colonies were more egalitarian than the Home Country but class still mattered, and education helped assure a better status.

Benedict was first sent to a school run by Dr. Jewett in the village of Montville, just south of Norwich.[10] Hannah pressed Jewett to instill in her son "the first rudiments of religion and enforce virtue and explode all manner of vice."[11] If young Benedict proved "backward and unteachable," she wrote, "pray don't be soon discouraged." She urged the schoolmaster not to "spare the rod and spoil the child." It is unclear how often that rod needed to be applied to this small boy, but applying it was standard practice at the time, considered a duty by parents and teachers intent that youngsters become God-fearing and virtuous adults. If Benedict resented Hannah's pious admonitions to her children to trust in God, and children easily tire of pious admonitions, he found himself echoing them when he had children of his own.[12]

In 1752 when Benedict was eleven it was time for more advanced schooling. With great pride and fanfare his mother and father arranged for him to go to Canterbury, Connecticut some twelve miles from Norwich to board with a relation of Benedict's father, the Reverend James Cogswell. Like many ministers of the time, Rev. Cogswell took in boys and schooled them in the classics.[13] The aim was to prepare them for higher education and, for some of them, the ministry. At Canterbury Benedict found himself laboring at the classic subjects required for learned men—Latin, the Bible, logic, mathematics, rhetoric, and history. Most of Cogswell's pupils were destined to be enrolled at Yale College in New Haven. That was presumably Benedict's parents' plan for him, but he was not to be one of those fortunate sons.[14]

He was a lively, even bold boy but didn't consider himself unruly or brave. Enemies then and since have told stories of misbehavior and even cruelty, behavior that might have been written off later as high spirits in any other boy. As the only son in a family of daughters, Benedict felt the need to prove his bravery, to play the manly part. Yet, keen as people were to find fault in later years he was remembered as having picked fights with the stronger boys, always protecting the weaker children.[15] However boisterous and spirited he was, Benedict loved and respected his parents. He carefully kept the letters his mother wrote him while he was away at school. Five of these survive.[16] They are full of a mother's reminders to be pious and diligent. "Keep a steady watch over your thoughts and actions," Hannah wrote him, "be dutiful to superiors, obliging to equals, and affable to inferiors, if any such there be. Always choose that your companions be your betters, that by their good examples, you may learn."[17] How many children of that time heard the same sound advice, perhaps in the very same words! Hannah then tucked shillings into that letter that he was to spend "prudently, as you are accountable to God and your father."[18]

In 1753 while Benedict was away from home boarding in Canterbury, a terrible plague descended on Norwich. The highly contagious and deadly disease, diphtheria, struck the town. Adults sometimes became sick from diphtheria and pulled through. Most of its victims were children. It was one of the three most feared childhood killers in an age of childhood scourges.[19] Hannah wrote to convey the dreadful news that his sisters Hannah, Mary, and little Elizabeth were deathly ill and that she and the captain were sick. His entire family was sick and possibly dying. Hannah's fears for her son's own health leap from the page: "My dear, God seems to be saying to all, 'Children, be ye also ready!'" She pleaded, "improve your time and beg God to grant His spirit, or death may overtake you unprepared. . . . Your groaning sisters give love to you. God may mete you with this disease wherever you be, for it is His servant, but I would not have you come home for fear it should be presumption." His distraught mother nonetheless closed her letter: "My love to you—beg you will write us. I have sent you one pound chocolate."[20]

Dr. Benjamin Rush, the renowned colonial physician, referred to diphtheria as malignant sore throat. It was commonly described as "throat distemper" since the white fibers it produced in the throat quickly covered it. Fever followed with a rapid pulse, breathing problems, and lastly paralysis of the throat and heart failure. Death usually occurred within a week. The disease was spread through respiratory droplets from a cough or sneeze, and once exposed symptoms began to appear in two to five days. There was no cure.[21] A deadly diphtheria epidemic struck Philadelphia in 1763, ten years after the Norwich outbreak, killing hundreds of children.

Hannah wrote to Benedict again on August 12 to tell him, "deaths are multiplied all around us and more daily expected."[22] In her letter of August 30 Benedict learned with some relief, "your poor sisters are yet in the land of the living." Mary, who had been "just stepping on the banks of time" was "something revived," but poor Hannah was "waxing weaker and weaker."[23] His father was "very poor" and his mother "had a touch of the distemper" although "through divine goodness it is past of [sic] light with me." How was a boy to concentrate on memorizing those Latin verbs and mastering mathematics while his sisters and parents were grievously sick at home?

As it turned out it was eight-year-old Mary, "something revived" on August 30 who died. Nineteen days later little four-year-old Elizabeth passed away. Miraculously his sister Hannah, who had been "waxing weaker and weaker," was spared along with his parents. Of the six Arnold children only Benedict and Hannah would survive to adulthood. It was a fearful toll.

Misery continued knocking on the Arnold door even after the sad loss of his two sisters. In fact, their troubles had begun even before the deaths of Mary and Elizabeth. Benedict's father's business was in serious decline. As a merchant who served as his own captain sailing from port to port on risky voyages buying and selling cargoes, everything depended on his energy, his skill, and his enterprise. His personal relationships with suppliers and customers were all-important. But Captain Arnold's hard drinking, typical of the time and seafaring vocation, gradually became more and more uncontrolled and debilitating. It is unclear whether his business decline had caused the drinking, or the drinking caused the business decline. The latter seems most likely since the 1750s were overall a prosperous time for American long distance trade. Sea travel had become generally less dangerous, port times had shortened significantly, and insurance costs had decreased dramatically.[24] The French and Indian War actually increased trade. Arnold's business ought to have been flourishing. Perhaps bad luck or overextending his resources was the cause of his difficulties. How was a young schoolboy to know or understand the true circumstances of his father's collapse? He only knew and felt the result. When Hannah wrote Benedict on August 12 of the dangers of the disease raging in Norwich and urged her son not to "neglect your precious soul, which once lost can never be regained," she may have been thinking of her husband's growing addiction. His hard drinking was increasingly interfering with his work and life and imperiling his very soul.[25] It was terrible for a wife to watch. The sudden and painful deaths of his two little daughters added to Captain Arnold's grief. Had their deaths been his fault? Was God punishing him for his pride or drinking by taking his children? Is that what his wife thought? Unworthy as he was, he had recovered from the disease that had killed his innocent little girls. In his despair Captain Arnold turned away from God and prayer, and to the bottle. Benedict's much-loved father was increasingly unable to lead or even support his family.

Captain Arnold was not alone in succumbing to drink. Drinking was, or was certainly thought to be, a serious problem in colonial Connecticut from the earliest times. The Connecticut Assembly tackled the problem repeatedly, to little effect. One set of laws punished being drunk, another frequent drinking. In 1650 and 1709 the assembly passed laws punishing drunkenness with a ten-shilling fine.[26] In 1676 the assembly turned its attention to habitual drinking with a law "to prevent the increase of drunkenness," ordering constables to take "special care to notice" every person who frequents taverns and bars and to require them to forbear frequenting the places." This law added, "if such person does not heed the warning and is found in such a place, he must forfeit five shillings or sit in the stocks for an hour." Thirty years later the fine for drunkenness remained ten shillings but with a five-shilling penalty for drinking after nine o'clock in the evening.[27] If the drinker was unable to pay he was to sit for one to three hours in the stocks. In 1716 the colony ordered that magistrates and other officials were to post the names of so-called "tavern-haunters" on the doors of every tavern in the town. Clearly this was a means of public shaming. Moreover, a listed tavern-haunter who entered a tavern was fined either twenty shillings, double the earlier fine or, if he could not pay, had to sit in the stocks for two hours unless he could find two sureties willing to take responsibility for his good behavior. A "common drunkard" could be incarcerated. For better or worse Hannah's Lathrop relatives owned a tavern in Norwich and presumably extended credit to the Captain until his name appeared on the shameful list of tavern-haunters. Drinking in moderation was accepted but excessive drinking was considered a grave moral failing. Norwich residents were regarded as conspicuous examples of "Connecticut Steady Habits," and moral failings were to be forcefully discouraged.[28] Colonial taverns were meant to be located near a church, the better for members to see who frequented them. The presence of the church, it was hoped, would be a silent admonition for those planning on entering a tavern. Captain Arnold's increasing alcoholism, with its eventual physical and mental deterioration threatened not only to destroy his shipping business but to bring very public disgrace to himself and his wife and children.

Poor Hannah! Despite her piety and prayers after losing two sons, she had just lost her two youngest daughters. There would be no further children. That terrible loss together with her husband's failing business, his depression, and increasing alcoholism, might have driven a weaker woman to drink as well. But Hannah was made of sterner stuff. She now shouldered responsibility for holding her family together and keeping her husband's business going. She was successful for a time.

In 1754, the year after his sisters' deaths, the Arnolds still managed to pay Benedict's school fees. In April his mother sent him fifty shillings and his father added twenty shillings for his personal expenses. But Captain Arnold's condition and with it the family business continued to deteriorate. In late summer Hannah wrote Benedict that his father's health was so poor he wasn't certain he could make the short sail to Newport, Rhode Island.[29] By the new year Hannah and Captain Arnold with great reluctance felt they had no choice but to give up their dream for their only son. Even by scrimping, they did not have the money to pay Benedict's school fees. The great expectations for his future, the chance for a college education that would place him among the colony's elite, vanished.

If it was a difficult decision for them it was worse for Benedict. He faced the humiliation of having to leave school and return home to Norwich. The return would be public. Everyone would know what had happened: his school friends, his neighbors, everyone. The cooper's son would have to start his career with no better advantage than his own father had. Worse actually, because while Grandfather Arnold was a respectable farmer of modest means with little to give his six children, Benedict had the bitter disappointment of a sudden collapse of his hopes, coupled with public shame and debt. If he was to acquire personal honor after this deep disgrace, Benedict would have to earn it himself.

THREE

Descent

I n the bitter cold of the new year Benedict packed up his clothes
and his books, reluctantly turned his back on his Canterbury
school, and journeyed home to Norwich. The bleak, frosty
weather mirrored his mood. The contrast between the bustling
life at the Canterbury school and the grim reality of his home was
stark. No more lively society of boys living away from home, bub-
bling over with chatter and pranks. No more camaraderie chafing
under the discipline of the Reverend Cogswell, laboring over the
subjects necessary to make them educated men. The arrival of his
mother's letters had linked the two worlds and punctured his Canterbury existence from time to time, bringing news of the troubles
at home. But Norwich had seemed very distant, quite out of sight,
and could be forgotten for hours at a stretch in the press of school
activities. Now there was no escape. As soon as he arrived he was
engulfed by those family problems, but too young to help resolve

them. Worse, his mere presence was a constant reminder to his mother and father of their own failure.

The spacious Arnold home seemed silent and empty without Mary and Elizabeth. The survivors, Benedict and Hannah, were grateful for each other's company, but the sad loss of their little sisters was impossible to forget. Benedict's father, with whom he had shared wonderful summers sailing in the family's vessels to exotic ports, had been transformed from a successful merchant and respected town official to a sick and irascible man, sunk in depression. Alcohol was robbing him of his personality and competence, yet his family could not stop him from dulling his mind with drink. Benedict's loving and kindly mother was preoccupied, frantically attempting to keep the shipping business and shop functioning, while running the household and struggling to pay the bills. When Benedict could be of no help to her it seemed best he stay out of the way. He wandered the town and its woodlands and meadows. He met the Mohegan Indian Chief Benjamin Uncas who befriended the boy and taught him native ways of fishing and hunting, of horseback riding and canoeing.[1] This very different education, more active and exciting, helped shape him into the confident warrior and outdoorsman he was destined to become. It also distracted him from the increasing anxiety he and his family were enduring.

The Arnold family's slide into indebtedness and disgrace might have passed undetected in a large city, but in Norwich little escaped public notice. Neighbors knew each other well. They met weekly in church and almost daily at the market or down by the docks. They enjoyed a good gossip. Public shame for questionable acts helped ensure that the people of Norwich behaved in a proper and moral manner. Morality encompassed the virtues of sobriety, piety, and fiscal responsibility. In this setting it was nearly impossible to disguise business failure or moral failings, especially any slippage by someone who had been prosperous and prominent, someone of whom more was expected. There was general sympathy for Benedict's long-suffering mother. But Arnold's father was a relative newcomer, a cooper who had married into money and position. That fact would not have passed unremarked.

This puritanical streak in its citizenry had not abated much from Connecticut's earliest days. The tendency was fortified and perpetuated by the colony's assembly that continued to demand godly behavior through relentless and detailed social legislation. Local justices of the peace were kept busy ruling on instances of alleged impropriety. The efforts of Richard Hide, a justice of the peace in mid-eighteenth-century Norwich, demonstrates what the Arnolds could expect. The case of a resident presented "for profane swearing" because he had "been heard to say at the public house— *damn me*," was typical. For this outburst he was fined six shillings and had to pay court costs of six shillings, three pence.[2] Another blasphemer received the same six-shilling fine for blurting out, "*Go to the devil.*" In 1771 two women reported a young woman for laughing during a religious service. Hide showed mercy to the young woman in question and she was dismissed with a reprimand. Ebenezer Waterman Jr. did not get off so lightly. He was hauled before a grand jury for profaning the Sabbath by talking "in the time of divine service in a merry manner, to make sport." He pleaded guilty and was fined ten shillings.

It was not just during church services that good deportment was expected. The entire Sabbath day was to be spent in religious observance or quiet activity. Five young residents—Asa Fuller, an apprentice, Ede Trap, Lemuel Wentworth, Hannah Forsey, and Elizabeth Winship, a minor—were hauled before Justice Hide after witnesses reported that "on the evening following the 27th of May last, it being Sabbath, or Lord's Day evening," the youngsters did "meet and convene together, and walk in the street in company, upon no religious occasion, all which is contrary to the statute of this colony in such case." It was in this setting Hannah Arnold and her two children were trying to shield Captain Arnold's alcoholism

THE TRAGEDY OF BENEDICT ARNOLD

from public scrutiny and the disgrace and punishment that must follow.

The year Benedict turned fourteen events came to a head. Hannah's attempt to run the family business with her husband's fitful help and to pay the bills failed, and that failure set in motion a new plan for Benedict's future. If any woman could have salvaged the Arnold business, Hannah was that woman. Under the law married women had little control over their own property, let alone an opportunity for business activity. Of course Hannah was better educated than most women and a capable and well-respected member of the community. Moreover, like many wives of seafaring merchants gone for months at a time, she had needed to assume financial responsibility when Captain Arnold was away.[3] As an Englishman explained it at the time, while a married woman's property rights were limited, a woman "in her husband's absence is wife and deputy-husband, which makes her double the files of her diligence."[4] Now, as her husband became less and less able to manage himself let alone his business, she took over as much as she could. The accounting and record-keeping could be managed, and maybe basic buying and selling.[5] The voyages were another thing. A great deal had depended on the Captain's quick eye for a bargain and his contacts among producers and other merchants. In the end Hannah was unable to keep the shipping business afloat. In a time of booming sea trade the Arnold business collapsed. Benedict's father could no longer pay his debts.

Failure to pay a debt was not just an embarrassment, it was a crime. There was no public bankruptcy law in Connecticut.[6] Men unable to pay their business or private debts were sent to prison until they could pay. Conditions in these prisons were awful. There were no separate prisons for the scores of convicted debtors unable to meet their obligations. They were simply tossed in with ordinary criminals to languish until somehow rescued.

The awful reckoning came one morning. The sheriff knocked at the door of the fine house Captain Arnold had built, demanding payment of the family debts.[7] They had to tell him they simply did not have the money. He immediately began seizing and removing their personal possessions to the value of the money owed. The Arnolds were able to keep basic items, since the law stipulated that a debtor was to be left "bedding, tools, arms, and implements of his household necessary for upholding his life."[8] The seizure of their possessions was very upsetting and very public. The sheriff warned that worse was in store. Unless Captain Arnold could come up with the funds he owed in twenty days his property would be sold at public auction.

In this wretched circumstance Hannah was either sufficiently desperate to plead for help from her Lathrop relatives, or they came forward unasked to spare her and her family the misery of public disgrace. Whichever it was, her Lathrop relatives came to the rescue. The Lathrops were an extraordinarily prosperous and generous family, especially brothers Daniel and Joshua Lathrop. Both had been educated at Yale College and Daniel had then sailed to England where he spent three years studying medicine. He had returned to set up an apothecary business with Joshua. The two were not only the first pharmacists in Norwich, but Dr. Daniel Lathrop was the first trained pharmacist in all of Connecticut. The business he and Joshua established was the sole apothecary business along the entire route from Boston to New York.[9] It provided a crucial service and the brothers prospered accordingly. They purchased shiploads of medical goods from England and grew their own medicinal herbs in large gardens. Gossip reported that a single shipment of drugs they imported was worth £8,000.[10]

With a close relative about to be dispossessed and jailed for debt, Daniel Lathrop agreed to pay the £300 needed to keep Captain Arnold out of prison and save his possessions from public auction.[11] The Lathrops also took over the mortgage on the Arnold house to ensure the family would not lose their home. But their timely rescue also involved young Benedict. The Lathrops accepted the fourteen-year-old Benedict as an apprentice. They promised to look after him and instruct him in their trade. Benedict's parents readily agreed and signed a standard seven-year apprenticeship contract that would provide their only son preparation for a lucrative career. It would also bind him to work for the Lathrops until he was twenty-one.

For Benedict this was a dramatic transition. It meant moving from his tense and depressing family home to Dr. Daniel Lathrop's waterfront Georgian mansion with its lavish formal gardens, and beginning professional training. If Benedict's parents were unable to give him a university education, they were at least providing him something far better than the training his own father had. The apothecary profession was respected and respectable. The Lathrops would also teach Benedict how to run a business. He would start out in life far better off than any cooper's apprentice. Leaving home was also a financial relief for his hard-pressed parents. And he hadn't moved far. He remained in the same town as his family and could keep in close contact. However he may have felt about his father's behavior and incompetence, however much he regretted being deprived of higher education, Benedict never uttered any condemnation of the man whose weaknesses led to the family ruin and his own diminished hopes.

Life with the Lathrops was more than comfortable. Both Daniel and his wife Jerusha treated him like a son.[12] The couple had no children of their own. Their wealth hadn't spared them from domestic tragedy. Some years before Benedict's arrival their own three little children had died in infancy. Daniel and Jerusha were happy to have youngsters to raise and were ready to lavish their affection upon them. Benedict was very fortunate. Jerusha was the daughter of Joseph Talcott, the first native-born governor of Connecticut.[13] She was a few years younger than Benedict's mother, but like Hannah, she was an educated and cultivated woman. The latest books filled the house. While Benedict missed the opportunity for a formal university education he was being schooled in the behavior and culture of a gentleman. There was another boy, Solomon Smith, who was also being trained by the Lathrops in the apothecary trade along with Benedict. How strange to be living in luxury not far from where his parents and sister were struggling to make ends meet and to avoid further shame. It was important to make a success of his training and through his own hard work repay the Lathrops for their loan and kindness, and benefit himself and his mother, father, and sister.

Life went on. The Arnold family scrimped, tried to control the Captain's drinking, and managed. Benedict worked hard for the Lathrops. He was attentive and serious about learning the basic concepts and particulars of their interesting profession. He had to memorize the virtues and composition of a great variety of medicines. The apothecary workshop was full of the scent of drying herbs and lined with shelf after shelf crowded with bottles of elixirs and powders. Observing how the Lathrop brothers ran their booming business was also fascinating. There was constant activity. Ships unloaded cargoes and set sail again. Their warehouses were kept busy receiving and unpacking stock, then packing wagons for delivery to customers along the coast and into the interior. It was complex and interesting work. Between his responsibilities as an apprentice and his efforts to help his family he was fully occupied. But when Benedict was sixteen the outside world suddenly intruded.

Military disaster loomed. The French were threatening to seize control of New York, imperiling New England. He was old enough to enlist in the Connecticut militia and anxious to participate. This first military experience would be brief. Yet the terrible events that occasioned his service and the furious anti-French feelings they provoked colored the rest of his life. Years later when Arnold wrote to his fellow Americans to explain why he had abandoned their cause, he was to blame it on the alliance they had forged with the French.

FOUR

The Fortunes of War

War between the French and English peoples had
been going on in Europe for as long as anyone could
remember. Once each country had colonies in North
America the competition quite naturally spread across the Atlantic.
England's colonies suffered repeatedly from full-scale conflicts and
sporadic raids on their settlements by the soldiers of New France
and their Indian allies. The French and Indians would swoop down
the Atlantic coast or along the rivers of the western frontier plundering, burning houses and barns, terrorizing and slaughtering the
men, women, and children. New Englanders, in particular, lived
with the dread of invasions from Canada. Ordinarily the colonists
were left to defend themselves. Every colony had a militia of able-
bodied men between the ages of sixteen and sixty.[1] Its members
were required to keep arms and ammunition at the ready and were
drilled several times a year. They were no match for professional,

29

European regulars, but they had the advantage of being men fighting for their homes and farms on ground they knew.

This new war was different. For the first time the British sent a large, professional army to the New World to defend their colonies. They hoped to evict the French from the Ohio Valley and carry the battle to New France. The French, for their part, sent reinforcements to Canada. In 1754, the year Benedict had to leave Canterbury, the war that Americans would call the French and Indian War broke out. In Britain it was dubbed the Seven Years War as the North American conflict expanded to become part of a worldwide struggle between the two ancient rivals. An ambitious young Virginian whom Benedict would come to know so very well, Colonel George Washington, played a prominent role in the events on the American frontier that triggered the war. Both the British and the French reinforced their troops by mobilizing local militia and recruiting Indian tribes as allies. The French, however, would fight, as they often did, with Indian warriors who were difficult to control and notorious for their brutal tactics. Some warriors traveled from beyond the Mississippi River to fight for the French with the promise of plunder and trophies. French commanders made a point of using their Indian allies' reputation for atrocities to terrorize the colonists. Most of the fighting was concentrated along the frontier where many tribes lived and in New York around Lake Ontario, the Mohawk Valley of central New York, and the colony's eastern watershed of Lake Champlain and Lake George.

Norwich men had been involved from the beginning. Connecticut had mobilized its militia as Benedict was beginning his apprenticeship in 1755. It called up militia recruits again the following year, 1756, to assist the British regulars. Every town had a quota of men to contribute. Bachelors were conscripted first, young men with no dependents. Some were poor men but many were merely waiting to inherit family property and marry. Benedict was busy with his apprenticeship both years and anyway he was too young to participate.[2] But in 1757 when he turned sixteen there was a sudden emergency. The war had taken a frightening turn. With dismay verging on panic New Englanders learned that the French seemed about to gain control of upstate New York.

It was not as if the British had done well in 1756. In May of that year Major General Louis-Joseph de Montcalm arrived in Montreal to command French forces bringing additional troops. He moved quickly and methodically. Barely three months after his arrival he attacked Fort Oswego some 250 miles away at the western end of Lake Ontario. The fort fell. Montcalm captured 1700 prisoners and 121 cannon. The loss of Fort Oswego upset British plans to attack French forts on Lake Ontario and to invade Canada.

In contrast to Montcalm's focused strategy, British campaign plans had been a confusion of orders, counterorders, fits, and starts. A new British commander in chief, John Campbell, Lord Loudoun, had arrived like Montcalm in 1756. He was replacing William Shirley, governor of Massachusetts. Shirley had planned an expedition against French forts on Lake Ontario for 1756 but when Loudoun finally reached Albany in late July he canceled Shirley's plan.

With winter coming on, the French would have been expected to wait for spring to begin a new campaign. Instead they spent the winter harassing British forts and settlements. The Marquis de Vaudreuil, governor of New France, incited Indian tribes to attack British settlements on the frontier while his own troops went after British forts and supplies. He was much more enthusiastic about the use of Indians than Montcalm, who disliked the Indian insistence on fighting in their own way and the brutality they practiced. He had only a slightly better opinion of the Canadian militia, but the shortage of trained troops would force the general to employ both.[3] While the French were busy eroding British strength and morale, British commanders continued to plan to no effect. Loudoun spent the winter organizing a summer campaign against Quebec, the capital of New France, proposing to leave some troops at Fort William Henry to mislead Montcalm. But as he was working out the details for his 1757 campaign, counterorders arrived from London. William Pitt, secretary of state for the colonies insisted the fortress at Louisbourg in Nova Scotia be attacked first. Loudoun dutifully changed course. As he was approaching the new target, however, he discovered that a French fleet had eluded the British blockade of France and was already at anchor off Louisbourg. If he attacked he would be seriously outnumbered. Taking the prudent course he abruptly called off the operation and returned to New York City. As for protection of New York's forts and waterways, it was not until July of 1757, the middle of the traditional campaign season, that a new British general, James Abercrombie, reached Albany. Abercrombie, like Loudoun, was a careful man and reluctant to take any important action without Loudoun's approval.

Of course the English colonists, including the people of Norwich, didn't know why the British army was on the defensive with no victories and no clear campaign goal. What was startlingly clear, however, was that the French with their Indian allies were destroying western settlements and were poised to take key forts in New York State. They captured and demolished Fort Bull, one of the small forts the British had built in central New York to protect their supply line. Critical amounts of war materials stored in the fort fell into French hands, including forty-five thousand pounds of gunpowder. Without the fort and supplies British plans for the 1757 season were hampered from the start.

The real focus of French attention that summer was Fort William Henry. It stood on the southern shore of Lake George north of Albany guarding the gateway from New France south to Albany and then down the great Hudson River to New York City. British possession of Fort William Henry was vital.

The French laid their plans to seize Fort William Henry with skill and daring. In January they ambushed British rangers near Fort Ticonderoga, which guarded the southern end of Lake Champlain where the La Chute River enters Lake George.[4] The next month they made a surprise attack on the supplies and outbuildings outside the walls of Fort William Henry by crossing a frozen Lake George. It was a great success. By early August when Montcalm descended on the fort in earnest with some seven thousand troops and Indians it was already weakened. The French were careful to keep their objective secret. British scouts went on fruitless forays trying to track the French army's movements. By the time the target was clear it was late in the day to send help. On August 3 French and Indian troops encircled the fort and Montcalm called upon its commander to surrender.

Word of French attacks on key British supplies and settlements had been reaching Connecticut all summer. The flood of refugees streaming east from the Ohio Valley, carrying whatever they could save, brought with them tales of horrible Indian atrocities. Now the French were threatening a key British fort. When General Daniel Webb, the British commander at Fort Edward, just sixteen miles from Fort William Henry, realized Montcalm was closing in on the neighboring fort he dashed off messages to the governors of New York and New England urging them to send their militia as quickly as possible. More fighters were essential to attack Montcalm's army and reinforce his own garrison at Fort Edward. Montcalm's assault was judged the "most dangerous threat to the frontier in fifty years."[5] If Fort William Henry fell, the way would be open for the French to strike deep into New York. England's hold on the entire region would be in grave peril. Fearful for Fort Edward itself, General Christie at Albany pleaded with New York Governor Thomas Pownall: "Let us save that, Sir, otherwise New York itself may fall, and then you can judge the fate of the Continent."[6]

The call for help was quickly answered, at least in Connecticut. General Loudoun had been scathing about the quality of the New England militia the previous year, describing them as "frightened out of their senses at the name of a Frenchman."[7] Nevertheless, for the 1757 campaign he had originally asked Connecticut to send fourteen hundred men and all of New England to contribute some four thousand. But now Connecticut alone was raising five thousand men, fully twenty-five percent of the colony's militia. What energetic and courageous sixteen-year-old boy with much to prove could resist the call to save his country? Not young Benedict Arnold. The Lathrops and his parents gave him permission to leave his apprenticeship temporarily and enlist in the Norwich company. There was no time to waste. Within a week of receiving Webb's request, the Connecticut militia set out. Off Benedict marched with the men of Norwich, some 154 strong, as their families and friends waved farewell and prayed fervently for their safety and their success.[8]

Massachusetts responded with urgency as well, mobilizing the militia of the four western regiments to march to New York and alerting all the colony's twenty-six battalions "to hold themselves in readiness to march at a minute's warning."[9] By August 12 more than seven thousand Massachusetts men were speeding to Fort Edward. More than forty-two hundred New England men were already encamped outside the fort.[10]

Benedict was swept up in the excitement and desperate haste. The Connecticut recruits were organized into companies and rendezvoused with militia from other towns, then as a body they set off for Albany over 150 miles away. More than half of the men were on horseback, an extraordinary number, but key to a rapid response.[11] Men on foot struggled to keep up, mile after mile. [12]

As they poured into Albany, relieved to have reached their destination, they discovered all their haste and effort had been for nothing. General Webb's call for help had been sent too late.[13] As thousands of Connecticut men were marching off leaving their homes Fort William Henry was already surrounded. By the time the exhausted Connecticut recruits reached Albany it was all over. Fort William Henry's garrison had surrendered. Terrible and deeply frustrating as that news was, there was worse. The Indian allies of the French had behaved in an outrageous and dishonorable manner, violating the terms of surrender and slaughtering many members of the defeated garrison.

The garrison at Fort William Henry was commanded by Lieutenant Colonel George Munro, a fifty-seven-year-old Scots-Irish soldier. His forces had been strengthened that spring, and General Webb had responded to his pleas. On August 2 Webb sent more men, bringing their numbers to 2,372. Still they were no match for the eleven thousand men Munro thought Montcalm had.[14] On the other hand Munro had reasonable supplies of food and ammunition and eighteen heavy cannon and other artillery.[15] He could hold out if reinforcements arrived quickly to raise the siege.

At first the siege proceeded with all the European niceties of war. On August 3, while Montcalm's soldiers and Indian allies ranged around its walls and brought their artillery into range, he sent a messenger to Munro under a flag of truce. He called upon Munro to surrender the fort and avoid the inevitable bloodshed that would follow a successful assault: "Humanity obliged him to warn [Munro] that once [the French] batteries were in place and the cannon fired, perhaps there would not be time, nor would it be in [his] power to restrain the cruelties of a mob of Indians of so many different nations."[16] While Montcalm awaited a reply, his Indian allies congregated before the walls shouting insults at the defenders.

Munro had tried to avoid his present predicament. He had written to General Webb three times informing him that Montcalm was about to besiege Fort William Henry and requesting his help. If the fort was to hold out it was imperative a relief force from Fort Edward attack the French before they encircled the fort, or come in strength and force them to lift the siege. Webb had originally been very helpful. He had sent some reinforcements before the siege was complete and a letter assuring Munro that he was "determin'd to assist you as soon as possible with the whole army if requir'd."[17] The situation was desperate once the fort had been encircled but Webb might still arrive with a relief force. Munro therefore replied that he and his men would fight "to the last extremity."[18]

But once the fighting started Webb changed his mind. He decided he could not afford to send help and weaken his own garrison until he had been reinforced by militia. At noon on August 4 Webb's aide-de-camp set out from Fort Edward with a letter to inform Munro that General Webb "does not think it prudent (as you know his strength at this place) to attempt a Junction or to assist you" at present.[19] Webb added that should militia not arrive at Fort Edward in time to assist him, Munro "might make the best Terms" of surrender he could.[20] Webb's messenger was tracked by one of Montcalm's Indian scouts and killed. The letter, stained with the man's blood, was found hidden in the lining of his coat and brought to Montcalm. The French commander read it and had it delivered to Munro on August 7 with the suggestion that he take Webb's advice. By that time the fort's walls had been weathering days of heavy bombardment from the French artillery, most of Munro's own cannon had burst from overheating, and his men had been up five nights in a row.[21] Morale was collapsing. He had had to threaten to hang cowards from the fort's walls, or anyone arguing for surrender.[22] Now he knew there would be no relief column. If Webb was not going to come to his aid there was little point in holding out further. Munro agreed to negotiate a surrender.

Montcalm was prepared to make terms and by 1:00 P.M. on August 9, while some Connecticut militia were just starting out on their forced march to Albany, the agreement was concluded. Munro agreed his entire garrison would remain on parole, that is take no part in the fighting, for eighteen months. In return Montcalm guaranteed a French escort would provide safe passage to Fort Edward for the entire garrison, soldiers, their families, and camp followers.[23] The French also pledged to care for anyone too sick and injured to travel and to repatriate them once they were well. In return the British were to return all French prisoners to the French at Fort Carillon by November.

Perhaps all would have gone according to their arrangements if Montcalm's Indian allies had been a party to the talks. But they were only told of the terms just before Montcalm signed them. The terms gave them nothing. They had been promised plunder, war trophies, and captives to ransom. Instead they were not to harm the defeated British, or plunder their possessions or even take the supplies left in the fort. Where was their reward for fighting for the French? The Indian chiefs listened to the terms in silence.

That afternoon after the British surrendered the fort and moved to an encampment where they were to remain until the march to Fort Edward the next day, the Indians struck. They rushed into the abandoned fort searching for plunder. Finding little they attacked the seventy sick and wounded men left behind.[24] They would have scalped them all had not some French soldiers and missionaries managed to stop them. Next they moved to the camp where the rest of the garrison was awaiting their escort. Throughout the night they plundered the terrified people gathered there. What happened at dawn the next morning is graphically described by historian Fred Anderson:

> As the regulars prepared to lead the column down the road to Fort Edward, hundreds of warriors armed with knives, tomahawks, and other weapons swarmed around them, demanding that they surrender arms, equipment, and clothing. Other Indians entered the entrenched camp, where the provincial troops and camp followers anxiously awaited the order to march, and began carrying off not only property but all the blacks, women, and children they could find among the camp followers. When at last the column began to move out, at around 5:00 A.M., the regulars in the lead marched alongside the column's French escort and thus were spared the worst of the violence that followed. The provincials at the rear of the column, however, lacked all protection and found themselves beset on every side. Within minutes, Indians had seized, killed, and scalped the

wounded from the provincial companies and stripped others of clothes, money, and possessions. As noise and confusion mounted, discipline disintegrated. Terrified men and women huddled together, trying as best they could to defend themselves. Then, with a whoop that witnesses took to be a signal, dozens of warriors began to tomahawk the most exposed groups, at the rear of the column.[25]

Men, women and children ran in all directions trying desperately to escape. Montcalm and the French soldiers did try to stop the massacre and managed to snatch some captives from the Indians. Later other captives, whom the Indians had carried back to Canada and had not yet murdered, were ransomed by the French, hoping to restore some semblance of their own honor. Their Indian captors were sent off with ransom that included thirty bottles of brandy each, canoes and other gifts.[26] Vaudreuil did not want to alienate the warriors, therefore he did not interrupt the Indian practice of "the ritual eating of a prisoner" outside the city of Montreal on August 15. On the other hand Montcalm had had his fears about the use of Indians justified, and two years later when some 1,800 Indians offered to help defend Quebec, he used them as little as possible.[27]

In a kind of rough justice the triumphant Indians carried more than ransom prizes with them as they returned to their tribes. Some, greedy for scalps, had dug up graves at Fort William Henry and scalped the corpses. Many of these had died of smallpox. As the warriors paddled those new canoes back to their tribes in the upper Great Lakes the deadly virus traveled with them.

For the British military and the American militia who had come to protect the fort it was far too late to restore French honor. As survivors trickled into Fort Edward and details of the massacre reached Benedict and the Connecticut militia at Albany there was tremendous rage and revulsion directed at the French military for this shameful and despicable act. The militia was wild with anger and frustration.

General Webb kept the militia that had reinforced Fort Edward until he was sure that Montcalm would not attack. In the meantime he had no proper provisions for them. Having seen the desperate survivors of the massacre who managed to reach Fort Edward, the men were eager to avenge the victims. But Webb would not permit them to pursue the French. Instead they had to await Webb's pleasure without tents, blankets, and with only the most basic provisions. By August 14 most of the New Yorkers would stay no longer and simply headed home, warning their officers they would be shot if they tried to stop them.[28] Captain James Delancey, lieutenant-governor of New York, responded with orders to shoot the deserters. One sergeant was shot and others were arrested.[29] The confusion finally ended on August 17 when Webb sent the militia home.

At Albany the militia was less mutinous, but the men were deeply bitter about what they regarded as French duplicity. Although Montcalm was retreating north, the Connecticut militia, like the New York militia, was prevented from pursuing him and simply sent home. They got back to their towns and families between August 23 and August 25. Their eighteen days of service had cost the colony about £15,000. [30] But it had more long-lasting costs. Anti-French and anti-Catholic hatred increased exponentially. New York's lieutenant-governor, afraid for the safety of French prisoners and "Neutrals" in New York City, ordered them jailed for their own safety and assigned a militia company to guard them.[31] After the massacre at Fort William Henry no British commander would offer a French force the opportunity to surrender with the full honors of war.[32]

For Benedict it was a horror not to be forgiven or forgotten. The French had dishonored themselves, behaving in a dastardly way toward helpless captives. They had tolerated, probably even encouraged, the atrocities of savage Indians. It was a strange and unsatisfying first experience of war. The militia played no part in the fighting, indeed were prevented from the revenge they sought. But it was a taste of the drama and uncertainty of war. He had been swept up in the urgency of the moment and as a participant in the drama, equally swept up in the outrage at the result. Deep within there were lessons being learned about the key to leading men into danger, about the difficulties of inadequate provisions, the frustration of dithering orders, the general desire that some scope be offered for bravery, for glory, for honor. Meanwhile his task was to return to what now seemed the more humdrum duties of his apprenticeship at home. His family's problems, however, turned out to be far from humdrum.

FIVE

Taking Charge

T he war continued but Benedict's brief part in it was over. His life in Norwich returned to the basic concerns of work and family. The town sent recruits off to fight in succeeding years, young men he knew, but he could take no more time from his apprenticeship. Everyone breathed a sign of relief as the war took a turn for the better during 1758, with the British forces making solid advances while the French suffered a series of problems. By 1760 the fighting was largely over. The British were well on their way to evicting the French from the eastern region of North American. It was an amazing result.

Benedict did play a further, if indirect, part in the grand victory through his work. The Lathrops sold pharmaceuticals and surgeons' supplies to the British army and the militia. Even in the midst of war their business flourished as did that of other Connecticut shippers. Because Connecticut merchant shipping was largely concerned with British mainland colonies and the West Indies the conflict with New France didn't interrupt the colony's trade as much as might have been expected.[1] Benedict learned that the Lathrops and other shippers were benefitting from increased efficiencies that his father would have envied—smaller crews, the decreasing risk of pirates and privateers, and shorter port times.[2] With these conditions Connecticut sea trade was growing steadily, especially along the Atlantic coast and with the West Indies. In 1748–49, when Captain Arnold's business was still prosperous, sixty-seven Connecticut ships had sailed to the West Indies.[3] By 1756 the number of the colony's ships trading with the West Indies had increased to 98 and by 1771 it would increase again, to 250.[4]

The Lathrops were unusual in trading with Europe as well as the Caribbean. Most local merchants had little chance to trade with Europe simply because Connecticut had little the Europeans wanted. But for the Lathrops the British trade was essential. British medicinal products, books, and other goods were a large proportion of their stock in trade. In addition to Benedict's efforts to master the pharmaceutical profession, he was learning to recognize opportunities to buy goods for which there would be a ready market. He learned how to deal with producers and transact such purchases and, just as important, how to serve customers. As he gained knowledge the Lathrops gained confidence in him. They started sending their talented apprentice on voyages to purchase goods for them. As Benedict assumed these new responsibilities and handled them successfully his confidence grew. The impoverished young man from a small Connecticut port town burdened with reduced expectations and family problems was on his way to becoming an able and skilled pharmacist and businessman. All that was to the good, increasing his personal reputation and with it his sense of honor. On the other hand his family's personal fortunes were moving inexorably in the opposite direction in a downward spiral that threatened both.

★★★

While her son was maturing and learning, Hannah Arnold was becoming increasingly exhausted from the effort of coping with the family's reduced financial circumstances and raising her daughter Hannah while keeping her husband's alcoholism and poor health from getting worse. The tension and fatigue exacted a heavy toll on her own health. In mid-August, as Norwich residents were struggling with the relentless heat and the illnesses it brought, she fell desperately ill. The end came quickly. Benedict's loving mother died. She was fifty-one. It was unclear what disease gave her that final respite that she would have seen as ending her earthly trials. It was commonly believed that Hannah Arnold died of heartbreak.[5]

Hannah and her only son had been very close. She believed in him, came to rely upon him, and imbued him with her confidence that whatever the family misfortunes, he was destined for greatness. While her strict piety may have occasionally grated on Benedict, her unfailing kindness and concern made it easier to bear. As Captain Arnold's condition and mental state worsened, mother and son depended more and more on each other for support. The loss of his mother was a terrible blow. Benedict was now a young man of eighteen. Although still an apprentice, he became the head of the family. He immediately assumed responsibility for the care of his father and sister. He also arranged for his mother's funeral. Hannah was greatly admired by the entire community. Her husband's problems had, if anything, raised her in everyone's estimation for the brave, uncomplaining way she bore them. She was laid to rest in the Norwich churchyard. In the few words her gravestone permitted, Benedict described his mother: "A pattern of patience, piety, and virtue."[6] His younger sister, Hannah, was now to be the woman of the family and shoulder her mother's burden. It was heavy indeed. Brother and sister worked together to deal with their father's distress. Hannah's death seemed to snap a final connection for Captain Arnold. He became increasingly depressed, hopelessly alcoholic, and ever more difficult to control.

★ ★ ★

The new year, as new years do, brought its measure of joy and sorrow. For Benedict, its professional joys and accomplishment were balanced against further personal family humiliation. The growing pleasure of the increasing trust and responsibility he was given by the Lathrops was offset by his father's increasing slide into mental deterioration. Daniel and Joshua officially promoted Benedict to chief clerk of the trading part of their business. In that role, young as he was, he was sent on voyages to the West Indies and even to London to purchase goods. With the French and Indian War substantially over, the seas were safer and business opportunities abounded. On his arrival at a port he made contact with the Lathrops' business associates and scouted for new merchandise and new contacts. It was exhilarating to be sailing away from Norwich. He loved the sea and the excitement each journey brought. It took him back to those long-ago voyages with his father when he was a boy. But his absences meant that Hannah was left to cope with his father's erratic behavior without his help. He was home, however, when the law struck again.

On May 26, 1760 a justice of the peace issued a warrant for Captain Arnold's arrest on a charge of public drunkenness. Three witnesses appeared before the judge testifying that he was so drunk "that he was disabled in the use of his understanding and reason."[7] The judge ordered him to pay a fine and warned the scarcely cognizant man to amend his behavior. Making ends meet was difficult enough for the Arnolds without this fine, but far worse was the public shame Hannah and Benedict endured and the worry that their father was very likely to offend again. They were not the only ones concerned.

There was a great deal of concern among the members of the First Church of Norwich about the disgraceful behavior of one of their brethren. A month after Captain Arnold's arrest one of the church deacons asked the senior Arnold to appear before the congregation to be chastised and to repent of his sin.[8] The Captain flatly refused. The church next sent a committee to meet with him at his home. Presumably Hannah and Benedict were present to witness the interview and help their father. The upshot was that the committee had no better success than the deacon. They confessed that "they had not recovered him to his duty—that he was still impertinent and refused to make a public confession." The members of the congregation were out of patience with this badly behaved and obstinate member of their congregation. His shameful ways reflected on them. Church members voted to impose "a public admonition which renders him incapable of communion in special circumstances."[9] Still nothing would bring the Captain to heel. When there began to be suggestions that he ought to be excommunicated, their minister, Reverend Lord, who had baptized the Arnold children, intervened to try to sort things out himself. He asked his congregation to show Christian pity and assured them that he would write "this poor man . . . a pungent letter." When even the pungent letter had no better success, Reverend Lord explained to his exasperated congregation that the senior Arnold was suffering from "great disorder" and "great incapacity." It was too late to expect clear thought or orderly behavior. Time to show understanding and charity to someone who had once been a respectable and prominent member of the community.

The Captain's condition continued to worsen as the year went on. Before it came to a close Benedict was arranging another funeral. The Captain's passing was a relief to his children, but terribly sad as well. Their father had started life with few possessions but boundless enthusiasm. He had risen to a position of prominence and prosperity with a loving wife and children. Then business setbacks set in, followed by the deaths of his little daughters. He began a spiral of despair from which he could not recover. His growing depression and drinking did the rest. In the end everything he had accomplished in his lifetime was taken from him but the love and concern of his son and daughter. All he left them were debts and shame. Thanks to the good will of Reverend Lord, Captain Arnold was laid to rest in the cemetery of the church he had defied, next to the wife he'd loved.

The next New Year saw the end of Benedict's apprenticeship. He was twenty-one, a trained apothecary, and keen businessman. The end of an apprenticeship was traditionally marked by "freedom dues."[10] The customary freedom dues or payment consisted of "two suits, one new."[11] The Lathrops, however, in a final act of generosity, gave Benedict £500 to purchase stock with which to launch his own business. It was a substantial sum. He chose to start his career in New Haven, a bustling Connecticut port town. New Haven, on busy Long Island Sound, was larger than Norwich and home to Yale College. It was an excellent choice for selling both medical supplies and books for the students. If his father's business had remained prosperous, if his father had not become an alcoholic, Benedict would have arrived in New Haven years earlier as a student at that college. Now he would come to New Haven to sell books to the fortunate boys studying there. Still, he was full of hope that in this new setting respect and honor could yet be earned through his own hard work and his courage.

SIX

Smooth and Choppy Waters

B enedict's decision to launch his career in New Haven was
inspired. The city was booming. It was the fastest growing
port on Long Island Sound. He was joining a throng of
settlers to this co-capital of Connecticut, a throng that would
quadruple its population between 1750 and 1775. Its wharfs were
crowded with ships of all sizes loading and unloading cargoes from
perilous voyages across the Atlantic or picked up skimming the
length of the continent from the forests and rocky coasts of Canada
to the lush tropical islands of the Caribbean. Indeed, Connecticut
ports had seen an amazing growth in shipping during those years.
Despite their pretensions of gentility most of the town's old,
established families were descendants of seafaring merchants and
many were still deeply involved in trade. What a perfect setting
for an enterprising and daring young man with his reputation and
fortune to make.

Away from its hectic commercial wharfs New Haven was a pretty town. Its brick and wooden Georgian homes were encircled by neat gardens. On the western side of the handsome town green stood the buildings of Yale College chartered some sixty years before in hopes the "Youth may be instructed in the Arts and Sciences [and] through the blessing of Almighty God may be fitted for Publick employment both in Church and Civil State." So they had been, fitted for that and much else. The college was named after Elihu Yale, a merchant engaged in international trade, who donated the income from the sale of nine bales of goods along with 417 books to the college, together with a portrait of King George I. It was to Yale College that Benedict's parents had hoped to send their only son. But if Benedict resented those young men able, although not always willing, to devote their days to book learning he did not show it. He had no time for such regrets. He was a young man of action and intellect with much to do.

Happily his uncle Oliver, his father's brother, was living in New Haven and offered him a home and board while he got settled. That was especially generous since Oliver's was a bustling household with his aunt, uncle, and their five children crammed into a modest house in the midst of a small garden. Benedict would repay their kindness years later sending funds to support those children when his uncle's death after a long illness left his family destitute.[1] But that was in the future. For the moment he concentrated on locating a small store for rent. He found one on Chapel Street near the waterfront. Then off he sailed to England to purchase the goods to stock it, using the £500 the Lathrops had given him.[2] Back in New Haven with the shop stocked, he proudly hung a specially painted sign outside the shop door, "B. Arnold Druggist Bookseller &c. From London." The sign sported the Latin motto, *Sibi Totique*, "For Himself and for Everybody."

The druggist-bookseller label gave little hint of the range of goods crammed inside. Alongside the pharmaceuticals, medical instruments, and herbs of all sorts, Arnold's shop sold cosmetics, watches, earrings, stationery, maps, prints, and a large selection of books for Yale students and other town readers.[3] His books included the usual sober religious works and sermons of the period as well as law books. Customers also had their choice of the works of Ben Jonson, Dryden, Prior, Pope, Swift, Locke, Thomson's *Seasons*, *Clarissa*, *Peregrine Pickle*, *Tom Jones*, *Pamela*, plays, more novels, practical books such as one on midwifery, and classic works of Plutarch and Aristotle. The shop was the only one of its kind and a delight. Little wonder the business was such a success that twice in quick succession Arnold had to move his store to larger, more upscale quarters. His customers began calling him Dr. Arnold.[4]

Even before that, however, indeed that very autumn as soon as he had accumulated enough money, Benedict returned to Norwich to pay off his father's debts. Hannah was still living in their once grand family home. The Lathrops, unfailingly kind, had purchased their father's mortgage so Hannah would have a home. Benedict now bought the mortgage from them, sold the old house at a profit and moved his dear sister to New Haven, cutting their immediate ties to Norwich. With its humiliations behind them, they could both enjoy this fresh start in life and Benedict's growing success.

Hannah had grown into a lovely and refined young woman, capable and respected. For her entire life she would be her brother's faithful friend and helper. They barely looked like siblings. Where Benedict had thick, dark hair and gray eyes and was solidly built, Hannah was unusually tall and slender with blond hair but similar blue-gray eyes.[5] Despite all her virtues and attractions she would never marry. If rumors were to be believed, she might well have resented her brother's rather fierce interference with one early suitor. Shortly before Hannah joined Benedict in New Haven, she was being courted by a young Frenchman. Arnold, like many New Englanders, had an understandably passionate hatred of the French. His brief but bitter experience of them in the French and Indian War and before that—their tactics over many decades egging on their Indian allies to terrorize and massacre the region's settlers—left a permanent disgust. When Benedict learned about his young sister's French suitor he was livid. At the earliest opportunity he confronted the young man warning him never to see Hannah again. But, as the story goes, on another of his visits to Norwich Benedict spotted the Frenchman again at the family home. He bided his time and as the man emerged from the house fired a warning shot. This time the ardent Frenchman took flight and was never seen at the Arnolds' again. The two men would meet in the Caribbean years later with dramatic results.

Benedict quickly began moving in professional circles, seeking and finding business partners. He struck up a friendship with Adam Babcock, another young New Haven merchant, just a year older than Benedict, and the two formed a partnership. Their backgrounds were very different. Unlike Benedict, Adam hadn't come from a merchant family, hadn't known its constant worries and excitement as ships sailed off and returned from risky voyages, with them fortunes made or lost. Adam's father, Dr. Joshua Babcock of Westerly, Connecticut was a physician, a gentleman farmer, scholar, and eccentric, famous for his austere and regular habits.[6] A fellow doctor visiting him wrote that the senior Babcock had berated him for his breakfast coffee and toast, pointing out "better live as I do, out of this old silver porringer and with this spoon I have taken my breakfast for forty years." Perhaps it was this father so proudly regular, drinking exactly three cups of tea every teatime, eating only one main dish at dinner every day, that drove his son to seek a more exciting life in New Haven, sailing to foreign parts.

The two young men invested in a forty-ton sloop they named *Fortune*. A ship of their own gave the partners more flexibility to find good deals picking up and exchanging local cargoes. From early spring until late fall they sailed south to the Caribbean and north to Quebec. By the time Benedict was twenty-five he and Adam owned three ships. In addition to *Fortune*, they had bought two other ships. And with these came more time at sea, more opportunities, more profit.

From childhood summers spent sailing with his father, Benedict had loved the thrill of sea voyages. Adding to the sheer exhilaration of travel now came the game of spotting profitable deals for his business, trading goods from eastern Canada to New Yorkers and New Englanders and products from the West Indies to individuals and small manufacturers back home. He dealt in "large, genteel, fat horses," pork, oats, salt, hay, mahogany, and gallons and gallons of rum.[7] After Hannah joined him she helped with the day-to-day business of the shop while he was off on voyages. The New Haven shop became the headquarters for their lively, international business.

Another business connection of Benedict's was Comfort Sage, a prosperous merchant from Middletown. Comfort, ten years Benedict's senior, had been an officer in the Connecticut militia during the French and Indian War, rising from quartermaster of a troop of horsemen in 1757 to captain in 1763.[8] He was much respected in the region and served as a justice of the peace. The Arnold and Sage families were to become very close over the years. Although both Sage and Arnold were businessmen with families needing their support, both men joined the fight for independence when war came.[9]

Two serious hazards threatened this prosperous career. One Benedict foresaw, the other he did not. First, the increasingly burdensome British restrictions on trade and taxes were a growing threat to his business. Like many other New England merchants he began to resort to smuggling goods to circumvent British duties. The second hazard he understood from boyhood, that much rested on his personal involvement in the trade. He sailed himself, and although he hired other captains, the buying and selling, the spotting of opportunities depended on his insight. Anything that took him away from his shipping business for a length of time might sink his buoyant finances. He did not foresee the coming war or the part he would play in it.

Whenever he was home from his voyages Benedict plunged into New Haven's social scene. He was handsome and prosperous and a contemporary noted that he soon became, "a general favorite with the ladies, fond of their society, and floating in the gayest circles of the day."[10]

He was also gaining a growing reputation with the men. He was admitted to New Haven's Masonic Lodge in 1765 when he was twenty-four.[11] This honor required recommendation by two masons, a Recommender and a Master Mason who signed as Avoucher. They were to testify to his "reputation of unsullied honor and probity." He was elected by unanimous consent. With other masons he pledged to "live honorably, practice justice, love his neighbor, work unceasingly for the true happiness of humanity, and help human beings to emancipate themselves from the thralldom of passion and ignorance." With this membership Benedict had arrived.

Freemasonry was relatively new in the colonies. The lodge at New Haven, founded in 1750, was the state's first. Membership was open to any man over eighteen years of age who believed in a Supreme Being and was of sound moral character. In joining the freemasons Arnold was joining the secretive, benevolent society to which an extraordinary number of America's leaders and founders belonged, among them George Washington, Benjamin Franklin, James Monroe, John Jay, John Hancock, Paul Revere, John Paul Jones, and James Otis. At least nine signers of the Declaration of Independence and an equal number of signers of the Constitution were freemasons, as well as nearly half of the generals in the colonial army.

Samuel Mansfield, a prosperous merchant and high sheriff of the county was a fellow mason. Samuel was sufficiently impressed by Benedict to invite the younger man to dine with his family on several occasions. This brought Arnold into contact with Samuel's eldest daughter Margaret.[12] She would be his first love.

Samuel Mansfield was one of New Haven's most respected men, a graduate of Yale College, nevertheless his house was not far from his wharf and store, all were on East Water Street.[13] Margaret— Peggy—the Mansfield's oldest daughter was four years younger than Benedict. Their first child, Esther, had died in infancy. Margaret and three other daughters were born before Samuel and his wife Esther had two sons, Moses Samuel, who went by his father's name, Samuel, and Giles Daniel. Peggy was a shy young woman, attractive, amiable, and affectionate, and like Benedict's mother Hannah, devout.[14] She attended the city's strict North Church, a congregation her parents only joined after their daughter. Before the courtship of Benedict and Peggy could proceed politics and scandal intervened.

The issue was import duties. The British were becoming serious about collecting these duties. Not surprising, really, since the British public was increasingly upset by the burden of supporting the defense of their North American colonies. The French and Indian War had been a victory, but an expensive one. British debt incurred by the war has been estimated at £137 million, or over 1.3 billion pounds in today's currency.[15] It seemed only fair that the colonists who were, after all, the beneficiaries, should help maintain the British army in America. The Sugar Tax passed in April 1764 actually cut the duty on molasses from six pence to three pence a gallon. But a three-pence tax that is actually collected is worse than a six-pence tax that is not.[16] The Sugar Tax hit the molasses trade, key to the great New England rum industry. With West Indian molasses they produced thousands of gallons of rum. Benedict and other New England traders were especially dependent on the French islands in the West Indies for sugarcane and the new restrictions on that trade posed a serious problem. The general public tended to connive with the smugglers, in part because paying British duties raised the prices for goods, but also because they considered the taxes and trade restrictions unfair. The colonists were not represented in Parliament, of course, and had no say in their passage. The shipping business was essential to the prosperity of the little seaside cities and towns. "Connecticut cargo" became a popular expression for smuggled goods. Still another difficulty for merchants was the serious shortage in specie with which to pay taxes and business debts.

Adding insult to injury, the colonists deeply resented the tax being intended for the support of the British army now that the war was over. English tradition and the English Bill of Rights warned that keeping a standing, or professional, army in peacetime was a danger to liberty. Armies were the tool of tyrants. The patriotic sense of injustice certainly made smuggling seem respectable and even a public benefit. However, it did make smugglers vulnerable to anyone who had a grudge and might want to inform against them for the rewards offered.

On November 1, 1765 the Stamp Act was due to take effect and, even more than the Sugar Act it drove the tempers of Americans to a boil. It was an excise tax, rather than an import tax. It taxed paper used for official documents, newspapers, and playing cards. Merchants would need to use the stamped paper to record their cargoes. Mobs incited by the newly formed "Sons of Liberty" terrorized those officials brave enough to distribute the stamped paper for the government and collect the tax. A mob in New York City led by Isaac Sears, a shipmaster, frightened the lieutenant-governor so much the poor man sought refuge on a British warship in the harbor.[17] Not content, the mob went on to attack the fort at the Battery, then broke into the governor's coach house and destroyed his coaches.[18] Sometimes such crowd action ended peacefully, other times not. In Boston the stamp official was yanked from bed and his house ransacked. In South Carolina when Henry Laurens was suspected of being involved in Stamp Act distribution, his friends in disguise yanked him from bed and searched his house. Boston's stamp collector was burned in effigy and his shop destroyed.

In Connecticut the stamp official for New Haven was Jared Ingersoll, Benedict's friend and attorney. Ingersoll was a dutiful, law-abiding, and respected individual. But when the public learned of his new duties Ingersoll became the target of mob intimidation. In the autumn of 1765, when the hated Stamp Act was due to take effect, Ingersoll was confronted by an angry crowd. He quickly agreed to yield to the crowd's demands that he resign from the office and denounce the Stamp Act. [19] In addition he had to swear an oath "never to receive any Stampt-Papers, which may arrive from Europe, in consequence of any act lately passed in the Parliament of Great Britain, nor officiate in any manner as Stamp Master." For good measure he was further convinced to publically request "all the inhabitants of this his majesty's Colony of Connecticut . . . not to apply to me, ever hereafter, for any such stamped Papers." Mollified, the crowd asked him "to give Liberty and Property, with three Cheers," which he did, followed by the traditional three huzzas. For good measure they took him to the colonial assembly in Hartford and before its building he repeated his vow. Ingersoll's treatment and resignation made newspapers in Massachusetts, Pennsylvania, and New York.[20] He wrote an agent in London explaining, "I hope you will be the Colony's friend whatever some people may think of me . . . Whatever errors I have committed in public life, I have always loved my country . . . Whatever usage I have received from my country, it shall never make me break with her . . . I have received much unreserved favor and good at the hands of my country and shall I not bear with a little abuse, especially, upon so irritating an occasion as the Stamp Act?"[21] In March the following spring the British parliament withdrew the hated Stamp Act to great rejoicing in the colonies.

For Benedict it was various English restrictions and duties, especially on sugar, and the shortage of specie that were the problems. His politics are interesting. He was not a Son of Liberty, or one of Connecticut's leaders of that often intemperate group. Ingersoll's memoirs never name him as one. While Arnold was irate at British taxes and duties on imports and a devoted colonist, he never let his views poison his relationships with men and women who did not agree with him. Arnold and Ingersoll were, and remained, close friends. In January 1766, several months after Ingersoll's ordeal, one angry sailor threatening to turn informer pushed him into the public spotlight in dramatic fashion. Ingersoll came to his friend's aid.

Peter Boles was a sailor aboard Arnold's ship, *Fortune,* as it docked in New Haven harbor that January.[22] Boles knew, as did all the crew, that the *Fortune* was carrying molasses that had been loaded without the required duty. On their arrival in port he demanded Arnold pay him to keep his silence or he would report the smuggled goods to the excise official for the reward the government offered. The penalty for smuggling was stiff, confiscation of the ship's cargo and possibly the ship itself.

Benedict was furious and refused to pay the blackmail. Boles immediately followed through on his threat, stalking off to the customhouse. Luckily for Arnold the custom master was not there at the time. When Arnold found out about Boles's attempt he confronted him and frightened him into agreeing to leave town. But Boles didn't go. Two days later Arnold learned Bowles was still in New Haven drinking away his earnings in a local tavern.[23] Furious, Arnold got together a group of men and they marched to the tavern. Ingersoll's experience served as a template for Arnold's strategy. The crowd confronted Boles, handing him a statement in which he admitted to being "instigated by the Devil" in trying to inform against Arnold and "deserved a halter" for his "malicious and cruel intentions." He promised never to inform against any merchant and to immediately leave New Haven forever.[24] But, unlike Ingersoll who kept his vow, Boles violated his. When he was discovered four hours later still drinking in the tavern Arnold and an even larger group of men hauled him from the building to the public whipping post where they lashed him forty times then escorted him out of New Haven.

That was on January 2. There the incident might have ended, had not two members of the New Haven grand jury, John Wise and Titley Blakeslee, reported the incident to the county sheriff, Roger Sherman. An arrest warrant was duly issued the very next day charging Arnold and the rest of Boles's assailants with "unlawfully and notoriously" assembling with "intent with force and violence" and then did "assault, batter and evilly entreat the person of Peter Bowes," who the warrant oddly describes as "a transient person then and still residing in New Haven."[25] The warrant states that Benedict and the others:

> . . . then and there with great force and violence did
> unlawfully breach the dwelling house of John Beacher
> [Beacher's tavern] of sd New Haven . . . and did with
> some force and violence then and there assault the body
> of Peter Boles being in sd house in the peace of God and
> stripped him of his apparel and tied and fastened him to
> the whipping post in New Haven and him did beat and
> abuse in a cruel shocking and dangerous manner to his
> grievous damage and against the peace to the terror of
> his Majesties subjects.

The sheriff was ordered "forthwith to apprehend the Bodies of the above named Benedict Arnold and some 11 others and bring them before Roger Sherman, justice of the peace, at 3rd day of January 1766." Arnold was out of town when the hearing occurred but he was defended by Jared Ingersoll. Despite Ingersoll's defense Arnold was fined fifty shillings for disturbing the peace.[26]

The approach Arnold and the other merchants and sailors adopted to deal with the would-be informer was the same technique used earlier in dealing with men who had agreed to serve as collectors for the hated Stamp Act. Ingersoll had abided by his sworn agreement. Boles repeatedly violated his. Arnold could not let it rest. His reputation was at stake in the larger community and he wanted his version of events made public. As he wrote to the press, "finding the affair misrepresented much to my disadvantage," as there was an article in the Connecticut newspaper, he was anxious to publish his own account of the affair.[27] He stressed first that Boles "was used with the greatest humanity, on our return was paid his wage to his full satisfaction" and had told Arnold he meant to leave town immediately. But, Arnold stressed, he appeared instead at the New Haven customhouse two days later, intending to inform against his employer for the reward offered. Before he was able to meet with the custom master Benedict gave him what he characterized as "a little Chastisement" and Boles left town. But again Boles returned. Again Benedict confronted him and this time Boles "agreed to and signed" an oath swearing to "never hereafter make information, directly or indirectly, or cause the same to be done against any person or person, whatever for importing Contraband or any other goods into this Colony, or any Port of America." The language of the oath focused not on Arnold's own profits but on the threat informers posed to all colonial merchants. Boles promised to leave town immediately in return for Benedict promising not to tell the other sailors of his presence, which would jeopardize their livelihoods. But when Boles failed to leave immediately the sailors were informed, and with Arnold and others seized the man. "I then made one of the party and took him to the Whipping Post," Arnold concedes, and after his thrashing conducted him out of town. When Boles once again reappeared Arnold submitted the affair to Col. David Wooster and Mr. Enos Allen whom he describes as "Gentlemen of reputed good judgment and understanding." Both "were of opinion that the fellow was not whipped too much, and gave him 50s damages." Arnold concludes his letter to the press with a query:

Is it good policy or would so great a number of People, in any trading town on the Continent, (New Haven excepted) vindicate, protect, and caress an informer a character particularly at this alarming time so justly odious to the Public? Every such information tends to suppress our trade, so advantageous to the Colony, and to almost every individual both here and in Great Britain, and which is nearly ruined by the late detestable stamp and other oppressive acts, acts which we have so severely felt, and so loudly complained of, and so earnestly remonstrated against, that one would imagine every sensible man would strive to encourage trade and discountenance such useless, such infamous Informers.[28]

This was Arnold's entry into the political maelstrom that would lead to war.

This very public arrest was a striking contrast from his father's humiliating arrest for public drunkenness in Norwich. While Benedict had also disturbed the public order, he had acted together with a group of men to punish a would-be informer. Those responsible for law and order in New Haven were right to object to this vigilante approach, but the general shipping community would have supported, if not the whipping, the message it sent to others tempted to inform on merchants evading British duties. Arnold became a popular hero for the shipping community and its workers.

Later that year another of his father's problems would hit him—debt. Throughout 1766 Arnold wrestled with the predicament of staying solvent. He was careful in his business dealings but in these hard times sums owed to him were not being paid, sometimes not for years, and then he was unable to meet his own obligations. He wrote politely to those owing him money, and on at least two occasions, in 1763 and again in 1765, the Lathrops wrote on his behalf urging men with long outstanding bills to please pay him.[29]

His financial situation reached a crisis in the summer of 1767. But several months earlier, in the dead of winter, Benedict was blessed with new joy and a new obligation. He married the woman he loved, Peggy Mansfield.

SEVEN

Love, Marriage, Duels, and Honor

T he marriage took place on February 22 in the First Church, a conservative church on the New Haven town green. Peggy was twenty-two, Benedict twenty-six, good sensible ages for a first marriage. There were cynics who saw this marriage as a real coup for the young man from Norwich. But in fact Arnold's prospects were as sound as any in that difficult time, despite the headache of British duties. And after all, Peggy's father Samuel may have been sheriff of the county, but he was also a merchant whose wharf and store were not far from his handsome house.

It seems to have been a loving marriage, at least on Benedict's part. He was deeply in love with Peggy. Yet she had been aloof during their courtship, not replying to his letters. In May, 1766 he wrote complaining that he had been in the West Indies seven weeks but had "heard not one syllable from you since I left home."[1] Nonetheless she agreed to marry him, and he didn't seem concerned that his betrothed was such a melancholy, reluctant correspondent, perhaps attributing her behavior to her shyness. He quickly found that marriage did not make her more communicative. This was particularly hard because Arnold's shipping business meant he had to be away from home for months at a time on long and often dangerous voyages. He may have been away when, nearly a year to the day of their wedding, little Benedict was born. These absences were difficult for the newly married couple. Arnold wrote "his dear girl" as often as he could during these journeys, assuring her, "you and you only can imagine how long the time seems since we parted and how impatient I am to see you and the dear little pledge of our mutual love. God bless you both and send us a happy meeting soon."[2] He pleaded for news of his little family but, it was some two months later, while he was still in the Caribbean buying and trading cargoes, before he received a letter from Peggy assuring him that she and little Ben were well. [3] He occasionally got news of his family when he chanced to meet and quiz the captain of another New Haven vessel, but these ships seldom brought the longed-for letter from Peggy. In frustration he wrote complaining to his "dear girl," "I assure you I think it hard you have wrote me only once when there have been so many opportunities."[4] Still, he ended this letter on a loving note, asking that "the best of Heaven's blessings attend you, and may we both be under the care of a kind Providence, and soon, very soon, have a happy meeting is the sincere prayer of your ever affectionate husband."[5]

In August a year later Peggy gave birth to a second son, Richard. Three years afterward, in 1772, a third child, Henry, was born. His growing family made Arnold's voyages, with the attendant anxiety of partings and worries, all the more imperative. His wife, his sister, and his little sons were depending on him. These absences were the cost of a merchant trader's life, and New Haven and all other American ports were filled with families anxiously awaiting the return of their men. New England was known for the rooftop lookouts on its houses, the "widow's walk." Many mariners' wives helped keep the business records and handle various transactions while their men were off on voyages.[6] In Arnold's case it was his sister Hannah who helped. Peggy seems to have resented these long absences, for she rarely answered Benedict's letters pleading for news of her and their little ones. She also must have fretted about the debts her husband was working frantically to repay. He wrote her not to let creditors bother her, and please could she write to him.[7] But her letters never became more frequent. Indeed, in 1773, six years after they were married, Benedict's patience was exhausted. He wrote in exasperation from a business voyage to Quebec, "I am now under the greatest anxiety and suspense, not knowing whether I write to the dead or the living, not having heard the least syllable from you this last four months.[8] I have wrote you almost every post . . . have this three posts expected answers and been disappointed. I am now loaded and am set to sail tomorrow for Barbados." A few days later, still not having set sail for the long voyage south, he wrote again, "With an aching and anxious heart, I resume my pen. The post arrived yesterday and no letters. This I cannot account for . . . I have now given over any thoughts of hearing from you until I get to the West Indies . . . I sail this afternoon." Benedict left Quebec in October. He hoped to be home by December.

What of the much loved "dear girl." Certainly Benedict never understood her, never broke through her reserve. Shy, depressed Peggy must have wondered what the good of financial prosperity was if she was left without her husband for months at a time, left in the company of her sister-in-law Hannah and her own parents, raising her children alone. Most merchants hired captains to sail to the West Indies and negotiate the deals for them. But not Benedict. He did hire other captains but he also insisted on traveling himself. It was his shrewd eye for a bargain that made his enterprise such a success, but there was a toll to be paid for those long absences.

Peggy's silence while he was away became a permanent feature of their relationship. It was a difficult life Benedict had chosen, but one he knew and possessed a talent for. Torn as he was between being home with his family or at sea, he had little choice. He was desperate to make a success of his business and avoid his father's fate, arrest for debt. Most of all he was anxious to keep his reputation as a man of integrity and honor.

Like many hundreds of colonial traders Benedict found debt could not be avoided. Within months of his marriage to Peggy, Benedict's financial problems became worse. In fact, despite his hard work and careful calculations, he was slipping into debt even before his marriage. By 1767 he owed some £1,700 to his London suppliers.[9] In his father's day men who could not pay their debts were jailed, but in 1767 the Connecticut authorities decided that prisons overflowing with debtors made little sense when other means might be found to repay creditors. They came to agree with an anonymous Connecticut writer who argued in 1755 that it was unjust to imprison a man who "by the badness of the Time in Trade, or by the mere Providence of God, has been reduced."[10] The legislature decided to permit debtors to take an oath to keep working to repay their bills.[11] Happily Benedict was a beneficiary of this new approach. His friend and attorney, Jared Ingersoll, negotiated a deal with his London creditors permitting him to continue in business to repay the sums he owed them.[12] Benedict's sloop *Sally* and her cargo were to be held as security and payment "of one half of the demands." The deal included a schedule for repayment. Ingersoll was to approve the amount of security Arnold had to pay in case his next voyage did not turn sufficient profit and he needed another trip to raise the sum required. Ingersoll was also to ensure that Benedict was permitted sufficient time to sell the cargo. With the burden of this debt repayment schedule Benedict drove himself even harder, expanding the range of products he purchased. Sometimes he traded goods from one Caribbean island to another, rather than bringing products from the tropics back to New England. His hard work paid off. Despite British economic policies, he managed to repay his debt and once again prosper.

Ever in the background though, were the policies and taxes coming from London to regulate and benefit from American trade. Sometimes the news was hopeful, other times dismal. In 1766 a reluctant British Parliament withdrew the hated Stamp Act by a narrow majority. Immediately afterward, however, a large majority of MPs approved the Declaratory Act. Modeled on the 1719 Irish Act, the Declaratory Act reaffirmed Parliament's right to legislate for the colonies "in all cases whatsoever." In their joy over the repeal of the Stamp Act few Americans noticed this ominous legislation. They would be reminded of it in February 1767. While Arnold was desperately trying to regain solvency, Parliament passed the Townshend Act. Since the colonists objected to an excise tax the Townshend Act imposed the customary import taxes, this time on glass, paint, lead, paper, and tea. Parliament also acted to ensure more vigorous collection of these taxes. Customs officers assigned to monitor American imports who remained in Britain and hired agents to work in the colonies now were dismissed. The British government was intent on cracking down on the casual manner in which those who evaded the required duties were dealt with.

Many Americans were, as always, incensed by new taxes. They protested and organized boycotts of the taxed goods and of merchants who imported them. Boycotts did not satisfy the Massachusetts legislature, however. Members drafted a sharp letter denouncing the tax and sent copies to all the other colonial assemblies urging them to do likewise. The British government was fed up with this quarrelsome colony. Their response was swift and angry. Four army regiments were sent to Boston, one soldier for every four inhabitants.

This was a dangerous policy. The king's soldiers were resented and taunted. On March 5, 1770, a few dockside youths began throwing ice at a lone British sentry. The frightened soldier called for help. The rowdy crowd of his tormentors grew. A British officer and his men rushed to protect him from the disorderly mob. Shots were fired and five Bostonians were killed. It had not been premeditated. The soldiers had been harassed and endangered. But the Sons of Liberty promptly labeled the incident the Boston Massacre. Three local engravers, eager to make money from the tragedy, dashed off prints of the event. The most famous, by Paul Revere, was entitled *The Bloody Massacre perpetrated on King Street,* and sold like proverbial hotcakes. News of the shootings spread quickly and provoked fury throughout the colonies. The actual details of the event dropped away, leaving only the violence of the shooting, stark and awful. Armed soldiers had killed unarmed colonists.

Arnold was in the Caribbean when he learned of the incident. The news traveled from colony to colony quickly but was slow reaching him on St. George's Key as he explained in a letter to his New Haven friend Douglas:

> I am now in a corner of the world whence you can expect no news of consequence, yet was very much shocked the other day on hearing the accounts of the most wanton, cruel, and inhumane murders committed in Boston by the soldiers. Good God! Are the Americans all asleep; and tamely yielding up their liberties, or are they all turned philosophers, that they do not take immediate vengeance on such miscreants; I am afraid of the latter and that we shall all soon see ourselves as poor and as much oppressed as ever a heathen philosopher was.[13]

John Adams successfully defended the soldiers, but Arnold and the general population knew that even if this case could somehow be justified in law, such incidents were bound to happen when a professional army was bivouacked in the midst of civilians during a time of peace. Every common law tenet and the English Bill of Rights told them so. Local militia, made up of citizen-soldiers like

Comfort Sage and Arnold himself in 1757, could be trusted to have the welfare of their people at heart. Not so professional soldiers, especially foreign ones.

Voyages to the Caribbean may not have been as dramatic as war, but carried all sorts of hazards, quite apart from the fitful winds and turbulent seas. Arnold's long absences in the Caribbean, his growing success, his manner and politics bred jealousies and nasty gossip. And nasty gossip threatened to diminish his hard-won reputation. Late in 1770 news reached Arnold that someone was spreading a rumor in New Haven that he had contracted venereal disease while in the Caribbean the previous year. This outrageous claim was obviously false as he was in good health. But Benedict was furious. It had "hurt my good character here very much," he wrote, "and given my family and friends much uneasiness."[14] Poor Peggy and Hannah, both devout and refined women, suffered from the taunt that he had consorted with prostitutes and picked up this dreadful disease. However successful Arnold became, he could not let this or any smear on his reputation stand. Someone else might have just denounced the rumor as a lie and pointed to his own good health. Not Arnold. He tracked down the suspected source, a New Haven ship's captain, possibly a former employee, and had Ingersoll sue the man for libel. He got depositions from men with whom he had worked in the West Indies testifying that he was in "perfect health" when he was in Honduras, where he was supposed to have contracted the disease, and that he lived a temperate life while there, "eating, and drinking wine and punch, and any spirituous liquors as freely as any person" and keeping good company.[15] With his father's sad example before him, Arnold was painfully aware of the dangers of excessive drink. Arnold even fought a duel in the West Indies against a Mr. Brookman who was spreading the tale about "a whore I wanted to take from him."[16] Successful people tend to have detractors. Successful, feisty people have even more. Arnold was feisty and proud. All his adult life he was plagued by a variety of enemies ready to tarnish his name, compete with him for positions, and generally sully his honor.

In addition to the rumors of dissipation and disease, there were direct insults to his honor as a gentleman. In an era when perceived slights to a man's honor were considered serious, Benedict was typical of many men, especially self-made men, who resorted to duels to protect their reputations. The rough and tumble world of international trade in the West Indies was the perfect seed ground for misunderstandings among proud, independent men. The tale of a duel retold by generations of Arnold's own family was one he fought in Honduras against Captain Croskie, the British captain of a merchant ship. As Arnold was preparing to set sail Croskie invited him to attend a party. Preoccupied with numerous tasks before departure, Arnold simply forgot to send his regrets. However, he went to Croskie's home the next morning to pay his respects and apologize for this neglect. The apology was not enough for the British captain who snapped that Arnold was "a damned Yankee, destitute of good manners or those of a gentleman."[17] Benedict quietly removed his glove and handed it to Croskie. The arrogant Briton had demeaned him as an ignorant Yankee rube. Croskie also had sworn at Arnold, an offense that qualified as blasphemy back in Connecticut.

The duel was arranged for the next morning on a nearby island. It was agreed each man was to bring only a second and a surgeon. Arnold arrived at the appointed time and waited for Croskie to appear. After a long delay he was about to leave when Croskie arrived in a boat with six natives. Arnold insisted that only Croskie and his two attendants be permitted to dock. When Croskie objected Arnold stood on the beach, pistol in hand, forbidding the rest to come ashore. Croskie conceded and final preparations were made. As the challenged man Croskie had the first shot. He missed. Then Arnold fired and wounded Croskie. The injury was attended to by the surgeon and Arnold called to Croskie to resume his position and take another shot, warning,

"I give you notice, if you miss this time I shall kill you." At this point Croskie decided discretion was the better option, gave his hand to Arnold and apologized. The two men returned together, in the same boat.

There was a rumor that while he was in the Caribbean Arnold came across the young Frenchman who had courted his sister in Norwich, and challenged the young man to a duel. Whatever the truth of it, Benedict survived these tests of his manliness without physical injury and, the attitudes of the time being what they were, with his reputation and honor intact.

By 1772 when his third son was born, Benedict was once again prosperous, so prosperous that he got three acres of prime land on Water Street from his father-in-law and began building a house for his growing family. It was a fine site on a rise overlooking the harbor. The new house was built on a grand, even ostentatious scale, measuring forty-eight feet long by thirty-eight feet deep. The house was covered in traditional New England clapboard, painted white. On the roof was the equally traditional and poignant widow's walk.[18] The interior was finished in lavish style with mahogany panels and marble fireplaces. Around the house were formal gardens. Behind it stables for a large number of horses, a coach house, and an orchard. It was a show of wealth, of having arrived. But interestingly it also looked like the house Arnold's own father had built for his family, before his fortune collapsed and he became an alcoholic.[19] On Sundays when Benedict was at home he, Peggy and their little sons attended the First Church. Prayers for the Lord's blessings on that home and that family were certainly, if silently made, prayers that the widow's walk never be a lookout for an actual widow.

They hardly needed the clergyman to remind them that life and health were precious and transient. Fears for his fragile Peggy were in Benedict's mind in a letter to her of January, 1774.[20] He was alarmed and troubled to learn of the death of a neighbor, Adam Babcock's young wife, and another young woman.

It has been a few days since I heard of the death of Mrs. Babcock and Polly Austin, which surprise me much. They were in the prime of life and as likely to live as any of us. How uncertain is life, how certain is death.

Benedict prayed,

> May their loud and affecting calls awaken us to prepare for our own exit, whenever it shall happen. My dear Life, pray by no means neglect the education of our dear boys. It is of infinite concern what habits and principles they imbibe when young.

> I hope this will find you all well and that the Almighty may preserve you in health and happiness is the sincere prayer of, dear Peggy,

> Your loving husband,
> Benedict Arnold.

Life held unpleasant surprises beyond the death of the young. There was politics. On April 12, 1770, the month following the Boston Massacre, Parliament agreed to repeal the Townshend Act. But revenues were needed and the British taxpayer was tired of paying for colonial defense. Therefore, three years later, in 1773, Parliament passed the Tea Act granting the British East India Company a monopoly on importing tea to the colonies. Apart from the revenue, the monopoly was meant to help the company's finances. Again Americans responded with boycotts. These were made more difficult because the East India tea was actually cheaper than smuggled tea. When late that year three ships loaded with East India tea entered Boston Harbor the local Sons of Liberty feared if the tea were unloaded people would buy it. Their campaign against the tax would collapse. Unable to get the governor to prohibit the landing, a group disguised as Indians boarded the vessels. They broke open the 342 chests of tea, worth some £10,000, dumping the contents into the harbor. The British government was furious and demanded that the company be reimbursed. The Massachusetts assembly refused. After all, unknown "red Indians" had been the vandals. The British government decided it had no option but to make an example of Boston by punishing the town and the entire Massachusetts Bay Colony until restitution was made for the tea and for losses sustained by Crown servants, and until King George III himself had determined that "peace and obedience to the laws" had been restored.

In the meantime the punishment they devised was draconian. The Massachusetts charter, with its guarantee to residents of the rights of Englishmen, was revoked. The governor of Massachusetts was removed and replaced with the military commander for the colonies, General Thomas Gage. The governor's council was now appointed by the Crown, not chosen by the colonial legislature. The port of Boston was closed, town meetings forbidden without prior permission and the colonial government moved north to Salem. Trials of crown officials could be moved to another colony or even to Great Britain. More British troops were sent to reinforce those already in Boston. The Quebec Act, passed a few months later, settled how the British meant to govern Canada and was regarded as intolerable as well. Not only was the Catholic church permitted to remain the official church and French civil law to be retained for private affairs, but the act transferred to Canada the Indian territory that would later become the states of Illinois, Indiana, Michigan, Ohio, Wisconsin, and parts of Minnesota.

These "Intolerable Acts" shocked other colonies and alarmed the Second Continental Congress. Contributions of food and supplies were sent to the people of Boston. Protection was needed but the regular militia was in the hands of the government and of uncertain loyalty. Colonists in Massachusetts, Connecticut, and other colonies began to form voluntary groups of militia, prepared to act in an emergency, the Minutemen. They were prepared to defend their towns and families should the British take military action in Massachusetts or elsewhere. At the town of Concord, some thirty miles from Boston and away from the watchful gaze of General Gage and his army, they began feverishly assembling an arsenal, including cannon, for a militia army. Its task was to defend the colony should Gage send his men to attack the colonists and burn their homes and villages.

Arnold was outraged by the treatment of Massachusetts and the precedent it posed for other colonies. Once home he joined a group of sixty-five young New Haven men who formed themselves into a militia company and started drilling regularly. In March 1775 Connecticut officials adopted the group as the Governor's 2nd Company of Guards. The Guards, or Foot Guards as they preferred to call themselves, were asked to select their own officers. They chose as their captain that zealous, respected, and wealthy patriot, Benedict Arnold.

Barely a month later, on April 19th, 1775, General Gage moved. He sent eight hundred regulars west to Lexington to capture those renowned troublemakers, John Hancock and Sam Adams. The main task of the troops, however, was to march to Concord to destroy the weapons being assembled for a secret American army of some fifteen thousand. The military expedition into rural Massachusetts was meant to be a surprise, but was quickly discovered. When they reached Lexington some seventy men of the local militia stood on their little town green hoping to dissuade the regulars. The British officers ordered the men to drop their weapons and disburse. As they began retreating shots were fired. When the shooting stopped eight Lexington men lay dead, another ten were wounded.

As news of the British advance reached nearby towns their men came streaming into Concord. Others gathered along the route the army would take back to Boston. The King's men set fire to gun carriages and other weapons they were able to find at Concord and retreated into the town center as the local militia began shooting. When, after some delay the regulars began the retreat to Boston, they endured a withering fire as hundreds of local men joined the chase. In response the troops fired into houses and set others ablaze. Before they reached Boston and safety, the King's soldiers lost 19 officers and 246 soldiers, dead and wounded, the colonists some 90 men, fathers, brothers, friends, and neighbors. War had begun.

EIGHT

"My Country Called"

In the bleak, drizzly dawn of April 20 the men and women of Massachusetts awoke in a panic. Soldiers of the Crown lay where they had fallen the day before on the roads and in the fields from Concord all the way to Cambridge some fifteen miles to the east. Fathers, brothers and neighbors who perished fighting them were being hurriedly buried, some in mass graves covered in brush, so the British could not find them. Gage's troops were gone for now. They had retreated with their wounded to Boston leaving burnt-out homes and barns still smoldering. The chaotic militia regiments who had pursued the troops were blocking the narrow spit of land connecting Boston to the surrounding mainland, hoping to hem them in. But there was no doubt in anyone's mind that the regulars would burst through the American lines bent on revenge.

A frantic message from the Massachusetts Committee of Safety was being carried by riders galloping off to the colony's scattered towns and to the governor and towns of neighboring Connecticut with news of the battle and their present plight.[1] The message told of the trail of wreckage the regulars had left. At Lexington, they explained, "the regulars fired upon our men without any provocation"; at Concord they burned the magazine and supplies stockpiled there. The King's troops were the aggressors. Americans had fought to defend themselves and their families. "As the Troops have now commenced hostilities," the Committee felt it had no choice: "we think it our duty to exert our utmost strength to save our Country from absolute slavery. We pray your Honors would afford us all the assistance in your power . . . We pray God to direct you to such measures as shall tend to the salvation of our common liberties." They minced no words. "We conjure you by all that is sacred."[2] "Our all is at stake. Death and devastation are the certain consequences of delay. Every Moment is infinitely precious. An hour lost may deluge your country in blood and entail perpetual slavery upon the few of our posterity that may survive the carnage."[3]

News of the fighting with the plea for help reached New Haven the next day. How to weigh voyages not taken, business lost when the fate of family and liberty were at stake? What honorable man could ignore such a plea? Certainly not Benedict Arnold, Captain of the Connecticut Foot Guards. At his court-martial five years later Benedict explained how his life stood on that fateful day in April, 1775:

> When the present necessary war against Great Britain commenced, I was in easy circumstances, and enjoyed a fair prospect of improving them. I was happy in domestic connections, and blessed with a rising family who claimed my care and attention.[4]

Yet without hesitating he left the family he loved and a business dependent upon his personal attention for the uncertainty and hazards of war. Arnold explained, "The liberties of my country were in danger. The voice of my country called upon all her faithful sons to join in her defense. With cheerfulness I obeyed the call; I was one of the first in the field."[5]

And yet what of his loyalty to the Crown and the established government? What of the real possibility of being hanged as a traitor? True, there had been years of anger at British policy toward her American colonies, especially since the end of the French and Indian War, the victory that seemed to make everything worse. Americans at odds with British commercial policies that made their lives increasingly difficult and threatened their promised liberties did not blame King George for their sufferings or for the Intolerable Acts that robbed Massachusetts of its royal charter. Kings had granted them their charters that assured them of the rights of Englishmen. No, they blamed Parliament with its selfish commercial interests and callous indifference toward the colonies and they blamed the King's evil councilors. Allegiance was to the Crown alone, not to a parliament in which they were not represented. Back in 1766, as they were celebrating the repeal of the hated Stamp Act, an anonymous American author pointed out that the people of Britain had no more political connection with them than "with or over the people of Hanover, who are also subjects of the same King":

> . . . the people here still remain under the most sacred tie, the subjects of the *King* of Great-Britain, but utterly unaccountable to, and uncontrolable by the people of Great-Britain, or any body of them whatever, their compact being with the King only, to him alone they submitted, to be govern'd by him, agreeable to the terms of that compact, contain'd in their charter.[6]

It was a naïve belief that George III meant them well, hopeful but misguided. King George was, from the first, intent that the long-evaded navigation acts be enforced. He had endorsed the taxes heaped upon the Americans. Indeed, in November, 1774, months before Lexington and Concord, the King not only approved Parliament's punishment of Massachusetts but wrote: "The New England governments are in a state of rebellion, blows must decide whether they are to be subject to this country or independent."[7] Even had Arnold and his compatriots known or suspected this, it was diplomatic to assume his good intentions. A king who deprived his subjects of their liberties was a tyrant. No one need obey a tyrant, oaths of allegiance notwithstanding. History reminded them that Englishmen had had a similar experience with Charles I in the previous century. Then too they had first claimed Charles was misled by evil ministers and when war started insisted they were fighting against the king's armies on behalf of king and country. That pretence had ultimately collapsed and Charles's subjects had resorted to defending their rights as they saw them against a rogue monarch who had become a tyrant. George III, however, unlike Charles I, was acting in conjunction with his parliament. It was the right of the British government to rule the colonies that was at stake.

On the anniversary of the Boston Massacre a month before the bloodshed at Lexington and Concord Dr. Joseph Warren, a leader of the American opposition, spoke of liberty and tyranny and their fathers' resolve "never to wear the yoke of despotism."[8] He referred to the "mutilation" of the Massachusetts Charter that "made every Colony jealous for its own, for this, if once submitted to by us, would set on float the property and Government of every British settlement upon the Continent. If Charters are not deemed sacred, how miserably precarious is everything founded upon them." "Our enemies are numerous," he conceded, "but we have many friends determined to be free, and Heaven and earth will aid the resolution. . . . Your fathers look from their celestial seats with smiling approbation on their sons, who boldly stand forth in the cause of virtue."

★ ★ ★

With the Massachusetts report in hand the New Haven selectmen called an emergency town meeting to decide what action the town should take. The town elders were cautious, practical men. They persuaded the meeting to await more detailed information about the reasons for the fighting at Lexington and Concord before providing any help to Massachusetts.[9] There were hotheads in Massachusetts. Perhaps the colonists had provoked the fight. They had a point. It wasn't, and still isn't, clear who fired first at Lexington Green. The activists at Concord were amassing arms and supplies for an army of some fifteen thousand men. Treason, rebellion, call it what you will, it was not to be entered into lightly.

But Arnold had no patience for delay. This was an emergency. He called a muster of his Foot Guards for early the next morning. The men appeared in their smart blue-and-white uniforms before a cheering crowd. Arnold reviewed them to great applause and called for volunteers to join them in the march to Massachusetts. Men came forward including several Yale students.[10] The volunteers were not armed with military weapons and needed the gunpowder stored in the town magazine. Hearing that the selectmen and Committee of Safety were busy meeting in a local tavern, Arnold sent a lieutenant inside to ask for the keys to the powder house. General David Wooster, the commander of the New Haven militia and Arnold's military superior, came outside to discuss the matter. He flatly refused to hand over the keys and ordered Arnold not to march his men to Massachusetts. Backed by an enthusiastic crowd Benedict was not to be put off and, according to witnesses, insisted only God could prevent their marching. He gave Wooster five minutes to deliver the keys after which his men would break open the powder-house door and take the supplies. Wooster disappeared into the tavern and returned shortly with the keys. With the prayers and cheers from the assembled crowd ringing in their ears and the town's military equipment in their hands Captain Arnold and the Connecticut Foot Guard marched off to answer their country's call.

★ ★ ★

Massachusetts was calling for an army of thirty thousand men. Connecticut planned to contribute some six thousand men. Such orderly plans, indeed order itself, was difficult in the rush to respond. Thousands of men and boys converged on the headquarters of the impromptu army in Cambridge. Rhode Island sent three regiments. A New Hampshire troop marched fifty-five miles in just eighteen hours.[11] Far-off North Carolina raised two regiments of infantry and one of rangers, a guerrilla-style unit, and voted £140,000 in bills of credit for the conflict. Georgia sent a ship loaded with rice to Massachusetts. There were soon so many men that some units were turned back.

Arnold and his men had a 135-mile journey ahead of them. They marched briskly along bearing flags emblazoned with the Connecticut coat of arms and inscribed with the colony's motto, *"Qui transtulit sustinet,"* He who brought us hither will support us.[12] It was a version of the traditional motto of Europe's Protestant armies, "God with Us." To ensure discipline and emphasize the principles on which they meant to comport themselves the officers and privates of Arnold's guards subscribed to a "mutual covenant." They promised to "conduct themselves decently and inoffensively, both to their countrymen and to each other," and to obey all the rules and regulations."[13] "Drunkenness, gaming, profanity and every vice," were to be "avoided and discountenanced." Discipline was to be humane, obedience "not to be enforced by blows, but if any person guilty of any offence, after being admonished, should persist, such incorrigible person should be expelled, 'as totally unworthy of serving in so great and glorious a cause.'"

Their route cut north and east across Connecticut into the gently rolling hill country of central Massachusetts. On the way, in Pomfret, Connecticut, Arnold met the famous old warrior, General Israel Putnam, "old Put" to his men. When Old Put had learned of the alarm he left his plough in the field and hurried to join the growing army.[14] Tales of Putnam's bravery and exploits had regaled many an evening gathering, particularly the story of his tracking a wolf that had been preying on his sheep back to its den. He had crawled in after it on hands and knees. When he saw its eyes glittering in the dark he shot. He then pulled it out by the ears. During the French and Indian War Old Put had taken part in the attack on Fort Ticonderoga alongside the British army. General Howe's older brother, George, had died in his arms. Soon he would be fighting against another Howe.

A more consequential meeting during the journey took place when Arnold met Colonel Samuel Parsons. Parsons was returning from Cambridge to recruit men at Hartford. He complained to Arnold of the need for artillery if a siege of Boston was to be successful. Arnold had the solution. He recommended an attack on forts Ticonderoga and Crown Point in New York to seize the cannon and supplies stored there. These two forts were strategically important as they guarded the all-important water route to Canada, but they were only lightly garrisoned by the British. If the British continued to hold them they were a threat to New England and its communication with New York and the middle Atlantic colonies. If the colonists seized them it would give them a great strategic advantage and cut the communication lines between New York and Boston and British Canada. Arnold knew the area having visited Lakes George and Champlain as a boy. The notion of the expedition stuck in the minds of both Arnold and Parsons.

At Cambridge at last Arnold and his men found themselves swept up in a chaotic scene. Hundreds of men and boys were flooding into the little town across the Charles River from Boston. They were being housed wherever there was room. They crammed into Harvard College buildings and private homes, especially the houses of loyalists who had fled. Others slept outdoors without even the comfort of a tent. The college opened its kitchen to feed the men. Citizen-soldiers were busy drilling on the Cambridge common just across the road from Harvard. Arnold wasted no time laying claim to the best accommodations he could find for his troop and himself. Somehow he managed to take possession of the deserted home of Lieutenant Governor Andrew Oliver as his headquarters.

Even worse than the housing problem was the problem of discipline. An army without discipline is a mob, and that April the Americans gathered in Cambridge were still a mob. They gloried in the belief that men fighting for their freedom, and unlike the regulars, didn't need formal discipline. To add to the confusion there was a great deal of coming and going. Men living nearby went home when they pleased. Though they were brave they were inexperienced.

John Adams, one of the Massachusetts delegates to the Continental Congress meeting in Philadelphia, was painfully aware of the situation and struggled to get the assembly to adopt the army at Cambridge, Massachusetts as its own. "At present," he pointed out to the Congress, "this extraordinary martial assemblage was in the most singular condition ever presented by such a body. It could not be said that the officers commanded by any lawful title or authority, or that the rank and file obeyed otherwise than by virtue of their own willingness to do so. The whole existing condition of military as well as of civil affairs was based upon little more than general understanding and mutual acquiescence."[15] Congress finally agreed. In June, as George Washington was preparing to set out from Pennsylvania to take command, the Massachusetts Provincial Congress felt it advisable to send him a frank description of the men he would find at Cambridge:

> The greatest part of them have not before seen Service. And altho' naturally brave and of good understanding, yet, for want of Experience in military Life, have but little knowledge of divers things most essential to the preservation of Health and even of Life. The Youth in

the Army are not possessed of the absolute Necessity of Cleanliness in their Dress, and Lodging; continual Exercise and strict Temperance to preserve them from Diseases frequently prevailing in Camps, especially among those who, from their Childhood, have been us'd to a laborious Life.

Arnold's own men had been carefully drilled by a hired professional. They were also better behaved and had sworn to obey orders and live in a temperate fashion. But, like the great majority of men around them, they were nearly all inexperienced. Arnold himself, now aged 34, had only two weeks of prior service eighteen years before and no actual experience of warfare. But he was brave, confident, and with his extensive seafaring experience was used to facing dangers coolly and decisively. Like the rest he was eager to prove himself.

While the generals concentrated on building defenses and creating some sort of order, and the British in Boston awaited reinforcements, Arnold believed there was no time to waste. The forts of Ticonderoga and Crown Point with their precious artillery needed to be taken before the British realized the danger. He asked to meet with the Committee of Safety to get their approval of the attempt.[16] One member of the committee, Dr. Joseph Warren, became a firm friend of Arnold's. Warren had had such a plan in mind since early spring. John Brown, an agent sent by the Boston Committee of Safety in March to assess Canadian sentiment toward British rule, had recommended that Fort Ticonderoga be seized if hostilities broke out. Arnold was passionate and persuasive. The committee was won over to the plan and on May 3 Arnold was commissioned a colonel to undertake this "secret service." The new colonel was supplied with horses, equipment, and funds for the expedition and permitted to select two lieutenants to assist him. That very night he and his lieutenants set out for western Massachusetts with instructions to recruit four hundred men and attack the forts as quickly as possible.

Three days later, after nearly one hundred miles of hard riding, they arrived at the town of Stockbridge in the Berkshire Mountains of western Massachusetts only to find that an expedition to capture Ticonderoga was already on the march. Having had no time to begin recruiting his four hundred men, Arnold left his officers to that work and rode off hoping to catch up with the expedition already on its way. On May 8, after another hard three days' ride Arnold caught up with the Green Mountain Boys and volunteers from Massachusetts and Connecticut, well advanced in carrying out the very same mission.

NINE

The Race to Seize Forts

Arnold reined his exhausted horse to a halt when he caught sight of the Green Mountain Boys. There were nearly ninety of these "Boys," along with volunteers from Connecticut and Massachusetts on their way to seize the very fort Arnold had been commissioned to capture. The final group was about to set out when he reached them. Unfortunately their leader, Ethan Allen, had already gone on ahead, leaving Arnold to explain his commission to Allen's men. At this stage in the expedition the Boys and other men were not about to put themselves under the command of a perfect stranger. Captain Edward Mott, the leader of the Connecticut contingent in their midst wrote of their anger that Arnold "presumed to contend for the command of those forces which we had raised . . . which bred such a mutiny amongst the soldiers, as almost frustrated our whole design." After three days of hard riding to catch up with the group, Arnold had little choice.

He mounted his weary animal again and dashed off to overtake Ethan Allen.

Their meeting was tense. Arnold, the sturdy, successful seafaring merchant, was three years younger than the tall, lanky backwoodsman. Both men were feisty and cocksure. Allen, a land speculator and sometime entrepreneur, had also been born in Connecticut, first child of Puritan parents, Joseph and Mary Allen. The Allen family moved from Litchfield, where Ethan was born, to Cornwall on the Connecticut frontier. His parents were spared the sad experience of Benedict's mother and father, the deaths of their small children. All seven Allen youngsters survived to adulthood. Like Benedict's father, Ethan's was successful, in his case his wealth was in farmland. But unlike Benedict's father, Joseph Allen ended his life a prosperous and respected member of the community. Like Arnold, though, Ethan's education was cut short, in his case when his father died in 1755. Ethan managed to continue studying informally. He was especially fond of philosophy and later wrote a book on the subject.

During the French and Indian wars both Arnold and Allen had answered the call to save Fort William Henry. Both served short enlistments in the Connecticut militia. Neither had seen combat. Since then Arnold had built a fortune in the Atlantic trade. Allen had tried his hand at various enterprises, including running an iron foundry. In 1770 he had moved to present-day Vermont, then the New Hampshire Grants, and had gotten involved in the dispute over land claimed by both New Hampshire and New York, land actually intended to reward soldiers who had fought in the French and Indian Wars. Both New York and New Hampshire claimed jurisdiction over the land between the Hudson and Connecticut Rivers. After London decided in favor of New York in 1764 that colony insisted those who held grants from New Hampshire had to pay for their land again. Allen helped the New Hampshire grantees defend their rights in a New York court, aided by Arnold's own friend and attorney, Jared Ingersoll. At some point in the process

Allen laid down $50 to purchase some one thousand acres of the grants. The New Hampshire grantees lost in the New York court, a result that was hardly unexpected, but refused to give up. Allen returned to Bennington and helped found the Green Mountain Boys. The Boys then chose Allen as their leader. He turned out to be a great propagandist, and he and the Boys were soon heroes to the farmers and landholders in the disputed New Hampshire grants. Their methods of intimidation and evasion of New York claims, however, also made them vigilantes to New York officials, who branded Allen and the Boys the "Bennington mob," a "collection of the most abandoned wretches that ever lived."[1]

Now that war with Britain had started the Boys were patriots. But their interest in the New York forts was not merely patriotic. They hoped it would strengthen their claims against New York. As Allen later wrote, they hoped by seizing the fort "to annihilate the old quarrel with the Government of New York by swallowing it up in the general conflict for liberty."[2] With Benedict's arrival the two proud, combative men, bent on the same military errand, met, one armed with a commission, the other with men.

The situation was a perfect example of the confusion that reigned in the frantic days just after Lexington and Concord. The idea of an attack on Fort Ticonderoga had occurred to the Green Mountain Boys among others. They were plotting such an expedition when they gathered in early May in their usual haunt, the Catamount Tavern in Bennington. The tavern, where they had been founded, was named for a local wildcat. A member of the species was stuck on a pole outside the tavern, its dead gaze pointing toward the New York border.[3] As they were preparing for the expedition sixteen men from Connecticut and another forty from Massachusetts appeared bent on the same goal. The Connecticut contingent had been dispatched and privately financed by General Parsons and his friends, apparently on their own authority. Parsons had been convinced of the wisdom of Arnold's suggestion to him and put the idea into motion. The Massachusetts men had come with the same idea, inspired by John Brown. The three groups agreed to coordinate their efforts, and with Allen as their field commander and James Easton of Massachusetts as second in command they set off to surprise Fort Ticonderoga.

Arnold was a Connecticut native but his commission was from Massachusetts and was as official as anything at that time and place could be. Yet he hadn't had time to recruit the men he was authorized to raise. His lieutenants were busy doing that in western Massachusetts. Allen had the Boys as well as the Connecticut men sent by Parsons and the Massachusetts volunteers. In these circumstances Arnold's insistence that his commission gave him authority to take command was not persuasive. The time was late. The attack was planned for the very next day. Proud as Arnold was of his honor and rank, he was also a realist. He had little option at this point, only the expectation that his own recruits would appear soon and would follow him. But he had a commission and expertise and Allen had neither. A compromise was struck up. Arnold would go along with the group. It would be a joint command, Allen would lead but Arnold would march at his side.

They were now quite close to their destination. There was no time to waste. The command being settled, off they went hoping to reach the fort before the British realized their danger and reinforced its garrison. It was May 9, and the attack was planned for dawn on May 10.

Forts Ticonderoga on the eastern shore of Lake George and Crown Point, on Lake Champlain twelve miles to the north, guarded the American colonies' inland water route from French Canada. Ticonderoga, formerly Fort Carillon, had been built by the French in 1755 to protect the water passage from Lake Champlain to Lake George. The fort stood on a rise of land. It was constructed of stone in classic French military style, with four angular bastions protruding from its walls, and even a moat and drawbridge. Although the French had fought off a British attack on the fort they surrendered it in 1759 after an explosion destroyed its powder-house. General Amherst, who accepted the surrender, repaired the damage and renamed the fort with the Indian word, Ticonderoga, "place between two waters." Crown Point had also experienced a devastating explosion, in that case in the spring of 1773 when its powder magazine blew up, destroying much of its earthworks. After the fire the British headquarters there was moved south to Ticonderoga. As relations between Britain and the American colonies worsened the acting Governor of Canada, Major General Frederick Haldimand, and the Earl of Dartmouth at the Colonial Office in London both stressed the importance of rebuilding Crown Point, or at least bringing a couple of regiments from Canada to Crown Point and Ticonderoga to strengthen the small garrisons holding the two forts. If the forts were strengthened, Haldimand advised, they would provide "an easy access to the back settlements of the northern colonies and may keep them in awe should any of them be rash enough to incline to acts of open force and violence."[4] Good advice but resources were needed elsewhere. Nevertheless, in the fall of 1774 Lord Dartmouth ordered Gage to strengthen both forts. General Gage was busy keeping Boston under control but in any case he did not receive Dartmouth's orders before winter snows blocked the valleys and Lake Champlain lay covered in ice. By the time the Spring thaw occurred it was too late. Happily for the Americans hoping to conquer the fort that May, only fifty British soldiers held Ticonderoga.[5]

Forts Ticonderoga and Crown Point were strategically placed on what the Native Americans called the Great Warpath. And Great Warpath it was destined to be in the American Revolution. Arnold's participation in the attack on Ticonderoga would be only the first of a series of crucial battles he would fight along that warpath in the years ahead, battles that shaped his career and determined the fate of the American cause.

The expedition to Ticonderoga also brought Arnold into contact with two men who would join other expeditions of his and who quickly became lifelong enemies. The first was John Brown. The two met when Brown was attending Yale College in New Haven. He went on to become a lawyer and moved to Pittsfield in the western corner of Massachusetts. In February, 1775, two months before shooting began, a group of Boston activists sent Brown to Canada on a secret mission to find out whether Canadians would join the American colonists in protests or an eventual revolt. On his way north Brown spent some time in Albany and reported back on the importance of Fort Ticonderoga and its weapons. As for his mission to Canada, in what was to become an oft-repeated and always counterproductive American approach, Brown first tried appealing to their common grievances against the Mother Country. He then switched from good will and blandishments to the threat that "if a man of them should dare to take up arms and act against the Bostonians thirty thousand of them will march into Canada and lay waste the whole country."[6] Brown made a botch of his mission in other respects as well. The British quickly caught on to his plot and carefully tracked his movements. Brown pretended he was in Canada to deal in horses, but during his two months there never bothered to purchase a single animal.[7] Now Captain Brown, along with other Massachusetts men, was part of the expedition against Ticonderoga. For reasons best known to himself, possibly resentment against the pretensions of the New Haven "shopkeeper," Brown would become Arnold's most bitter and relentless enemy.

James Easton was also from Pittsfield, where he kept a tavern and was deep in debt. He was a boastful man, and head of the local militia who gave himself the title of colonel.[8] In Easton's case the enmity to Arnold can be traced to Arnold's impatience with the militia colonel. Arnold had chided Easton because during the attack on the fort he lagged behind, claiming to be worried about wet powder in his musket. Tempers flared and Arnold challenged him to a duel, which Easton declined. Arnold could not brook cowardice and gave Easton a couple of swift kicks.[9] This was sufficient to make Easton, like Brown, a long-standing enemy. Despite Easton's laggardly behavior, or perhaps to sooth his hurt feelings, Easton was given the honor of bringing the tidings about the outcome of the assault to the Massachusetts Provincial Congress.

The attack against Ticonderoga was to take place at dawn. A force of thirty men was dispatched to capture Major Philip Skene and his schooner docked nearby, while the rest of the men marched to a point of embarkation known as Hand's Cove, across the lake just northeast of Ticonderoga. There they were to await the boats. Some 250 men reached the embarkation point by dark but the boats were slow to arrive. Apparently no one had assembled the boats needed to ferry them across the lake.[10] By sunrise only two boatloads carrying eighty men had made the crossing. With the morning fog about to lift, revealing their presence to the soldiers in the fort looming above, Allen decided to act. "We must this morning either quit our pretensions to valor, or possess ourselves of this fortress in a few minutes," he exhorted the little group, "and, in as much as it is a desperate attempt (which none but the bravest of men dare undertake) I do not urge it to any contrary to his will. You that will undertake voluntarily, poise your firelocks."[11]

That said they set off in silence on the road that ran past their landing site and up to the base of the fortress. Once inside they entered a tunnel in one of the barracks that led up a flight of stairs to the parade ground at the center of the fort. The sentry guarding the entrance tried to shoot at them but his gun misfired. He turned and fled up the stairs. A second sentry dashing from the guardhouse charged at them with his bayonet. Allen coolly smashed him on the head with the flat of his sword but spared the desperate man on condition he point out his commander's quarters. Following his directions Arnold and Allen led the way racing up another flight of stairs to the top of another barracks with shouts of "no quarter." Allen would later claim that he had demanded the British captain surrender "In the name of the great Jehovah and the Continental Congress."[12] Witnesses reported that he actually shouted, "Come out of there you old rat." The "old rat" had little option but to surrender his garrison of forty-four men, two dozen civilians, and its eighty heavy cannon, twenty brass cannon, and other military supplies.[13] The next day while the Green Mountain Boys were busy pillaging the fort, enthusiastically breaking into the ninety barrels of rum stored there, Allen wrote the Massachusetts Provincial Congress at Watertown of the triumphal capture of Ticonderoga, omitting any mention of Benedict Arnold and effusively praising his men.[14] Arnold was busy writing to the Massachusetts Committee of Safety who had commissioned him, giving a very different picture of the present scene. "There is here at present near one hundred men, who are in the greatest confusion and anarchy, destroying and plundering private property, committing every enormity, and paying no attention to publick service."[15] He had no harsh words for Allen as leader of the Green Mountain Boys, but deplored the lack of discipline.

The confusion over commissions continued after the capture of the fort, with Allen assuming command of the fort, and the Massachusetts Congress demanding to see copies of Arnold's commission from the Massachusetts Committee of Safety and "every paper containing the appointment of Colonel Benedict Arnold" including "the instructions given him by you; of your engagements to him on behalf of this Colony, if any such authority was given him by you; his orders respecting the ordnance at Ticonderoga, and places on Lake Champlain, and every thing necessary to give the Congress a full understanding of the relation Colonel Arnold then stood, and now stands in to this Colony."[16] John Brown was a busy actor in this inquiry. The response of the Massachusetts Committee of Safety and the documents requested of them were to be delivered to the Congress by Brown himself. None of this was Arnold's fault, of course. He had presented his plan to the Committee of Safety and been commissioned and funded by them. But the sheer confusion of authority left him in a difficult position in the capture of Ticonderoga and the aftermath.

That position was to change. Arnold's recruits finally began to appear while some of Allen's Boys, having achieved their goal, began to turn toward home. Both Arnold and Allen were eager to build on their achievement. Neither was prepared to await further instructions or the results of deliberations by the competing Massachusetts bodies. This was entirely understandable. The British could be expected to reinforce their troops on Lake Champlain at any time. Any further efforts to wrest control and supplies from them could not stay for bureaucratic niceties, especially when tempting opportunities lay close at hand.

One of these tempting targets was at Skenesborough. Near the southern end of Lake Champlain lay the vast estate of Philip Skene. Although Skene was active in the Indian Wars, he was visiting London and while there had been granted the lieutenant governorship of Ticonderoga and Crown Point. His estate and village just south of Ticonderoga were not that important, but there was a schooner berthed at Skenesborough. A schooner was just what was needed. Allen sent a group of men to seize the ship. They captured it and planned to sail it to Ticonderoga where it would be renamed *Liberty*. As it happened the first group of men recruited for Arnold began to appear and arrived at Skenesborough just in time to take command of the *Liberty*. Although Allen's own men had no experience with such vessels, some of Arnold's did. They were given command of the *Liberty* and sailed it safely to the fort. Allen also sent a group led by Seth Warner, his second in command, north to capture Crown Point, where a garrison even smaller than that at Ticonderoga yielded without firing a shot.

Arnold fully appreciated these moves and the need to control the Great Warpath. Control required not only possession of key forts but of armed ships. He had believed the one armed vessel on the lake, the *Betsy*, was at Ticonderoga. When he got to the fort he learned the ship was berthed at St. Johns on the Richelieu River north of Lake Champlain and just over the border into Canada. Crossing that border did not deter him. He installed guns on the

Liberty and loaded his fifty men on board her and two bateaux. Off they sailed on May 14, just four days after the capture of Ticonderoga. At dawn four days later his men attacked the small garrison at St. Johns and seized the *Betsy*. There were also nine bateaux docked at St. Johns. Arnold knew he and his men could not handle that many boats as well as their own vessels. Rather than leave them to the British he ordered four bateaux immediately sunk and with the *Betsy* and the other five sailed away. The entire operation had taken only three hours. Speed was important because Arnold learned that British reinforcements were already on their way. He and his men were now in possession of the only armed vessels on Lake Champlain. While the Massachusetts committees were sorting out his credentials, Arnold had vastly improved their military position without a shot being fired.

As Arnold and his flotilla were sailing toward Ticonderoga they met Allen and one hundred of his men rowing north in four bateaux hoping to conquer St. Johns itself. The competition between the two leaders may be what induced Allen to make the attempt. Arnold tried to convince Allen that capturing the city was almost certain to fail, but Allen would not be dissuaded. Too late he learned that Arnold had been right. By the time Allen and his men docked across the river from St. Johns, British reinforcements had arrived and began preparations to open fire on Allen and his men. The vastly outnumbered Americans retreated in disgrace.

The Continental Congress was worried about these exploits. The capture of British forts and seizure of weapons, and the foray into Canada, gave the American uprising a more serious cast. True, they were prudent military measures and achieved without bloodshed. But at Lexington and Concord the Americans insisted that the British were the aggressors, the colonists merely defending their homes and families. The hope remained, and would persist until the vote for independence a year later, that there would be a negotiated settlement with the British and a peaceful resolution of the tensions. But there was no way to argue that seizing forts and even invading Canada were defensive measures.

Arnold was intent on military results and had little skill or interest in ingratiating himself with the men sitting on the provincial bodies in Massachusetts or in the Continental Congress. His detractors, however, especially Allen, Brown, and Easton who had no specific authorization to take Ticonderoga, were keen to advance their own reputations and diminish his. In fact it was necessary to diminish Arnold's if their less official behavior was to be seen as responsible for the triumph. Arnold had criticized the disorder and plunder that followed the capture of the fort of course, while Allen was keen to praise all those who had looked to him as their leader and anxious to make sure the Green Mountain Boys came away with glowing reputations. John Brown and James Easton, both of whom were praised in Allen's report for their bravery at Ticonderoga, were intent on vilifying Arnold to Congress and making it appear that he had no real role in the capture of the fort. Congress decided to give Allen control of Ticonderoga and ordered Arnold to fulfill his original commission, delivering the artillery from Ticonderoga to the army at Cambridge. Later when Allen left Arnold was given command and until properly relieved of his commission, was determined to maintain his post and carry out the plan to move the fort's artillery to Cambridge.[17] But the Provincial Congress was also insistent that he provide a detailed accounting of how he had used the money and supplies he had been allotted. Arnold was keen to hand over command to an appropriate officer, having accomplished the military tasks he had set himself. He had a family and business to get back to. He was ready to leave but there was still much confusion among the revolutionary committees and the three colonies involved.

On May 31st Arnold was informed that the Connecticut General Assembly had appointed a Colonel Benjamin Hinman to take command of the two forts, a mild man younger than him, whose military capabilities he did not rank very high.[18] A day later the

Massachusetts Provincial Congress finally gave long overdue recognition to Arnold assuring him that "They highly approve of and
take great satisfactions in the acquisitions you have made at Ticonderoga and Crown Point, on the lake, & c."[19] They were "sorry to
meet with repeated requests from you that some gentleman be sent
to succeed you in command, they assure you that they place the
greatest confidence in your fidelity, knowledge, courage, and good
conduct and they desire that you at present dismiss the thought of
quitting your important command of Ticonderoga, Crown Point,
Lake Champlain." Could he please remain and take command of
the additional troops Connecticut, Massachusetts and New York
were to send. They added that, now that the Continental Congress
was involved, he could only be relieved of his command by the
Congress sitting in Philadelphia.

News of Arnold's successes finally reached his family in New
Haven. Hannah wrote with sisterly pride and love, congratulating
Benedict on his success "in reducing Ticonderoga and making
yourself master of the vessels on the lakes."[20] The men "who went
under your care to Boston," she wrote, "give you the praises of
a very humane and tender officer." Her wish was that "all your
future endeavors to serve your country may be crowned with equal
success." Then in sisterly fashion she worried about "the fatigue
you must unavoidably suffer in the wilderness." Still, Hannah
judged, "as the cause is undoubtedly a just one, I hope you may
have health, strength, fortitude, and valor, for whatever you may
be called to." She ended with the prayer: "May the broad hand of
the Almighty overshadow you; and if called to battle, may the God
of Armies cover your head in the day of it." "If we are to meet no
more in time," she hoped "a wise preparation for eternity secure
to us a happy meeting in the realms of bliss, where painful separa-
tions are forever excluded."

Arnold was now following the orders of the Continental Congress sitting in Philadelphia. On Wednesday, June 14th that body
agreed to take control of the hodge-podge army assembled at

Cambridge. Two days later Hinman arrived, sent by Connecticut to take over Arnold's command. He came without his official orders which took two more days to catch up with him. At the same time Hinman's orders arrived a three man committee sent by the Massachusetts Provincial Congress appeared, led by one Walter Spooner, assigned to check on the situation of the forts, their importance, supplies and to judge Colonel Arnold's "spirit, capacity and conduct."[21] If they thought these attributes inadequate they were to order his "immediate return to Massachusetts to render an account of the money, ammunition and stores, he had received."[22] If he remained their orders were that "he was to be subordinate to Colonel Hinman."[23] The idea they were to assess Arnold was amazing since the Congress had just sent him a letter praising his work and pleading with him to stay in command. The Congress was also aware of the impertinence of Massachusetts and Connecticut organizing the seizure of forts in New York without seeking the agreement and help of New York's patriot assemblies. All very awkward along with the issue of which colony was to pay for the effort, presumably better Connecticut than Massachusetts. The Spooner committee did write the Continental Congress in Philadelphia of the vital importance of retaining control of the Champlain forts and the lake. The Continental Congress agreed to adopt the impromptu army gathered at Cambridge and on June 15th appointed George Washington of Virginia to be its commander. He would arrive at Cambridge to assume his command on June 23rd, the same day Arnold resigned his. Arnold considered the demand of the Massachusetts Congress that he present himself to them with an exact accounting of his disbursements insulting and demeaning. His reports had consistently detailed his disbursement and needs. Moreover, he regarded as outrageous their failure to provide the final small sums needed to make good various expenses. He reminded them he had advanced more than one thousand pounds of his own money to pay various expenses. Although he had repeatedly asked to be relieved of his post, he deeply resented these requests and was particularly upset that he was now to turn over the command of the forts and his men to a younger officer of the same rank. Worse James Easton was to take command of Arnold's men with John Brown as second in command. All this was sufficient to cause him "to decline holding my commission longer."[24] Rather than put the forts and vessels under the new commander and his men under Easton and Brown, he simply disbanded the men.[25] His men were pragmatic though. As they had not been paid for their services and were far from home, many agreed to enlist under the new officers.

However disgruntled the Spooner committee was with him, the residents of the Champlain area fully appreciated Arnold's contribution to their safety. Arnold had persuaded the Congress not to abandon the area forts and the local population. A group of residents wrote him just before he left on behalf of all the inhabitants of the region amounting, they explained "to about six hundred families." They were deeply impressed with a sense of your merit, and the weighty obligations which we lie under to you in your military capacity."[26] They thanked him for his "humanity and benevolence" toward them "supplying them with provisions in their distress" as well as "your polite treatment of such prisoners as have fallen into your hands." Indeed, they judged that his humane and polite manner had shown "your adversaries a bright example of that elevation and generosity of soul, which nothing less than real magnanimity and innate virtue could inspire." This gratitude was in sharp contrast to the aspersions cast on Arnold's conduct by Easton's version of events and by the Spooner committee.

While Arnold was being ordered to appear before the Massachusetts Congress to "render an account of his proceedings," John Brown, although also under investigation, was promoted to major in the Massachusetts force. On July 1 Arnold was at Albany on his way home. At the request of Major General Philip Schuyler he sent the Continental Congress a report of the situation of the army in the "Northern Department."[27] He did not mince words informing the delegates of the lack of provisions, none at all made for the growing numbers of sick men, scarcity of gunpowder and other concerns.

The lobbying against Arnold had helped convince the Continental Congress that Arnold should be recalled. It was a sober lesson learned, and it ended his military expectations for the moment. He had turned toward home, stopping at Albany to write a full report of his efforts to fulfill his commission. It was there that the news reached him. His dear wife, Peggy, was dead.

TEN

Buried in the Public Calamity

The news was a dreadful shock. Hannah's letter in June assured him "Your little family are all well."[1] Clearly Peggy's fever had come without warning. It was deadly. She had died while he was miles away, ignorant of her condition. Peggy had always been delicate, aloof, hard to please. But he was devoted to her. Now there was no chance to say goodbye, to tell her how much he loved her. He hadn't even been able to attend her funeral or comfort their three little sons. After the frustrating and contentious weeks at Ticonderoga Benedict had been longing to return to the refuge of his home and family, to what he called his "safe, happy asylum where mutual love and friendship doubled our joys and bears down our every misfortune."[2] He was just about to set out for that happy asylum when the awful news reached him. He bid a hasty farewell to General Schuyler and galloped off to New Haven, 114 miles from Albany as the crow flies, far longer on the crooked, dusty roads of a hot New England summer. He was anxious, exhausted, racing to get home but dreading that homecoming.

The scene that greeted Benedict at his journey's end was even more wretched than he expected. The grand house he had built for Peggy was, of course, hushed and darkened in deep mourning. It seemed empty despite the presence of his dear sister Hannah and his little sons. The letter that told him of Peggy's death also informed him of the Mansfield family's second tragedy. Peggy's father, Samuel, had been ill for a long time but Hannah's letter in June reported the good news that Samuel, "contrary to all expectation, is again able to ride out; and his physicians think he is in a fair way of recovering a comfortable state of health."[3] But, as is sometimes the way with illness, he took a fatal turn for the worse, no doubt badly shaken by Peggy's death. Three days after Peggy died her "papa" followed his dear daughter to the grave. Yet there was Hannah to welcome him, coping quietly as she had done when they faced their own mother's death and their father's alcoholism. She was there, thank God, to care for his three sons. Benedict, the eldest was just seven, Richard six, and little Henry was only three. Would they remember their mother, particularly Henry?

Samuel's business had been failing. In one of her rare letters to Benedict before fighting began, Peggy asked if they could help him out financially. Now Samuel's business would be left to his son and partners to manage. Benedict's own shipping business was in scarcely better shape. Although he had a partner who could take the lead, and Hannah was eager to help while he was away, the American shipping trade was about to become extraordinarily hazardous. In August George III would proclaim his American opponents rebels making their ships targets for every British vessel. At the moment Benedict was worried about his ship, *Peggy*, due to enter port at Quebec.[4] Would authorities there know of his earlier seizure of Canadian craft at St. Johns? Beyond these difficulties his own health became a problem. The gout that occasionally afflicted him suddenly flared up, probably provoked by the good food and drink of home. It kept him in bed with wretched pain for many of the few days he was in New Haven.

Much as he was needed at home though, Benedict could not stay. He had spent a good deal of his own funds to pay for the supplies his men needed at Ticonderoga. He asked to be reimbursed, but the Massachusetts Provincial Congress was more interested in his accounting for every penny of the public funds used for the campaign. Gulled by the attacks on Arnold, the Provincial Congress was exceptionally suspicious of his every expense. While Arnold was commanding the fort at Ticonderoga and Crown Point they sent the Spooner Committee to inspect the forts and assess his command. It had orders to pay only his men who were capable of further service.[5] "The very great hardship on the private men, who having served well near two months," an astonished Arnold protested, "are now to be mustered and if by sickness or hard labor they are reduced and not fit for service . . . they are to lose their former time and service, and reduced to the distress of begging their bread until they can get home to their friends."[6] The committee yielded, but only when the men at Crown Point threatened to mutiny after learning the sick or injured were not to be paid. Still, Congress demanded Arnold appear as soon as possible to account directly to them. It was certain to be a contentious confrontation. The delegates hadn't questioned the scurrilous reports John Brown and James Easton brought them of Arnold's behavior or their supposed heroism. Therefore, although Benedict had only been home a few days, he had no choice but to return to Watertown to report to the Massachusetts Congress. He was prepared to give them the financial reckoning they wanted, but meant to insist on being reimbursed for the large sum of £1,060 he had advanced to pay for supplies. In these uncertain times his family would need the money.

His few days in New Haven were busy sorting out affairs at home. Could Hannah manage the household and look after his three little sons? Was his business in as good shape as possible? Little time to grieve. Perhaps that was best. As he later explained, "every recollection of past happiness heightens my present grief, which would be intolerable, were it not buried in the public calamity."[7] And he was determined to bury himself in that public calamity. "An idle life under my present circumstances would be but a lingering death." If an expedition to Canada which he had recommended to the Continental Congress in June were to take place he wanted to play a part in it, otherwise he planned to join the army at Cambridge as a volunteer. Leaving his dear little family and his good friends with their prayers for his safety and swift return, he galloped off to confront the Massachusetts Provincial Congress and dedicate his life to the cause.

When Arnold hurriedly galloped off from his Albany mansion Philip Schuyler, commander of Washington's North Department, knew he had found his man. Schuyler was so impressed by Arnold he wanted him appointed the deputy adjutant general of his department.[8] This would have to be done with circumspection though, since the Continental Congress insisted upon its exclusive right to make military appointments. The Congress had had no doubts about its choice of Schuyler as one of its first four major generals. At forty-one Philip Schuyler was a brilliant choice to command the North Department—the principal magnate of the Albany-Hudson region of New York, a patriot although moderate, and a supremely able and talented man. He was tall, dignified, serious. To the sizeable estate he inherited from Dutch forebears, he added large tracts of land, building a vast farming and commercial empire. When he and Arnold met that July Schuyler owned some hundred thousand acres. But he was no mere aristocratic farmer in the British sense. He had also developed a manufacturing center at Saratoga and conveyed the produce of his farms to market in his own ships. He had married into one of New York's oldest and most influential

Dutch families. He and Catherine Van Rensselaer were to become the parents of fifteen children.

More pertinent in the present emergency, Schuyler's military experience rivaled that of George Washington. Both men had served with the British army during the French and Indian War. Schuyler was commissioned a captain authorized to raise a militia regiment. Serving under John Bradstreet, he had taken part in the capture of Ticonderoga and in the capture of Fort Frontenac. When Bradstreet was made quartermaster general of the British Army, Schuyler served in his department. That experience gave him expertise in the logistics of supplying military forces on wilderness expeditions. Schuyler also knew the Indians of his region well. There was just one potential problem with his appointment: this loyal and able man suffered excruciating bouts of pain from gout, and had serious breathing problems from pleurisy. But when in good health he was superb.

Schuyler had just returned from serving in the Continental Congress at Philadelphia when he and Arnold had their meeting. That assembly had brought the New York magnate into contact with George Washington of Virginia. The two men, alike in many ways, became firm friends and remained so after Washington was appointed commander in chief of the boisterous throng of volunteer-soldiers gathered at Cambridge, Massachusetts. Indeed, Schuyler was among those officers who accompanied Washington on the journey to Massachusetts before heading home to Albany.

On June 17 while Washington and the new officers were riding north the Battle of Bunker Hill took place. It had begun with an amphibious assault by the British across the Charles River from Boston, breaking out of the blockade the patriots had created. As they landed on the Cambridge beachhead the British set the nearby city of Charlestown aflame to punish residents who were shooting at them from their windows. With the smoke and flames of burning homes in the background, the regulars launched three punishing assaults up Breed's Hill, convinced the American volunteers crouching at its top would break and run. They did not. And although the regulars eventually won the day, they suffered about one thousand casualties, half of all the soldiers engaged. That number included nineteen British officers killed and another seventy wounded.[9] The Americans thought nothing of violating the European code of honor by targeting the officers. For their part the Americans taking shelter behind a barrier they had constructed in the darkness the previous night lost between four hundred and six hundred men, only retreating when their ammunition gave out. This battle was a far more serious encounter than the running fight in April as the besieged regulars retreated from Concord to Boston. With so much blood spilled could the two sides still reconcile? Many colonists and members of Congress desperately hoped they could.

Schuyler had heard of the aspersions on Arnold's character, but he had his own sources. Barnabas Deane, brother of Silas Deane of Connecticut, Arnold's friend and Schuyler's fellow delegate to the Continental Congress, had visited Crown Point in May. He assured Silas: "Colonel Arnold has been greatly abused and misrepresented by designing persons," adding, "had it not been for him everything . . . would have been in the utmost confusion and disorder; people would have been plundered of their private property and no man's person would be safe that was not of the Green Mountain party."[10] As a New Yorker it wouldn't have taken much to convince Schuyler that the Green Mountain Boys, along with their claims against Arnold, were to be treated with skepticism. He wrote privately to Deane in July asking whether he could get Arnold appointed his deputy adjutant general for the Northern Department.[11] He "dare not mention it in Congress," he wrote, "and would not have it known that I had ever hinted it, as it might create jealousy. Be silent, therefore, with respect to me." Arnold was the capable, daring and resourceful man he needed for the expedition that he and Washington had been discussing to conquer Canada. In fact during their meeting Arnold had explained to Schuyler his idea of an attack on Quebec cutting through the Maine wilderness and making use of the river systems flowing north to the St. Lawrence. But first Arnold had to deal with the Massachusetts Congress.

On August 1 Arnold presented himself at the Watertown Meeting House to report to the Massachusetts Provincial Congress assembled there. The confrontation was every bit as frustrating as he had feared, the meeting in a church doing nothing to quiet the irascible attitudes of the delegates. They even chastised Arnold for going home to New Haven before reporting to them. The sudden death of his wife apparently was no excuse. The Provincial Congress, as was their habit, appointed a committee to deal with him. In this case its five members were led by Dr. Benjamin Church. Unbeknownst to his colleagues at the time, that good doctor interrogating Arnold was secretly passing information to the British. Church's duplicity would be discovered several weeks later and he would be arrested. In the meantime he and his committee were busily probing Arnold's use of public funds in minute detail. For two and a half weeks the committee audited his every expense while Congress refused to reimburse him in full for the money he had contributed. The committee recommended nearly £200 less than Arnold claimed. Silas Deane and Washington continued to urge members of the Congress to reconsider their parsimony but it was not until several months later, in the dead of winter, when Arnold lay wounded in Canada, that they finally agreed to make amends. All this relentless scrutiny would have tried Arnold's patience even further had he not slipped off during a quiet interval to meet with General Washington. He wanted to press for a new, more important mission, the invasion of Canada.

Arnold took advantage of the Provincial Congress's proximity to Cambridge to visit the headquarters of George Washington, the new commander in chief. He was keen to tell him of his ideas for an expedition against Quebec and with its capture, control of Canada. Washington's headquarters on Brattle Street was near Harvard College in the elegant, three-storey mansion of John Vassall, a wealthy

Tory who was then in Boston sheltered under British protection.[12] The entire area surrounding Harvard College was filled with the men and boys who had answered the Committee of Safety's desperate call for help keeping the British bottled up in Boston after April 19. The college flanks the Cambridge green, the town common. Harvard had sent its students home and opened its doors to as many of the citizen-soldiers cramming the town as possible. Four of its buildings were housing many of the men while others slept outdoors or were put up in private homes. The college was making other contributions to the cause. The lead on the roof of its main hall was being stripped and melted down to make bullets. Its kitchens were feeding the men nearby. The library collection and other college treasures, however, had been sent to the northshore town of Andover, out of harm's way.[13]

Washington and Arnold made quite a contrast as they greeted each other: the tall, dignified, handsome Virginian, and the shorter, stockier, impetuous Connecticut Yankee; the plantation owner and the shipping merchant both now turned soldier. Both had had to acquire learning and gentlemanly skills without the advantage of a college education. Both had an unabashed entrepreneurial spirit and a zeal for the cause. Washington had wanted the appointment to command the new army. While the other delegates to the Continental Congress wore ordinary civilian clothes to their meetings, he appeared daily in the buff and blue uniform of the Fairfax militia. Washington was an aristocrat but he was not a snob. He was anxious to make use of capable, talented men where he found them. God knows he needed them. While he waited a few days before giving Arnold his approval, he knew immediately Benedict Arnold was one of these.

Arnold had conceived of a plan for an attack on Canada's capital, the fortress city of Quebec, while commanding at Fort Ticonderoga. For years he had traded with the Canadians, sailing his ships from New Haven north to Halifax and other Canadian ports. He made a point of keeping informed about Canadian affairs, asking friends traveling there and others he knew in Canada for reports on British military strength and Canadian attitudes toward British rule. He had secured Ticonderoga, Crown Point, and Lake Champlain, at least for the moment, but garrison duty did not suit him. He was too restless, too keen for new challenges, for dramatic action. He was full of ideas to advance the American cause.

On June 13 while still at Crown Point he wrote directly to the Continental Congress on the peril to America with Canada in British hands and the need "to take possession of Montreal and Quebec."[14] He was convinced this would not be difficult, informing the delegates of the exact British strength in these key cities and laying out a plan of action. He estimated that two thousand men "might very easily affect it." Arnold concluded his proposal with an apology for his impetuousness in writing them, hoping "the urgency of the times and my zeal in the service of my country will apologize for the liberty of giving my sentiments so freely on a subject which the Honorable Congress are doubtless the best judges of, but which they in their hurry may not have paid the attention to which the matter requires." Rather than rebuilding Ticonderoga, he argued, it would be better to protect the thirteen colonies from attack from the north. "If no person appears who will undertake to carry the plan into execution (if thought advisable)," he added, "I will undertake, and, with the smiles of Heaven, answer for the success of it." With many delegates ambivalent about the capture of Ticonderoga and Crown Point, and desperately wanting reconciliation with Britain, Arnold ventured that "the reduction of these places [Montreal and Quebec] would discourage the enemies of American liberty" and would help restore "that solid peace and harmony between Great Britain and colonies." On the importance of securing control of Canada, Arnold was right, of course. Its continuing possession under British control threatened the American colonies for the remainder of the war and led to some of its key battles.

Arnold's idea struck a chord. His planned expedition though, aimed to use a customary route through Lake Champlain, the Great Warpath.[15] The strategy was first to attack Montreal, then move east to Quebec. Schemes to also attack Quebec directly by way of the rivers through the Maine wilderness or, conversely, for a French attack on New England along the same inland route had been pondered by the British and the French for years.[16] A trail between Quebec and the Maine coast through the river system actually appeared on a French map of 1682. During the French and Indian War there was a British plan to send two thousand regulars to attack Quebec using that route through the wilderness of Maine by way of the Kennebec and Chaudiere Rivers. Once war broke out in 1775 there were rumors the British might use that route to descend from Canada and attack New England. In fact a scouting party from Falmouth [now Portland] led by two experienced woodsmen, Remington Hobby and John Gatchell, was sent up the Kennebec River to check whether any Canadians or Indians were on their way south by means of the Maine rivers.[17] The two men traveled only as far as they could up the Kennebec, assuring themselves no one was coming down the river to attack Maine. The only man known to have traveled the entire route and surveyed it was a British army engineer, Colonel John Montresor. He had taken a party of Indians on that journey in 1761 and was at the present with General Gage in Boston. Washington was able to get a copy of Montresor's journal and maps but key material had been blocked out.[18] Even more unfortunate, Montresor's official journal neglected to mention the misery he had suffered as he and his party maneuvered through the forest around the many carrying places between navigable waterways. Years later Montresor recalled how during the journey he was "suffering from a loss of appetite from derangement of my System, for having been distressed by Famine for 13 days."[19]

If the Canadians could be persuaded to make common cause with the Americans it would be an immense advantage. Continued British control of Canada posed a constant threat to New York and the New England colonies. Whether Arnold knew it or not when he and Washington met, the Continental Congress had already agreed to a secret expedition to Canada. General Schuyler had been placed in overall command. What Washington had in mind for Arnold was not the full plan Arnold had laid out to the Continental Congress for attacking Montreal, but the daring expedition through the little-known rivers of Maine that he had outlined to General Gates, adjutant-general of the forces in Cambridge.[20]

Washington was enthusiastic about securing Canada and intrigued by the idea of launching a secret expedition through the Maine wilderness. The main force, led by Schuyler, would take the customary route north and capture Montreal, which was only lightly defended. It would then move east to Quebec where the two armies would meet to capture the citadel. The march through the wilderness along the river systems with their frequent carrying places was daunting, but Arnold was eager to lead such an expedition. Neither he nor Washington knew the problems and suffering Montresor had kept out of his official journals, problems Arnold was soon to find out for himself.

Preparations for the campaign to Canada were already under way. General Schuyler, who was to personally lead the main army of the Canadian expedition knew the area well. His expertise was ideal for the expedition. Washington assigned Schuyler some of the best officers he could spare. Chief among these was Brigadier General Richard Montgomery. Montgomery, like Horatio Gates, Charles Lee, and several other Continental Army officers, was a former British career soldier. And he was familiar with the Canadian region as well. During the French and Indian War he served under General Jeffrey Amherst at Ticonderoga, Crown Point, and their present target, Montreal. When that war ended he was stationed in New York. Seeing no opportunity for military advancement during peacetime, Montgomery sold his commission in 1772 and prepared to begin a new life in America. He bought land and married into a prominent New York family, determined to leave politics and the military behind. But as tensions with Britain mounted he was sent as a delegate to the New York provincial congress and then to the Second Continental Congress. Unlike Washington who actively sought a military role in the coming conflict, or Arnold who was anxious to prove himself by undertaking daring expeditions for the cause, Montgomery simply wanted to live the peaceful life of a landowner. He was done with soldiering. Yet he could not disentangle himself from the world about him. As he explained to his wife in despair:

> When I entered your family I was a stranger in your country . . . yet without my wish or knowledge they appoint me to the committee from Duchess[county]. The times were such I could not refuse however reluctant . . . Now without consulting me they have made me general. In this capacity I may be of service for a just cause. Can I refuse? . . . Honor calls on me. [21]

Washington made Montgomery second in command to Schuyler. Two inveterate foes of Arnold's from the Ticonderoga campaign, John Brown and Ethan Allen, also were to be in Schuyler's army. Allen joined Schuyler's forces assembling at Crown Point. Brown, whom Schuyler had sent to Canada several times to spy out the strength of British forces and the sentiment of English Canadians, eventually joined the expedition. While neither Brown nor Allen would serve in Arnold's wilderness expedition, they were all destined to meet when the two American forces converged before Quebec.

Arnold's expedition, the march through the wilderness, was designed to surprise the Canadians and assist the main army. Washington and Arnold met several times to discuss the plan. The commander was aware of the various complaints against Arnold but had been reassured by his friend Silas Deane and trusted his own instincts. Nevertheless he insisted Arnold meet three conditions before appointing him to lead an army through Maine. First, Arnold had to sort out his problems with the Massachusetts

Provincial Congress by presenting them with his full report. Second, he was to put himself under General Schuyler who was in overall charge of the Canadian campaign. And third, he was to treat the Canadians as fellow Americans joining in a common cause against British oppression. To these Arnold readily agreed, and by August 20 Washington had made up his mind. He sent an express letter to Schuyler that a second expedition would be sent through Maine to distract General Carleton and help capture Quebec and that Benedict Arnold would lead it.[22] He assured Schuyler of Arnold's "enterprising and persevering sprit," adding: "The merit of this gentleman is certainly great and I heartily wish that fortune may distinguish him one of her favorites."[23]

Washington estimated that one thousand to twelve hundred men would be sufficient for Arnold's army. He carefully selected those officers he thought best able to venture with Arnold on this perilous trek. These included four New Englanders: Major Christopher Greene of Rhode Island, Lieutenant Colonel Roger Enos of Connecticut, Major Return Jonathan Meigs of Connecticut and Major Timothy Bigelow, a blacksmith from Worcester, Massachusetts. Among the volunteers was Aaron Burr who would become vice president of the new republic and wage a murderous duel with Alexander Hamilton. Now, like the rest, he was a young man seeking adventure.

Washington also planned to have three frontier rifle companies on the expedition. By September he had six such companies in Cambridge. To avoid upset about which were to go and which were to remain he decided there should be lots drawn. The three winning companies were Daniel Morgan's men from the Virginia frontier and two companies from the then Pennsylvania backwoods, Captain William Hendricks's company from Cumberland County and Captain Matthew Smith's Lancaster County company. These frontier riflemen were a rough but impressive group. It would take an inspiring and courageous leader to win their obedience and respect.

Daniel Morgan would become the de facto leader of the three rifle companies in Arnold's army. He was a colorful character, six feet tall, two hundred pounds, broad shouldered, brawling, a survivor of some five hundred lashes inflicted for disorderly behavior while serving with the British as a teamster during the French and Indian War. Morgan was immensely popular in Virginia, captain of his local militia company. While Congress specified that each company in their army was to have sixty men, Morgan's had ninety-six. And they were impressive. When ordered to join the forces gathered at Cambridge off they marched, taking only three weeks to complete the six-hundred-mile journey. Morgan was an excellent man to have on a dangerous expedition and deserved his growing reputation as a daring military leader.[24] Arnold's two other rifle companies of tough backwoods sharpshooters were equally formidable. The company led by Captain William Hendricks of Cumberland, made the 441-mile journey to Cambridge in twenty-six days including stops to see the sights and to tar-and-feather the occasional loyalist they came upon.[25]

The three rifle companies were markedly distinct from the rest of the troops in their equipment and dress. Each man arrived in Cambridge carrying a long rifle, and with a long knife and a tomahawk at his waist. Their dress was a knee-length hunting shirt of linen or deerskin in a natural linen color, or blue or red usually fringed at the neck, with breeches and boots or moccasins.[26] As one of Arnold's riflemen wrote, their clothing was "by no means in a military style," but aped "the manners of savages."[27] Yet it was practical and comfortable for wilderness work.

They had one other distinction—even among the self-reliant Americans these backwoods men stood out as fiercely independent. John Joseph Henry, a young member of one of these companies, wrote they were "of as rude and hardy a race as ourselves, and as unused to the discipline of a camp, and as fearless as we."[28] Washington found it especially difficult to get them to conform to military discipline. They resented being ordered to shoulder routine military duties such as digging trenches. Their officers either would not, or could not, control them. In one incident described by a New England officer, a member of Captain Ross's company was sent to the guardhouse for his refusal to carry out a task.[29] Furious at his arrest thirty-two of his comrades marched with loaded guns to the guardhouse swearing they would release him or lose their lives. The sentinels at the guardhouse immediately sent word to Washington who ordered five hundred New England recruits to dash to the guardhouse, weapons loaded. When the angry riflemen arrived they found themselves surrounded by the New England troops armed with muskets, bayonets fixed. Two of the rebellious ringleaders were bound and the disorder ended.

There were six frontier rifle companies in Washington's army at Cambridge by September and he was determined to send three of them with Arnold. One wonders whether Washington chose these rifle companies for Arnold's army, not merely for their knowledge of wilderness survival but also to remove troublesome men from his own camp.

This was the human material that comprised Arnold's army. Yet by the end of their frightful wilderness expedition every journal writer among the group praised Arnold's courage and leadership.

With plans laid and officers assigned the preparations for the assault on Canada began in earnest. As these arrangements began in August it was already late in the year to launch an attack on Canada before the Canadian winter, which always came early. In addition the British had been given additional time to reinforce their Canadian army. But it was the weather that was to prove the most formidable. General Schuyler had been working feverishly, mobilizing troops and amassing supplies and boats, keenly aware how crucial this planning would be to their success. He arranged for the building of powder mills to provide ammunition along with the construction of boats, docks, roads, and hospitals. While all this was going on Schuyler also took time out to negotiate with the Iroquois.[30] By the end of August he had sixty boats ready to launch, able to carry thirteen hundred men and a three-week supply of food.[31]

Arnold began his own arrangements immediately after Washington appointed him on August 20. He started assembling his army and wrote Captain Colburn, a Maine militia officer with a boat building business in the Kennebec Valley, to find out how soon two hundred light bateaux, each capable of carrying six or seven men with their provisions and baggage, could be purchased or built.[32] Colburn replied that he couldn't even begin building these until September 6. That was not just unfortunate but disastrous, as the speed with which the boats now had to be built meant they would not be made of seasoned wood or well constructed. Amid all his other concerns Arnold insisted that at least his men look like soldiers. Benjamin Thompson, a New Hampshire militia officer, observed them before their departure and, while finding the rest of the American army "not very badly accoutered, but most wretchedly clothed, and as dirty a set of mortals as ever disgraced the name of a soldier. They have had no clothes of any sort provided for them by the Congress," except, he added, "the detachment of 1,133 that are gone to Canada under Col. Arnold, who had each of them a new coat and a linen frock served out to them before they set out."[33]

Arnold ordered his men to rendezvous at the north shore town of Newburyport. From there they were to sail up the Maine coast to the Kennebec River to get their bateaux. On September 14, the day before the final contingent of troops reached Newburyport, Washington wrote to Arnold laying out his mission in detail, being careful to emphasize how important its success and their behavior was to their personal honor and reputation: "You are intrusted with a command of the utmost consequence to the interest and liberties of America. Upon your conduct and courage and that of the officers and soldiers detached on this expedition, not only the success of the present enterprise and honor, but the safety and welfare of the whole continent may depend."[34] He charged, "you therefore, and the officers and soldiers under your command as you value your own safety and honor and the favor and esteem of your country, that you consider yourselves as marching not through an enemy's country, but that of our friends and brethren." The men were to behave with scrupulous care toward both Canadians and Indians, paying for anything they needed, behaving with strict discipline and courtesy, showing respect for the Catholic religion, treating any prisoners with "as much humanity and kindness as may be consistent with your own safety & the public interest." Once in Canada Arnold was to distribute "addresses" written by Washington to Canadians and to convince "those people & such Indians as you may meet with by every means in your power . . . that we come at the request of many of their principal people, not as robbers or to make war upon them, but as the friends and supporters of their liberties as well as ours."[35] "Come then, ye generous citizens" Washington urged Canadians, "range yourselves under the standard of General Liberty, against which all the force and artifice of tyranny will never be able to prevail."[36]

With so much at stake, on September 19 Arnold and his little army set sail from Newburyport for the trip along the rocky Maine coast to the Kennebec River, where they were to pick up their bateaux. Private Abner Stocking described the expedition's departure as the nine hundred men with their equipment and supplies crowded onto nine vessels:

> This morning we got under way with a pleasant breeze, our drums beating, fifes playing, and colors flying. Many pretty girls stood upon the shore, I suppose weeping for the departure of their sweethearts. [37]

After this noisy leave-taking the secret expedition cleared Newburyport harbor at eleven o'clock bound for the Kennebec River, there to follow Montresor's route through the wilderness to Canada.

ELEVEN

Honor in a
"Direful Howling Wilderness"

A rnold was right, Canada was vulnerable. Certainly General Sir Guy Carleton, the British commander and governor of the colony, was painfully aware of the danger. Carleton was an experienced career officer, third of four sons of a proud but poor Irish Protestant family. His father died when Guy was fourteen and he and his brothers went into the army.[1] Military families tended to have sons and Carleton himself would have nine. He served in the French and Indian Wars under the brilliant leadership of General James Wolfe. The two men had become close friends and Carleton was with Wolfe during the triumphant British assault on Quebec. Both men were wounded in that engagement, Carleton badly, Wolfe fatally. When the war ended Carleton returned to Britain to recuperate, then served with the army in expeditions to the Bay of

Biscay and to Cuba where he was wounded twice. While in Cuba Carleton served alongside a neighbor of his from Ireland, Richard Montgomery. The two officers were fated to face each other again, but this time on opposite sides in another battle for Quebec.

In 1766 Carleton was appointed administrator of the new British colony of Canada. On his journey to Quebec he docked at New York to visit General Gage, commander of British forces in the New World. Carleton advised General Gage that, if necessary, force should be used to keep the American colonies in check.[2] In preparation for that eventuality he suggested the British army use Quebec and New York as their bases and fortify the routes connecting the two, which could, if advisable, isolate New England. Carleton estimated it would cost about £68,000, a vast sum, to build a citadel at Quebec, but argued it be undertaken and that they suppress factious men in the North American colonies who "might not be ready to do their duty."[3]

Guy Carleton was a fine choice to command in Canada. The post required a knowledgeable and sensible man. Conquering the largely French-Catholic province was hard enough, governing it just as difficult. Carleton had a keen appreciation of the military and civil challenges he faced forging a workable government with longtime enemies whose language, law, and culture were at odds with Britain's. The task was made more urgent by the dangerous tensions between Britain and its temperamental North American colonies. Carleton knew the country, knew the people. He counseled London to tread carefully in their new province, permitting the French-Canadians, the great majority of residents, to preserve their own traditions. And he was listened to. He had the satisfaction of being in London in 1774 when Parliament took his advice. The Quebec Act eased French-Canadian anxieties though at the cost of heightening the dismay and anger of Britain's thirteen colonies to the south. The Act enlarged the Canadian borders absorbing America's "northwest territory" into Canada and dropped all reference to the Protestant faith from the new Canadian oath of allegiance. Indeed, the Quebec Act allowed the Catholic Church to continue tithing and continued the use of French civil law.[4] All this deference to French-Canadians occurred at the same time and in the same Parliament that was drafting the so-called Intolerable Acts to punish Massachusetts Bay residents by depriving them of civilian government and cherished rights.[5]

Britain was walking a fine line. If it treated the French-Canadians more harshly they were more likely to be susceptible to the blandishments of the cantankerous colonists to the south, or simply to rebel against the small occupying army of their new masters. Britain could not afford either. Parliament decided to treat the Canadians with every consideration and deal with the Americans as their rebellious behavior deserved.

In the spring of 1772 during one of Carleton's stays in Britain the then forty-eight-year-old soldier married Maria Howard, daughter of an earl from another military family, a young woman nearly thirty years his junior. In the fall of 1774 Carleton and his wife sailed to Canada to begin the process of implementing the Quebec Act.

The Continental Congress, fuming about the Quebec Act, wrote that October to the people of Montreal urging "our brave enemies" to "become our hearty friends" and explaining that the Act promoted Catholicism, was undemocratic, and deprived the Canadians of the common law benefits of habeas corpus and trial by jury. Carleton was aware of these overtures and of John Brown's secret visits to English merchants in Montreal, including a trip in early 1775 to persuade British merchants in Canada to send delegates to the Second Continental Congress in May. Still Carleton did nothing to interfere. Before the Congress met the battle of Lexington and Concord would occur. And no Canadian delegates were sent to the Congress.

Now, in 1775, blood had been shed and the military situation in all of North America was precarious. Thomas Gage, based in Boston, was calling for three British armies, one in Boston, a second in New York, and a third in Canada. The last was to be made up of British regulars, Canadians, and Indians.[6] Carleton would have been happy to have a large army. He asked for ten thousand to twelve thousand men. But in June 1775 he had a mere six hundred able-bodied rank-and-file soldiers and not one armed ship.[7] The French-Canadian militia no longer functioned and while Carleton welcomed the arrival of more regulars he quietly ignored the order to recruit the Indians. He was only too aware what doubtful allies they could be, fighting in their own way with sometimes terrible brutality.[8] Opposing his troops the rebellious colonists to the south had a large, eager force of citizen-soldiers in Massachusetts itching for action. He spent the summer strengthening his defenses, especially at Fort Saint Jean, bracing for an assault. In September it came. An American army led by Schuyler and Carleton's old comrade Montgomery crossed the border and besieged Fort Saint Jean. A month later Arnold's little army began its own trek north.

Arnold's expedition did not begin well, but not because the expedition was a badly kept secret. Even before Arnold's men had left Cambridge, Gage was writing Vice Admiral Samuel Graves of the Royal Navy asking that warships intercept Arnold's fleet at sea.[9] Gage didn't reckon on the wilderness route Arnold meant to take, however, and thought that the expedition must be heading for Halifax, Nova Scotia.[10] Arnold's army didn't meet with any British vessels as they put to sea. But there were other, natural dangers. The night of August 19, that first night out of port, a fog arose and the ships lost each other in the mist. In the dark the schooner *Swallow*, with about one hundred men aboard, became surrounded by rocks and ran aground. Young Private Abner Stocking on board the foundering schooner believed the pilots had had too much to drink.[11] With the morning light Arnold gathered his fleet and rescued the soldiers aboard the *Swallow*, distributing them among the other ships and ordering the *Swallow*'s crew to follow with the cargo as quickly as they could. The fleet now sailed north to the mouth of the Kennebec River.

Arnold's plan was more daring than Gage imagined. He and his men were to travel up the "very troublesome" Kennebec River forty-nine miles to Gardiner, where the bateaux he had ordered were awaiting them.[12] They were then to voyage up the Kennebec as far as practical, that is to Fort Western, deep into Maine opposite the present state capital of Augusta.[13] This part of the plan went relatively smoothly and they arrived at Fort Western on September 23. From Fort Western they were to ascend the Kennebec to the "great carrying place" where the bateaux, each weighing four hundred pounds, and their hundreds of pounds of supplies would have to be carried overland for miles through rough terrain between that river and the Dead River. There were, in fact, several other carrying places such as rapids where the boats had to be carried. These began with rapids a quarter-mile above Fort Western, where with the aid of teams of men and animals from the area they hoisted their boats and supplies overland. Eighteen miles further along the Kennebec lay the Ticonic Falls, and then came Five Mile Falls where the river abruptly descended thirty-four feet.[14] At Skowhegan Falls the river descended through a crevice in the rocks and the boats needed to be hauled up the steep rock face. Once at the Dead River they were to turn west, then carry their boats over the summit of the Maine Appalachian ridge that divides the New England rivers from those flowing into the St. Lawrence. On their descent they were to put their boats in the Chaudiere River and navigate it to Quebec. Their knowledge of the country was sketchy. It proved extremely rugged in many places, without even a trail. Worse, they had to carry their heavy boats through bogs and over rocky passes, while often enduring wet and freezing weather as the winter of the northeast began to descend, all this taking much longer than the supplies Arnold had would last. Indeed, the wet weather and water washing over their food spoiled much of it.

Arnold kept his promise to Washington to write regularly of their progress. His letters and the journals of several of his men catalogue their trials. Arnold explained, for a start, that the bateaux were smaller than he had ordered and "very badly built" using green timber. He thought it necessary to order twenty more just to carry supplies.[15] Another delay was caused when "many of the vessels were detained in the river by running aground & headwinds." He sent two advance parties ahead to scout the route while he traveled back and forth between the groups in a birch canoe. Everything took more time than Arnold and Washington had hoped.

On October 2 Arnold arrived at Norridgewock Falls where he spent the next seven days directing the troops around the falls. On October 12 he ordered a hospital to be built for sick and injured men at the starting point of the Great Carrying Place. On October 13 he wrote Washington again to explain their problems after leaving Fort Western: "We have had a very fatiguing time, the men in general not understanding bateaus [which needed to be poled rather than rowed] have been obliged to wade and haul them more than half way up the river."[16] He reported that he had ordered supplies delivered to secure their retreat. While this was expensive, he wrote that "when set in competition with the lives of liberty of so many brave men I think it trifling, and if we succeed the provisions will not be lost."[17] Arnold then added a postscript:

> Your Excellency might possibly think we have been tardy in our march, as we have gained so little, but when you consider the badness & weight of the bateaux and large quantity of provisions etc. we have been obliged to force up against a very rapid stream, where you would have taken the men for amphibious animals, as they were great part of the time under water, add to this the great fatigue in portage, you will think I have pushed the men as fast as they could possibly bear.

Arnold kept up his men's spirits as they worked their way down the Dead River, going back and forth in a canoe to check on their progress. None of them knew he had underestimated the distance to Quebec thinking it to be 180 miles, which was less than half the actual distance.[18] Happily for all their spirits they were unaware of that problem or that other difficulties were soon to come.

On October 19, six days after Arnold's letter to Washington, it began to rain. Over the next three days it poured. Days of water from what was a hurricane came surging down the river, raising its level nine feet.[19] The men scrambled to save themselves and their provisions, hauling them to a high point and then lighting fires to dry out. On October 23 they set out again, but the river water was turbulent and one of the bateaux collided with another, overturning it and starting a chain reaction. Seven boats were swamped and the provisions they carried completely lost. That evening Arnold and his officers met and decided that the sick and weak should turn back. With the sparse rations left on hand only the strongest men would survive.[20] Arnold wrote advising colonels Enos and Greene, who were farther back with their men, to bring only those who were fit and for whom they had fifteen days of supplies. But Enos had had enough and against orders turned back with all his men.

For Arnold and those who continued there was more suffering to come. Their provisions ran out. On November 1 twenty-year-old Dr. Isaac Senter wrote that their greatest luxuries "now consisted in a little water, stiffened with flour in imitation of shoemaker's paste."[21] A poor dog that accompanied the group was seized by desperate men and eaten. Senter saw men trying to eat shaving soap, lip salve, the leather of their shoes, and cartridge boxes. On November 2 Private Abner Stocking found that "many of the company were so weak that they could hardly stand on their legs. When we attempted to march, they reeled out like drunken men, having now been without provisions for five days." Stocking continued:

As I proceeded I passed many sitting, wholly drowned in sorrow, wishfully placing their eyes on every one who passed by them, hoping for some relief. . . . The circumstances of a young Dutchman and his wife, who followed him through this fatiguing march, particularly excited my sensibility. They appeared to be much interested in each other's welfare and unwilling to be separated, but the husband, exhausted with fatigue and hunger fell victim to the king of terrors. His affectionate wife tarried by him until he died, while the rest of the company proceeded on their way. Having no implements with which she could bury him she covered him with leaves, and then took his gun and other implements and left him with a heavy heart.[22]

But just at this point help appeared. Arnold had gone on ahead, found friendly Frenchmen, and purchased supplies to send back to his men. That very evening Stocking and his comrades met cattle coming up the river "sent to us for our relief. This was the most joyful sight our eyes beheld."

One of the men, Shafer, a drummer with poor eyesight, became the butt of many pranks and jokes on the trek, struggling to pick his way through the gullies and ravines with the rest of the men. When the men were able to cross a gully by means of a log Shafer sometimes tumbled off it.[23] Some men even stole the last of his cakes, but then took pity and gave him a cup of flour. Nevertheless poor Shafer, starving and pitiful, "bore his drum uninjured to Quebec when many strong and hale men died in the wilderness."

Through it all Arnold was purposeful, energetic, dedicated to the success of his mission, yet always considerate of his men. John Joseph Henry, a seventeen-year-old private from Pennsylvania, wrote that on November 7 he simply could walk no farther while the other troops passed on.[24] In the rear came Arnold on horseback.

He knew my name and character, and good-naturedly inquired after my health. Being informed, he dismounted, ran down to the riverside, and hailed the owner of the house, which stood opposite across the water. The good Canadian, in his canoe, quickly arrived. Depositing my gun and accoutrements in the hand of one of our men, who attended upon me, and had been disarmed by losing his rifle in some of the wrecking's above, and Arnold putting two silver dollars in my hands, the Frenchman carried me to his house.

The young man was cared for by the kindly Frenchman and later rejoined his comrades.

To supplement his reduced numbers, Arnold met with local Indians. He managed to persuade Chief Natanis and his brother Sabatis to join his army, bringing fifty warriors with them. Natanis was struck by Arnold, this vigorous, driven man, dark haired with light eyes, and named him "The Dark Eagle."[25]

On November 8 Arnold arrived at Point Levi. Across the river lay Quebec. The journey done he wrote to Schuyler reporting on the arduous trek through the wilderness, extolling not his own achievement, but the bravery and courage of his men:

> . . . thus in about eight weeks we completed a march of near six hundred miles, not to be paralleled in history, the men having the greatest fortitude and perseverance hauled their bateaux up rapid streams, being obliged to wade almost the whole way, near 180 miles, carried them on their shoulders near forty miles, over hills, swamps, and bogs almost impenetrable, and to their knees in mire, being often obliged to cross three or four times with their baggage. Short of provisions, part of the detachment disheartened and gone back, famine staring us in the face, an enemy's country and uncertainty

ahead. Notwithstanding all these obstacles, the officers and men, inspired and fired with the love of liberty and their country, pushed on with a fortitude superior to every obstacle, and most of them had not one day's provision for a week.[26]

Of the 1100 men who had started the journey 675 remained with Arnold on the banks of the St. Lawrence awaiting Montgomery's arrival for the attack on Quebec.[27]

The main American army led by Philip Schuyler and Richard Montgomery had quite a jump on Arnold and his men. Schuyler had journeyed to Ticonderoga in July and Montgomery joined him the following month. There they assembled the twelve hundred men, most from the nearby states of New York and Connecticut, for their campaign. Happily for Arnold and, as it turned out, unhappily for these two commanders, John Brown and Ethan Allen were among that number. Brown had been sent to Canada on yet another spy mission and reported the dire news that the British were building two gunboats at St. Johns. The *Royal Savage*, a schooner with twelve cannon and ten swivels already lay at anchor in the harbor. There was no time to waste. Schuyler moved his men out, and on September 4 they reached Isle La Motte, at the northern end of Lake Champlain. At this point, just as they were about to continue their march, Schuyler's old illnesses, gout and pleurisy, struck hard. A sick man, he headed back to Ticonderoga to work on the supplies and logistics for the expedition, leaving the reluctant soldier, Richard Montgomery, to face Carleton, his old British army comrade.

Montgomery's first target was Fort St. Johns on the Richelieu River. Its defenses were made of earth and logs. With too little time to strengthen the walls Carleton had fortified the fort's key buildings instead. Now a series of moves and countermoves by the two rival commanders began. Before attacking St. Johns Montgomery tried to cut its communication with Fort Chambly. He failed and retreated to Île aux Noix. He then attacked St. Johns directly. In preparation, he sent John Brown and Ethan Allen into Canada to rally the Canadians on his behalf. That proved a disastrous decision.

Brown managed to raid the British supply lines, but it was Allen who typically claimed great success raising large numbers of recruits. Reporting to Montgomery on September 20, he assured the commander, "You may rely on it that I shall join you in about three days, with five hundred or more Canadian volunteers. I could raise one or two thousand in a week's time, but will first visit the Army with a less number, and if necessary will go again recruiting."[28] "Those that used to be enemies to our cause," he added, "come cap in hand to me." Montgomery, unable to take the fort by force, now began a prolonged and costly siege, costly because the season was quickly heading toward the bitter Canadian winter. Allen and his recruits never appeared.

Lengthy sieges were not for Allen. It occurred to him that with his small contingent of recruits he could take Montreal immediately. On September 24, four days after writing to Montgomery and without that commander's knowledge, Allen began his march with some two hundred men, a number that quickly shrank to eighty. He chanced to meet John Brown with two hundred recruits of his own on the south shore of the St. Lawrence, opposite Montreal. With his eighty recruits, some thirty Americans and Brown's promise of support Allen crossed the river in a collection of boats to attack Montreal, a city of nine thousand residents. Although it had a tiny garrison of only sixty it did have several hundred local militia willing to oppose them.[29] Typically, where Brown and Allen were concerned the former was timid, the latter full of bravado. Quite in character, Brown never showed up to support his friend, "an omission," historian Eliot Cohen finds, "never satisfactorily explained."[30] The result was a rout. General Prescott rallied his little garrison and three-hundred-man militia, a force sallied out to attack Allen, and he and his men quickly surrendered. Allen later claimed two Indians had tried to kill him but using a British officer as a shield he was soon rescued, although he and thirty-five of his men were taken prisoner. Allen insisted he had been "very merry and facetious" throughout and when taken to the commandant of Montreal, General Prescott, who shook his cane at him and called him "many hard names," Allen had shaken his own fist in the general's face and warned him not to use the cane. General Prescott retorted, "I will not execute you now. But you shall grace a halter at Tyburn, God Damn you."[31] In the event Allen was put in chains and shipped off to England for trial.

Allen's foolish attack on Montreal harmed the American cause as Canadians and Indians became more reluctant to support Montgomery and his men. Montgomery deplored Allen's "imprudence and ambition." And when the commander in chief himself learned of Allen's fiasco he wrote General Schuyler, "Colonel Allen's misfortune will, I hope, teach a lesson of prudence and subordination to others who may be too ambitious to outshine their general officers and regardless of order and duty rush into enterprises which have unfavorable effects to the public and are destructive to themselves."[32] The *New England Gazette* summed up the general opinion: "Allen is a high flying genius, pursues every scheme on its first impression, without consideration and much less judgment."[33] Arnold could be grateful that despite the natural obstacles his army had to overcome, he did not have Brown and Allen in their midst. Brown, however, would reappear once the two armies met.

St. Johns lay between two old French forts, Île aux Noix on an island in the river, and Fort Chambly, near Montreal. With his supplies growing short and six hundred of his men now ill, Montgomery sent a raiding party to Chambly. It was held by 150 men but surrendered, the first Canadian fort to fall.[34] Its 88 officers were captured along with the desperately needed supplies—six tons of gunpowder, 6500 musket cartridges, 125 Brown Bess muskets, three mortars, 80 barrels of flour, 134 barrels of salt pork, and a large amount of rice and peas. Montgomery sent the captured standard of the British 7th Regiment of Foot to Congress.[35] This success saved Montgomery's expedition, enabling him to hold out. On November 2, after a siege of fifty days St. Johns surrendered. Among its five hundred soldiers was John André, whose path would cross tragically with Arnold's a few years later.

The long siege had provided the British more time to get reinforcements and left the Americans with a winter campaign in the field. With the loss of St. Johns Carleton retreated from Montreal to Quebec taking most of his forces with him and leaving Montreal virtually defenseless. Despite the shortage of manpower, Carleton refused to recruit Indians, writing Lord Dartmouth in October that he meant to treat the rebels with "as much Humanity as our own Safety would permit."[36] Nor did he let them cross into the bordering colonies "lest cruelties might have been committed, and for fear the innocent might have suffered with the Guilty."[37] On November 12 it fell to Montgomery, along with the eleven ships in its harbor and all the military supplies in the town. In celebration Congress made Montgomery a major general. However, Montgomery had no illusions about the achievement, writing his father-in-law, Robert Livingston, a delegate to the Congress: "until Quebec falls, Canada is unconquered."

Time and disease had depleted both American forces and the men's enlistments were due to expire. Montgomery marched quickly to rendezvous with Arnold. On December 3 he and Arnold met at Quebec and immediately began preparations to assault that fortress city. There was no time to waste. On the last day of the year, in a blinding snowstorm, their two armies attacked.

TWELVE

A Fierce Attack, a Winter Siege

Quebec, the chief city of British Canada, was a formidable target. Samuel de Champlain had an excellent eye for a perfect defensive site when he founded the city in 1608. Only General Wolfe's brilliant and skillful battle plan had enabled the British to scale its heights unseen and capture it in 1759.

Quebec stands on the north shore of the St. Lawrence River near its conjunction with the St. Charles River. The St. Lawrence River valley is low and flat, and Quebec's port and narrow, lower town is at water level. But steep cliffs loom over the lower town and on their summit stands the upper town, protected by stout stone walls giving its defenders a commanding view of the river. Added to this challenging location for would-be conquerors, the region's long, frigid winter gave it additional protection for much of the year. And that frigid winter was beginning.

Arnold's army on the southern bank of the St. Lawrence was threatening the city, but first he had to get across the river controlled by British ships. While he awaited the arrival of Montgomery, he learned with joy that Montreal had been taken. Unfortunately in the process the British Commander, General Carleton, had managed to slip away, but a victory was a victory. Just Quebec lay between the Americans and control of Canada. Still, Arnold was impatient to make some attempt on the Canadian capital, formidable as the task was. There was no time to lose. Winter was fast approaching. Far better to weather it in the confines of the city than enduring a miserable winter siege. Worse, the enlistments of the American troops ended with the end of the year.

Guy Carleton had his own share of troubles at that moment. He had abandoned Montreal but with one American army surrounding it and another across the river from Quebec where was he to go? He and his officers agreed he was needed at Quebec, some 160 miles to the east, despite the difficulty of slipping past enemy lines to reach it. His best option seemed to be to trust his safety to Captain Jean Baptiste Bouchette, a French-Canadian merchant and river pilot, who agreed to smuggle him down the river in a flat, open whaleboat. The general boarded the vessel disguised as a French-Canadian peasant, a *habitant*.[1]

On the night of November 16 the boat managed to evade the American sentries and docked at Trois-Rivières where Carleton learned the bad news that Americans had reached Pointe-aux-Trembles, a few miles above Quebec. Thoroughly exhausted, he risked leaving his party and found a bed in the home of a local family. In the middle of the night he awakened to the noisy arrival of American soldiers also looking for shelter. Thanks to his disguise and passable French they didn't recognize him. He slipped out and returned to the whaleboat. With all aboard her lying in the bottom of the boat, their hands over the sides, paddling as silently as possible, they rowed down the river hoping to look like a drifting log. Once beyond Montgomery's men they met and boarded the *Fell*, a friendly merchant ship. Three days after setting off Carleton arrived at Quebec to the great joy of the garrison and friends of the British. He immediately took charge, but the city's troops had wasted no time and were fully prepared to mount a vigorous defense, agreeing to defend Quebec "to the last extremity."[2]

Carleton counted some 1,178 more or less reliable men and reckoned they had enough supplies to last them until spring. He quickly dispatched a messenger to London, however, asking that when the river was passable the government send supplies and reinforcements as well as prefabricated boats that could be assembled to sail down Lake Champlain and bring the war to the Americans. Despite all this he was pessimistic, writing Lord Dartmouth, "I think our Fate extremely doubtful, to say nothing worse."[3] There were enemies inside the walls, hostile French and reluctant Canadian militia. Would they support the regulars?

Carleton made what repairs he could to the blockhouses and placed cannon on the walls. Residents hostile to the British regime were given four days to quit the city and had to leave the entire district by December 1 or be treated "as rebels or spies."[4] All these preparations were not a moment too soon. On December 2 he was informed that Montgomery and Arnold had joined forces. Quebec was sealed tight and ready for the assault Washington had ordered.

If Carleton was pessimistic, Washington was hopeful. Montgomery had taken St. Johns and Montreal. Arnold had managed to bring his valiant little army through the wilderness, and it was now poised, when the two armies met, to attack Quebec. It was a triumphant and satisfying moment for Arnold as well. A flurry of letters all written on December 5 to him and from his superior officers to each other were full of his praise. Washington was in a jubilant mood writing Arnold, "It is not in the power of any man to command success, but you have done more—you have deserved it, & before this I hope, have met with the laurels which are due to your toils, in the possession of Quebec—My thanks are due

& sincerely offered to you, for your Enterprising & persevering spirit—To your brave followers I likewise present them."[5] He added the prayer that "the Almighty may preserve & prosper you in it [the enterprise] is the sincere & fervent prayer of Dear sir. &c." In a postscript Washington expressed his surprise that Enos had returned to Cambridge with the division under his command, adding, "I immediately put him under Arrest & had him tried for Quitting the Detachment without your Orders—He is acquitted on the Score of provisions." Washington extolled Arnold's achievement writing Schuyler the same day: "The merit of that officer is certainly great and I heartily wish that fortune may distinguish him as one of her favorites. He will do everything which prudence and valor may suggest, to add to the success of our arms."[6] Montgomery also wrote Schuyler about their two armies meeting, pointing out that his own vessels carried only "the few troops equipped for a winter campaign, about 300." On the other hand he added, "I find Colonel Arnold's corps an exceedingly fine one. Immune to fatigue and well accustomed to cannon shot, there is a style of discipline among them much superior to what I have been used to see in this campaign."[7]

Arnold and Montgomery agreed it was time to take action. Protocol and good sense demanded that they first attempt to persuade the city to surrender. On December 13 with a flotilla carrying five hundred men Arnold set off to cross the river, taking great care to evade the British frigate and sloop nearby. They landed safely in Wolfe's Cove where he hoped to cut off the city's supplies and to send a messenger to call upon the city to surrender. A surrender would ensure defenders and residents better treatment and avoid bloodshed. The response was uncharacteristically abrupt. Carleton ordered his men to shoot at the messenger. Montgomery tried a somewhat different tack to negotiate a surrender. His first message to Carleton that general tossed into the fire. Next he sent a woman to Carleton calling for the surrender of the garrison. Carleton's answer was to have her arrested.[8] Frustrated, Montgomery and Arnold besieged the city although Arnold tried going himself to request surrender. Again the document he carried was burnt and Arnold left amid a chorus of insults.

As the year was drawing rapidly to a close and with it their men's enlistments, the two American commanders planned their assault. The British and Americans were about equally matched in numbers, although the British had by far the best strategic position. The American attack was planned for Sunday, December 31. It was to be four-pronged, with Arnold's men advancing from the northeast with his division of "Famine proof Veterans," Montgomery's from the west and south with most of the troops from Montreal.[9] Colonel Livingston and his Canadian regiment were to attack the wall at St. John's gate. Another attack was to take place at the riverbank near the end of the city walls.[10] The signal to advance was three rocket blasts. Their men were to identify themselves with a strip of white paper pinned to the front of their hats bearing the words, "Liberty or Death." They slept that night with their weapons.

At four in the morning in the pitch dark, shrouded by blinding, heavy snow they moved out. Snow on the ground might have helped them see their way, but a storm was different. John Henry, one of Arnold's men, wrote, "The snow was outrageous and the cold wind extremely biting. In this northern country the snow is blown horizontally into the faces of travelers on most occasions— this was our case."[11] Montgomery was leading an advance party. They plunged through the snow, their mission to push their way through the stout pickets at the edge of the riverbank and attack a blockhouse guarded by regulars armed with muskets and cannon. Abner Stocking explained that Cape Diamond around which they were to climb was a precipice. At its base next to the river enormous and rugged chunks of ice had piled making the route nearly impassable. Their path up was so narrow they had to climb single file. When they reached the wooden pickets Montgomery began pulling them out with his own hands shouting to his troops, "Men of New York, you will not fear to follow where your General leads. March on!"[12] They charged. The blockhouse's cannon were lit. Cannon balls exploded all about them. Montgomery and a group of his soldiers were killed instantly. The rest of his men turned and fled.

Across town with a cacophony of bells, drums, and muskets making a mockery of a predawn Sunday surprise, Arnold led another small advance group followed by the rest of his men toward Sault-au-Matelot. He expected some small batteries ranged against them before reaching the lower town where the two wings of the American army were to meet. Enemy muskets blazed. Arnold, in the vanguard, was struck by a musket ball that entered his left leg just below the knee. Refusing to leave the field, he continued marching, dragging his bleeding leg.[13] Once the rest of his men caught up he turned back toward the hospital a mile away, urging on his men as he passed them. Unlike Montgomery's soldiers, Arnold's kept advancing. When they ran out of ammunition they advanced with bayonets drawn.

Dr. Isaac Senter, based at the hospital, reported that within an hour of the attack the wounded came pouring in.[14] Later the enemy began venturing out of the city capturing American horses, carriages, and supplies. Dawn was just breaking when Arnold arrived at the hospital supported by two soldiers. Dr. Senter was able to remove the musket ball from where it was wedged in a muscle near Arnold's Achilles tendon. Shortly after, the doctor and his patients learned the grave news of Montgomery's death and the "fall" of two young officers of his army. Arnold wept when he learned of Montgomery's death. More bad news followed. The enemy was outside the city walls and advancing on the hospital. Men were ordered into the street with field pieces to repel them and managed to put them to flight. There was no news of Arnold's men, and it was assumed they were dead. The doctor and officers in the hospital urged Arnold to leave for the country where he could not as easily be discovered. He would have none of it. Dr. Senter writes:

He would neither be removed, nor suffer a man from the hospital to retreat. He ordered pistols loaded, with a sword on his bed adding that he was determined to kill as many as possible if they came into the room. We were all now soldiers; even to the wounded in their beds were ordered a gun by their side, that, if they did attack the hospital, to make the most vigorous defense possible.[15]

The snowstorm continued. Requests for help from local militia fell on frightened ears. A message was sent to Congress pleading for immediate assistance, but Philadelphia was a long way off on a winter's day.[16] Senter found the prospect "gloomy on every side. The loss of the bravest of Generals, with other amiable officers smote the breasts of all around with inexpressible grief."[17]

As the ranking officer Arnold, wounded and in pain, was in command at Quebec. Americans held Montreal, however, where Brigadier General Wooster, Montgomery's second in command, had a garrison of five hundred men. Wooster and Arnold were both from New Haven. Wooster, then sixty-five, had a long career interspersed with military action, from the attack on Louisburg in 1745 through the French and Indian War. He had brought a contingent of Connecticut men to this campaign. Arnold wrote him the following day of their losses and his desperate need for Wooster to replace him, bringing reinforcements and cannon. "I am in such excessive pain from my wound . . . Your presence will be absolutely necessary."[18] But bold as Wooster may have been in his youth, he was now an older and more cautious man. He was reluctant to come to Arnold's aid himself or even to send any of his men to the siege outside Quebec. He would eventually send a few New York troops but without their equipment—no weapons, uniforms, or even snowshoes to help them manage the deep drifts. Not until April did Wooster arrive to replace Arnold.

On January 4 Arnold, still hopeful help would arrive, agreed to be moved to a safer, more comfortable location behind the lines. He was taken by sleigh to Montgomery's former headquarters. Now, for the first time, he felt able to write Hannah of their predicament and his injury. He apologized for not having written sooner but, "a continual hurry of business has prevented me. The command of the army, by the death of General Montgomery, has devolved upon me; a task," he confessed, "I find, too heavy under my present circumstances."[19] He described how he had been wounded and his painful walk back to the hospital "under the continual fire of the enemy from the walls." Hannah wrote back anxiously asking when he meant to return home. Arnold was clear, he would not consider it "until I first enter it [Quebec] in triumph. My wound has been exceedingly painful, but is now easy and the Providence, which has carried me through so many dangers, is still my protection. I am in the way of my duty and know no fear."[20]

How is one to explain the courage, dedication, and fortitude of Benedict Arnold, the proud, determined, seafaring merchant from New Haven? How account for the military brilliance, the confidence to lead, the ability to inspire men, to see military opportunities, and dare to take them? He may have felt he had little to live for except the cause to which he was fiercely dedicated. Perhaps it was simply his trust in Providence, instilled by his mother, sister, wife, and his own experience of overcoming tremendous odds. Certainly he often referred to the protection God had been pleased to grant him. And there was his absolute dedication to personal honor. Washington was fortunate to have such an obstinate man in his army, America to have such a natural and dedicated soldier in her cause. But bravery alone could not achieve this particular victory. A long winter lay ahead as the depleted American force suffered cold, smallpox, discouragement, despair.

Snow continued to fall all day, as Carleton directed the city's defense. At dawn he sent a search party to gather the wounded and dead. Someone found a frozen hand just visible above the snow at the barrier. It was Montgomery's. His body lay between those of two of his aides, MacPherson and Cheeseman.[21] Carleton learned of the death that afternoon and ordered Montgomery's body to be brought into Quebec. The man had, after all, been a fellow officer and a comrade. They had served together. One of Carleton's officers wrote of Montgomery's death, "Those who knew him formerly in this place, sincerely lament his late infatuation. They say he was a genteel man, and an agreeable companion."[22] Carleton was determined to give Montgomery a proper military funeral. At sunset on the evening of January 4 with Carleton and a few other British officers in attendance, General Montgomery, the reluctant warrior, was laid to rest in a flannel-lined coffin in the city's St. Louis bastion. It was a simple, dignified ceremony. Two other Americans were buried in the same plot. Under a flag of truce Carleton later sent Montgomery's widow, Janet, his watch and seal.[23]

But that was not the end of the story for this fine soldier, loved and respected by both sides. Some forty-three years later, as his wife stood on her porch at Rhinebeck, New York, a barge bringing Montgomery's remains from Quebec paused in the river below his old home before moving on to New York where they were laid to rest at St. Paul's Church. Congress ordered this first national monument, erected there in his honor, where passersby on the street could see it and remember. Benjamin Franklin arranged for the French sculptor, Caffieres, to design it, and personally composed the inscription for this final tribute.[24]

Arnold's men had not been killed as at first feared, they had been taken prisoner. Much to Arnold's surprise Carleton treated them very humanely, hoping to convince them of the wisdom of giving up rebellious notions. One of them, Major Return Meigs, was permitted to retrieve their baggage from the American lines. As he prepared to return to the city Arnold handed him a substantial amount of his own money to distribute among his imprisoned officers.[25]

The three long winter months that intervened before Wooster came to Arnold's aid were particularly trying ones. The weather was terrible, one of the most severe winters in memory. His men were sickening as smallpox raged through the ranks. He and Schuyler both wrote Congress pleading for money and supplies, Arnold pointing out, "We have been obliged to beg, borrow, and squeeze to get money for our subsistence."[26] He also asked for someone to take charge of financial matters and accounts. "The multiplicity of accounts which daily arise here, and many which originated in the life of Genl Montgomery, together with those of the commissaries & quartermasters . . . and do not immediately fall under any particular department, renders it impossible for a commanding officer to pay that attention to them which they deserve and at the same time do his duty as a soldier."[27] He requested that a paymaster or committee take charge of the accounts. It was a sensible request, especially after the fiasco about finances and supplies at Ticonderoga. But despite this plea Arnold would later be charged with not having kept careful accounts of expenditures during the wilderness expedition and afterward. Arnold was frank with Washington: "The severity of the climate, the troops very ill clad and worse paid, the trouble of reconciling matters among the inhabitants, and lately an uneasiness among some of the New York & other officers, who think themselves neglected in the new arrangement, while those who deserted the cause and went home last fall have been promoted, in short the choice of difficulties I have had to encounter has rendered it so very perplexing that I have often been at a loss, how to conduct matters."[28] The men were hungry and resorted to stealing from the locals and scrounging for firewood which, of course, turned the local residents against them. Of Arnold and Montgomery's combined force only eight hundred men remained and half of these were new French Canadian recruits.

Apart from such major problems there were smaller but vexing irritants. His old enemies from the Ticonderoga campaign, Major John Brown and Colonel James Easton, who had been in Montgomery's army, were now under Arnold's command. Brown, typically unreliable and insubordinate, refused to obey Arnold's orders to bring in the six siege mortars left at St. Roch's after the battle, thus abandoning them to the British. Brown was obviously a poor choice for that mission, never having been keen to put himself in harm's way.

Brown also claimed to have been promoted to colonel and therefore deserved an independent command. Easton, as always, backed Brown's claims. Brown insisted Montgomery had promised to promote him to colonel. But Arnold, writing to Hancock of this claim, pointed out that Montgomery had informed him that "Colonel Easton and Major Brown were publicly impeached with plundering the officers' baggage taken at Sorrel, contrary to articles of capitulation and to the great scandal of the American Army, he could not, in conscience or honor promote him until these matters were cleared up."[29] Montgomery then had sent for Brown to tell him this. Arnold noted, several officers were witness to the conversation and the episode was well known to the officers and men at Montreal. Arnold advised that while Brown and Easton had "a sufficient share of modest merit to apply to the Honorable Continental Congress for promotion . . . I believe it would give great disgust to the Army in general if those gentlemen were promoted before those matters were cleared up." He added in a postscript that he did not mean the contents of his letter to be kept from "the gentlemen mentioned therein." This episode added to the festering bitterness Brown and Easton felt for Arnold, hatred that would plague him for the rest of his career.

In contrast to Brown's claimed promotion, Arnold actually was promoted. When Congress learned of Arnold's fortitude leading his men through the wilderness and valor in the assault on Quebec they voted unanimously to promote him to brigadier general. He thanked Congress for the honor that he would "study to deserve."[30] Washington and Schuyler exchanged letters commiserating about the failure to take Quebec and the deaths and injuries caused in the attempt. "I condole with you on the fall of the brave and worthy Montgomery," Washington wrote, adding, "I am much concerned for the intrepid and enterprising Arnold."[31] He wrote Arnold, "Wishing you a speedy recovery & the possession of those laurels, which your bravery & perservance justly merit."[32] Arnold replied promising his "utmost exertions shall not be wanting to effect your wishes in adding it [Canada] to the United Colonies."[33] He was now "able to hobble about my room," and "though my leg is a little contracted and weak; I hope soon to be ready for action." He intended to continue the blockade of Quebec, informing Congress on January 11: "I expect General Wooster from Montreal with a reinforcement every minute."[34] In February, with Arnold still in the hospital, Wooster wrote Washington marveling that Arnold, "to his great honor, kept up the blockade with such a handful of men that the story when told hereafter will scarcely be believed."[35] That situation, however, failed to convince Wooster to come to Arnold's aid. Instead he informed Arnold he could not leave Montreal.[36] Arnold still hoped for someone else to take command writing Washington, "I hope soon to have the pleasure to seeing Genl Lee or some experienced officer here."[37] Grim as his army's situation was, since Arnold expected Wooster to appear with reinforcements and anticipated additional help from Washington and Congress. He began planning for an attack in early spring. It was essential to capture the city before the British could reinforce Carleton.

For his part Carleton preferred to await reinforcements in the spring rather than attack the weak American force that winter. He had no confidence his Canadian militia would do well in an open battle, and even if they did, bringing American prisoners, some suffering from smallpox, into the city was irresponsible. Nor could he afford to risk losing Quebec. Happily for the Americans, apart from the occasional skirmish outside the walls, the British sat tight throughout the winter.

At last, on April 1 Wooster appeared at Arnold's camp to take command. Arnold had still not completely recovered from the shot to his leg and a day after Wooster's appearance was hurt when his horse fell as he rode to one of the outposts. Nevertheless, as he wrote General Schuyler, he was keen to take "an active part" at Quebec. But, he complained, General Wooster "did not think proper to consult me." Arnold requested permission to leave Quebec and take command of Montreal.[38] Wooster agreed. This would not be the last time Arnold chafed under the supervision of a superior officer who was cautious and indecisive. Arnold's very energy and boldness seemed to cause such men to resent and distrust him.

Arnold's estimation of Wooster's passivity turned out to be sadly accurate. Once Arnold left for Montreal, an historian found, "all vigorous efforts in the field to capture Quebec and unite the Canadas with the United Colonies terminated."[39] Perhaps no amount of military skill and vigor would have saved the campaign. When Enos and his division abandoned the trek through Maine, Arnold lost a third of his own army. Those additional men might have tipped the balance. Now British Canada would prove, as Washington feared, a powerful weapon against the American cause.

No sooner had Arnold taken command at Montreal when three commissioners sent by the Congress appeared there—Benjamin Franklin, then seventy years old, and Samuel Chase and Charles Carroll, both from Maryland. Carroll's brother, the Reverend John Carroll, first Roman Catholic Archbishop of the American colonies, came with them hoping his presence would reassure French Catholics that Americans welcomed those of that faith. Arnold greeted the commissioners warmly with a special reception and a resounding cannonade from the fortress. Their mission was to persuade Canadians that the Americans meant to defeat Carleton and enable the Canadians to pursue their own liberty.[40] The commissioners' description of the army they found mirrors Arnold's:

> The army is in a distressed condition, and is in want of
> the most necessary articles—meat, bread, tents, shoes,
> stockings, shirts, etc. They said they were obliged to
> seize by force flour to supply the garrison with bread.[41]

But help was on the way. As Arnold was planning for a spring offensive Washington wrote that Major General John Thomas was on his way to take command in Canada, replacing Wooster. He also informed Arnold of the great success at Boston.[42] Cannon hauled from Ticonderoga during the winter had permitted Washington to threaten General Gage and the British troops besieged in Boston. In late March the British army evacuated the city sailing to the north. The worrisome aspect of this victory was that the British army and fleet were likely headed for Halifax. Washington hoped Quebec would be in American hands before the ice on the St. Lawrence River broke that spring enabling the British to reinforce Carleton.

It wasn't just the affiliation of Canada that was at stake. If Carleton and the British retained control of Canada their next move would be to attempt to take command of Lake Champlain and advance down the Hudson River to New York. In fact they were arranging to bring over some thirteen thousand troops from England, Ireland, and Germany to do just that.

In addition to all his other concerns that spring Arnold was confronted with a terrible dilemma.[43] He had stationed some four hundred men under Colonel Bedel at The Cedars, a point thirty-six miles from Montreal on the north side of the river. In May a British force of 150 English and Canadian soldiers and 500 Indians came down the river under Captain Foster. Colonel Bedel "fled" to Montreal to get reinforcements, leaving Major Butterfield in charge. Butterfield was terrified of the Indians and keen to surrender without a fight. Arnold immediately sent Major Sherburne with 140 men to relieve the post and followed himself. But Butterfield surrendered just before Sherburne arrived and Sherburne and his men were ambushed by the Indians. Some fifty-two men were killed, even some who had surrendered. Furious at this, Arnold dashed to St. Anne just in time to see the Indians taking their prisoners to the mainland from an island three miles away. Since his own boats had not yet arrived he was unable to pursue them but sent a friendly Indian chief to demand that if the prisoners were not returned, "he would destroy their villages, and pursue and put to the sword any one who fell into his hands."[44] Back came the reply refusing to give up their prisoners and threatening that if Arnold followed them and attacked they would immediately kill all the prisoners. As soon as his boats appeared Arnold made straight to the island where his men had been held. He found five men, stripped and starving. Two others who were very weak had been killed. Arnold was furious and would not be deterred. His little fleet of boats tracked the British and found them camped for the night. Arnold was determined to attack at dawn when a message came signed by Major Sherburne for an equal exchange of prisoners, the British prisoners to be sent to Quebec, but the American hostages when released were to return home and not fight against the British again. Arnold was again warned that if he did not agree the American prisoners would be killed. Arnold had the men to make good an attack but was reluctant to sacrifice the hostages. He finally agreed to the exchange of prisoners provided they were on equal terms, writing to the British captain, Foster, that if he refused the equal terms "my determination was to attack him immediately; and if our prisoners were murdered, to sacrifice every soul which fell into our hands."[45] Arnold wrote Congress:

Words cannot express my feelings . . . torn by conflicting passions of revenge and humanity; a sufficient force to take ample revenge, raging for action, urged me on, on one hand; and humanity for five hundred unhappy wretches, who were on the point of being sacrificed if our vengeance was not delayed, plead strongly on the other.

Captain Foster agreed to Arnold's demand for equal treatment. Congress was upset about honoring this extorted agreement though Washington was prepared to honor it. In the end the British lost interest. Arnold and his men returned to Montreal.

If Congress was upset about this incident, Arnold was in anguish about the terrible situation that he was dealing with. At the end of May he wrote Horatio Gates of his dismay:

> I shall be ever happy in your friendship and society, and hope with you, that our next winter quarters will be more agreeable, though I must doubt it, if affairs go as ill with you as here. Neglected by Congress below; pinched with every want here; distressed with the small-pox; want of Generals and discipline in our army—which may rather be called a great rabble—our late unhappy retreat from Quebeck and loss of the Cedars; our credit and reputation lost, and great part of the country; and a powerful foreign enemy advancing upon us; are so many difficulties we cannot surmount them. My whole thoughts are now bent on making a safe retreat out of this country; however, I hope we shall not be obliged to leave it until we have had one bout more for the honor of America.[46]

He hoped they could make a stand and keep control of Lake Champlain but admitted, "I am heartily chagrined to think we have lost in one month all the immortal Montgomery was a whole campaign in gaining, together with our credit, and many men and an amazing sum of money. The commissioners this day leave us as our good fortune has long since, but as Miss, like other Misses, is fickle, and often changes, I still hope for her favors again; and that we shall have the pleasure of dying or living happy together."

The following day, as the British began reinforcing Carleton, Arnold admitted there was no hope for the Canadian expedition's success. Already, as Arnold wrote Gates, General Thomas and his army had been forced to retreat from Quebec and were pursued up the river. Arnold conceded to Schuyler in a letter of June 13 that "The junction of the Canadas with the colonies is now at an end."[47]

"Let us quit them," he advised, "and secure our own country before it is too late." Typically he considered what the honorable approach was in the circumstances. He had changed his mind about wanting one more bout. "There will be more honor in making a safe retreat," he ventured, "than in hazarding a battle against such superiority; and which will be attended with the loss of men, artillery, etc., and the only pass to our country." Just in case Schuyler should think him cowardly for the recommendation, he added, "These arguments are not urged by fear for my personal safety: I am content to be the last man who quits this country, and fall, so that my country may rise. But let us not fall altogether."

And so it turned out. General Sullivan, who replaced General Thomas who had died of smallpox on the retreat, abandoned Canada leaving only Arnold's forces at Montreal. It was the last place in American hands. Before leaving the city Arnold confiscated "a quantity of goods for use of the army," from local merchants, "some bought, some seized," sending these on to St. Johns.[48] "Everything is in the greatest confusion," he admitted to Schuyler, "Not one contractor, commissary or quarter-master. I am obliged to do the duty of all."[49] This seizure of goods would later be seized upon by Arnold's enemies claiming Arnold was plundering to enrich himself.

Arnold led the retreat to St. Johns, scene of Montgomery's triumph eight months earlier, breaking down all the bridges once his army had passed, to slow the advancing British. After all his men were safely aboard ships heading south he and a single comrade, young Captain James Wilkinson, rode to the shore. Night was coming on. They saw the British troops approaching. Arnold galloped back to the shore, stripped his horse of its saddle and bridle and shot the animal to prevent the British seizing it. As night enfolded him he boarded the boat, the last man to leave Canada.

THIRTEEN

Defending the Lakes

Arnold didn't keep his promise to Hannah. He quit Canada without entering Quebec in triumph, without even the "one bout more" against the British he had hoped for, but he was not prepared to return home. It was a fateful decision. Hannah was bitterly disappointed that he meant to continue risking his life far from home. "I am sorry to hear you are going upon the lake," she wrote on August 5, "but if after all your fatigues, & dangers you think it best, must be silent, have been hoping you would quit the service but it seems you have no such intention."[1] Appealing to him as a father she added: "Little Hal sends a kiss to Pa and says, 'Auntie, tell Papa he must come home. I want to kiss him.'"[2]

She and Benedict remained close confidants, writing every two weeks despite the hundreds of miles between them and his enormous workload. He relied upon her to take care of all the tasks at home, mothering his three small sons, passing on news

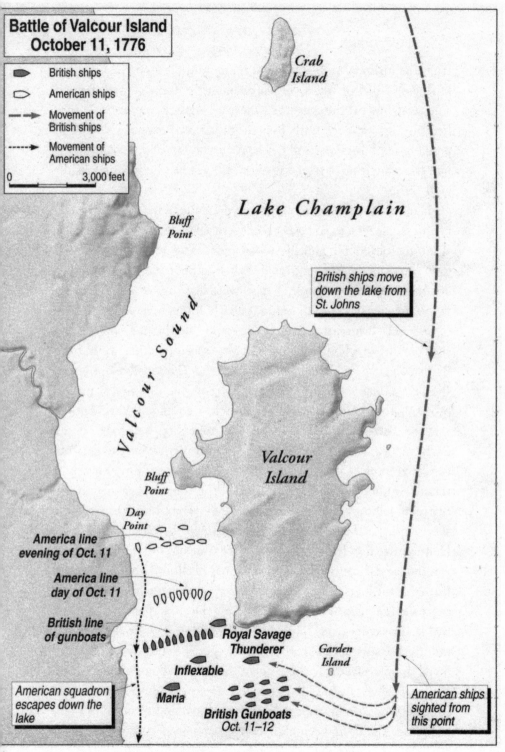

The Battle of Valcour Island, October 11, 1776.

from his military colleagues and managing his complex shipping business. This last was a very problematic enterprise with British ships trawling off the coast for American prizes.[3] Her letters betray her fraying patience with Benedict's absence on hazardous and possibly fatal missions and her growing doubts about a cause that had started with a patriotic protest but was fast becoming a bitter civil war.

Hannah obediently took over responsibility for all family and business matters, as she was asked. Arnold had his pay sent to her. Running the shipping business was unusual for a woman, although their own mother had done it when their father became increasingly debilitated. But their parents' days were less tumultuous. With so many men away Hannah found it nearly impossible to find a crew for Arnold's brigantine. Even if she could find the men, merchants she consulted reckoned the odds of an American ship running the British blockade no better than one in ten.[4] The sensible option, as she saw it, was to sell the brigantine. This she did, investing the proceeds in annuities in New York. How could she have known that the British would soon make New York City their major base? Early reports from the city had been optimistic that the patriots would triumph.[5] Once in British possession in late summer it would remain in their hands until the end of the war, the last city in the thirteen colonies they were to evacuate. The annuities invested there, risky at best, were almost certain to become a total loss. Hannah also decided to sell the stock of rum and sugar in Benedict's warehouse assuming their value would decline if she kept them. But with the blockade creating a scarcity, those commodities were more likely to become increasingly valuable. She then lent some of the cash receipts from their sale at "good interest for three to six months," assuring her brother she was getting sound security. She made these decisions without consulting Arnold, hoping "you will not disapprove of what I have done." Despite the family's uncertain finances, she paid his bills meticulously, no doubt mindful of their father's bad debts and Arnold's own shaky start. The sums involved were sizeable, "upward of £1000." "If you ever live to return," she warned him, "you will find yourself a broken merchant, as I have sold everything upon hand." None of this can have been a comfort to Arnold. His sister was ruining his business and devastating his finances, but what could he do? She was coping with a perplexing situation as well as she could. He had asked a great deal of her. How could he complain? Anyway, by the time he learned of these sales and payments it was too late to stop them.

Was this Hannah's way to remind her brother of her distress and resentment at being left to manage alone? While she appreciated Arnold's dedication to the cause, as hopes for a negotiated settlement vanished and the fighting escalated, she was increasingly distraught about the terrors of civil war and the real prospect he might never return. Even New Haven was unsafe. She wrote him that roofers were afraid to come there to fix the leaky roof of their home.[6] Sending news of the fight for New York City on September 1 she wrote, "'tis said thousands on both sides have lost their lives," she wrote in despair: "Good God! What havoc does ambition make amongst your noblest works—brother slain by the cruel hand of brother, mothers weeping for their darling sons, sisters for affectionate and perhaps only brothers . . . The dear little boys yet remain . . . blessed in ignorance. . . Oh, that their future life may be unclouded."[7] What *"havoc does ambition make amongst your noblest works?"* His noblest works? His ambition? Even if she had insisted he abandon the struggle he was unlikely to do so. But she could not refrain from reminding him of the terrible toll this fight against the British was taking. At the end of the letter she wrote of deaths among their friends at home. A "dysentery" was raging in New Haven: "'Tis very sickly here 3 or 4 funerals every day, but mostly children." These children were fortunate, she insisted in despair, "privileged by fate, to shorter Labours & a later date, yesterday receiv'd the gift of breath, order'd this day to return to Death. Happy! Thrice happy exemption from the cares, pains, and anxiety of a protracted life."

Arnold's decision to remain in the forefront of the struggle was fateful for him as well as Hannah. Even as he was exerting every ounce of energy to defend New York State, old enemies were relentless in wanting to blacken his reputation. The wonder is not that Arnold ignored Hannah's plea to return to his family and rescue his business, but that he stuck with the cause, despite its perils and bitter attacks on his honor. His nautical expertise was critical to the survival of the American cause that summer, but John Brown, an old enemy with new grievances, along with a clutch of junior officers managed to haul him before a court-martial on a battery of charges of Brown's creation, indifferent to the fact that Arnold was fully engaged in protecting the Lake Champlain-Lake George corridor from an imminent attack by the thirteen thousand British, Irish, and German troops massing in Canada.

To protect New York State, the vital link between the New England and the Middle Atlantic states, Arnold proposed immediately building a fleet of ships to guard the corridor of lakes from Canada to Albany. Arnold's ships were designed to be more maneuverable than Britain's large deepwater vessels and able to operate in the shallower waters of Lake Champlain. Constructing and manning a fleet before British ships descended the lake was a formidable challenge. Franklin, then chairman of the Pennsylvania Committee of Safety, convinced the scheme was crucial, authorized the building of two galleys, measuring seventy to eighty feet long, each with two masts. New York's Committee of Safety asked Arnold to take charge of building the fleet but chose Captain Jacob Wynkoop to command the lake. How could playing the father and businessman in New Haven compare with the excitement and importance of saving the nation?

From the moment Arnold issued his first orders on July 10 he was a whirlwind of activity as his reports to Gates make clear. At best he had only two or maybe three months. He had to construct a fleet in upstate New York, far from ship fittings, knowledgeable carpenters, and sailors. He notified Gates that he had "made a draft of the artisans needed," was organizing ships carpenters into gangs of fifteen each; was dispatching armorers to Ticonderoga; had personally selected over twenty thousand boards and timbers from local timber mills, and was sending Gates some four tons of lead with more to follow.[8] It was difficult to get experienced sailors to volunteer, although the coast of New England and New York had many part-time seamen. Indeed, with Washington busy defending New York against a huge British army and navy, they were needed elsewhere as well. John Glover's superb Marblehead regiment was with Washington and would save the army that August by ferrying the men from Long Island back to Manhattan.

Gates was relieved to have Arnold take the lead, admitting he knew little about ship building and was "entirely unacquainted with the Lake below Crown Point." He was anxious to have Arnold with him at Crown Point "as soon as possible" in order "to drive directions to putting our whole squadron afloat. It seems they are very tardy about it, but am entirely uninformed as to Marine affairs." Gates fretted over the slow pace of his carpenters and disliked New York's choice of Wynkoop to command. Neither Gates nor Arnold had any illusions about the urgency of their task. "We shall be happy or miserable," Gates wrote Arnold, "as we are or are not prepared to receive the enemy."[9]

If Arnold jealously guarded his personal honor and reputation, so too did other men of his generation, especially men of more modest status. The fact that he rather cavalierly injured the reputation of Colonel John Brown, however deserved, festered within Brown. He needed to destroy Arnold's reputation to regain his own. While Gates and Arnold were frantically creating a fleet to fend off a British naval attack, Brown's machinations began to bear their bitter fruit. To humiliations from their Ticonderoga days, Brown had added a spate of new complaints from the Quebec campaign. On December 1, six months earlier, he had drawn up thirteen accusations couched as charges and sent them to Gates. Most of these concerned personal slights against himself. Brown accused Arnold of slandering him, depriving him of a promotion, calling him a liar and defaming his character.[10] To these he added accusations of more general concern claiming Arnold had spread smallpox in Quebec by permitting inoculation—a technique known to reduce fatalities by giving the inoculated individual a milder case of the disease. A year later Washington would take the dire step of inoculating his entire army to protect them from the ravages of smallpox. Brown accused Arnold of starving his army at Quebec, plundering Montreal on his retreat, and robbing British prisoners, laying waste whole villages and illegally exchanging prisoners.[11]

Gates brushed these accusations aside but agreed to place them before Congress "who will, when they think proper, give such orders as they think necessary thereupon."[12] General Schuyler was just as dismissive: "if courts martial would severely punish officers for illiberal abuse of their superior officers, such violent and ill-founded complaints as you mention to be made by Lieutenant Colonel Brown against General Arnold would soon cease."[13] Schuyler added the shrewd insight: "The latter gentleman will always be the subject of complaint, because his impartiality and candor will not suffer him to see impropriety of behavior with impunity." Brown found members of Congress, by nature suspicious of their military commanders, more sympathetic. A group of officers, all junior to Arnold in rank, were selected to investigate. On July 26 Arnold was summoned to a court-martial at Fort Ticonderoga to answer Brown's charges.

The court was stacked with Arnold's enemies and friends of enemies. It was chaired by Colonel Enoch Poor of New Hampshire, a friend of Lieutenant Colonel Enos, the one division leader of Arnold's expedition to Quebec who had taken his men and turned back.[14] While Arnold had not called him to account for this others had. Arnold was also unpopular with some officers because of his friendship with the wealthy and aristocratic General Schuyler.

The New Englanders were particularly vicious in their attacks on Schuyler, who wrote in despair to Washington: "Suspicion and envy had followed me, from the moment I came to the command, I have experienced the most illiberal abuse, in many of the colonies, and even in the Army I command."[15] Their hostility to Arnold was equally if not more intense. Poor's brigade surgeon, Dr. Beebe, thought a court-martial too good for Arnold, preferring "to make the sun shine through his head with an ounce of ball or lead."[16]

Of Brown's charges the looting of Montreal was the most serious. Washington had asked Arnold to take what he needed for his army during their retreat. Arnold had purchased supplies and sent goods on to Colonel Moses Hazen at Chambly. It was Hazen's failure to protect the goods that led to a dispute between the two men who traded allegations of looting and disobedience. Hazen would become another of Arnold's lifelong enemies. Hazen was born in Massachusetts, fought in the French and Indian War, and was commissioned into the British army at its end. He moved to Quebec and invested heavily in land there, settling down near Montreal. He was obviously in a quandary over his allegiance when Montgomery and Arnold invaded Canada, hoping to land on the winning side. Hazen was a courier to Carleton for the British, was arrested by the Americans, rescued by the British then arrested by them, and finally fled to Quebec where he again sided with the Americans.[17] Arnold's first impression was that Hazen was "a sensible, judicious officer."[18] Their relationship went downhill from there. Hazen, never notable for personal courage, loudly opposed Arnold's efforts to rescue the men from his Canadian outpost who had been taken prisoner by the British. Arnold went ahead anyway but while his assault at La Chine failed he convinced the British to negotiate for their release.[19]

As for the goods Arnold had taken from Montreal merchants, he wrote in consternation to General Sullivan that they had been carefully labeled and that he had ordered Hazen to see they were guarded and stored at Chambly. Hazen refused, leaving everything in a heap where the goods were plundered. When Hazen finally agreed to place guards over the property it was in such disarray that Arnold found it impossible to sort out whose property was whose, or to settle with the proprietors.[20] "This is not the first or last order Colonel Hazen has disobeyed," Arnold wrote Sullivan, explaining, "I think him a man of too much consequence for the post he is in." He filed for a court-martial against Hazen, but Colonel Poor focused instead on Arnold, blaming him for the looting. Arnold was hard-pressed to locate supporting witnesses who had helped transport the goods during his desperate retreat from Canada. But he needn't have bothered since the court-martial refused to allow Major Scott, his best witness, to testify. The Court insisted Scott was "so far interested," never explaining what that interest was.[21]

The Ticonderoga court, more kangaroo court than impartial military tribunal, dragged on for precious days. Arnold's patience was exhausted. He protested the court's refusal to permit Scott, his sole witness, to testify on his behalf: "As the court have refused accepting my principal evidence, Major Scott, after my having declared to them, on honor, that he had punctually obeyed my orders respecting the goods he had in charge from Montreal to Chambly, and of course is not in the least interested in the event of Colonel Hazen's trial, I do solemnly protest against their proceedings and refusal as unprecedented, and I think unjustified."[22] The court's reaction was to label Arnold's protest "illegal, illiberal and ungentlemanlike." They demanded he apologize for his "error." This response was unprecedented and taken by Arnold as an assault upon his honor, as indeed it was. On August 1 Arnold wrote, refusing to apologize, attacking Colonel Poor for "ungenteel and indecent reflections on a superior officer," and warned that Congress would "judge between us."[23] For good measure Arnold challenged the officers on the court-martial to duel. Congress, or at least its president, John Hancock, had heard from Horatio Gates two days earlier that Arnold had "most nobly undertaken to command our fleet on the lake."[24] Gates added, "I have committed the whole of that department to his care, convinced that he will thereby add to the brilliant reputation he has so deservedly acquired." Washington, not knowing Arnold had already been selected to command on the lake wrote Gates, "I trust neither courage nor activity will be wanting in those to whom the business is committed. If assigned to General Arnold, none will doubt of his exertion."[25] Clearly Gates had had enough of the Brown/Hazen controversy. He needed Arnold to take command. Congress agreed. The court-martial, however, acquitted Hazen of dereliction of duty and by war's end he had been promoted to brigadier general.

Horatio Gates, like Montgomery and Charles Lee, was a former British career officer whose path was blocked by lack of the money to achieve higher command and who, angry and discontented, had joined the American cause. Gates had the misfortune to lack the look or bearing of a commander. Only fifty, he was stooped, with a double chin, whispy gray hair, and weak eyes that required him to wear spectacles that tended to end up at the tip of his nose. To his men he became known as Granny Gates. He was also more administrator than adept field commander but very ambitious for high command. In this instance Arnold's daring and skill suited Gates's temperament perfectly. Later, at crucial points, he would deeply resent the younger man's charisma and courage.

Lake Champlain's soft blue waters rise from a creek near Lake George and flow north for 125 miles to the Richelieu River in the southern part of Quebec before emptying into the St. Lawrence River, dividing the eastern fringe of New York's Appalachian Mountains on the west from Vermont's Green Mountains on the east. Its 490 square miles of fresh water is fourteen miles at its widest point, 400 feet deep in spots, with peaceful inlets and shallows backed by purple-hued mountains on both shores, and festooned with a scattering of islands. Into this beautiful and deceptively placid waterway Arnold led his hastily built little flotilla.

The American vessels were a mix of flat-bottomed "gundolas," enormous rowboats common on American rivers, with two square sails amidships carrying a crew of forty-five men and three cannon; galleys eighty feet by twenty sporting two masts with lateen sails, ten to twelve guns, and a crew of up to one hundred men; the two-hundred-ton, twelve-gun schooner *Royal Savage*, eight-gun schooners *Revenge* and *Liberty*, and ten-gun sloop *Enterprise*. The *Royal Savage*, a British vessel captured by Montgomery when he laid siege to St. Johns, now became Arnold's flag ship. These ships plus four newly finished galleys carried a combined weight of metal—all the cannonballs they could fire at once—of 703 pounds.[26]

At St. Johns the British fleet was being just as hurriedly constructed, in this instance in less than three months from sections shipped over from Britain. It was commanded by Lieutenant Thomas Pringle although Carleton was to sail with it, and staffed by some of the royal navy's most able officers and experienced sailors. By contrast to Arnold's 703, Pringle's ships had 1300 pounds of metal, nearly twice as much. The greater size of the British vessels did make them less maneuverable but also made them less vulnerable to attack. The two largest British ships *Inflexible* and *Thunderer* carried six twenty-four-pound guns and twenty-four twelve pounders respectively. The British fleet had twenty gunships and five large sailing vessels including the *Inflexible* with its three masts and the *Thunderer* which, at 423 tons, was the largest ship ever seen on Lake Champlain. Its two howitzers could produce as much fire as all Arnold's eight gundolas together. The coming naval battle was clearly a mismatch. But Arnold had spent considerable time scouting the lake and taking soundings. He had a plan.

Before he could put it into effect, however, the typical American confusion over who was properly in command occurred. A day after Arnold arrived at Crown Point word came that British advance troops were spotted targeting Arnold's men gathering timber for oars. He immediately ordered an expedition of one hundred men to protect them and sent the schooners *Revenge* and *Liberty* to head south to escort the expedition and help bring the threatened workers back to the fort. Just as the two ships were setting off, Jacob Wynkoop stopped them with a shot across their bows: "I know of no orders," he insisted, "but what shall be give out by me. If our enemy is approaching I am to be acquainted with it and know how to act in my station."[27] Arnold was incensed, dispatching a stinging rebuke to "Captain" Wynkoop, pointing out Arnold was commander of the navy on the lake, having "received this appointment from my rank in the Army and as Commander-in-Chief of this post. It is your duty to obey my orders which you have received and executed for some time past."[28] With one of those explosions of temper that earned him enemies, he added: "You surely must be out of your senses to say no orders shall be obeyed but yours. Do you imagine that Congress has given you a superior command over the Commander-in-Chief or that you are not to be under his direction? If you do not suffer his orders to be immediately complied with, I shall be under the disagreeable necessity of convincing you of your error by immediately arresting you." He signed himself B. Genl & Commr-in-Chief of the Fleet on Lake Champlain.

Arnold and Wynkoop both wrote to Gates, Wynkoop laying out his claim for command and insisting if anyone else was given that post he "wished to be dismissed from the service. . . for I am resolved to go under command of no man."[29] Gates ordered Wynkoop to be arrested and brought to his headquarters at Ticonderoga, telling Arnold to warn other officers of the fleet "that such of them that do not pay an implicit Obedience to your Command, are instantly to be confined and sent to me for trial."[30] Although Schuyler had originally accepted Wynkoop as fleet commander, he pointed out that Wynkoop was appointed when the army was in Canada and the ships few, but the man was not the best commander for the task at hand.[31] Schuler assured Gates that he too was "extremely happy that General Arnold has undertaken to command the fleet. It has relieved me from very great anxiety, under which I labored on that account."[32]

Gates's orders as Arnold prepared to set out with this fleet were straightforward: "Should the enemy come up the lake and attempt to force their way through the pass you are stationed to defend, in that case you will act with such cool, determined valor as will give them reason to repent their temerity."[33] All those who would later argue that Arnold was merely a greedy, self-server cannot explain why, in that case, he bravely set sail on an exceedingly dangerous and near-hopeless mission. True to Gates's orders Arnold was to exhibit that coolness and determined valor the confrontation commanded, however slim its hopes of success. Neither man had any illusions however. The Americans could at best hold the British fleet off for a time before being forced to retreat, but Arnold, Gates, and their men were determined to make as good a show as possible. "I am confident your, and their [his other officers] zeal for the Public Service will not suffer you to return one Moment sooner than in Prudence and Good Conduct you ought to do it," Gates wrote Arnold on October 3. Eight days later the two fleets met.[34]

Arnold's plan for confronting a superior British fleet required choosing a location where he might protect his own smaller force while taking the British by surprise. No smaller military force since Agincourt in 1415 and before, could afford open ground or open water where it could be enveloped. Arnold decided to place his fleet at the southern end of the narrow channel between Valcour Island and the New York shore. The northern end of that channel had hidden rocks and was only five feet deep, while the southern end, where the American fleet would wait, had an underwater ledge three hundred yards long.[35] In fact the one British map of the lake didn't even have Valcour Island on it.[36] Not only would Arnold's fleet be hidden from the main channel of the lake, but he ordered his ships painted red to blend with the autumn leaves and camouflaged with boughs of spruce trees around the bulwarks, sharpened to points to protect his gunners from snipers and discourage enemy sailors from boarding them. A British fleet sailing down the lake would be unlikely to spot them until they had sailed south of the island. At that point, with the American fleet behind them the big British vessels would have to turn and tack back to confront them. Britain's square-sailed vessels would find that difficult. The channel where the American ships would be lined up in a crescent formation would be too narrow for more than one large enemy vessel at a time to fire at them and that vessel would face the entire American fleet. As Napoleon would later point out, his aim was always to win before the battle. In Arnold's case winning might not be a realistic option, but holding one's own against formidable odds was. There was a serious problem with Arnold's plan however. If all went as he hoped the British fleet would be south of his own. His line of retreat would be blocked by British ships. In addition the Canadians and Indians were coming down the New York shore of the lake in hundreds of canoes making any retreat by land just as hazardous.

On August 24 Arnold, on board the *Royal Savage*, led his ships north. On September 23 his sixteen vessels took up their position in the shadow of Valcour Island where they waited to confront the powerful British fleet descending from Canada.

At eight o'clock in the morning of October 11 Arnold's lookout ships sighted the British fleet, its battle flags flying in the morning breeze. Arnold's ships lay hidden behind the bluffs of Valcour Island. Not until the British were five miles south of the island did they spot his ships and at that point their own ships were strung out over almost ten miles of the lake.[37] The signal went out and British ships turned to confront the American vessels, their larger ships falling behind. Arnold decided to attack the smaller vessels before the more formidable ships could come to their rescue. Aboard the *Royal Savage* and leading the three galleys he set off toward them and opened fire. He meant to lure the British vessels into the channel where his ships would be waiting. As the firing started a south wind caught the British ships. It also caught Arnold's *Royal Savage* as it struggled to get back to the American lines. Although the three galleys made it back to the American line the *Royal Savage* did not. Britain's mighty *Inflexible* got within firing range of the *Savage* and aimed its powerful guns at Arnold's flagship with devastating effect, ripping its sails, rigging, and lines until it was nearly impossible to maneuver. A sudden powerful gust drove the crippled ship into the island's southwest shore, leaving her stranded on a reef. Impervious to the fire from the other American ships, the *Inflexible* moved in for the kill, pounding the *Royal Savage*, leaving her grounded and keeling onto her side. Arnold quickly switched to the *Congress* in the center of the tight American line as the *Savage*'s commander, Captain Hawley, lowered lifeboats. Some of Hawley's crew managed to scramble aboard the boats, others leaped into the lake and swam for the island where Indians awaited them. Hawley tried hard to shift his ship off the shallows, to no avail. The crew of the British *Loyal Convert* moved in and boarded the *Savage* taking twenty men prisoner and carrying off Arnold's papers. For good measure they turned the *Savage*'s guns on her sister ships. That night they would set her on fire.

At half past twelve the fighting became general. The noise of the cannon was terrific and heard as far as Crown Point thirty-five miles to the south. Smoke and debris filled the air accompanied by the shouts of commanders and their men along with the cries of those injured. Arnold fought on, keeping up a blistering barrage on the British fleet, inspiring his men with his daring and determination.[38] Lacking experienced gunners he personally aimed all the *Congress*'s guns himself. One of these guns, aimed at the *Maria*, sent a shot between General Carleton and his brother Thomas. Both men threw themselves onto the deck. Pringle, the fleet commander, fearing for their safety, ordered the *Maria* to back off and sent in gunboats. Arnold's ships peppered them with a withering fire. One shot from an American ship hit the magazine of a Hessian gunboat causing a huge explosion. Another British ship, the *Carlton*, got caught in the narrow Valcour channel, and was pounded by a fierce barrage from the American line. Its anchor line was severed, leaving her drifting helplessly into the guns of the American ships, her commander and first mate both casualties. She was eventually rescued by two longboats whose men were able to catch a tow line and drag her out of harm's way. Other ships moved in to try their luck. The *Inflexible,* which had devastated the floundering *Royal Savage,* was forced to withdraw to be replaced by the *Thunderer,* the two most powerful ships in the British fleet. The battle raged for six hours. The American ships were badly damaged, the gundola *Philadelphia* was sunk, and Arnold's flagship, the *Congress,* had taken seven shots between wind and water, the mainmast hit in two places, the hull twelve times, and the rigging cut to pieces.[39] The galley *Washington* was badly damaged, its first lieutenant killed, the captain and master wounded. All the *New York's* officers except her captain had been killed. The *Philadelphia* was so badly damaged it sunk an hour after the fighting stopped. About eighty of their men had been killed or wounded, and they had used up three-quarters of their ammunition. As the sun slipped down behind the mountains the British ships drew off for the night, taking up a position that blocked the American ships in the Valcour channel. They continued firing at Arnold's ships until dark. Carleton was confident they would finish the destruction of the American fleet the next morning. Darkness fell over the lake, the rising mist punctuated only by the flames of the *Royal Savage* glowing in the night sky.

FOURTEEN

Don't Tread on Me

General Waterbury and Colonel Wigglesworth rowed through the black waters that night to meet Arnold aboard the *Congress*. They were despondent, but Arnold had prepared for this moment. He had a plan, a desperate but doable plan. The fleet would escape that evening by slipping between the British ships blocking the Valcour channel then dash south to Crown Point and safety. It was an exceedingly risky strategy. Many of their vessels were badly damaged, some were leaking. The little fleet with its five hundred sailors had lost some eighty men killed or wounded, including many officers, with twenty others captured. If any of the British crews spotted them they would be vulnerable and readily destroyed. But what other option did they have?

It was a moonless night. They set out at seven o'clock. A heavy autumn mist rising from the lake shrouded the American ships as they began moving in single file. Their oars were muffled in shirts, their wounded kept below decks so their moans would not alert the enemy. Each ship was completely dark except for a small lantern in the stern and a shrouded one in the bow. A chalk mark on the rear rails, lit by a slit in the rear lantern, made the vessel's stern just visible to the ship immediately behind. Wigglesworth in the galley *Trumbull* led. One by one the gundolas and smaller vessels followed in silence. The *Congress*, with Arnold aboard, and the *Washington* were last in line. The procession passed so close to the *Carlton* that they could hear its sailors chatting as they glided beside it. They were in luck. The British had moved their three large men-of-war a mile out from the western shore of the lake, inadvertently leaving a passageway for the American ships to slip through.[1]

The British commander woke with a shock the next morning to find the American fleet gone. Writing General Burgoyne, Carleton admitted he had gone to sleep "expecting in the morning to be able to engage them with our whole fleet, but to our great mortification," he confessed, "we perceived at daybreak that they had found means to escape us unobserved by any of our guard boats or cruisers."[2] At first Carleton assumed his intended prey had gone north up the Valcour channel aiming to cut the British fleet off from the their land forces under Burgoyne. Had Carleton's information on the depth of the northern end of the channel been better he would have realized escape in that direction was impossible. At any rate the British lost time sailing north rather than south looking for the American convoy.

Once the British turned south, they were hampered by a strong south wind making the journey upstream even more of a struggle. The wind played no favorites though, and slowed the Americans down as well. They had given the British the slip at Valcour Island but were still twenty-eight miles from Crown Point, plenty of time for the powerful fleet to catch them.

Arnold and his bedraggled fleet made for Schuyler Island seven miles south of Valcour Island to reconnoiter and make what repairs they could. The *New York* and the *Providence* were so badly damaged Arnold had their ordnance transferred to other vessels, then the two ships were towed off and sunk.[3] The *Jersey*, so water-logged it could not be towed or even burned, was allowed to sink where it was. Arnold, reporting to Gates, explained, "We remained no longer at Schuyler's Island than to stop our leaks and mend the sails of the *Washington*. At two o'clock P.M., they weighed anchor, with a fresh breeze to the southward."[4]

During the night the wind moderated. The British ships moving through the dark gained on them. The following day they caught up. In a last attempt to hold them off and protect the rest of his fleet Arnold turned his flagship, the *Congress*, and the *Washington* galley commanded by Waterbury to meet the enemy ships. The two ships fought fiercely while the rest of the fleet got away. Both ships took a terrible beating. The *Washington* was surrounded and badly damaged. Arnold explained, "The *Washington* galley was in such a shattered condition, and had so many men killed and wounded, she struck [her flag] to the enemy after receiving a few broadsides."[5] Waterbury decided to surrender to save his crew of some one hundred men. That left Arnold in the *Congress* to fight on alone. The British ships, in Arnold's words, "kept up an incessant fire on us for about five glasses [hourglasses, in this case four hours], with round and grape shot, which we returned as briskly." The *Congress*, surrounded by seven enemy ships, began receiving broadside after broadside. Through the smoke her flag, "Don't Tread on Me," could be glimpsed still flying. "The sails, rigging and hull of the *Congress* were shattered and torn in pieces," Arnold reported, "the First Lieutenant and three men killed." He was out of ammunition, twenty-seven of his seventy-man crew were dead or wounded.[6] Still he would not surrender. Somehow he managed to break through the encircling ships with his little gundolas and made for a creek on the Vermont shore where the British vessels could not follow. Having run his ships aground Arnold ordered the crews to take their firearms and leap overboard. Holding their guns aloft, they waded to shore. That done he set fire to the *Congress* and the gundolas, while his men fired their weapons to keep any smaller British vessels at bay. Arnold stayed watching the fire until he was sure it had spread to all the vessels. The *Congress*'s flag was still flying as the flames consumed it. Leaping from his ship's bow Arnold led his 150 exhausted men through the forest. They took an unusual route that enabled them to escape the waiting Indians. Thankfully they reached Crown Point safely.

There was no real safety at Crown Point though. The fort was vulnerable to an attack from the British fleet. Still, at least it was a temporary respite for Arnold and his weary officers and men. Exhausted as they were, their only option was to retreat further south, to Ticonderoga. Off they set trekking overland for another twenty miles, carrying their wounded in slings made from sails. On October 15, two days after Arnold's fierce defense aboard the *Congress*, they reached Ticonderoga.

Five days later Carleton arrived at Crown Point. On November 3 he captured the fort. It was snowing heavily on the lake and the surrounding mountains were white with snow. The onset of winter gave Carleton a difficult choice. He could press on and attack Ticonderoga or retreat back to Canada and launch an invasion south again the next campaign season. Pressing on though, he risked his fleet becoming iced in on Lake Champlain, while he and his men faced a bitter winter in a remote part of northern New York. Carleton was a cautious man. He reckoned retreat made more sense. In early December he and his fleet headed north. Some of his bateaux and long boats had already left. On November 2 Lieutenant William Digby, with this group, reported that when they had gone some seventeen miles north a stiff wind forced the boats to take shelter in a creek.[7] The British sailors dubbed the spot Destruction Bay when they discovered it was where Arnold's men had endured the British bombardment. "Some of their dead," Digby wrote, "were then floating on the brink of the water just as the surf threw them." The British, out of decency, took time to retrieve the bodies and bury them. That evening snow fell softly, covering the newly dug graves.

The British fleet had been triumphant, but the obstinate defense Arnold's men had put up meant there would be no British conquest of New York State, at least for that year. Arnold's heroism, capping his astonishing trek through the Maine woods the previous year, was widely celebrated. Gates, writing to Schuyler with Arnold's report, was relieved and delighted: "It has pleased Providence to preserve General Arnold. Few men ever met with so many hair breadth escapes in so short a space of time."[8] In Gates's general orders on October 14 he gave thanks "to General Arnold and the officers, seamen and marines of the fleet for the gallant defense they made against the great superiority of the enemy's force."[9] Even Arnold's critics would later praise him. Jared Sparks writing some years later of Arnold's life and treason, marveled, "There are few instances on record of more deliberate courage and gallantry than were displayed by him, from beginning to end of this action."[10] When Lieutenant James Dacre reported in London on the naval battle he pointed out that Arnold's disposition of his force, his defense against a more powerful enemy, and the management of the retreat did him great honor.[11] J. W. Fortescue, in his classic history of the British army, berates Carleton for failing to attack Ticonderoga rather than retreating adding: "Very different would it have been if the British had been commanded by such a man as Arnold, whose amazing skill, gallantry, and resource make him undoubtedly the hero of this short campaign."[12] At Ticonderoga Colonel Varick described Arnold's escape as "a blessing from Almighty God." America's newspapers carried detailed accounts of the naval battle against the British and Arnold's gallantry, often quoting Arnold's original report.[13] It was stirring stuff. The battle of Valcour Island was not a victory but was an inspiring example of colonial heroism and resistance in the face of superior force, an inspiration badly needed that autumn. Washington's army had been beaten on Long Island in August and had been retreating ever since, into New York, New Jersey, then Pennsylvania. The only positive aspect of Washington's continuing retreat was that the American army was still intact.

What Hannah made of her brother's death-defying leadership on the lake and his near-miraculous escape can be guessed. Although relieved and thankful that God had spared him, she could not be happy at the way he risked his life, time and again. At any rate Arnold was heading home at last. He left Saratoga in November to set out for New Haven but never got there. On his way he stopped at Albany to pick up his cash box and confer with General Schuyler. He also needed to attend a hearing brought by Hazen claiming Arnold had harmed his reputation by alleging he had sold rum meant for the troops for his personal profit. The hearing on December 2 concluded that there was no real proof that Hazen had sold rum improperly. Arnold now hurried south to catch up to Gates. As always his celebrity and unflinching honesty caused problems that threatened his sense of honor. He was a hero, and deservedly so. The American public honored Arnold, his men loved him, but his pride and even, or especially, his success made for a growing number of enemies. John Brown, the oldest and most persistent, was not satisfied with the collapse of the summer's court-martial against Arnold and was still lobbying the New England delegation in Congress, accusing him of plundering. Arnold was jealous of his reputation, but so were his enemies. And he had in one way or another reflected badly on them, sometimes just indirectly by making them look inadequate. They would not let it rest. The ranks of these men, determined to diminish him in order to exonerate themselves, continued to grow with every year, and would bedevil him for the remainder of his career in the American cause.

But there was a deeper problem, one quite beyond Arnold's control. Arnold's amazing military triumphs and continuing problems with personal enemies became tangled in the widespread suspicion of military officers. His very success made it worse. Even if he had been more willing to pander to the politicians in Massachusetts and Philadelphia it is uncertain that would have solved the problem. Yet experienced volunteers were needed if the British were to be defeated. And Arnold shared the increasing exasperation officers and soldiers felt at criticism and the woeful neglect of the army by civilians. He was loyal and had repeatedly risked his life and devoted his fortune to the cause. Why should politicians sitting smugly in their committee rooms doubt his dedication and look for flaws?

Arnold was anxious about the continuing accusations of John Brown, who had somehow managed to convince Congress to grant him the promotion and pay of a colonel, and to make this retroactive to November 29, 1775, the day Montgomery had originally promised it to him, before learning he had been plundering British prisoners. To preserve his own honor and reputation, Arnold decided to change his plans for returning home immediately and instead go with Gates to join Washington. He could then continue on to petition Congress and finally clear Brown's charges against him.

The two men headed south marching their Ticonderoga regiments through the rolling mountains of New York, New Jersey, and Pennsylvania in the freezing winter weather, struggling through heavy snows. Just before they reached Washington's camp a dispatch arrived from the commander asking Arnold to set out for Rhode Island immediately, as the British had invaded the state. A large British fleet had entered Newport harbor on Aquidneck Island followed by an army of seven thousand troops. There was no real resistance. The location had great strategic value for the British as Newport was the only harbor in the northern states that could be entered directly from the sea by large vessels without their having to wait for favorable winds. It also gave the British ships an opportunity to prey on colonial shipping. Rhode Island's government had retreated to Providence where the state militia and the few regiments Washington could spare were housed at the College of Rhode Island, today's Brown University.

Arnold decided to continue on to Washington's camp before turning back north, assuming Washington would deal with

Congress on his behalf. He and Gates caught up with the commander in chief on the Pennsylvania side of the Delaware River. Arnold hadn't met with Washington since setting off on the trek to Quebec. Because of the need for him to head to Rhode Island the two were together for only three days. Arnold took the opportunity to plead with Washington to hasten an exchange for the American prisoners still being held in Quebec. He brought to Washington's attention three men in particular, Daniel Morgan, John Lamb, and Eleazer Oswald. In January 1777 all three men were officially exchanged and able to return to active service in the American cause. He also encouraged Washington to pursue his plan to attack the lightly guarded Hessian posts in New Jersey. Gates gave Washington quite the opposite advice, urging him to continue retreating to the hills and bide his time before contemplating an attack. Gates always seemed to prefer a defensive approach. Washington was more in tune with Arnold's view and welcomed the Ticonderoga troops to his camp on December 21, just in time to take part in the dramatic crossing of the Delaware and the triumphant capture of the Hessian posts, and the battles at Trenton and Princeton that followed.

On his way to Rhode Island Arnold was, at long last, able to visit his family in Connecticut. He had been away a year and a half. Veterans from the Quebec campaign who were captured and had already been exchanged welcomed him with tears of thanks. Other veterans of his march through the wilderness of Maine turned out just to shake his hand. At every Connecticut town he entered—at Hartford, Middletown, and New Haven—he was hailed as a hero by admiring crowds. Cannon were shot off in salute.[14] His old Foot Guards were assembled on the New Haven town green to salute him. And of course Hannah and his three little sons, now eight, seven, and four were delighted to have him home. After only a week, however, surely to their dismay, he was off again, although this time he would be based much closer to home.

One of Arnold's new tasks was recruiting, a task for which his fame made him ideally suited. A new regiment was to be raised, and Arnold suggested Washington appoint John Lamb to head it. Lamb, now promoted to colonel, was one of those men imprisoned in Quebec and freed through Arnold's good offices. Congress had promised to advance money to equip the new regiment, but when it hadn't arrived Arnold wrote a note for the £1,000 needed and sent it to Lamb. Arnold's brother-in-law, Samuel Mansfield, who had been with his fleet on Lake Champlain was, at Arnold's urging, now made a captain. Arnold went on to raise some six thousand militia who were to join Washington at his winter camp in Morristown, New Jersey.

Arnold had been a widower now for more than a year. In his travels to Boston to recruit men he met and fell in love with Elizabeth DeBlois, a lovely young woman of sixteen. Party affiliation seems not to have mattered, as Elizabeth's merchant father was a loyalist who had fled Boston when the British evacuated it in March. Perhaps Arnold's visit to Hannah and his children reminded him of the need for a wife for himself and a mother for his sons, for a real home. Oddly, while Arnold was a daring military commander coolly facing death, he had never been especially successful with women. His wife Peggy had been aloof and plainly less in love with him than he with her. At any rate he approached Miss DeBlois delicately and indirectly, writing to Lucy Knox, the wife of Colonel Henry Knox and presumably a friend of the young lady, to pass along a letter to "the heavenly Miss DeBlois."[15] "I shall remain under the most anxious suspense until I have the favor of a line from you," he wrote her, "who if I may judge, will from your own experience consider the fond anxiety, the glowing hopes, and chilling fears that alternately possess the heart of . . . your most obedient and humble servant, Benedict Arnold."[16] The answer came, equally indirectly, in mid-April when he was next in New Haven. The heavenly Miss DeBlois, as Lucy Knox explained in a letter to her husband, had "politely refused to listen to the general."[17]

★ ★ ★

That winter the Rhode Island theater of war ground to a standoff. Arnold had suggested a more aggressive approach but Washington was against it. Instead, the militia lobbed cannon balls into the British garrison and occasionally sent raiding parties to Aquidneck Island. The British did not seem interested in expanding their territory, but for their part occasionally raided the mainland for supplies or to burn houses.

As Arnold bustled about in Massachusetts and Connecticut recruiting men for Washington's army and fretting over John Brown's success with Congress, the Congress reached a crisis in its attitude toward the army. The discussion got to the heart of Arnold's real problem with authorities. It was more fundamental than Arnold's prickly nature, although that didn't help, or his sensitivity about honor, which was commonplace among men at the time, or even his friendship with Schuyler and Washington and reluctance to pander to the delegates of Congress. The real problem was the prevailing attitude of Americans toward full-time soldiers. Arnold knew that antipathy well. He shared it. Indeed, it was virtually bred in the bones of an Englishman. Englishmen had been fearful of royal mercenaries since the time of Magna Carta. More recent events had justified that hostility as professional soldiers in the pay of kings had destroyed individual liberties and representative assemblies on the Continent. England, as an island nation, was spared that fate since it was better able to dispense with a professional army, at least during peacetime. Englishmen preferred to rely on a citizen-militia, local men officered by local gentry. Only the crisis of civil war in the mid-seventeenth century convinced Parliament to create its own army and the results had been terrible. After defeating the armies of Charles I, General Oliver Cromwell, backed by Parliament's soldiers, evicted its members and seized power. One-man government backed by military force had followed until the restoration of the monarchy. The English Bill of Rights of 1689 was adopted after another English monarch with a large standing army was deposed. To prevent this happening again that document insisted there could be no standing army in time of peace without the consent of Parliament. In addition, to ensure parliamentary control when armies were raised, Parliament passed the Mutiny Act forcing army commanders to return annually to Parliament for authorization to discipline their men and to get funding.

Yet fears persisted, as an English peacetime army became a fact of life. British pamphleteers in the eighteenth century penned tract after tract on the dangers of standing armies. These were widely read in America. In *Commentaries on the Laws of England*, a best seller in America as well as Britain when it appeared in 1765, William Blackstone, the great authority on common law, warned: "In a land of liberty it is extremely dangerous to make a distinct order of the profession of arms."[18] Blackstone advised Englishmen to look upon their own professional soldiers "as temporary excrescences bred out of the distemper of the State, and not as any part of the permanent and perpetual laws of the Kingdom."[19]

Americans had had their own problems on that score. From 1660 more than half the men selected as colonial governors were army officers who had served as garrison captains in England.[20] During the recent French and Indian War thousands of Americans serving alongside British regulars became disgusted with the low character of many soldiers, the brutal military discipline, and the way Americans were treated by British officers. Once the war finished the colonists were dismayed that the British government was stationing regulars in their major cities, sometimes quartering soldiers in their homes. Tensions between the soldiers and the colonial population were inevitable. Samuel Adams was quick to remind Americans that a professional army was "always dangerous to the Liberties of the People." Soldiers would come to feel themselves a group apart from the community and become more attached to their officers than to their government. They learned to obey orders in an unthinking fashion. Adams warned that a standing army's power "should be watched with a jealous Eye." All these worries came to a head with the so-called Boston Massacre of 1770 where soldiers fired on a raucous dockside crowd, killing five civilians. Paul Revere quickly produced an engraving of the massacre driving home that lesson.

With this background in mind, with the example of the English Parliament's disastrous experience with its own army, it is understandable that the Continental Congress was reluctant to accede to Washington's call for longer-term enlistments and a more professional force. Just as the seventeenth-century English Parliament had found though, there was constant tension between having an effective military and maintaining civilian control. But this was an emergency. Britain had sent a fleet and troops of unprecedented size to suppress the rebellion. Washington was calling for recruits who would serve longer terms, three years or for the duration of the war, and would become experienced soldiers and permit more rational campaign planning. The solution, it seemed to the delegates, was to tighten still further their control of the army so it would never become a threat.

To ensure their army would not slip the reins, the Continental Congress insisted upon micromanaging every aspect of the war. That winter of 1776–1777, the delegates devised new measures to tighten their control. In December they promoted Thomas Conway from brigadier general to major general. Washington had opposed the elevation of the arrogant Irish soldier of fortune when there were so many more deserving and more senior American officers. Nevertheless, they made Conroy inspector general of the army in charge of drilling and training. And Conway was to report directly to the Board of War, not to Washington. Horatio Gates was appointed president of the Board. In sum, Washington was to be overseen and second-guessed by this new board staffed with officers junior to him. The lines of authority were confused and cumbersome and insulting.

But Congress was not done imposing controls. While Arnold was in Rhode Island and Massachusetts recruiting men for Washington's army, Congress wrangled over new rules for army promotions, power that would ensure they made these decisions, not Washington. The commander in chief had assumed that in a republican army officers would be promoted though the ranks based on seniority and merit. There would be no buying commissions, the practice in the British army. But Congress viewed the emphasis on seniority and merit as depriving them of the power to decide promotions. They voted to deprive Washington of the power to appoint or discharge general officers. This suited John Adams, who argued during the debate: "I have been distressed to see some members of this house disposed to idolize an image which their own hands have molded. I speak here of the superstitious veneration that is sometimes paid to Genl Washington. Altho' I honor him for his good qualities, yet in this house I feel myself his Superior. In private life I shall always acknowledge that he is mine. It becomes us to attend early to the restraining our army."[21] After further discussion they agreed on February 19 that in making promotions they pay "a due regard" to three criteria; the line of succession, the merit of the persons proposed [both Washington's sensible criteria] and lastly the quota of troops raised by each state.[22] Although not stating it in so many words, this last criteria tied the number of major generals a state could have to the number of men from that state in the ranks. Certainly the first two criteria were unexceptional. The third, however, worked against those and left the door open to lobbying and favoritism. Often it was favoritism that was to prevail.

The very day the debate concluded Congress acted. It promoted five officers to the rank of major general. Arnold was a brigadier general. He easily had met the first two of their three criteria. He was the senior brigadier general, and there was no doubt he had demonstrated great merit. Yet he was passed over for promotion while five officers junior to him in rank, one only a militia officer, were promoted.

FIFTEEN

"Besmirched Honor"

T he year began badly. It would end with Arnold's greatest military triumph, but as in the past, his extraordinary exploits on the battlefield were quickly followed by struggles to defend his honor against a growing number of angry fellow officers. The more Arnold achieved, the deeper the resentment he seemed to arouse among less brilliant officers and wary members of Congress. The year 1777 was no different.

It was puzzling why the hero of Quebec and Lake Champlain was passed over for promotion. True, neither campaign ended in victory, but in both instances Arnold's behavior was exemplary. At the Lake his defense managed to protect upstate New York from invasion that year. Arnold wondered whether John Brown's continued allegations that he had plundered the merchants of Montreal was the problem. Brown was busily distributing a pamphlet in his hometown of Pittsfield, Massachusetts, vilifying

Arnold. Did Arnold's reluctance to lobby Congress and the Massachusetts delegates turn them against him, or had he engaged in too much unskillful lobbying? Others, including Horatio Gates, lobbied delegates to Congress far more, and more successfully. Had Washington exerted too much pressure on Arnold's behalf, or not enough? Actually Washington had not pressed for Arnold's promotion, doubtless considering it a foregone conclusion. He had, however, recommended Benjamin Lincoln who was promoted to major general although only a militia officer. The commander in chief was as puzzled as Arnold at his being bypassed. As Congress reluctantly agreed to expand the army and lengthen enlistments, it was even more determined to micromanage the force and, in this case, hadn't the courtesy to inform Washington about the promotions. The commander learned of his new major generals from a newspaper article. When Arnold's name was not among them his first thought was that there must have been some mistake. Certainly if bypassing Arnold was intended, it was a terrible slight and he worried that Arnold would resign forthwith. Washington wrote him on March 3: "We have had several promotions to the rank of major general," and confessed "I am at a loss whether you had a preceding appointment, as the newspapers would announce, or whether you have been omitted through some mistake. Should the latter be the case, I beg you not to take any hasty steps in consequence of it, but will allow time for recollection, which I flatter myself will remedy every error that may have been made. My endeavors to that end will not be wanting."[1] Despite his sense of humiliation Arnold did as Washington advised and bided his time.

Washington was as good as his word. Three days later he wrote Richard Henry Lee, a Congressman and friend from Virginia: "I am anxious to know whether General Arnold's non-promotion was owing to accident or design, and the cause of it."[2] "Surely," he reminded Lee, "a more active, a more spirited, and sensible officer fills no department in your Army." Washington feared, "not seeing him then on the list of major generals, and no mention made of him, has given me uneasiness, as it is not to be presumed (being the oldest brigadier) that he will continue in the service under such a slight." Arnold has been accused of being unusually sensitive about rank and precedent. Yet this was not the case. Washington himself saw the failure to promote him as a serious slight. And later that year other Continental officers were even more irate at what they regarded as an unwarranted promotion. When Generals Greene, Sullivan, and Knox heard a report that Congress had appointed a French officer, Ducondray, a major general in the army, all three wrote directly to Congress on the same day requesting permission to resign.[3] "If the report be true," Greene warned the legislators, "it will lay me under the necessity of resigning my commission, as his appointment supersedes me in command." Faced with losing three outstanding officers, Congress backed off. That did not happen in Arnold's case. Other good officers resigned in anger when passed over for promotion.

That same February Congress also passed over John Stark, a tough veteran of the French and Indian War who played a crucial part in the victory at Trenton, choosing instead for brigadier general a well-connected man with little military experience. Stark, unlike Arnold, did resign in fury, stating, "I am bound on Honor to leave the service, Congress having tho't fit to promote Junr. officers over my head."[4] Stark returned to his farm. [5]

Washington's letters were waiting for Arnold on his return to camp several days later. He replied on March 11 thanking Washington "for interesting yourself so much in my behalf in respect to my appointment, which I have had no advice of and know not by what means it was announced in the papers."[6] After acknowledging Congress's right to promote "those whom from their abilities, and their long and arduous services, they esteem most deserving," he found "their promoting junior officers to the rank of major general I view it as a very civil way of requesting my resignation, as unqualified for the office I hold." This was, in fact, the understanding of officers of that era when they were passed over for promotion, a means of forcing their resignation.[7] "My commission was conferred unsolicited and received with pleasure only as a means of serving my country," he continued. "With equal pleasure I resign it, when I can no longer serve my country with honor." On the question of honor Arnold held, "The person who, void of the nice feelings of honor, will tamely condescend to give up his right, and retain a commission at the expense of his reputation, I hold as a disgrace to the Army and unworthy of the glorious cause in which we are engaged. When I entered the service of my country my character was not impeached. I have sacrificed my interest, ease and happiness in her cause. It is rather a misfortune than a fault that my exertions have not been crowned with success. I am conscious of the rectitude of my intentions."

He requested a court of inquiry into his conduct. His countrymen might be ungrateful, he noted, but "every personal injury shall be buried in my zeal for the safety and happiness of my country." Washington must have been greatly relieved that Arnold agreed not to take any hasty step "that may tend to injure my country." That is not a promise other officers who felt themselves slighted made. In a second letter Arnold pointed out that his being superseded "must be viewed as an implicit impeachment of my character" and repeated his request for a court of inquiry into his character.[8]

When Washington replied on April 2 he was able to tell Arnold that he was indeed passed over because Congress had decided numbers of general officers from each state were to be proportionate to the number of troops enlisted from that state and Connecticut already had two major generals.[9] This was, Washington judged, "a strange mode of reasoning," but added, "it may serve to show you that the promotion that was due to your seniority, was not overlooked for want of merit in you." He judged the situation "of so delicate a nature, that I will not even undertake to advise, your own feelings must be your guide." This was an explanation, but little comfort. If the intention was to win the war it made little sense to ignore merit as well as seniority. Still, Washington counseled him, "as no particular charge is alleged against you, I do not see upon what ground you can demand a court of inquiry."

Although Washington found no "particular charge alleged" against Arnold, Arnold was right, the constant criticism of him from a growing number of sources may have had an impact on whether Congress chose to promote him. Among Arnold's new critics was Brigadier General David Waterbury, who had commanded a ship alongside Arnold's on Lake Champlain. Waterbury was clearly defensive about having surrendered his ship and crew. In a letter to Gates and in complaints to others he laid out his version of the battle and charged Arnold with recklessly wasting the ships and disregarding the lives of his men.[10] This was a transparent attempt to exonerate himself and blame others for his own perceived failing. Arnold never accused Waterbury of cowardice, but his own heroic behavior made Waterbury's conduct look unworthy. Making matters worse Waterbury's views were then echoed by Brigadier General William Maxwell of New Jersey, an inveterate malcontent. Another retired British officer just recently promoted to brigadier general, Maxwell had objected to the promotion of Arthur St. Clair before him and accused both Gates and Arnold of incompetence.[11] Maxwell, like Waterbury, accused Arnold of needlessly sacrificing the fleet and crew on Lake Champlain. In a private letter to Governor Livingston of New Jersey, Maxwell branded Arnold "our evil genius to the north" who "with a good deal of industry, got us clear of all our fine fleet" which were, Maxwell insisted, "by far the strongest."[12] He argued that Arnold should have retreated before the British fleet and, by not doing so, Maxwell implied, had disobeyed Gates's orders. In fact, Gates had instructed Arnold to make the best defense he could, for as long as he could, and was delighted at how Arnold had managed to carry out those instructions against a far superior force.[13]

In sum, although Washington did not find any particular charge causing Congress not to promote the hero of Lake Champlain, Arnold was probably nearer the mark in attributing it to the charges circulating of recklessness and self-serving that turned his achievements into failings. Even Washington's friend, Richard Henry Lee, who had praised Arnold's heroism initially, by November was describing Arnold as having behaved in a "fiery, hot, and impetuous" manner, an officer who "without discretion, never thought of informing himself how the enemy went on, and . . . had no idea of retiring when he saw them coming, though so much superior to his force!"[14] Arnold's mission on Lake Champlain and Gates's instructions to him were grossly distorted by these allegations. Maxwell's odd assertion to the contrary, the British force was bound to be superior to any fleet the Americans managed to cobble together. Indeed, there was no point building a fleet, only to retreat when the enemy appeared. Arnold's critics chose to ignore the crucial fact that Arnold's obstinate defense convinced the British to retreat to Canada for the winter.

Whether because Washington agreed with Arnold's not Gates's military advice or because Gates was preoccupied with his own advancement, he had little incentive to correct the general understanding of his orders to Arnold. The day after Arnold was passed over for promotion Congress asked Gates to resume the post of adjutant general, a desk job. They intended that St. Clair, just promoted to major general, take his place as Schuyler's second in command. This was not at all what Gates wanted. His aim was Schuyler's post commanding the northern army. He now bent his efforts to persuade Congress to appoint him to replace Schuyler.

As to Arnold's critics, it is surprising how successful they were, branding his heroic actions as merely rash and self-serving, when he had repeatedly risked his life for the cause. Where his British opponents were impressed by his skill and bravery in the battle on Lake Champlain, some American officers and congressmen saw only vainglory.

Undeterred by Washington's caution, Arnold decided to petition Congress and left his Rhode Island post heading south. En route he went home to spend time with Hannah and his sons. While in New

Haven he hoped to improve his financial affairs. Given British vessels were preying upon American ships, the best opportunity was investing in privateering. Privateers, really licensed pirates sailing in armed merchant ships, preyed in their turn upon British vessels. If they managed to capture a ship bringing supplies to British forces, they could sell the cargo for a handsome profit. Arnold's ship, *Polly*, was already engaged in privateering.[15]

He hadn't long to concentrate on financial matters, however. Early on March 26 a breathless courier arrived at Arnold's home with news that the British were invading Connecticut. Some twenty-six ships were spotted off Norwalk making for Compo Beach, twenty-five miles south of New Haven. Their obvious object was the supply depot at Danbury that was only lightly defended. Generals Wooster and Silliman leading six hundred militia had already marched off hoping to protect the supplies at Danbury. Arnold rushed to join them. The officers and men arrived at Bethel four miles from Danbury at two in the morning, only to learn that the depot was already in flames along with many houses in the town. The British, led by William Tryon, Governor of New York, having accomplished their goal were gone.[16]

The American leaders were determined to head them off. They divided their exhausted troops intent on pursuing the British but unsure which route they meant to take. Pursuers and pursued struggled through driving rain. Members of the Connecticut militia were proud to rally behind Arnold, and joined him. The British were heading for Ridgefield and seemed well informed. At Ridgefield they set the homes of known patriots ablaze and torched the Presbyterian church where munitions were stored. Wooster had taken two hundred men along another route aiming to get behind the enemy. He did catch up with the British but in the fighting the elderly general received a fatal wound.

Arnold and Silliman began a forced march to Ridgefield with five hundred militia. They caught up with the regulars at eleven that morning. Their troops were greatly outnumbered by the two thousand British soldiers, but Arnold was determined to cut off the British retreat to their ships. He ordered his men to throw up a barricade of wagons, logs, stones, and earth.[17] Behind this makeshift barrier they were able to hold off three charges. They were finally forced to retreat when a British force flanked them. During one of the charges Arnold's horse was shot, trapping him under it.[18] A young local Tory dashed up to him, bayonet fixed, shouting "Surrender, you are my prisoner!" With a mighty effort Arnold freed himself from the horse replying, "Not yet," and drawing his pistol shot the man in the chest. He then leaped over a fence and ran through a swamp, bullets spraying all around him. The following day Arnold sent off a message to General McDougall to prepare to waylay the regulars from the front, while Arnold and his men attacked them from the rear.[19] The British learned of the ambush and managed to circumvent it, but were harassed and fired on by Arnold's men while Arnold had yet another horse killed under him. When the retreating regulars reached Compo Beach they counterattacked, driving off the militia just long enough to board their ships.

In recognition of Arnold's immediately taking action to rally the militia to drive the British out of Connecticut, on May 2 the members of Congress voted to promote him to major general. His appointment read:

In CONGRESS
The DELEGATES of the UNITED STATES
TO
Benedict Arnold, Esquire
We reporting special Trust and Confidence in your
Patriotism, Valor, Conduct, and Fidelity, DO by these
presence, constitute and appoint you to be
Major General

No issue, now, of the numbers of major generals Connecticut already had. However, Congress did not agree to restore Arnold's seniority over the five men who had been promoted to major general in February.

Washington was delighted that Arnold had been "restored" to the Continental Army and on May 8 asked him to take command at Peekskill in the Hudson Highlands.[20] This was a key location as the fort sat high above the Hudson River guarding the Hudson Highlands from any British move north from New York City. The threat was real. In March there had been a British raid on the fort. Some five hundred regulars with two field guns were put ashore to destroy the supplies there. The American garrison retreated burning the supplies as they left. A small force attacked the British the next day but the British withdrew, having accomplished their mission. The episode left Washington anxious to protect the region in case the British chose to move in that direction during the coming campaign season.

Before Arnold took up the commission at Peekskill, he wanted Congress to appoint a committee to investigate the charges against him. He paid a visit to Washington with that request. Washington understood the concern and sent along a letter to Congress pointing out that "if any such aspersions lie against him, it is but reasonable, that he should have an opportunity of vindicating himself and evincing his innocence."[21] He added that Arnold was concerned that Congress had failed to grant him the seniority he was due. Arnold wrote Congress himself asking for an opportunity to justify his financial claims against the charges "of a catalog of crimes which, if true, ought to subject me to disgrace, infamy, and the just resentment of my countrymen."[22] Congress agreed to hold a hearing.

Arnold made his case to the Board of War the following evening, producing documents from the Canadian expedition. He reminded Congress that they had ignored his plea for a paymaster. The chaotic situation of his troops to and from Canada made careful record-keeping nearly impossible. Some funds that were to go to divisional commanders had been captured with the financial records during the expedition to Quebec, other records were destroyed when the

Royal Savage was captured and burned. Many members of Congress regarded his requests for funds unreasonable and insisted that rather than owing Arnold restitution he owed them $9,000.[23] They did, however, concede he had lost horses in battle and granted him money for new mounts. The New Englanders had always been among the most skeptical of Arnold. But even John Adams, who chaired the Board of War, sympathized with Arnold against Brown's claims. On May 30 Adams wrote of meeting with Arnold and acknowledged he had been "basely slandered and libeled."[24] Still Congress would not restore his seniority. Arnold had had enough and in July wrote to resign his commission.

Military threats to the American cause were especially dire that summer. A major British invasion from Canada, this time led by General John Burgoyne, was advancing on Albany. On June 26 Burgoyne reached Crown Point. The small garrison there fled to Ticonderoga with the British only a few days behind them. In the dead of night on July 6, with British cannon on a nearby hill poised to fire on Fort Ticonderoga, its garrison slipped away. The great fort fell without a shot being fired. Its commander, Arthur St. Clair, along with General Philip Schuyler would face a court-martial for abandoning it. By July 10 the British army was at the north end of Wood Creek laying plans for proceeding to the Hudson. A second British army had taken another route from Canada and was threatening central New York's Mohawk Valley.

Arnold's letter of resignation crossed with Washington's recommending that Arnold be sent to assist Schuyler in the emergency. Indeed Schuyler had asked for Arnold's assistance. Once again Arnold gave way, putting the defense of the cause ahead of his personal honor. Once again worries about rank and reputation took second place to his loyalty to his country. After he set off on this key commission Congress voted on a resolution to restore his seniority. It was voted down.

SIXTEEN

Savage Warfare

A rnold's desperate naval battle against the British fleet on Lake Champlain bought the patriot cause time. But time was now up. Back came British armies that summer, streaming down from Canada in even greater force than before, determined to seize New York State and cut the New England states off from the mid-Atlantic and southern states. Their campaign was more elaborate this time, more ambitious, better equipped. It was planned in Britain early that year by King George himself with Lord Germain, secretary of war, and Major General John Burgoyne. General Burgoyne, Gentleman Johnny as he was affectionately known to his troops, was the new commander in charge. Back in London for the winter meeting of Parliament where he represented a friend's pocket boroughs, Burgoyne jockeyed hard to replace Carleton as field commander in Canada.[1] The two men were a study in contrasts. Where Carleton was modest and pragmatic, expert on the Canadian situation, Burgoyne was flamboyant and cocksure. After a stint of active duty in Portugal where he led some three thousand men to victory in Valencia de Alcántara, Burgoyne had "made himself conspicuous chiefly by ornate speeches" in Parliament.[2] He was regarded as a good soldier on both sides of the Atlantic, but also as a vain and pompous man. He had arrived in North America in 1775 to reinforce General Gage at Boston. Now he wanted Carleton's job leading the expedition from Canada, and he got it. King George and Lord Germain agreed Burgoyne was more enterprising than Carleton. The task before him, though, was more formidable than he or his superiors in London realized.

The British campaign plan was three-pronged. Burgoyne was to lead the major force south up Lake Champlain to Albany. Where Carleton depended on a fleet Burgoyne would have a large combined force of British and Hessian regulars as well as Canadians and Indians. At Burgoyne's suggestion a second assault force would create a diversion, traveling west up the St. Lawrence to Lake Ontario and Oswego, then sweeping south to the Mohawk River in central New York and east to link up with the main army. Lieutenant Colonel Barry St. Leger, forty-four and a veteran of frontier warfare, was to command this expedition. It was his first independent command and would be his last. The third, and more important prong, was the support of General Howe, Britain's North American commander based in New York City. Howe was to bring his army up the Hudson to join Burgoyne in Albany. New York State would be sliced apart. Since many New York residents were loyalists, the British commanders counted on large numbers of them joining their armies.

There were two serious problems with this strategy, the first created by Lord Germain himself. On March 3, shortly after Germain had agreed Howe would move his army north to link up with Burgoyne in Albany, he also approved Howe's suggestion that he attack Philadelphia to the south. Germain presumably believed Howe could capture Philadelphia quickly and then reverse direction and speed north to link up with Burgoyne.[3] There was also a sense that perhaps Howe's assistance wasn't essential for Burgoyne, that the expedition from Canada needed no assistance. Indeed, before he set out from Canada Carleton had showed Burgoyne a letter from Howe warning that he would be unable to help Burgoyne unless Washington moved his army north.[4] Burgoyne doesn't seem to have been particularly worried by this. But Howe's double mission was one of those battle plans that look perfectly logical until actually put into practice.

Burgoyne's second problem was manpower. He worried, quite rightly, whether he would have sufficient men for the task and feared he could barely spare the small detachment of men for St. Leger's campaign.[5] To fill his ranks Burgoyne resorted to recruiting Indians. While he counted on their participation to terrorize Americans into surrender, he was concerned that any atrocities they perpetrated would damage, if not destroy, his hopes of attracting American loyalists. Indian massacres of men, women, and children when they were France's allies during the French and Indian War were seared into everyone's minds. There had been recent Indian atrocities as well. The Declaration of Independence charged George III with "endeavoring to bring on the inhabitants of our frontiers, the merciless Indian Savages, whose known rule of warfare is an undistinguished destruction of all ages, sexes and conditions."

Burgoyne's solution to the problem was to lay down rules for his Indian recruits rewarding them for live captives while "calling them to account" for scalping innocent victims. Before the expedition set out in June he met with the Indian chiefs warning: "I positively forbid bloodshed, when you are not opposed in arms. Aged men, women, children and prisoners must be held sacred from the knife, hatchet, even in the time of actual conflict."[6] On the other hand he felt it necessary to placate Indians disappointed by the order:

> In conformity and indulgence of your customs, which have affixed an idea of honor to such badges of victory, you shall be allowed to take the scalps of the dead

when killed by your fire and in fair opposition, but on no account, or pretence, or subtilty, or prevarication, are they to be taken from the wounded or even dying; and still less pardonable, if possible, will it be held to kill men in that condition on purpose, and upon a supposition that this protection to the wounded would be thereby evaded.[7]

What the Indians made of this became clear in the following days.

While Burgoyne was trying to keep his Indian allies in check, he had no reservations about threatening awful retribution against Americans who persisted in "the Phrenzy of Hostility." His first proclamation to the Americans, printed on June 24, invited them to return to their allegiance and with it the blessings of legal government but then warned that he had "but to give stretch to the Indian forces under my direction, and they amount to thousands" who would overtake "the hardened enemies of Great Britain."[8]

I trust I shall stand acquitted in the Eyes of God and Men in denouncing and executing the Vengeance of the State against the willful Outcast. The Messengers of Justice and of Wrath await them in the Field, and Devastation, Famine, and every concomitant Horror that a reluctant but indispensable Prosecution of Military Duty must occasion, will bar the Way to their Return.[9]

This approach was unlikely to succeed with Burgoyne's Indian recruits or the Americans.

Arnold, Washington, and Schuyler, preoccupied with their own problems, would have taken some comfort had they known of those besetting the British. In addition to a smaller force than he asked for, Burgoyne was short of horses. His wagons were hastily built of green wood and kept breaking down, and there were too few of them to carry tents or the soldiers' baggage. Yet rumor had it that twenty wagons were being used to haul Gentleman Johnny's "necessaries," a silver dining service, his wardrobe of fresh uniforms, and numerous cases of champagne.[10] Worse, the expedition was only able to carry two weeks' supply of food. Supplies would have to be found for hundreds of men along the way. He had personnel problems in addition to the difficulty of controlling his four hundred Indians. A crowd of some two thousand women and children were accompanying the troops. The British and Hessian officers disliked each other. Nonetheless it was a formidable force with thirty-seven hundred British and two thousand German troops and several hundred artillerymen.[11] Burgoyne had hoped for two thousand Canadians but got only two hundred.[12] The adviser he selected to work with the Indians, La Corne St. Luc, proved a regrettable choice if he meant to "keep up [the Indians'] terror and avoid their cruelty."[13] True, La Corne had decades of experience leading Indian raids on the frontiers but also, most notoriously, at Fort William Henry in 1757, where the Indians violated a truce agreement and slaughtered hundreds of men, women, and children promised protection by the French. When war between the British and Americans broke out La Corne offered his services to both sides. The Americans regarded him with suspicion and brought him to Philadelphia while they investigated his background. They found nothing and released him. April found him recommending to William Tryon, royal governor of New York, that he loose the Indians on the "miserable rebels," urging, *"Il faut brutalizer les affaires"* ("We must brutalize the business").[14] It is hard to believe Burgoyne was unaware of La Corne's views when he put him in charge of the expedition's Indians. Perhaps he felt confident La Corne and his Indians could be induced to change their ways.

The patriot forces had their own problems with competition and animosity among generals. As the awful threat of the British invasion hung over their cause that summer the long-simmering friction between Horatio Gates and Philip Schuyler grew more virulent. It began a year earlier. Schuyler was commander of the northern army and Gates was given command of the American forces in Canada, just as they were retreating to America. There was therefore some confusion about Gates's role. Indeed, Gates has been judged "possibly even more ambitious and political than Burgoyne."[15] In that sense they were two of a kind, as officers, however, Gates could not match Burgoyne for actual field experience and daring. He insisted on overall command of the northern army in place of Schuyler. Schuyler objected and Congress supported Schuyler. That winter Gates didn't participate in Washington's spectacular victories in Trenton and Princeton, having advised his commander to retreat to the hills instead. In February 1777 Congress appointed Gates as George Washington's adjutant general to train the new three-year recruits. Gates refused the commission in high dudgeon. Congress then gave him an independent command of Fort Ticonderoga.

When he reached Albany on his way to Ticonderoga, he discovered, to his delight, that Schuyler had gone to serve as a delegate from New York to the Continental Congress in Philadelphia. Schuyler, a proud and diligent man, had grown increasingly dismayed by the vicious aspersions on his character Congress was hearing and upset by delegates' insulting reaction to his complaints. Like Arnold he resolved to defend himself in person to clear these stains on his honor. He traveled to Kingston to inform the New York convention. After hearing his concerns the members appointed him one of their delegates to the Congress. He arrived in Philadelphia in April writing his secretary that the reports had "gone too far, and all that stands on their journals injurious to me must be expunged or I quit the service."[16]

Gates never completed his journey to Ticonderoga. He took advantage of Schuyler's absence to seize the coveted command of the northern department. This was a step too far for Congress. Despite Gates's many supporters among the New Englanders who liked Gates and resented the imperious manners of this Dutch

New Yorker, Congress made it clear they wanted Schuyler in that post. A committee had looked into the allegations against Schuyler, and he had been vindicated. Gates was outraged and returned to Philadelphia to protest in person. On June 17 he was given permission to address the Congress and used the occasion to launch so vicious an attack on the New York delegation that he was asked to leave the chamber. One observer characterized his manner as "ungracious, and totally devoid of all dignity; his delivery incoherent and interrupted with frequent chasms, in which he was peering over his scattered notes; and the tenor of his discourse was a compound of vanity, folly and rudeness," adding, "I can assure you that notwithstanding his conduct has been such as to have eradicated from my mind every sentiment of respect and esteem for him, I felt for him as a man, and for the honor of human nature wished him to withdraw before he had plunged himself into utter contempt."[17] Congress ordered Gates to report to Washington who offered him the post of adjutant general once again, which again Gates refused.

While Congress and Washington were dealing with Gates's determination to replace Schuyler, all was going well for the British. On July 1 Burgoyne's advance corps led by Brigadier General Simon Fraser had come in sight of Fort Ticonderoga. By July 3 they had cut the fort off from its hinterland and two days later had dug a road up Sugar Loaf mountain overlooking the fort and planted a British flag on the summit. With cannon installed on the mountain they were poised to bombard the fort. Arthur St. Clair was commanding the besieged garrison. Like Gates and Montgomery, St. Clair was a veteran of the British army who had resigned his commission, married an American, and settled in the colonies. When war broke out Congress appointed St. Clair to the rank of colonel. He led a Pennsylvania regiment that supported Arnold's retreat from Canada ,and was then promoted to brigadier general. Unlike Gates, St. Clair took part in Washington's daring crossing of the Delaware and subsequent battles. St. Clair was assigned to serve at Ticonderoga under the command of General Gates. When Gates abandoned that commission in his zeal to take command of the northern department, the command of Ticonderoga fell to St. Clair. He took up the post on June 12 and found to his dismay that emergency repairs on the fort were still incomplete and the garrison of 2,200 far too weak. St. Clair believed at least ten thousand troops were required. Even those few soldiers based at the fort were poorly supplied. Had Gates actually assumed the post as ordered, some of the problems might have been rectified. Good officer that St. Clair was, he had no stomach for a desperate and unequal fight. The day after spotting the British flag on the mountain, he and his outnumbered troops abandoned Ticonderoga without firing a shot. Americans were shocked at the news. They had regarded Ticonderoga as impregnable. St. Clair and Schuyler and their men began battling their way south on a hundred-mile retreat.

While the British campaign to capture New York State was advancing nicely, Arnold lingered in Philadelphia to deal with Congress's humiliating inquiry into John Brown's complaints about his military expenditures. How outrageous that he who had willingly paid his men from his own pocket, left his shipping business to flounder, and risked his life time and again for the cause, should have to suffer this. Congress had begun an investigation but was in no hurry to get on with it. On July 11, with Washington bracing for an attack by Howe, Schuyler desperately trying to stop Burgoyne's advance into New York, and St. Leger forging up the St. Lawrence, Arnold resigned his commission. In his letter to Congress Arnold explained that he was forced to take this step by a sense of the injustice he had suffered. He dearly loved his country and was ready to risk his life for it again, but "honor is a sacrifice no man ought to make; as I received, so I wish to transmit it inviolate to posterity."[18]

Just the day before Arnold submitted his resignation, Washington wrote John Hancock, president of the Congress, about the dire situation in New York and his inadequate force to defend it.

He was uncertain whether Burgoyne had captured the forts along his route, but there was "an absolute necessity" for the militia "turning out to check General Burgoyne's progress, or the most disagreeable consequences may be apprehended."[19] Washington was painfully aware of Arnold's frustration with congressional charges of financial impropriety and his threat to resign. He needed an officer of Arnold's obvious talents badly. Politely but firmly he advised Hancock that since Arnold was the very man to animate the militia in this crisis, military necessity ought to take priority over any issue Congress might have with Arnold:

> Upon this occasion, I would take the liberty to suggest to Congress, the propriety of sending an active, spirited officer to conduct and lead them on. If General Arnold has settled his affairs, and can be spared from Philadelphia, I would recommend him for the business, and that he should immediately set out for the northern department. He is active, judicious, and brave, and an officer in whom the militia will repose great confidence. Besides this, he is well-acquainted with that country, and with the roads and more important passes and gorges in it. I do not think he can render more signal services, or be more usefully employed at this time, than in this way.[20]

Washington then reminded Hancock of the high esteem in which he held Arnold and what Arnold had done for the cause: "I could wish him to be engaged in a more agreeable service, to be with better troops, but circumstances call for his exertions in this way. And I have no doubt of his adding much to the honor he has already acquired."

Hancock wasted no time. The following day he wrote Arnold, ignoring the letter of resignation and ongoing financial investigation, but enclosing an extract of Washington's letter calling for "a brave, active, and judicious officer" to be "immediately employed in collecting the Militia" to oppose Burgoyne. The Congress, Hancock added, "concurring in opinion with General Washington, who had strongly recommended you for this purpose, have directed you to repair immediately to headquarters to follow such orders as you may receive from him on the subject."[21]

Once more Arnold responded to a call to arms and withdrew his resignation.

Arnold reported to Washington, who ordered him to take command of Fort Edward. The fort stood just fifty miles north of Albany at the first navigable place on the Hudson River that Burgoyne would reach as he moved south. Arnold arrived at the fort on July 21. Two days later Congress cleared him of all John Brown's charges. The conditions Arnold found when he arrived at Fort Edward were grim.[22] The woods around the fort were already full of Indians, Canadians, and regulars. He needed better intelligence but didn't even have enough supplies to equip scouts. The Indians were scalping men they caught. A day after Arnold arrived he wrote Washington they "attacked our picket guard, killed & scalped five men, wounded nine and took one prisoner. On the 24th they killed & scalped two officers" and two days later one of Arnold's pickets was attacked in force. A lieutenant and five privates were killed and scalped. That same day, Arnold reported, Indians seized two women from a house near the fort and brutally scalped and mutilated one of them, a young woman named Jane McCrea. Arnold immediately sent out one thousand men hoping to ambush the Indians, but a heavy rainstorm soaked their weapons and ammunition providing the Indians time to retreat.[23] News of the scalping of poor Jane McCrea spread quickly throughout the country provoking just the sort of outrage Burgoyne most feared, with important repercussions for Arnold and his cause.

There has been confusion over many details of Jane's murder, but this much seems certain. She was the daughter of a Scots minister in a family of five sons. Three of her brothers would fight for the American cause, two for the British. The family lived in

New Jersey but after her parents died Jane, then sixteen, moved to New York to live with her brother John on his farm near Fort Edward. She was described as a beautiful and well-mannered young woman with striking long reddish hair.[24] In her new home she was reunited with a childhood friend, David Jones. They fell in love and planned to marry. Her brother John had joined the militia while Jones joined the British. With the fighting closing in John's family fled to Albany, but Jones asked Jane to wait for him. She moved in with Mrs. Sarah McNeil, an elderly widow and cousin of British general Simon Fraser. With the British army close to Fort Edwards Jones sent for Jane and arranged for an Indian chief and his men to protect her as she walked the four miles to the British camp.

Unfortunately the day she set out a band of Hurons massacred the nine members of loyalist John Allen's family then attacked Arnold's picket led by young Lieutenant Tobias Van Vechten, chasing them into Jane's path. A letter related the fate of Van Vechten and his men: "Lt Van Vechten was most inhumanly butcher'd and Scalped, two Serjeants and two privates were likewise killed and Scalped—one of the latter had both his hands cut off."[25] Jane fled back to Mrs. McNeil's house. Just as the two women were climbing into the cellar the Hurons broke into the house and seized them, then set out with them to Fraser's camp. On the way the Hurons ran into Jane's Indian escort. The two groups of Indians argued. In a fit of anger the Huron chief threw his hatchet, striking Jane and killing her.[26] He then scalped her, stripping and mutilating her body. A British officer in Fraser's camp wrote that in the evening her bloody scalp and that of Van Vechten's were brought into Fraser's camp by the Indians "which they danced about in their usual manner."[27] He added, "the cruelties committed by them were too shocking to relate, particularly the melancholy catastrophe of the unfortunate Miss McCrea, which affected the general and the whole army with the sincerest regret and concern for her untimely fate. . . . She fell a sacrifice to the savage passions of these blood thirsty monsters." Jane's fiancé was horrified when he recognized her splendid hair. He pleaded to be discharged from the army. When this was denied he fled to Canada where he is said to have lived a solitary life.

This terrible incident was damning in itself, but Burgoyne's response was worse. He was outraged at first and went to the Indian camp to demand Jane's murderer be handed over to be hanged. But La Corne advised him that if he persisted the Indians would desert en masse and were likely to commit further atrocities on their way north.[28] Fraser agreed. Burgoyne decided it was wiser to leave punishment to the Indian chiefs. The result was no punishment at all.

The story of the lovely young woman basely slaughtered and mutilated by Burgoyne's Indian allies spread quickly by word of mouth, by letters, and then newspapers from Massachusetts to Virginia.[29] The terrible atrocity effected the military fortunes of both sides. Indeed Jane's brothers served on both sides. While her wanton murder was just one of dozens committed by Burgoyne's Indian allies against friend and foe alike, it caught the imagination of her countrymen as an especially horrible example of the terror the King intended to let loose. Suddenly there was new passion to volunteer for the militia, new determination to fight more fiercely rather than suffer a similar fate, and, most fatal to Burgoyne's hopes, disgust among loyalists about aiding an army whose Indian allies were butchering entire families of the King's loyal supporters.

With the British campaign for New York closing in on Albany and the Mohawk River Valley, Washington decided Arnold was more badly needed at Fort Stanwix than defending Fort Edward. Even before Arnold's first report from Fort Edward Washington was recommending to Schuyler that Arnold "or some other sensible spirited officer," be sent to Fort Schuyler, the renamed Fort Stanwix, "to take care of that post, keep up the spirits of the inhabitants, and cultivate and improve the favorable dispositions of the Indians."[30]

Fort Stanwix was destined to be a prime target for St. Leger. Its garrison was frantically preparing to withstand a siege.

This was a terrible time for confusion over the command of the northern department, but Gates and his supporters were busy in Philadelphia lobbying hard to replace Schuyler. In Arnold's letter to Washington from Fort Edward, he expressed his wholehearted support for General Schuyler, despite the loss of Ticonderoga and the long, discouraging retreat south. Arnold was aware of the chorus of Schuyler's detractors and could fully appreciate the anguish this caused his commander and friend: "Justice obliges me to observe I believe Genl Schuyler has done everything a man can do in his situation. I am very sorry to hear his character has been so unjustly aspersed & slandered."[31] Washington too supported Schuyler, alerting him a year earlier to "insidious diabolical acts and schemes" which he believed were spread about by Tories to create division and dissension."[32] Schuyler was accused of neglecting the troops in Canada to ensure their defeat, and embezzling money. While Congress was being regaled with all Schuyler's supposed failings, Schuyler was desperately trying to slow Burgoyne's advance. He had one thousand men at work felling trees along the British route and diverting marshes to flood their path. To deprive the British troops of supplies, he resorted to a scorched-earth strategy, leaving no crops, cattle, or supplies along their path. But with all this Schuyler had not forgotten the plight of Fort Stanwix, and shared Washington's fear that it might not be able to hold out against St. Leger's army.

St Leger had left Montreal on June 23. Like Burgoyne, St. Leger's Indian recruits were to play a key role in his campaign. He was even more dependent on the Indians than Burgoyne since he had only 340 regulars and Hessians, and 800 loyalists and Canadians. The remainder of his 2,000-man army, some 860 men, were Indians. St. Leger was in such a hurry to launch his expedition. There was a portage problem between Lake Ontario and the Mohawk River.

He hadn't brought artillery necessary for a proper siege. He had been warned by Indians that Fort Stanwix was being strengthened and had a garrison of nearly six hundred men, but he didn't believe the reports. The rebuilding of the fort and strengthening its garrison was still underway when St. Leger came within sight of it. His advance force reached Fort Stanwix just in time to see a convoy with two hundred more men and additional supplies disappear inside.

The surrender of Ticonderoga made the prospect of losing Fort Stanwix more devastating. St. Clair had taken responsibility for the surrender of Ticonderoga and the wisdom of his decision had become clear. Gates's supporters now shifted their argument claiming that the New England militia disliked Schuyler and would refuse to volunteer if he remained in command. This was a terrible aspersion on the loyalty of New Englanders, especially now that their region was threatened by the British army and its terrifying Indian allies. In the end neither Arnold's nor even Washington's views mattered to the delegates in Congress. Gates had lobbied long and hard for the honor of commanding the northern department. He had neither the temperament nor the experience necessary. His penchant for lobbying rather than remaining in the field, his pudgy body, balding head, the glasses perched at the end of his nose earning him the name "Granny Gates," were a startling contrast to the dignified presence and selfless dedication of Schuyler. But lobbying and contacts paid off. On August 1 the New England delegates sent a message to Washington asking that he remove Schuyler and appoint Gates.[33] Washington had had enough personal contact with Gates to politely pass the decision on to Congress.

But the war would not wait for these machinations. A day after the New Englanders approached Washington St. Leger called upon the garrison at Fort Stanwix to surrender. Three days later Congress acted, appointing Gates to replace Schuyler. On August 19 Gates arrived at Albany to take command. Despite Gates's personal attack on his abilities, Schuyler, the man New Englanders branded imperious, graciously offered to help Gates in any way he could. In a response that betrayed the measure of the man, Gates spurned the offer, treating Schuyler in a rude and disrespectful manner.

The garrison at Fort Stanwix was commanded by two experienced officers, young Colonel Peter Gansevoort from Albany and his second officer, Lieutenant Colonel Marinus Willett. Both had served under Montgomery at Montreal and Quebec. Gansevoort had been in command of Fort George for most of the previous year. St. Leger made the mistake of trying to intimidate the garrison by parading his troops around the fort's walls. It was particularly counterproductive since the Americans took note how few regulars he had and how many Indians. Their disgust at the scalping of Jane McCrea made them all the more determined to stand fast. St. Leger's call for surrender was spurned. The officers were awaiting a force of militia some eight hundred strong led by Brigadier General Nicholas Herkimer to relieve the siege. St. Leger had learned of the relief force and dispatched four hundred loyalists and Indians under the command of Chief Joseph Brant of the Mohawk Indians to ambush Herkimer and his men.

Herkimer had met with Brant in July to try to convince him that the Mohawks should remain neutral in the struggle between the American and British forces. He failed, and the Mohawks sided with the British. Now Brant was leading the men bent on decimating Herkimer and his militia to prevent them reaching the fort. It was Brant's sister, Molly, who warned St. Leger about the relief force. Herkimer was worried about an ambush at Oriskany where the road descended into a ravine. It was the shortest route to the fort though. When other officers actually questioned his patriotism and time being of the essence, he decided to chance it. The trap was sprung. Despite the advantage of surprise St. Leger's men had, a fierce, six-hour battle ensued. Herkimer's horse was shot and the ball penetrated into his leg shattering it below the knee. With extraordinary presence of mind and great personal courage, he sat propped up against a tree calmly smoking a pipe while he directed his men. When the British force finally withdrew with considerable losses, Herkimer was taken home, a painful forty-mile journey over rough ground. His wound never healed. His leg was amputated several days later, but the blood vessels were not properly sealed, and he died. The relief force on which the fort depended, however brave, was not able to complete its mission. On the other hand one third of St. Leger's force at Oriskany was lost.

Fort Stanwix's commanders had taken advantage of the absence of some of St. Leger's men—one group to ambush the relief force and another to cut a road through the forest to bring up artillery—to raid his camp. St. Leger's remaining troops were taken by surprise and many fled. Twenty-four wagonloads of British food, drink, blankets, clothes, tools and ammunition were hauled into the fort.

Schuyler, like Washington, was afraid the fort might fall. After the loss of Ticonderoga another surrender had to be avoided. Time was running out for the defenders, but there were fears a relief force might be ambushed just as Herkimer's was. "Gentlemen, I am willing to take responsibility upon myself," he told his assembled officers, "where is the Brigadier who will take command of the relief? I shall beat up for volunteers tomorrow."[34] This task was just the sort of challenge Arnold couldn't resist. Much to Schuyler's satisfaction, he immediately volunteered.[35] By noon the next day eight hundred men from General Learned's brigade were ready to march with him to rescue the fort.

Shortly after Arnold and his men left Schuyler was removed and Gates took command. Gates arrived at Albany on August 19, immediately writing Arnold for information about his progress, quite anxious to have his help in Albany. The message caught up with Arnold at German Flats, the location of the town of Herkimer. He sent word that his force had grown to twelve hundred Continentals and militia, and that he was continuing that very morning to the besieged fort. "Nothing shall be omitted that can be done to raise," he assured the new commander. "You will hear of my being victorious or no more and as soon as the safety of this part of the country will permit I will fly to your assistance."[36]

Despite his assurances to Gates Arnold was afraid he might not arrive before the fort surrendered. He needed a quicker alternative. As luck would have it an opportunity presented itself. A Dutchman, Hon Yost Schuyler, a distant cousin of Philip Schuyler, had been arrested and sentenced to hang for rallying men to assist the British. Yost had a reputation of being wild, even out of his wits. His mother and brother rushed to Fort Dayton where he was being held and pleaded with Arnold for mercy. At the suggestion of one of his colonels, Arnold agreed to pardon Yost if he would bring a message to Fort Stanwix telling the British that Arnold was approaching with a huge force. Yost's coat was shot full of holes to make his story of fleeing the death sentence more convincing. An Oneida Indian, from an area tribe that had allied with the Americans, agreed to accompany him, and Yost's brother was left with Arnold to ensure his good behavior.

Off Yost and his Indian assistant went. Upon reaching the British army they headed for a council where St. Leger's Indians were deciding whether to stay with the expedition after their losses fighting Herkimer. Yost told them Arnold was arriving with a huge force, and when they asked how many men Arnold had, Yost gazed up at a nearby tree and pointed to the leaves. The Oneida accompanying Yost confirmed this tale.

This was more than enough for St. Leger's Indian allies. They fled, pausing only long enough to break into the liquor supply and plunder some clothing. With half of his men having fled or been killed, St. Leger concluded he had no choice but to abandon the mission. He and his army promptly retreated, some say fled, back to Canada, abandoning much of their equipment, tents, and artillery. By the time Arnold and his men arrived at Fort Stanwix the enemy had disappeared. It was a wonderful, bloodless victory. Arnold could now return to Gates's army and the coming battle against Burgoyne. It was to be the high point of his career and decisive to his nation's cause.

SEVENTEEN

Defending New York, Again

"He was dark-skinned, with black hair, and middling height; there wasn't any waste timber in him; he was our fighting general, and a bloody fellow he was. He didn't care for nothing; he'd ride right in. It was 'Come on, boys'—'t wasn't 'Go, boys.' He was as brave a man as ever lived."
—An old soldier who fought alongside Arnold at Bemis Heights, *Isaac Newton Arnold*, p. 29.

The chilly nights and spreading splashes of gold and red leaves warned Gentleman Johnny that New York's brief summer was coming to an end, and with it his chances of success. Like Carleton before him, he must conquer or retreat. But how could he return to Canada without a battle? Writing gloomily to Lord Germain on August 20 from his camp near Saratoga he listed the many reasons the campaign was now likely to fail. "When I wrote more confidently," he explained, "I little foresaw that I was to be left to pursue my way through such a tract of country and hosts of forces, without any co-operation from New York." In truth when he left Canada he felt relatively confident he could manage without such help, but now his troops were dwindling, his supplies likewise. He was marooned with little sense of where the other British armies were. Two messengers sent to Howe had been captured on their journey and hanged. He wrote Germain that Howe's messengers to him had doubtless met the same painful end.[1] As his expedition marched farther and farther south, he now realized what ought to have been obvious from the start, that manning the forts he captured "would fall to my share alone." He was particularly concerned with holding Ticonderoga: "A dangerous experiment would it be to leave that post in weakness, and too heavy a drain it is upon the life-blood of my force to give it due strength."[2] Yet the fortress was essential to secure a line of retreat. And retreat might be necessary.

He also had new respect for the locals. Those living in the Hampshire Grants, present day Vermont whom he judged "the most active and most rebellious race of the continent," were threatening "like a gathering storm upon my left."[3] As for the loyalists who, he had been assured, would join his troops in large numbers, few were willing, and with good reason he doubted the sincerity of those who did. Instead he was marooned in hostile country where most people favored the Congress "in principle and in zeal." Wherever he moved, he complained, within twenty-four hours the militia mobilized to oppose him, then returned to their farms. Further, Schuyler's scorched-earth policies had removed cattle and destroyed crops so successfully that he was constantly short of supplies. Burgoyne had little respect for General Gates, but he reckoned the "old midwife," had a larger army than his and "as many militia as he pleases."[4]

Burgoyne concluded his letter defensively: "I submit my actions to the breast of the King, and the candid judgment of my profession, when all the motives become public, and I rest in the confidence that, whatever decision may be passed upon my conduct, my good intent will not be questioned."[5]

How could Germain read this letter other than as his general's excuse for impending failure? Still, Burgoyne had glossed over one bit of very bad news that contributed to his morose mood, the costly failure of his expedition to seize the enemy supply depot at Bennington, Vermont, insisting it had "little effect upon the strength or spirits of the army." That was not quite true.

On Arnold's return to northern army headquarters at Stillwater, flushed with joy at the bloodless victory at Fort Stanwix, he immediately focused on the larger threat to New York, Burgoyne's army. He respected Schuyler and supported him, yet he had worked amicably enough with Gates a year ago as he prepared to challenge the British fleet on Lake Champlain and was ready to serve him again. Despite his own experience clashing with bitter personal enemies, Arnold was too preoccupied, perhaps too naïve, to appreciate the intense animosity Gates felt for Schuyler and for Arnold's other patron, George Washington. Gates was expecting exclusive loyalty, not respect for his competitors. Arnold quickly found himself on the wrong side of his new commanding officer, whose passionate resentment would drive Arnold into disobedience and nearly cost the American cause its biggest victory.

The immediate cause of friction between them was Arnold's appointment of additional staff. When Schuyler lost his command the young men of his staff lost their posts. Certainly Gates was unlikely to accommodate them. As a favor to Schuyler, Arnold agreed to add the capable and well-connected young men to his personal staff. Matthew Clarkson, then eighteen, from a New York mercantile family close to the Schuylers, already served Arnold as his aide-de-camp.[6] Now he added nineteen-year-old Major Henry Brockholst Livingston, son of New Jersey's governor, and twenty-four-year-old Lieutenant Colonel Richard Varick, Schuyler's military secretary.[7] Gates expressed his displeasure at these additions but Arnold did not dismiss them, angering Gates. Their two staffs were so personally hostile they got into brawls. Their vicious gossip stoked Gates's resentment of Arnold. On such petty grievances great events ride.

Arnold, like Burgoyne, was alarmed that his correspondence seemed to have been intercepted. Since returning from Fort Stanwix he had written twice to his friend, John Lamb, but learned his letters had never arrived. "I am convinced," he wrote Lamb, "by some villainy in the post riders, or negligence in those who carry letters; one-half of those directed to me, and those which I send, never come to hand. I have received but three letters, out of seven, wrote me by my sister."[8] Apart from Hannah's letters with news of home, she had sent two horses to Peekskill for Arnold. Neither arrived. Although a well-bred horse was a more tempting target in the chaos of war than a letter, someone may have been keen to get his correspondence. At this dangerous time, facing what might be his last battle, he was cut off from news and support from home and friends. He wrote Lamb that September of the military situation and plans predicting: "This month, I believe, will be very important in the annals of America."

Bad as the hand Burgoyne was dealt, he made matters worse by poor decisions. The delay in reaching Fort Edward from Skenesborough, due to taking the advice of Major Skene, a loyalist, was one. Instead of using the water route south through Lake George to transport his supplies, bateaux, and artillery, he ordered his men to cut a road through rugged terrain and thick forest. The speed and skill with which his army managed the twenty-mile construction was astonishing. In twenty days the troops built over forty bridges, some very lengthy. It was a superb effort but it delayed his progress and exhausted his men and supplies. That was the reason he launched the raid on Bennington's supply depot some thirty miles southeast of Fort Edward. Burgoyne was badly in need of supplies. When his army crossed the Hudson all the supplies except for the basic essentials were left behind.[9]

Mistake two was his choice of the commander and troops to launch the surprise attack on Bennington. He could only spare five hundred men, but their success might have been greater had they not been led by Colonel Baum, a German officer who, as one of the members of the expedition sarcastically put it, "qualified for marching through a country of mixed friends and foes by speaking no English."[10] Baum's expedition comprised 50 British sharpshooters, 100 German grenadiers and light infantry, and a mix of 300 loyalists, Canadians, and Indians, 170 German dragoons hoping to find horses, and, oddly for a surprise raid, a German band. Still, the officers were experienced, many having served in the French and Indian war. The Indians led the column.

The expedition came as no surprise to residents. Two outstanding local officers, John Stark and Seth Warner, rushed to Bennington's defense. John Stark was an officer in Arnold's mold and, maybe for that reason, had experienced some of the same treatment from Congress. In contrast to Arnold's privileged boyhood on the coast though, Stark was raised in New Hampshire and came from a poorer family. He was at home in the forests of New England. During the French and Indian War Stark had served in Rogers' Rangers, an innovative troop trained in guerrilla-type warfare. When the Revolutionary War broke out he rushed to Cambridge to help. It was Stark who commanded the American troops at Bunker Hill with fortitude and foresight. Like Arnold he was a daring field commander undeterred by the danger from constant fire. Burgoyne, who was present at that battle, described the orderly and defensive retreat Stark led, admitting it was "no flight, it was even covered with bravery and military skill."[11] None of this persuaded Congress to promote him. Indeed, so worried was Congress over officers becoming too popular, popularity probably worked against him. Like Arnold, Stark was passed over when five lower-ranking men were promoted to major general. Instead Congress promoted Benjamin Lincoln, a hefty farmer from a prominent Massachusetts family who had served in his father's regiment but had seen no action. Unlike Arnold, however, Stark resigned his commission and went home, informing Congress, "I am bound in Honor to leave the service, Congress having tho't fit to promote Junr. officers over my head."[12]

With Burgoyne's army threatening his home region, Stark offered to help, but only on condition he report to the New Hampshire legislature, not to the Continental Congress.[13] With that caveat he proceeded to raise some fifteen hundred men in less than a week. He sent one thousand men to Seth Warner, a leader of the Green Mountain Boys, in Manchester. When Schuyler, who was still in command, ordered Stark to put some of his men under the command of now Brigadier General Lincoln, however, he flatly refused. Stark pledged however, he would beat the invader or "before night Molly Stark would be a widow."[14]

Baum made the serious mistake of believing the country people who came to the British claiming to be friends, demanding weapons and assuring him that most of the people in Bennington were loyalists.[15] One of his lieutenants wondered, "How Colonel Baum became so completely duped as to place reliance on these men, I know not." As Baum and his men approached open country they heard musket fire and an advance patrol sent to investigate came rushing back in dismay. "[T]hose whom we had hitherto trusted as friends had only waited till the arrival of their support" to advance. Baum became alarmed at the number of militia he was facing and Burgoyne sent him German reinforcements. Fierce fighting broke out. After an initial skirmish the Americans decided to encircle the British force, but were delayed a day by heavy rain. When the rain stopped heavy firing resumed and the plan was put in place. Stark reported to Gates that the two-hour battle was "the hottest I ever saw in my life. It represented one continued clap of thunder."[16] The British, protected by two breastworks, were forced to retreat, abandoning their field pieces and baggage. Seth Warner's men, fresh to the scene, pursued them through the forests. Fierce fighting continued until dark. The upshot was that instead of

Burgoyne's army capturing desperately needed supplies it was the Americans who captured British supplies—four cannon, hundreds of weapons, drums and about seven hundred prisoners including Baum.[17] Between killed and captured Burgoyne had lost 15–20 percent of his troops.[18]

On September 1 Gates held a war council on Van Schaick Island in the midst of the delta where the Mohawk River empties into the Hudson. Arnold and Gates agreed Burgoyne was heading for Albany. Gates ordered Arnold to Loudon's Ferry on the south bank of the Mohawk River, five miles from where it joined the Hudson, to take command of the brigades of Generals Poor and Learned, and Morgan's Virginia battalion of sharpshooters. On September 9 he put the New York and Connecticut militia under Arnold's command. Yet Gates was still brooding on Arnold's unwillingness to dismiss Schuyler's aides, and a day later in his general orders to the army Gates commanded the three New York militia regiments to report to General Glover's brigade instead. John Glover was a fine commander whose Marblehead seamen had performed yeoman service rescuing Washington's army at Long Island and later conveying it across the ice-choked Delaware. But the coming battle was not a river crossing. When Arnold complained that the sudden change "placed me in the ridiculous light of presuming to give orders I had no right to do, and having them publickly contradicted," Gates pretended it was a mistake, but failed to correct it.[19] Arnold's new aides also suffered ill treatment from Gates and his supporters in Congress. An officer who attacked Varick and tried to stab him was not punished, and when Schuyler had given Livingston the honor of bringing news of the victory at Bennington to Congress, members refused to give Livingston the usual promotion, and had all record of the incident erased from the congressional record. [20]

Gates's approach to warfare was timid and defensive. He was a very competent administrator, but had little actual battlefield experience and little desire to get any. His plan was to confront

Burgoyne's army with a defensive stand at Stillwater, his present headquarters, a low, open area where the Mohawk meets the Hudson. Arnold was uneasy with that choice. Taking with him Thaddeus Kosciuszko, the army's brilliant young Polish engineer, he went searching for a better location. He found it four miles farther north on the west side of the Hudson. Bemis Heights was a bluff overlooking the Hudson. The road Burgoyne had to take to Albany ran alongside the river beneath the Heights. On its other side the Heights was protected by ravines, ridges, and rough ground and flanked by forests. This was the perfect spot to confront the British who preferred fighting in open fields. Gates was typically cautious about the switch, and sent Wilkinson and Udney Hay to survey it. When they found it suitable he went himself, then gave his approval. Although willing to move his headquarters, Gates selected a spot for his new headquarters some distance south of the new breastworks, well behind Bemis Heights. He seemed unconcerned that he would be unable to see the battle from that location. Thirty years before, he and Burgoyne had served in the same regiment.[21] Now their armies were pitted against each other in a battle that would decide the fate of the Revolution.

Thousands of men were immediately sent to prepare the Heights for battle, building redoubts and earthworks, digging trenches, and felling trees for barricades. Another group, led by Colonel Jeduthan Baldwin, built a nine-hundred-foot-long bridge of rafts across the Hudson for bringing supplies and artillery for the army. Breastworks three-quarters of a mile long were erected to protect the troops and the ground near the river and the bridge was fortified.

On September 12 the army took up its position on Bemis Heights. Arnold chose the home of John Neilson, a local farmer, for his headquarters. A day later Burgoyne crossed the Hudson with seven thousand men. Arnold led a scouting party to survey their camp. Two days afterward the fortifications on Bemis Height were complete. Nine thousand American soldiers and militia steeled themselves to confront the British army. Arnold, like many others, wrote his will.

Impatient as always for action, Arnold began sending men out to skirmish and worry the enemy. While all eyes were focused on the coming engagement near Saratoga, General Lincoln, who turned out to be a very competent commander, quietly sent three squads of soldiers to retake Forts Ticonderoga, Anne, and Edward, effectively cutting off Burgoyne's line of retreat.

September 19 dawned cold and damp. Lower-lying areas were blanketed in fog. The two armies were so close they could hear each other's drums. As the fog lifted American pickets could see the British beginning to advance. Gates had given Arnold command of the left wing of the army, an excellent force with Poor's and Learned's men, Morgan's sharpshooters, and light infantry commanded by Dearborn, with some New York and New Hampshire troops and Connecticut militia. The army's right wing, comprised of Glover's, Nixon's, and Paterson's Continentals was to be commanded by General Lincoln. Lincoln was absent at the moment so Gates took charge.

Burgoyne began by sending some loyalists, Canadians, and Indians to take possession of an undefended height overlooking the American army. His main army was to advance in a three-pronged attack: one column led by the German General Friedrich von Riedesel would advance along the river while Burgoyne would lead the center group and General Simon Fraser the wing. Fraser's men were to make a wide arc and together with Burgoyne turn the American flank with their columns meeting up near Freeman's Farm. These three columns were to set off at the same time. Once they were in place three heavy guns would fire signaling the attack was to begin. The coming battle was to focus on Isaac Freeman's modest farm, with his cabin and fifteen acre clearing.

The terrain had been wisely chosen by Arnold and favored the Americans, since Burgoyne's troops had to advance through thick woods and cross two large ravines in sight of the American forces. Despite these advantages Gates intended to take a defensive position. This is what Burgoyne had anticipated. He later wrote Germain that he expected the ever-cautious Gates to "receive the attack in his lines," affording him an opportunity to establish "a position he could have maintained." It was Arnold who altered that strategy.

American lookouts high in the trees were watching British movements. By ten o'clock in the morning the news reached Gates's and Arnold's headquarters that the British were advancing and, as predicted, were struggling with the rugged terrain. They were vulnerable, yet Gates preferred to sit back and wait. Arnold, on the other hand, was eager to attack, and after much pleading got Gates's permission to send Morgan's sharpshooters and Dearborn's light infantry to scout the enemy. Arnold advanced with them to select their positions. Just after noon they spotted the British advance force of Canadians and Indians. Morgan's marksmen, hidden in the trees, couldn't resist firing. Their rifles were more accurate than the Brown Bess smoothbore muskets of the British, and their withering and deadly attack killed or wounded every officer but one in the group, sending the British troops into a panicky retreat. In great excitement Morgan's sharpshooters threw caution aside and pursued the survivors right back into a main force of British infantry who were in the process of bringing up a cannon. Now Morgan's men were being bloodied in their turn. Off they fled leaving Morgan, according to some reports, "alone and almost in tears." Pulling himself together he blew loudly on his signature turkey call and managed to rally his troops. Additional regiments quickly joined them. Despite Gates's insistence on playing defense, the battle became more general. Fighting was intense.

Burgoyne and his column reached Freeman's Farm as Fraser continued trying to turn the American left wing. Arnold led his division into the thick of the fighting, trying to cut Fraser off from Burgoyne. One of Dearborn's soldiers saw Arnold, "riding in front of the lines, his eyes flashing, pointing with his sword to the advancing foe, with a voice that rang clear as a trumpet and electrified the line."[22] Another described how Arnold fell upon the foe "with the fury and impetuosity of a tiger," encouraging his troops "by voice and action."[23] Initially Fraser had greater numbers than Arnold, but Arnold was reinforced and, screened by the woods, emerged to attack Fraser again, trying to break through his lines where he was most vulnerable. Now other units including the troops led by Philips rushed to reinforce Fraser. The noise of guns and artillery was tremendous. "Such an explosion of fire I never had any idea of before," a British officer wrote.[24] "For four hours a constant blaze of fire was kept up." General Glover was convinced "both armies seemed to be determined to conquer or die."[25] Field pieces were taken and retaken, the men "often mingling in a hand to hand wrestle and fight."[26] At this crucial juncture, with victory in the balance, Arnold urged Gates to send more reinforcements, in particular to help Poor's brigade. Gates flatly refused. Desperate, Arnold dashed up to Learned's regiment and asked for three hundred volunteers to assist Poor. Four companies were quickly mustered. Arnold returned to headquarters to plead with Gates for an all-out attack on the British lines. Gates finally sent reinforcements but refused to order his men to be fully engaged.

Night fell. In the growing dark the British nearly fired on a troop of their own German soldiers. The armies drew back leaving the wounded and dead where they lay on the damp ground between the two armies.[27] Gates and the men under his direct command never took the field.

Before dawn on September 21 Burgoyne received a most welcome letter from General Clinton agreeing to lead his army from New York City to attack south of West Point. Believing he was finally to get some relief and that Clinton meant to march north to join him, Burgoyne decided to postpone another assault and wait for relief to come. He urged Clinton to hurry as he could not hold off longer than October 12 before retiring to Ticonderoga for the winter. Not until a British prisoner escaped from the American camp did Burgoyne learn that the Americans had retaken Ticonderoga. While Burgoyne anxiously awaited help from Clinton, Clinton never received Burgoyne's letter urging haste, or Howe's ordering him to take his men 160 miles up the Hudson.[28] Ignorant that these letters had been intercepted, Burgoyne dug in to await relief.

The continuing praise for Arnold's valiant part in the battle in contrast to the little attention given Gates's own role only stoked the commander's jealousy and anger. Gates was not only a timorous and unimaginative leader, he was vindictive and jealous, and now determined to punish Arnold regardless of the impact on the success of their mission. The day after the battle he reverted to his defensive mode. Arnold, as always, was eager to renew the attack and, probably unwisely, wrote Gates in his bluff manner: "The army is becoming vigorous for action." The militia, some one-quarter of the force, were "threatening to go home." Even a fortnight's inaction, he argued, "will, I make no doubt, lessen your Army by sickness and desertion, at least four thousand men, in which time the enemy may be reinforced and make good their retreat."[29] Arnold added, "I have reasons to think that had we improved the 20th of September, it might have ruined the enemy. That is past; let me entreat you to improve the present time." While this may have been sound advice it was not a letter designed to endear Arnold to his commander.

In retaliation his report informing Congress of the battle never even mentioned Arnold. Gates's loyal aide and deputy adjutant general, James Wilkinson, furthered his commander's vendetta against Arnold by writing Arthur St. Clair shortly after the battle that Arnold had remained in camp during the entire action. [30] Still Gates was not satisfied. On September 22 he removed Morgan's corps from Arnold's command. Deeply upset, Arnold burst in on Gates to protest, and a shouting match ensued. Gates claimed he didn't know Arnold was a major general and since General Lincoln was returning as a division commander, Arnold was no longer needed. Arnold returned to his own headquarters where he wrote a stinging letter to Gates laying out the history of his orders that Arnold take command of Morgan's men among other units.[31] As to the recent battle, he reminded Gates that when the enemy was advancing Arnold had followed orders in sending out Morgan's men, eventually needing to send his whole division. "No other troops were engaged that day except Colonel Marshall's regiment of General Paterson's brigade," he added. Nevertheless he had learned that in Gates's report to Congress his troops were merely described as "a detachment from the Army" and in the orders of the day Morgan's corps were said not to belong to any division and ordered to report directly to headquarters. This report was insulting to him and to the men of his division. "I mention these matters as I wish justice due to the division, as well as particular regiments or persons."[32] Gates failed to take his advice, behaving toward him with "the greatest coolness at headquarters" where he was "often treated in such a manner as must mortify a person with less pride than I have and in my station in the Army." Gates had now told him that once Lincoln returned, "I should have no command of a division, that you thought me of little consequence to the Army and that you would with all your heart give me a pass to leave it whenever I thought proper." Since Lincoln had arrived Arnold asked for a pass to join Washington where he "may possibly have it in my power to serve my country, though I am thought of no consequence in this department." Gates refused instead, sending Arnold an unsealed note addressed to John Hancock granting him permission to report to Congress where Gates had strong support.

Arnold's aide, Henry Brockholst Livingston, wrote Schuyler in desperation that Arnold was to leave the army "at this important crisis."[33] Arnold was, he argued, "the life and soul of the troops. Believe me, Sir, to him and to him alone is due the honor of our late victory. . . He enjoys the confidence and affection of officers and soldiers. They would, to a man, follow him to conquer or death. His absence will dishearten them to such a degree as to render them of but little service." He explained that Arnold had received dismissive treatment from Gates but "has pocketed many insults for the sake of his country. Which a man of less pride would have resented." Livingston attributed Gates's hostility to "simply this—Arnold is your friend." What Schuyler's staunch friend expected him to do is unclear, but his description of the dismay the troops felt about Arnold's impending departure was not exaggerated. A petition, signed by every officer except Gates and Lincoln, was presented to Arnold, pleading with him to stay. Moved and keenly aware that a British attack was expected at any time, Arnold agreed to remain. It was unclear what his role would be. Gates still refused to recognize Arnold's status and denied him any command. So Arnold remained, braced for what must be the pivotal British attack, without any command but with the hopes and deep respect of the officers and men who were depending upon him to lead them.

EIGHTEEN

The Fatal Blow

Confined to his tent by General Gates, left without a command while the very ground was shaking from the deafening pounding of the great guns, the air filled with the acrid smoke and cries of battle, Arnold could tolerate no more. Mounting his powerful, dark horse he dashed toward the battlefield shouting to his aides, "No man shall keep me in my tent to-day. If I am without command, I will fight in the ranks; but the soldiers, God bless them, will follow my lead. Come on, victory or death!"[1] He galloped straight into the thickest of the fighting, pursued by Major John Armstrong, who Gates had ordered to bring him back. But Arnold was faster. Catching up with the rear of Learned's brigade, he asked the men who their officer was. A soldier shouted, "Colonel Latimer's, Sir." Arnold was delighted: "My old Norwich and New London friends. God bless you! I am glad to see you. Now come on, boys; if the day is long enough, we'll have them all

216

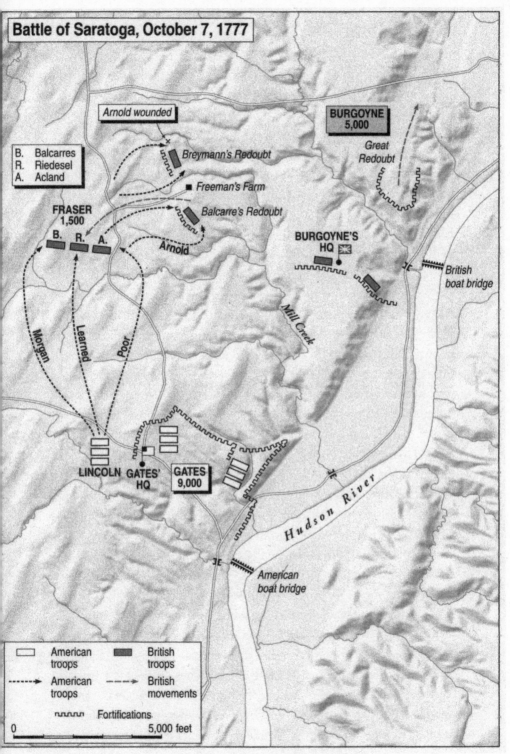

Battle of Saratoga, October 7, 1777

B. Balcarres
R. Riedesel
A. Acland

Arnold wounded

Breymann's Redoubt

Freeman's Farm

Balcarre's Redoubt

FRASER
1,500

B. R. A.

Arnold

BURGOYNE
5,000

Great
Redoubt

BURGOYNE'S
HQ

British
boat bridge

Morgan

Learned

Poor

Mill Creek

LINCOLN

GATES'
HQ

GATES
9,000

Hudson River

American
boat bridge

American
troops

British
troops

American
troops

British
movements

Fortifications

0   5,000 feet

The Battle of Saratoga, October 7, 1777.

in hell before night."[2] A cheer went up as he put himself at their head, galloping back and forth on his splendid horse, brandishing his sword over his head.

Until one o'clock that afternoon of October 7 there had been an uneasy quiet as the American army awaited the next British attack. Gates's resentment of Arnold had been festering since the first fierce battle against Burgoyne eighteen days earlier. Arnold had been the hero, the fighting general. As one captain remembered: "Nothing could exceed the bravery of Arnold on this day, he seemed the very genius of war. Infuriated by the conflict and maddened by Gates's refusal to send reinforcements, which he repeatedly called for, and knowing he was meeting the brunt of the battle, he seemed inspired with the glory of a demon."[3] How to understand what drove Arnold's fearless and brilliant leadership, his infectious spirit that carried men with him, forgetful of their own safety, straight into the guns of the enemy? His was a rare talent especially when combined, as it was, with true military genius, qualities Arnold possessed and Gates did not. And Gates, the cautious, ambitious administrator, knew it. Beyond this is the larger question, which was what persuaded Arnold to remain in camp facing such humiliating conditions? Honor demanded he leave for Washington's army or resign his commission and return home to family and business. Scores of officers had done just that with less provocation. Had he been as self-serving or prickly as he was accused of, that is what he would have done. Instead the only explanation is that he put the cause ahead of personal honor, ahead of his life.

Around one o'clock they heard two signal guns from the British camp two miles away. The British were on the move.[4] Arnold and other officers were dining with Gates as their troops "beat to arms," the entire army shouldering their weapons. Lieutenant Colonel John Brooks remembered that one of the dishes on the table was an ox's heart.[5] They could now hear the firing of their pickets. Arnold asked Gates's permission to see what was happening. Gates bluntly snapped that he did not trust Arnold. But when Arnold promised not to commit the army unless the advance troops needed support, Gates agreed, although sending Lincoln to accompany him. They returned with the report that the British were advancing in three columns as in the previous battle. Gates ordered Morgan and Dearborn's units forward to try to outflank them. Arnold urged him to commit a much stronger force. Gates, always favoring defense, refused, curtly telling Arnold, "I have nothing for you to do, you have no business here."[6] However, when Lincoln agreed with Arnold, Gates ordered Learned's and Nixon's brigades into action. Arnold set off to see what was happening but Gates ordered him to return to his quarters and remain there. And there he stayed, increasingly agitated as the sounds of battle grew. Chafing under Gates's humiliating treatment since the last battle, Arnold had only agreed to remain in camp, without command, for the sake of the men and the cause. But there was no point remaining if he sat in his tent while the crucial battle was raging. Gates, for his part, was quite happy to stay in his own tent while his army clashed with Burgoyne's British in a fierce battle for American independence. Wilkinson, a Gates partisan, wrote that rather than focusing on winning a crucial victory for that cause Gates actually spent the time in his tent trying to persuade Burgoyne's wounded aide, Sir Francis Clarke, of the merits of the Revolution.[7] When an aide dashed into Gates's tent for orders during the battle, he found the distracted general upset that Sir Francis continued to disagree with him.[8]

Burgoyne had delayed any further assault on the American lines as long as he had hopes that Clinton would at least send a detachment from New York City to create a diversion on the Hudson. He knew Howe had set sail for Pennsylvania leaving Clinton, as that general stressed, with a reduced force to hold New York City. Clinton, like Gates, was a cautious general, referring to himself as "a shy bitch."[9] The news that Clinton had received reinforcements at last, sent in a message tucked into a silver bullet, never reached Burgoyne. Clinton's messenger, Daniel Taylor, was spotted swallowing something just as he was captured. His captors forced him to vomit up the bullet.[10] Clinton's message for once had been optimistic: "Nous y voici and nothing now between us but Gates. I sincerely hope this little success of ours will facilitate your operation."[11] Clinton closed with his hearty wish for Burgoyne's success. On October 3 Clinton had taken three thousand men up the Hudson seizing an undermanned Fort Montgomery and overwhelming the desperate garrison at Fort Clinton. After those losses Fort Constitution was abandoned. But it was all too late. Even this small diversion came to a halt when Howe asked Clinton for reinforcements. Clinton wrote Burgoyne on October 6 that he thought "it impossible General Burgoyne could really suppose Sir Henry Clinton had any idea of penetrating to Albany with the small force he mentioned to him in his letter."[12] Clinton abruptly abandoned the forts he had just taken and returned to New York City leaving Burgoyne alone to carry out his mission or extricate his army.

Apart from Clinton's military support Burgoyne's other hope, actually expectation, was that loyalists would rise in force to assist him. When questioned by Parliament on his return to England, Burgoyne challenged his examiners:

> Would the Tories have risen? Why did they not rise round Albany and below it, at the time they found Mr. Gates army increasing . . . Why did they not rise in that populous and, as supposed, well-affected district, the German Flats, at the time St. Leger was before Fort Stanwix? . . . A critical insurrection from any one point of the compass within distance to create a diversion, would probably have secured the success of the campaign.[13]

Good questions.

On October 7 Burgoyne decided to make one final effort to turn the American army's left wing and move south to Albany, daring to take only fifteen hundred men from the protection of the camp despite facing a far larger army. He started in the late morning to permit any retreat to be made under cover of darkness. Burgoyne divided his troops into three groups with the Germans in the center, the British under Philips and himself respectively, on either side. All were focused on the American left wing. He also sent a small group of provincials and Indians to sneak through the woods and attack the rear of the American force. Gates split his troops in three directions, with Morgan and Dearborn to the left, Learned to the center, and Poor to the right. Instead of surprising the American flank as Burgoyne had hoped, he found Morgan's men attacking his own left, and was soon confronted by some four thousand of the enemy.

Poor's brigade, first on the scene, took up a position in the woods and were met with cannon fire. Major Acland, the British officer facing them, followed the artillery barrage with a series of gun volleys, then ordered his men to fix bayonets "and charge the damned rebels."[14] Poor's men under Colonel Joseph Cilley also fixed bayonets and charged, sending Acland's grenadiers retreating. Cannon were fought over, taken, and retaken. At one point Colonel Cilley leaped on a captured cannon waving his sword, and dedicating the gun to "the patriot cause," turned it on the enemy.[15] In the intense fighting the Americans forced Burgoyne's right wing under Fraser to pull back.

The fighting became increasingly fierce as men retreated and attacked, each side moving to take advantage of an opening. The Americans had a huge numerical advantage as thousands of militia had rushed in to help. On the other hand the British had the advantage of experienced professional troops, while only America's Continentals were as tested.

Burgoyne's provincials and Indians managed to get to the American rear and, helped by grenadiers, drove the Americans back to their lines. But the Americans rallied, and with help from

Morgan's men drove the British center back. And in the midst of it all was Arnold, commanding and coordinating the assault wherever he saw an opening; ordering Learned's men to the attack, some against a British redoubt, the rest on the front. He then dashed to the left ordering some of Wesson, Livingston, and Morgan's troops to combine in a general assault. When American lines gave way Arnold rallied the men, riding to wherever there was a need for direction. When he noticed how vital General Fraser was to the British troops attacking the American flank, he pointed that out to Morgan. It was not chivalrous to aim at Fraser, but that officer's death, he stressed, was critical to British morale and to American victory. Morgan promptly sent some of his sharpshooters forward into a group of trees. They took aim and within five minutes Fraser's horse was hit twice. One of Fraser's aides, worried that Fraser was being marked, suggested, "might it not be prudent for him to retire from this place?"[16] Fraser, the dedicated officer, responded, "My duty forbids me to fly from danger." Immediately afterward he was shot. Arnold was right though. Seeing him fall the British line collapsed in disorder. Burgoyne was also a target of Morgan's men who managed to hit his hat and coat but not the man.

Burgoyne understood that despite their fierce efforts his men could not prevail, and trying to save his fortified lines sent an order for his artillery to pull back. This was accomplished although six cannon had to be abandoned since all the men and horses attached to them had been shot. The British troops withdrew inside their entrenchments.[17] "Had Gates only been in command of the Americans that day, the British military historian J. W. Forestcue judged, "the combat might have ended at that moment; but Benedict Arnold, with true military instinct, seized the opportunity to order a general attack upon the British entrenchments."[18] Of course Gates was officially in command, but he was not commanding, Arnold was. It is surely one of the rare if only times when a major battle was coordinated and commanded by an officer on the field without authority, indeed against the wishes of a commanding officer who never saw the battlefield. It is a testimony to the men's respect, actually love, for Arnold that they followed his orders and fought fiercely and successfully at his direction.

At the head of parts of Glover's and Patterson's brigades, Arnold led an assault on the British works being held by light infantry under Earl Balcarras.[19] A first attack on Balcarras's line was beaten back but a second, with bayonets fixed, drove the British light infantry from their barricade. The Americans attempted to force their way into the British camp but were repulsed.

Leading Brooks's regiment Arnold attacked the German breastworks and the Breymann Redoubt. Constantly aware of the shifting logistics, even in the heat of battle, Arnold now spotted the sally port where the British lines opened up for any needed retreat. It was a critical weak spot in the enemy line and Arnold, as always heedless of his personal safety, led his men straight at it. The terrified Germans facing them fled, firing a final volley as they went. One bullet hit Arnold's great dark horse, killing him. The animal fell, pinning Arnold. Now a musket ball hit Arnold, shattering his leg bone just above the knee, the same leg he had injured in the assault on Quebec. John Redman, an American private who saw Arnold fall, rushed to bayonet the German soldier who had shot him. But Arnold shouted to Redman from the ground where he lay helpless and in excruciating pain, "Don't hurt him, he did but his duty; he is a fine fellow!"[20] As he fell Arnold shouted to his men, "Rush on, my brave boys, rush on!"[21] And they did, streaming over the British redoubt.

The British had fought well. Their officers had distinguished themselves. Two rifle balls had gone through Burgoyne's clothes but the general was unharmed. Sir Francis Clarke, who Gates could not convince of the virtue of American independence, died some hours later on Gates's bed. Many other British officers were dead or wounded. British Lieutenant William Digby's own captain and sincere friend, Wight of the 53rd Grenadiers, was shot in the bowels early in the action and lay wounded and helpless between the two battling armies until the next day when he was brought into the American camp.[22] After Colonel Breymann was killed commanding the German Grenadiers and light infantry, his men continued to fight on until they were finally defeated as dark brought the fighting to an end.

Fraser though gravely wounded lived until the following day, but without hope for his survival. Shortly before he died he asked that he be buried at six o'clock in the evening in a redoubt they had built on a hill near the battlefield.[23] As the sun was setting on October 8 his body was carried to the hill by the grenadiers of his division, followed by Burgoyne and the staff officers. The procession was spotted by the Americans, who in the dim light simply saw soldiers moving. They aimed their artillery at the little assembly. The chaplain continued to intone the final ritual, "Dust to dust," as the dust of the bombardment burst around him.

As the evening of October 7 approached, Burgoyne realized he had no option but to retreat. With the enemy positioned on his right flank and his army badly mauled their position was untenable. Under cover of night, as the American army had done on so many occasions, the British forces withdrew, hauling their cannon and baggage to heights closer to the river. "It was done with silence," William Digby wrote, "and fires were kept lighted to cause them not to suspect we had retired from our works where it was impossible for us to remain."[24] Ebenezer Mattoon, a Continental officer writing General Schuyler, focused not on his army's achievement but on the horror he felt as darkness covered the living and dead: "The gloom of the night, the groans and shrieks of the wounded and dying, and the horrors of the whole scene baffle all description."[25]

Arnold was carried from the field bleeding and helpless. He waved away the officers who hurried to help him. When Captain Dearborn asked where he was hit he replied, "In the same leg. I wish it had been my heart."[26] Armstrong now caught up with Arnold intent on taking him back to headquarters. That did not happen. The men of Asa Bray's Connecticut militia company, caring for one of their own, gently placed Arnold on a litter and carried him to the field hospital. Gates never set foot on the field during the battle that day, nor did Lincoln, the second in command.

NINETEEN

The Wages of Victory

Arnold spent three months in the hospital in Albany before he was finally able to sit up in bed.[1] It was another month before he was strong enough to begin the long, exhausting journey home to New Haven, carried in a litter to his carriage. When only a day's journey from New Haven he stopped for some weeks to convalesce at the home of his old friend, Comfort Sage, in Middletown, Connecticut. The two men discussed the business options still available for the shipping trade in seas patrolled by the British navy, and Arnold began learning to walk with crutches. As he was slowly regaining his strength, his spectacular victory at Saratoga was roiling the American Congress and the courts of Europe. Thanks to the surrender of Burgoyne's army in October while the wounded hero of the battle convalesced, the fortunes of the American cause changed dramatically.

The fates of three nations were at stake as France and Britain competed to woo the American Congress. France had been secretly sending supplies to the Americans. Now convinced the Americans had a chance of winning, her government began supporting them openly. It was the perfect opportunity for the French, still smarting from Britain's capture of Canada, to humiliate the British. Uncoupling Britain's American colonies would be sweet revenge and afford a chance to attack other British possessions. Britain, on the other hand, was anxious that no agreement be concluded between her rebellious colonists and her old enemy. An alliance between them would mean war with France not only in North America but, even worse, in the English Channel itself, and everywhere across the world where the two countries had colonial territories and ambitions. With the surrender of the British army at Saratoga that terrible possibility seemed likely. The Continental Congress, for its part, was anxious for France's help but fearful of being tied to a powerful ally that would manipulate the fledgling states and draw them into European wars. Worries all around.

As 1778 began events moved quickly. On February 6, while Arnold and his doctors were awaiting their own merciful separation, representatives of the French government and the Continental Congress, meeting in Paris, signed two treaties. One focused on trade, putting the two countries on a most-favored-nation status. In the second, France recognized the independence of America and formed a military alliance. Louis XVI also renounced French territorial ambitions in North America, including Canada, and in return was promised a free hand attacking the rich British possessions in the Caribbean. The sugar and rum they produced were more valuable than any products from their other colonies. Both signatories agreed not to sign any peace treaty with Britain without mutual agreement. Whether either government would adhere scrupulously to these terms was unclear. What was clear was that the Americans had a powerful foreign ally and while they were wary of being exploited by the

French, they were delighted to have their considerable help and recognition.

Washington learned of the treaties in April with tears of joy.[2] "It has pleased the Almighty ruler of the universe," he informed his troops, "propitiously to defend the cause of the united American States and finally, by raising us up a powerful friend among the princes of the earth, to establish our liberty and independence upon lasting foundations. . . ."[3] War, like politics, makes strange bedfellows. For years the colonies had suffered savage raids by French troops and their Indian allies swooping down from Canada attacking isolated villages on the frontiers and towns along the Atlantic coast, burning homes and slaughtering or carrying off men, women, and children. Terrorizing the settlers was French policy. In particular, New Englanders abhorred the dishonorable betrayal of the hapless British soldiers and civilians during the French and Indian War when Fort William Henry surrendered to the French in 1757. The English soldiers and American civilians had been promised safe passage by the French commander but as they marched out, France's Indian allies butchered every man, woman, and child they could lay hands on. That particular atrocity took place during Arnold's first military service. In addition, the liberty-loving colonists had an English sense of freedom, and grew up mocking the French for their slavish subordination to an absolute monarch supported by a large, professional army. Now, ironically, George III was the tyrant, Louis XVI their liberator.

At the beginning of May Congress ratified the treaties with France, and on May 6 Washington and his army celebrated. The men mustered at nine o'clock in the morning to hear the treaties read. Thirteen cannon were then fired, their boom and smoke followed by the firing of muskets in sequence. The soldiers gave three cheers, "Long Live the King of France." Each man was given a gill of rum for the occasion. If Washington had reservations about the collaboration, they were not apparent. John Laurens, son of the president of the Congress, reported that the commander "wore a countenance of uncommon delight."[4] The French officers, on the other hand, would be singularly unimpressed with their first sight of Washington's Continentals and thought even less of state militiamen.

John Adams had been fretting about an alliance with France as early as 1775.[5] He hoped any negotiations would be conducted with "great caution," fearful of "any alliance with her which should entangle us in any future wars in Europe." As for the broader strategy, he added, "it never could be our interest to unite with France in the destruction of England, or in any measures to brake her [England's] spirit or reduce her to a situation in which she could not support her independence."[6] Any alliance with either Britain or France, he judged, would make the states "too subordinate and dependent on the nation." Foreign powers "should find means to corrupt our people, to influence our councils, and in fine we should be little better than puppets danced on the wires of the cabinets of Europe."[7] During the negotiations with France three years later Adams reckoned the French foreign minister was prepared to keep "his hand under our chin to prevent us from drowning, but not to lift our heads out of water." [8]

The British were in a panic over the surrender at Saratoga and the pending alliance between the Congress and France. "[F]rom the moment when the news of Saratoga arrived," J. W. Fortescue wrote, "all thinking Englishmen were filled with apprehension for its possible influence on the policy of France."[9] In December the British port cities of Manchester, Liverpool, Edinburgh, Glasgow, and Aberdeen began raising battalions of eleven hundred men at their own expense to defend them from the French.[10] Some Scots nobles also offered to raise regiments. The British Cabinet and Parliament were deeply divided about what to do next, but the Cabinet was well aware of American negotiations with the French, as Benjamin Franklin's secretary was a British agent. On February 17, just before the final treaties between France and America were announced, Lord North submitted a proposal to Parliament for a royal commission to negotiate a peace treaty with Congress. It was dubbed the Carlisle Commission for Frederick Earl of Carlisle, one of its three members. The commission would be empowered to offer concessions that met the original American complaints. The Coercive Acts and all revenue acts passed since 1763 were to be repealed, any claims from war damage would be forgiven. No standing army would be placed in the colonies in time of peace; no change would be make in any colonial charter except at the request of the assembly of the colony concerned; judges would be appointed during good behavior as they were in England; and Parliament would consider giving the colonies representation in the British parliament or, if Americans preferred, would recognize the American Congress. What the commission was not to offer was independence.

Edmund Burke had proposed these concessions two years earlier when they might have been accepted.[11] Oddly misreading the Americans, many British leaders were convinced that the proposed terms would be happily accepted and peace restored. Lord Germain, Secretary of State for America, wrote Sir Henry Clinton on March 8 that his information about American opinion was that "the generality of the people desire nothing more than a full security for the enjoyment of all their rights and liberties under the British Constitution." There could be no doubt, Germain added, "that the generous terms now held out to them will be gladly embraced."[12] Should the Congress fail to accept these generous terms and "the horrors and devastations of war should continue," the commissioners were to warn, "we call God and the world to witness that the evils which must follow are not imputed to Great Britain, and we cannot without the most real sorrow anticipate the prospect of calamities which we feel the most ardent desire to prevent."[13]

After three years of brutal warfare, after a major British defeat and with an alliance with France, these concessions were too little too late. Nevertheless, after Britain had expended so much blood and treasure, many members of Parliament felt the terms were much too generous. To Horace Walpole, "The Astonishment of a great part of the House at such extensive offers, precluded all expression."[14] Lord Chatham, affectionately known as the "Great Commoner," though in failing health, made a desperate appeal to the House of Lords against the commission: "Shall we tarnish the luster of this nation by an ignominious surrender of its rights and fairest possessions? Shall the great kingdom, that has survived whole and entire the Danish depredations, the Scottish inroads, and the Norman conquest, that has stood the threatened invasion of the Spanish Armada, now fall prostrate before the House of Bourbon?" "If we must fall," he concluded, "let us fall like men."[15] Despite all these misgivings and the treaties Americans had already concluded with the French, the Carlisle Commission set sail for the New World hoping for a peace agreement.

In addition to the agreed-upon concessions the commissioners were secretly authorized to offer bribes to American leaders starting with Washington. Sir John Dalrymple, a shrewd observer, compared Washington to George Monk, the parliamentarian general who changed sides to restore Charles II to the English throne in 1660.[16] Dalrymple suggested the ministers or the king himself should write to Washington, "to remind him of the similarity between his situation and Monk's, desiring him to ask terms for America fair and just, and they should be granted, and that the terms for himself should be the dukedom like Monk received and an appropriate revenue to give dignity to the man who generously gave up his own power to save his country." This popular view of Monk was in Arnold's mind when he, like Monk, became disillusioned with the cause he had supported.

On March 17 Britain declared war on France. In April the British fleet refrained from challenging a French fleet under the Comte d'Estaing as it set sail for North America, for fear of weakening the British vessels in the English Channel. France, with an army far stronger than its navy, was actually considering landing forty thousand men on the British Isles but decided against it.

The Carlisle Commission's mission was undercut by the British government itself when, without notifying the commissioners, it ordered General Clinton to send eight thousand troops, one third of his men, to the Caribbean and Florida and to evacuate Philadelphia. The commissioners reached Philadelphia just as the British army was withdrawing. They were shocked and angry. Without that military presence, the commission lost much of its credibility. There was little chance they could accomplish their mission in any case. Washington vehemently urged delegates to Congress to oppose the British terms. He branded the commissioners' offers and powers a "malignant influence."[17] They were authorized to deal with any assembly or person or persons, to grant pardons and set up royal government in any agreeable colony. This was clearly intended to undermine American unity should Congress fail to accept their terms. "Nothing short of independence," Washington wrote, "can possibly do. A peace on any other terms would, if I may be allowed the expression, be a peace of war."

Washington needn't have worried. Congress agreed with him completely. They had just concluded an alliance with France recognizing their independence. Congress refused to meet with the Carlisle commissioners unless they agreed to independence first. And of course the commission was not authorized to grant that fundamental concession. Given the standoff, the commissioners never met with Congress at all, but lingered in New York until the end of 1778, hoping some change in the military situation might persuade Congress to deal with them. Also hoping, no doubt, that some leading American politician or general might be persuaded and bribed to support the British cause.

In addition to their proposal the commissioners had sent a packet of private letters for individuals with English friends. One went to Joseph Reed, president of the Pennsylvania executive council and a member of Congress. Washington passed these letters on to Congress, writing Henry Laurens that if any of them were addressed to persons Laurens did not know, "it may not be improper to open them."[18] George Johnstone, one of the three commissioners and a former governor of West Florida, wrote Laurens that if Congress failed to meet with the commissioners, "I shall hope from private friendship that I may be permitted to see the country and the worthy characters she has exhibited to the world."[19] The opportunity these visits would give him to stir disaffection was obvious. Johnstone's letter and Laurens's planned answer were both published in the *Pennsylvania Gazette*. Laurens's reply was blunt: "Until the basis of mutual confidence shall be established I believe, Sir, neither former friendship nor any other consideration can influence Congress to consent that even Governor Johnstone, a gentleman who has been so deservedly esteemed by America, shall see the country."[20] The problem of disaffection was serious. This was, after all, a civil war and Congress knew it.

Congress was delighted with the alliance but worried about the loyalty of its military. Three days before the treaties were concluded, the Continental Congress resolved that every military officer and all those holding government office take a loyalty oath. Congress had drawn up a loyalty oath after declaring independence in 1776. The signatory had to swear that the United States were "free, independent and sovereign states, and declare that the people thereof owe no allegiance or obedience to George the Third, King of Great-Britain," and would "support, maintain and defend the said United States against the said king George the third and his heirs and successors, and his and their abettors, assistants and adherents, and will serve the said United States in the office of which I now hold, with fidelity, according to the best of my skill and understanding. So help me God."[21] The new oath was similar, adding after mention of King George the additional phrase, "I renounce, refuse and abjure any allegiance or obedience to him."[22]

The timing of this oath for army and navy officers and civil servants three years after war had started may have been prompted by the pending alliance with France and the new pressure from

Britain to reconcile their differences. Congress was, as always, fearful of its own military and now, apart from the blandishments of foreign powers, had good reason to be. It was a bitter time for the woefully neglected army barely surviving at Valley Forge that winter. Washington put off asking his officers to take the oath from February until early May. As he confessed to Henry Laurens on May 1, "In compliance with the request of Congress I shall call upon the officers of the Army to take the Oath of Allegiance and Abjuration. This I should have done, as soon as the Resolution was passed, had it not been for the state of the Army at that time, and that there were some strong reasons which made it expedient to defer the matter."[23] That winter at Valley Forge was so miserable and with the army increasingly mutinous, he feared many officers would refuse to sign. Once the French alliance was publicly announced with its promise of proper support and funding, men would be more willing to take the oath. It had to be taken before the end of May. Arnold was fit enough to return to duty shortly before that deadline.

There were other concerns about the French alliance that troubled Americans. General John Lamb, in his memoir, referred to the "great diversity of opinion" in the army about the use of French land forces.[24] Major Samuel Shaw, aide to General Knox, worried:

> How will it sound in history that the United States of America, could not, or rather, would not, make an exertion, when the means were amply in their power, which might at once rid them of their enemies, and put them in possession of that liberty, and safety, for which we have been so long contending? By Heaven! if our rulers had any modesty, they would blush at the idea of calling in foreign aid! 'Tis really abominable, that we should send to France *for soldiers*, when there are so many sons of America idle. Such a step ought not (had these great men any sensibility) to have been taken, until the strength of

ABOVE: The Arnold home, New Haven, Connecticut, built in 1771. BELOW: Colonel Arnold, who commanded the provincial troops against Quebec. *Courtesy of the New-York Historical Society.*

MAJ. GEN. BENEDICT ARNOLD.

ABOVE: Benedict Arnold, now a Major General. *Courtesy of the New-York Historical Society.* BELOW: Benedict Arnold's Oath of Allegiance, May 1778. *Courtesy of Record Group 93, War Department Collection of Revolutionary War Records; National Archives and Records Administration, Washington, DC.*

I *Benedict Arnold Major General* do acknowledge the UNITED STATES of AME-RICA to be Free, Independent and Sovereign States, and declare that the people thereof owe no allegiance or obedience to George the Third, King of Great-Britain; and I renounce, refuse and abjure any allegiance or obedience to him; and I do *swear* that I will, to the utmost of my power, support, maintain and defend the said United States against the said King George the Third, his heirs and successors, and his or their abettors, assistants and adherents, and will serve the said United States in the office of *Major General* which I now hold, with fidelity, according to the best of my skill and understanding.

ABOVE: *Major General Horatio Gates,* by Gilbert Stuart. *Courtesy of The Metropolitan Museum of Art.* BELOW: Arnold falls at the Battle of Saratoga. *Courtesy of the New-York Historical Society.*

ABOVE: *Surrender of General Burgoyne to General Horatio Gates at Saratoga* by John Trumbull, October 16, 1777. *Courtesy of Yale University Art Gallery.* BELOW: Mrs. Benedict Arnold (neé Peggy Shippen) and Child. *Courtesy of the Philadelphia History Museum at the Atwater Kent.*

ABOVE: Major John André. *Courtesy of the New York Public Library.* BELOW: *Panoramic view of West Point New York showing American encampments on the Hudson River* by Major Pierre L'Enfant, ca. 1780. *Courtesy of Library of Congress, Rare Book and Special Collections Division, Printed Ephemera Collection.*

ABOVE: Major John André going from the *Vulture* to the shore of Havershaw Bay, 1780. *Courtesy of the New York Public Library.* BELOW: The meeting of Arnold and André. *Courtesy of The New-York Historical Society.*

ABOVE: Arnold tells André to hide plans of West Point in his boot, September 21, 1780. *Courtesy of the New-York Historical Society.* BELOW: Pass found on Major John André. *Courtesy of the New York State Archives.*

ABOVE: *Self Portrait* by Major John André, awaiting execution. BELOW: Parade with figures representing Arnold and the Devil on the streets of Philadelphia, September 30, 1780. *Courtesy of Library of Congress, Rare Book and Special Collections Division, Printed Ephemera Collection.*

the country had been nearly exhausted, and our freedom tottering on the brink of ruin.

Shaw had no problem with getting help from the French navy, "because we can not get one seasonably among ourselves" but added, "do let us unless we are contented to be transmitted to posterity with disgrace, make an exertion of our own strength by land, and not owe our independence entirely to our allies."[25] Support for the treaties prevailed and history has recorded the consequences.

The victory at Saratoga also had serious repercussions for Arnold's commander and supporter, George Washington. Gates had been proclaimed the hero of Saratoga and his supporters in Congress, mainly from New England, were quick to point out how their favorite general had been victorious while Washington had been defeated at Brandywine and Germantown and failed to oust the British from Philadelphia.[26] Washington had sent troops to reinforce the Northern Department against Burgoyne instead. John Adams also saw Washington's popularity as a danger to liberty, writing, "The people of America have been guilty of idolatry in making a man their God." This judgment was circulated anonymously.[27] The solution of this group was to replace Washington with Gates. Washington was aware of their criticism and attempt to reduce his power or replace him. A copy of Adams's comment was sent to Patrick Henry who passed it on to Washington. Further, little more than a month after the battle of Saratoga, Congress reorganized the Board of War to more closely monitor the army. Gates was appointed to head the board, giving him administrative oversight over the daily operations of the army and thus over Washington himself. Another member of the Board of War was Thomas Mifflin, a former aide to Washington and later quartermaster general, who resented Washington's decision to send reinforcements north rather than assaulting the British army in his home city of Philadelphia. As quartermaster general He proved himself woefully incompetent in supplying the army at Mount Vernon, focusing instead on scheming against the commander.[28]

The issue over command of the army came to a head when Washington learned of a letter to Gates from Thomas Conway shortly after the surrender at Saratoga, commending Gates and remarking, "Heaven has been determined to save your Country or a weak General and bad Councellors would have ruined it." Conway, an Irishman connected with the French army, had been commanding a brigade under Washington. He was critical of Washington's leadership at the battle of Germantown but boasted of his own efforts, and wrote Congress requesting a promotion to major general. Conway told members of Congress that in his view while Washington was a perfect gentleman, "or appeared to more advantage at his table, or in the usual intercourse of life . . . his talents for the command of an army . . . they are miserable indeed."[29] Washington, usually politely deferential, vehemently opposed Conway's promotion, explaining to Richard Henry Lee, a Virginia delegate to Congress, that the promotion of Conway would be as "unfortunate a measure as ever was adopted. I may add (and I think with truth) that it will give a fatal blow to the existence of the Army."[30] In Washington's opinion, "General Conway's merit, then, as an Officer and his importance in this Army, exists more in his own imagination, than in reality." Moreover, he argued, that as the youngest brigadier general in the service, Conway "should be put over the heads of all the Eldest? And thereby take Rank, and Command Gentlemen, who but Yesterday, were his Seniors, Gentlemen, who, I will be bold to say . . . are of sound judgment and unquestionable Bravery?" Washington was sure these men would refuse to serve under Conway. He stressed that while his officers were loyal and did not dispute the right of Congress to make promotions, "the service is so difficult, and every necessary so expensive, that almost all our Officers are tired out. Do not, therefore, afford them good pretexts for retiring: No day passes over my head without application for leave to resign." Unfortunately, Lee was one of the congressmen critical of the commander. Washington seemed as tired as his officers, and hinted he might resign: "I have been a Slave to the service: I have undergone more than most Men are aware of, to harmonize so many discordant parts, but it will be impossible for me to be of any further service, if such insuperable difficulties are thrown in my way."[31]

Then on November 8 Washington was informed of Conway's letter praising Gates for his victory and bemoaning the current "weak general." The letter's content was leaked by a drunken James Wilkinson, Gates's adjutant, on his leisurely journey to Congress to report the victory at Saratoga. The day after learning of the comment Washington wrote Conway a terse note citing the insulting paragraph. Gates later feigned innocence and asked Washington's help in "tracing out the Author of the Infidelity which put Extracts from General Conway's Letters to me into your Hands."[32] Wilkinson denied he was the source and Gates accused Alexander Hamilton, Washington's brilliant young aide, of glancing at his personal correspondence when alone in Gates's room on a visit to Albany.[33] Gates even informed Congress that Hamilton had "stealingly copied" his correspondence. At that point Washington informed Gates through Congress that the "Author of the Infidelity" was his own aide, James Wilkinson. Gates may have been upset by the news but Congress was not and made Wilkinson secretary of the Board of War. Conway offered his resignation to Congress but instead Congress passed it on to the new Board of War. Adding insult to injury in December, over Washington's vehement objections, Congress promoted Conway to major general and appointed him to the new post of inspector general in charge of drilling and training the Continental Army. Rather than reporting to Washington, Conway was to report directly to the Board of War, staffed by men hostile to the commander. When Conway appeared at Valley Forge to take up the assignment, Washington treated him so coldly that he stalked off in a huff.

This so-called "Conway Cabal" ended on January 19, 1778, after Washington's officers informed Congress of their complete confidence in him while Gates and Conway refused to provide the controversial letter to Congress. In mid-February Gates wrote Washington assuring him he was not involved in any faction. Congress sent Gates back to the Northern Department in April, where the general hoped to lead an attack on Canada. When that idea was dropped he was ordered west to protect New York's Mohawk Valley. He refused. A benefit of his transfer to New York, however, was to keep Gates and Washington apart, presumably pleasing both men.

While the political and military world Arnold knew was in flux, his zest for life was returning. At Middletown he and Comfort Sage visited taverns to discuss the problems he had seen in the army and explore business options. Arnold's shipping trade was ruined. Hannah had sold his ships and he had advanced his own money to support his troops, leaving little for himself and his family. Congress, typically behind in paying the army, had not paid his salary for over two years. As for investment opportunities, he learned that some men were making good profits outfitting merchant ships as privateers, licensed to seize British vessels as prizes. With the help of Sage he was able to buy a quarter share in a large, captured British transport ship, the ten-gun *General McDougall*. The *McDougall*'s new task as an American privateer would be capturing other British vessels. The Sage and Arnold families were old and steadfast friends. With Arnold only a day's journey from home, Hannah and Arnold's sons must have visited him while he was at Middletown. The reunion, while upsetting, as her dear brother was so badly wounded, was a time of relief for Hannah that he was for the moment out of harm's way, and joy for the boys in seeing their father again.

Feeling more optimistic Arnold decided to renew his unsuccessful courtship of young Betsy DeBlois. He was facing a return to his old home without a wife to love and to share raising his three young sons. With the prospects of profits from his privateer he bought a gold ring with four diamonds for Betsy.[34] He wrote a passionate letter to her on April 8 comparing his "trembling hand" penning the letter to his heart so often "calm and serene amidst the clashing of arms and all the din and horrors of war." As a national hero he obviously hoped the reference would help win the fair lady. He reminded Betsy of his former courtship: "Long have I struggled to efface your heavenly image," but "neither time, absence, misfortunes, nor your cruel indifference have been able to efface the deep impression your charms have made." Arnold asked whether she would now "doom a heart so true, so faithful, to languish in despair?"[35] The young lady and her family, especially her mother, were prepared to do just that, replying coolly that he "solicit no further" for her affections. Politics in addition to the lack of personal attraction may have played a part as Betsy's father had fled to British-controlled Halifax. Still Arnold was not easily put off and solicited again two weeks later, conceding that "the union of hearts" was necessary to happiness and his infatuation was one-sided but explaining that when there is "tender and ardent passion on one side and friendship and esteem on the other," happiness would ultimately result.[36] He even tried writing to her father to ask for her hand, all to no avail.

Arnold finally traveled on to New Haven arriving home on May 1 to a joyous welcome. He had been away a year. For whatever reason, his impatience to be back in action, the excitement that only military activity could bring him, the comparative dullness of New Haven life, he remained only two weeks. On May 21, still hobbling on crutches, he was at Washington's side at Valley Forge. He was not fit enough to lead a field army, but Washington now had another post in mind. In response to the French entry into the war, General Clinton was about to evacuate Philadelphia. The timing seemed perfect. Washington needed an officer to ensure the orderly, peaceful return to American hands of the largest American city, site of the Continental Congress and the executive council of Pennsylvania.

On May 28 he appointed Arnold military governor of Philadelphia. Two days later, on the very last day allotted for taking the new loyalty oath, Arnold swore to "support, maintain, and defend the said United States of America with fidelity, according to the best of my skill and understanding." The new assignment to reconcile residents who had remained while the British were in occupation and those who had fled required tact and diplomacy, not skills the blunt, impetuous Arnold possessed. Moreover, Congress had never been enamored of the man, despite his obvious martial valor, or maybe because of it. Nor did many delegates like his defenders, George Washington and Philip Schuyler. The Pennsylvania state government's Executive Council was dominated by radicals anxious to punish moderates and anyone suspected of British sympathies. Council members were imperious, touchy about their prerogatives, suspicious of military men. It was perhaps the worst assignment Washington could have chosen.

TWENTY

The Eye of the Storm

I nto the hornet's nest Arnold went, into the wreckage of the once fine city of Philadelphia, just abandoned by the British army. When Washington selected Arnold as the military governor of Philadelphia, it seemed the perfect post while Arnold's leg healed. He could not yet ride a horse let alone take the field. But Washington was certainly aware that for all Arnold's genius as a military leader, he was impetuous, impatient, clearly no politician. He lacked Washington's near inexhaustible deference to the sensitivities and procrastination of civilian leaders. Nor had Washington any illusions about what his protégé would face in Philadelphia, the largest city and busiest port in the United States. The state's politics were a volatile tangle. In addition to the raw ideological divisions between loyalists and patriots, the patriots themselves were bitterly divided between radicals and moderates. Although the Pennsylvanians had ultimately agreed to the Declaration of

Independence, there had been considerable debate almost until the final vote in Congress. However tactful Washington was about the city and its people in public, in private his opinion of nearly all Philadelphians was scathing. He reckoned, "Speculation, peculation, and an insatiable thirst for riches seem to have got the better of every other consideration and almost of every order of men."[1]

Arnold's task, as Washington explained it, was delicate. He was to maintain order in Philadelphia after the British army evacuated the city in June, 1778. On May 30 Arnold officially accepted the post, taking the oath of fidelity to the United States at Valley Forge before General Henry Knox. His exact instructions were "to take every prudent step in your power to preserve tranquility and order in the city and give security to individuals of every class and description. Restraining, as far as possible till the restoration of civil government, every species of persecution, insult or abuse, either from the soldiery to the inhabitants or among each other."[2] In the wake of the nine-month-long British occupation this was no easy task. As they prepared to abandon the city and their local supporters, the British had counseled Philadelphia loyalists to seek some accommodation with Congress. This casual abandonment of Americans who assumed the British would protect them was alarming. Washington and the British commander had this in common. Washington also hoped Congress would make some accommodation for the Philadelphia loyalists. He was sorry Congress, not in a forgiving mood, did not offer them some protection when the British left, rather than suffer the loss of "thousands of valuable artisans and their goods."[3] As Washington had predicted, three thousand local loyalists, among them many of the city's most prominent families, terrified of retribution, frantically dragged what goods they could to the departing British fleet and sailed off in a chaotic exodus.[4] Behind them the once fine capital lay shrouded in smoke from the fires the British set as they left.

In good military style the British force had burned any equipment they could not move, including ships under construction.

The fires burned for two days. Arnold and the first contingents of Continental soldiers entered the city on June 19 to the cheers of residents. What awaited them and thousands of returning refugees was a ruined, filthy, and stinking city: six hundred houses had been destroyed, piles of garbage and excrement blocked alleys and court-yards, public buildings and churches were stripped and desecrated, and shops were boarded up, while a vast store of rations lay rotting in the commissary.[5] As British officers left, many looted the city's homes they had used. John André, whose path was to cross Arnold's with tragic results, had been living in Benjamin Franklin's home. As André packed to leave, Lord Gray, his superior, asked him to take a variety of Franklin's possessions including paintings, books, and a printing press.[6] Houses that had been used as soldiers' bar-racks were in worse shape. The soldiers had cut holes in the floor, using these as their privy. Little wonder many outraged residents, horrified at what they found on their return, were likely to take revenge on neighbors suspected of collaboration.[7]

Anticipating confusion if not looting and violence after the British exodus, Congress required that all items be secured until the army inventoried them. It was Arnold's duty to enforce this act. He was to find that restoring order as civilian authorities returned and assuring peaceful reconstruction was made especially difficult by the rift between Pennsylvania's radical and moderate patriots. It is questionable whether anyone appointed to this task with these instructions could have avoided the wrath of the state's governing executive council. The radicals, among them Joseph Reed and Timothy Matlack, the executive council's president and secre-tary respectively, were spoiling for revenge. More moderate men, mostly Quakers and Anglicans, men like John Dickinson, Robert Morris, Benjamin Rush, and James Wilson, were true patriots but wanted forbearance and reconciliation. Unfortunately they were not in power.

Within a week of their return to the city the executive council members were upset with Arnold. Back in March, in preparation for the British evacuation, the exiled state legislature had passed "An Act for the Attainder of divers traitors" ordering twelve individuals who they claimed supported the British to appear and be voted guilty of high treason.[8] This procedure, simply voting someone guilty of a crime, was deemed so offensive by the drafters of the future American Constitution that they specifically banned it.[9] It also seems to have been banned by the 1776 Pennsylvania constitution that required a jury trial before anyone could be found guilty of a criminal offense.[10] The executive council didn't seem to care. In addition, between early May and June 18th, in three separate proclamations, the Pennsylvania executive council broadcast the names of some 332 people who they intended to prosecute.[11] They were also eager to confiscate the property of loyalists or suspected loyalists who had fled.

Even before the British seizure of Philadelphia the Pennsylvania government had required all white men eighteen years or older to take an oath of allegiance to the new order.[12] Anyone who failed to comply was unable to appear in court, serve as a guardian, executor or administrator, receive a legacy, or make a will, and for good measure was liable to paying double taxes. Further, those refusing to subscribe to the oath would be imprisoned for up to three months or fined £10 and had to leave the state within a month, forfeiting their goods and chattels to the Commonwealth and their real property to their legal heirs.[13] The disabilities refusal to take the oath imposed were to last for life.

Under these onerous penalties even those unenthusiastic about the revolution were likely to take the oath. Now, after the British had left, nonresidents needed a permit issued by Congress, the Executive Council, or Washington just to enter the city or face a fine of up to £50 and imprisonment at the pleasure of the court. Arnold, like Washington and many leading patriots, was more moderate and more charitable. His instructions, after all, were "to preserve tranquility and order in the city and give security to individuals of every class and description." Rounding up and arresting large numbers of leading residents and charging them with the heinous crime of treason or disloyalty was not the way to accomplish that task. Washington himself might not have been able to reconcile the executive council to a more generous approach. Certainly Arnold was not. The councilors were furious when Arnold refused to arrest this list of "known" enemy sympathizers.[14] Joseph Reed charged Arnold with attempting to protect loyalists.

The relations between Arnold and the executive council were made still worse by personal jealousies and prejudices. Arnold was Washington's man and Reed was one of Washington's harshest critics. Arnold was a Continental Army officer and a popular hero. History, as Congress and the council were keenly aware, demonstrated that unless armies are carefully controlled they can be a threat to liberty. Popular generals were especially worrisome. No one wanted another Oliver Cromwell, the parliamentary general who overthrew the English parliament in 1653 and made himself a virtual dictator with the support of the army. To avoid a similar attempt, Congress wanted Continental Army troops, and especially leading officers, subjected to strict civilian control. As one of the army's greatest heroes any signs of arrogance on Arnold's part had to be crushed. Indeed, Congress specifically authorized "the supreme executive powers of every State" to monitor "the conduct and behavior of all Continental officers, civil or military" and to notify the Commander in Chief of any "reprehensible conduct."[15]

In addition to political differences with the Pennsylvania governing council, there were social antagonisms. Arnold was tired of the austere life in the army and resentful of the sacrifices he and other officers made, risking their lives while civilians, like many Philadelphia "patriots," led comfortable lives or even made profits on the war. After years of hardships and dangers in camp and battle, grievously wounded and in almost constant pain, he felt entitled to live large. He was not willing to comport himself in the humble fashion the Pennsylvania councilors and Congress felt was appropriate.

Arnold's lively new aide, Major David Solebury Franks, was to get him into trouble on this score. Franks had been at Arnold's side during his hospital stay and preceded him into Philadelphia, entering immediately after the last British soldier crossed the Delaware. Arnold ordered Franks to select his new headquarters. Franks chose the mansion of the Penn family.[16] It was imposing, elegant, and probably the largest house in the city.[17] It was a double house that, with its offices, stretched 120 feet back. It had been General Howe's headquarters during the British occupation but they had stripped it as they left. Arnold needed to refurbish it immediately to make it suitable for his duties. That expenditure would be resented. So too would the fact he was driven around the city in a liveried coach-and-four, just as Howe had been. Arnold was also anxious to replenish his depleted fortune and immediately began taking advantage of every opportunity his position afforded to do that. All of this offended the watchful council.

To cap it off, while serving as commandant the crippled widower, father of three young sons, courted and miraculously won the hand of the beautiful eighteen-year-old Philadelphia belle, Peggy Shippen, daughter of a prominent family that had stayed in the city throughout the British occupation.

Margaret Shippen, Peggy, was an unusually able and educated young woman. She grew up in a literary household reading the great works in her father's well-stocked library, as well as the newspapers and political pamphlets of the day. This was a far cry from the lighter fare deemed suitable for most young women of her class. Peggy was born in 1760, the fifth child and fourth daughter of Edward and Hannah Shippen. The Shippens were one of the richest and most distinguished families in America. Peggy's father and grandfather were judges. The first Shippen in the New World, another Edward, arrived in 1688. He docked in Boston bringing with him a small fortune earned in trade and a knack for investing it wisely. When he married a Quaker they fled Puritan Massachusetts Bay for religiously tolerant Rhode Island where they were granted sanctuary by Governor Benedict Arnold, Arnold's great-grandfather.[18] The Shippens later moved to Pennsylvania, the great Quaker refuge, where they lived on a riverfront estate some two miles deep, investing in land and trade. William Penn's colonial charter named Edward Shippen the first mayor of Philadelphia. Shippen also served as speaker of the colony's assembly.

The Shippen men had a reputation for plain speaking and absolute integrity. Peggy's grandfather was a founder of both the University of Pennsylvania and the College of New Jersey, now Princeton University. He was a kind and jolly gentleman, much beloved by his granddaughter.[19] Peggy's own father had followed the same legal career. He held a slew of public offices, many simultaneously. In 1758 he was appointed a vice admiralty court judge. Governor Penn appointed Shippen to the upper house of the legislature. The post of admiralty court judge turned out to be an uncomfortable one as complaints grew about British governance and, in particular, the reliance on admiralty courts to avoid jury trials. In 1776 with passage of the Pennsylvania Constitution, Shippen lost his post of vice admiralty judge and his other offices as well, putting the family in some financial distress. As the political crisis worsened, Peggy's father refrained from taking a public stand. In 1777 as a suspected loyalist he was put on parole and took his family to their country house on the Schuylkill River.[20] In August he was once again free and moved back to Philadelphia. Although often labeled a loyalist, his Quaker background as well as his cautious nature may have been behind his neutral stance. John Adams and George Washington dined at the Shippen table, but so too did British officials.

When war broke out, remaining neutral was exceedingly difficult, especially living in Philadelphia, seat of the Continental Congress. Neutrals risked alienating both sides. Edward Shippen's best efforts, however, were unable to keep the younger men of his family from getting involved in the fighting. Neddy Burd, the fiancé of Peggy's sister Elizabeth, fought in the American army.

He was captured by the British in the battle for Long Island in 1776 and held prisoner on a British ship. Peggy's brother, Edward, on the other hand, joined the British army. He was at Trenton, and when Washington captured it in December 1776, he was taken prisoner. Edward was personally freed by Washington, for which his father was very grateful. However, the senior Edward never forgave his son for his reckless act and stripped him of all financial power over the family business. Edward's responsibilities were given to Peggy, a testament to her father's belief in her good sense and ability.[21] When the British occupied Philadelphia the Shippens remained while other families fled. And they remained when the British left.

Peggy grew into a beautiful young woman, dainty and blond with gray eyes. Lord Rawdon, General Howe's young chief of staff, reckoned Peggy Shippen the most beautiful woman he had ever seen in England or America.[22] She was devoted to her father and seems to have been his favorite. While often described as a rich belle, one of her friends explained that she did not frequent parties, nor behave in a frivolous manner, at least not until the British army took over the city. When the British occupied Philadelphia seventeen-year-old Peggy, rich, attractive, and accomplished, was unable to resist the gala entertainments—the dinners, balls, parties, and theater performances organized by British officers—that transformed the dour, wartime city. A royal navy captain who sometimes escorted her later admitted, "We were all in love with her."[23] That year Peggy's father began despairing of his sensible and frugal daughter who was turning heads and whose head was turned in turn.

As the British occupation wore on, the darker side of British military behavior became more glaring. General Howe was engaged in a very public affair with a married woman and many officers boasted of fathering illegitimate children. Fortunately for the American cause, during those months devoted to pleasure Howe and his men never attacked Washington's destitute and starving army, bivouacked only a few miles away at Valley Forge.

When the British withdrew after months of partying, the city was left in appalling condition. Thousands of residents who enjoyed those months of gaiety now fled with the British. Others like the Shippens remained to face the wrath of Congress and Pennsylvania's radical government and of neighbors returning to despoiled homes. It was Arnold's delicate task to keep order and some semblance of harmony as the refugees returned.

In the process of tackling his new responsibilities, Arnold met and fell deeply in love with Peggy Shippen, belle of the British occupation of Philadelphia. They met at a gala on July 4 to celebrate the second anniversary of the Declaration of Independence. Over the dinner table and in the newspapers Peggy had learned of Arnold's daring military exploits in 1776 and 1777. A new ship commissioned for the Pennsylvania navy was named for Arnold.[24] It was scarcely more than two months since Arnold was pressing his unwanted attentions on Betsy DeBlois. Whatever Miss DeBlois's attractions, however, they surely paled in comparison to Peggy's. For Arnold it was love at first sight; for Peggy it was the flattering attention of the war's daring and wounded hero, military commander of her city. In September he wrote Peggy the same letter of passion and commitment he had sent to Betsy. Why waste such an excellent letter? This time it was to meet with a more positive response, although not at first. As custom and courtesy demanded, Arnold also wrote to her father explaining that his "fortune is not large, though sufficient (not to depend upon my expectations) to make us both happy. I neither expect nor wish one with Miss Shippen."[25] He mentioned his reputation, "My public character is well known: my private one is, I hope, irreproachable," and referred to his three "lovely children." Arnold then addressed "Our difference in political sentiments," hoping that would be "no bar to my happiness . . . I flatter myself the time is at hand when our unhappy contest will be at an end, and peace and domestic happiness be restored to everyone." Differences in "political sentiments" seem not to have been a bar, or at least not the only bar for Judge

Shippen, although Arnold was refused at first. Arnold continued his siege of fair Peggy, and by February the two were betrothed.

Meeting Peggy in July did not divert Arnold from seeking a more suitable post, even one that would take him away from her. The navy appealed to him. Unlike a field command his injury would not be such a handicap, and he had a lifetime's experience with sailing. Privateering also would help refurbish his sadly diminished fortune. On July 19 he wrote to Washington pointing out that although his wounds "are in a fair way and less painful than usual," he saw "little prospect of my being able to take the field for a considerable time."[26] Since he had been "obliged entirely to neglect my private affairs since I have been in the service," he wished to retire from public business, "unless an offer which my friends have mentioned should be made to me of the command of the Navy to which my being wounded would not be so great an objection as it would remaining in the Army." He asked Washington's "sentiments respecting a command in the Navy." Despite all Arnold's sensible arguments and the extraordinary skill he had demonstrated in building and commanding the little fleet on Lake Champlain, despite his unsuitableness for his post in Philadelphia, Washington demurred, replying on August 3 that he was happy to hear Arnold's wounds were healing and wishing a situation for him where he "can be of the greatest advantage and where abilities like yours may not be lost to the public." However, Washington claimed to be "no competent judge in marine matters to offer advice on a subject so far out of my line." Instead of agreeing to a naval command Washington responded that Arnold was the best judge in the case.[27] It is unclear why Washington took this line. Perhaps he wanted Arnold to remain in the army. Arnold was his best field officer and one whose loyalty he could count on. Congress would have had to make the naval appointment in any case, but Washington's help would probably have sealed the deal since the authorities were already unhappy with Arnold as military commander of Philadelphia and would have been relieved to see him off to sea. A chance was lost that might have been beneficial to both the American cause and Arnold's future. Instead he was doomed to remain at his post in Philadelphia or retire from the army. He remained at his post. Sadly, the dye was cast.

With the option of a naval post quashed for the time being, Arnold proceeded to take advantage of opportunities that came his way to replenish his personal funds. His eagerness to do so clearly had many causes. His recent visit home made clear how depleted his fortune was and how few prospects wartime provided to restore it. How could Arnold forget that his father had become a debtor, bringing deep humiliation to his family? Arnold had been pulled out of boarding school and lost the opportunity to attend college. Certainly that disgrace and hardship must not happen to his own sons. Arnold himself had been bankrupt briefly, but with help and hard work had managed to recoup his losses. Others depended on him for support. He had a sister and three children and hoped to marry a young woman used to luxury. As for the propriety of seeking profit, he and other members of the army, including Washington, were thoroughly disgusted with the profiteering, complacency, and even scorn of civilians living in comparative safety while the troops who fought for them endured hardship, mortal danger, and penury. Congress had not paid him for three years but that didn't keep delegates from demanding that he scrupulously account for every penny that had been advanced for his military campaigns. Now his opportunity to serve his country and his pocketbook with a command at sea had been denied. Other expedients were necessary to secure his and his family's future and he took them.

Some of Arnold's questionable decisions as commander of Philadelphia were made with an eye for turning a profit, others were simply done from a sense of justice to injured parties. The result was a series of misadventures that made him even more toxic, if possible, in the eyes of the executive council. For example, Congress had ordered all the shops in Philadelphia closed until the army could inventory the contents. But Arnold needed to refurbish the Penn mansion promptly, which he did in grand style. The army badly needed clothing. He made a private deal with the clothier general of the army, James Mease, and his assistant William West to purchase goods for the army and other items at their own risk. These other goods were to be sold for the benefit of Arnold, Mease, and West.[28] The shops of other merchants, however, were still ordered to be closed. While this would be one of the charges of the executive council against Arnold for abusing his position, apparently the practice was not unusual for commanding generals at the time.[29] Historian Carl Van Doren points out that other American generals "paid in falling currency at a time of falling prices, even engaged in speculations, like many citizens whose love of country did not interfere with their love of profits."[30] In Arnold's case it's unclear whether the sale of items for profit ever took place.

A naval venture involving the sloop *Charming Nancy* began in June when Arnold was still at Valley Forge before leaving for Philadelphia.[31] The ship's owner, Philadelphia merchant Robert Shewell, asked permission to sail the ship and her cargo out of the Delaware River, then held by the British, to a port held by Americans. That day he approached Arnold Congress voted that no property was to leave Philadelphia until it was clear who the owners were. Arnold is unlikely to have known of this act and on his own initiative gave Robert Shewell a safe conduct pass for the *Charming Nancy*. With Arnold's pass the ship set sail with a cargo of commodities that would have been subject to the order of Congress. Shewell's two partners were from New York, then in British hands, and had brought their ship to Philadelphia planning to sell the cargo to the British. Arnold doesn't seem to have had a financial interest in the ship at that time although he did later. In any event his protection failed to shield the vessel from American privateers. A New Jersey admiralty judge released the ship from its captors back into the hands of its owners.

Arnold also involved himself in the conflict over the proper ownership of a prize ship. In early September Gideon Olmsted from Arnold's home state of Connecticut and three other Americans were seized and impressed by the British navy for their trade ship *Active* on a voyage from Jamaica to New York. Since a British prison likely awaited them when they docked, the four Americans managed to take over the ship, locking the officers up and overpowering the crew. They then sailed for Egg Harbor, New Jersey. When they were off Chestnut Neck, New Jersey, the *Active* was captured and brought to shore by the privateer *Convention*, owned by Pennsylvania. Another American privateer also claimed to have assisted in the capture. There were doubts whether the four Americans could have overpowered the captain and crew of the *Active*. The fight over profits from the sale of the ship and its cargo became a legal landmark. A Pennsylvania judge and jury awarded the four mutineers just one quarter of the value of the prize. Arnold took up their cause advancing money for an appeal to Congress in return for splitting any award. A committee of Congress did find in their favor ordering the monies from the ship's sale to go to Olmsted and his three colleagues. But the Pennsylvania court refused to back down.[32] Congress was unwilling to contest the result and Arnold lost his considerable advance.

When British vessels attacked Egg Harbor in October, burning houses and ships, Arnold got involved in another seemingly innocent action that would come to haunt him. He ordered a militia regiment of one hundred men to march to Egg Harbor and defend it. Only fifty men turned out, a totally inadequate number. A ship owner with a cargo at Egg Harbor pleaded with Arnold to save his cargo. Arnold agreed to help if he got half of the profit from the goods.[33] Wagons for public use had been assembled in Pennsylvania and some were idle at the time. Arnold ordered twelve of these wagons to retrieve the private property at Egg Harbor that was likely to fall into British hands. Although these wagons were otherwise idle and he paid for their use, by October Arnold was so unpopular that everything he did was seen as improper.[34]

If all this were not enough to damn Arnold, he also managed to trample on the wrong toes. The Council charged him with "imposing menial offices upon the sons of freemen on militia duty." The relations between the militia and members of the army were touchy. Militia units with their short enlistments and variable training, their own officers, and uncertain behavior in battle didn't always mesh smoothly with the Continentals and could be resented by the regulars. The militia in turn sometimes shared the assumption that only money induced Washington's men, the so-called dregs of the earth, to enlist. The incident that exposed these issues involved Arnold's aide, Major Franks. Franks had asked a militia soldier to fetch a barber for him, and when the barber did not appear ordered the man to fetch him again.[35] The young militia sergeant found the order demeaning for a free man and complained to his father. It turned out the insulted young man was the son of the particularly powerful secretary of the Pennsylvania Executive Council, Timothy Matlack. The first Arnold knew about this tempest in a teapot was when the young man complained to Arnold directly. Arnold responded that orders given by him or his aides to any man in service were to be obeyed. Later that same day Arnold received an outraged letter from the sergeant's father, Secretary Matlack.[36] Their exchange of letters highlights a key difference of perspective on the priority of the cause that engaged them all and the public's often demeaning attitude toward the Continental regulars. Matlack's letter pointed out to Arnold the key role of militia who he insisted be treated "in such manner as to make the duty as agreeable to them [as] is consistent with the service in which they are called." How, he asked, would Arnold have felt when he served in the militia if ordered to summon a barber? "Free men," Matlack insisted, "will be hardly brought to submit to such indignities; and if it is intended to have any of the respectable citizens of the state, in service in the militia, military discipline in such instances must be relaxed." He considered that "Military duty of every kind is rather disagreeable; and perhaps, to free men, garrison duty more disagreeable than any other. The sergeant above mentioned entered the service to discharge his duty; and as an example to other young men of the city, and not from necessity, in any sense of the word." Matlack asked that Arnold prevent any further complaints of this kind.

The next day Arnold replied. "No man has a higher sense of the rights of a citizen and free man than myself: they are dear to me, as I have fought and bled for them, and as it is my highest ambition and most ardent wish to resume the character of a free citizen whenever the service of my country will permit. . . . At the same time," he added, "I beg leave to observe, that whenever necessity obliges the citizen to assume the character of a soldier, the former is entirely lost in the latter, and the respect due to a citizen is by no means to be paid to the soldier, any further than his rank entitles him to it. This is evident from the necessity of military discipline, the basis of which is implicit obedience, and however the feelings of a citizen may be hurt, he has this consolation, that it is a sacrifice he pays to the safety of his country."[37] During his own militia service Arnold wrote, "my feelings were hurt not only as a citizen, but more so as a soldier: they were however sacrificed to the interest of my country. The event proved unfortunate to me; but I have the satisfaction to think I rendered some service to my country." He argued that any order not against the laws or principles of the Constitution should be obeyed. Matlack was still not satisfied, insisting the order in question should have been made to a menial servant. He was "mortified" to find Arnold justifying the order.[38] If such offensive orders were issued in the future, he warned, "it is my duty as a father, to withdraw my son from a service in which commands are to be given him which to obey would lessen him in the esteem of the world; and I shall consider it a duty which I owe to myself to acquaint my fellow citizens of my reason for so doing."

Arnold replied that "if the declaration that you will withdraw your son from the service and publish the reasons is intended as a threat, you have mistaken your object. I am not to be intimidated by a newspaper."[39] Matlack's complaint would be one of the charges the executive council levied and broadcast against Arnold. It should be added that Arnold had always been very popular with the militia. Washington had specifically sent him to New York State to ensure that militia rallied to the defense of the state from Burgoyne.

In September as relations with the Pennsylvania authorities worsened, Arnold tried once again to switch from his army post in Philadelphia to the navy. He sent Congress a plan to capture one of Britain's Windward Islands and use it as a base to intercept British shipping.[40] He offered to serve as commodore of the new fleet of privateers that would be based in New London, Connecticut. Congress agreed to consider the scheme but never acted on the plan. Once again Arnold's efforts to find a position that would enable him to serve his country and remove him from the constant harassment of the Pennsylvania council came to nothing.

By December Arnold was so disgusted with the aspersions on his honor by council members and members of Congress's new Board of War that he had challenged some of them to a duel. When Washington learned of this he wrote to Arnold on December 13, seriously worried. After mentioning that he was sending a regiment to help guard stores in Philadelphia and Trenton, since the local militia "complained of the hardship of being turned out for these purposes," Washington added that he had "(. . . never heard, nor is it my) wish to be acquainted with the causes of the coolness between some gentlemen composing the Board of War and yourself."[41] Of course Washington himself had causes of coolness with the Board of War. He expressed the hope these unnamed causes "may never rise to such a height as to oblige either party to make a public matter of it, as I am under more apprehensions on account of our own dissentions than of the efforts of the enemy."[42] But public it was to become.

In January Matlack and Arnold had an exchange about the wagons Arnold had sent to transport goods from Egg Harbor. Arnold provided Matlack with the official reports and in response to aspersions on his personal conduct replied in exasperation, "I shall only say that I am at all times ready to answer my public conduct to Congress or General Washington, to whom alone I am accountable."[43] This was too much for the self-important Pennsylvania council. Reed wrote the president of Congress, then John Jay, demanding Arnold's removal from his command in Philadelphia for unspecified charges he labeled "willful abuse of power and criminal acts."[44] Congress was unwilling to take action without more information and appointed a committee to investigate.

From the start the Pennsylvania councilors were determined to bring the proud shopkeeper-made-general down a peg. With the army and Congress dependent upon the cooperation of their state, whose capital they shared and whose capitol building they occupied, the Pennsylvania authorities had the leverage to manage it. Arnold would find that out to his detriment. For the moment though he set off for New York State to investigate possible land purchases with an eye to retiring from the service.

In February, 1779, after months of fuming, the Council drew up eight formal charges against Arnold. As regulations required they forwarded their complaints of Arnold's misuse of public wagons and other infractions to General Washington, but also, as Washington feared, made a point of publishing them in the *Pennsylvania Packet*, a newspaper with a wide circulation. To elevate their various complaints to some higher principle the Council summed up Arnold's tenure in their city as "oppressive to the faithful subjects of this state, unworthy of his rank and station" and "disrespectful to the supreme executive authority." Disrespectful, that is, to themselves.[45] They demanded Arnold's punishment and removal.

Arnold learned of the charges on February 6 during a meeting with Washington at Middlebook, New Jersey. A day later the

Pennsylvania council, determined to destroy his reputation, had their charges published in the newspaper and sent copies of their charges against him to the governor of every other state. Matlack, father of the aggrieved militia sergeant, was especially nasty, dredging up two-year-old charges that Arnold had plundered Montreal when his army retreated from Canada, charges long ago dismissed, and sending these anonymously to the *Packet*.[46] Matlack admitted to Arnold the flimsy basis for his allegation: "When I meet your carriage in the street, and think of the splendor in which you live and revel . . . of the purchases you have made, and compare these things with the decent frugality necessarily used by other officers in the Army, it is impossible to avoid the question, From whence have these riches flowed if you did not plunder Montreal?"[47] The charges concluded by damning Arnold's brief service in Philadelphia as "highly discouraging to those who have manifested their attachment to the liberties and interests of America, and disrespectful to the supreme executive authority."[48] They went further. They called on the attorney general of Pennsylvania to prosecute Arnold "for such illegal and oppressive conduct cognizable in the courts of law."[49] As long as Arnold remained in command in their capital city they refused to pay for any charges of the army or to mobilize the militia except during an emergency.

How the slander rankled. The Council president, Joseph Reed, formerly serving with Washington, had become one of Washington's bitter critics. He and these other politicians, tending home and business, questioned Arnold's attachment to liberty, he who had repeatedly risked his life for his country and had a crippled leg and ruined family business for his trouble. London's *Royal Gazette* gleefully reported that once Arnold was wounded, "Congress . . . considering him unfit for any further exercise of his military talents, permit him to fall into the unmerciful fangs of the Executive Council of Pennsylvania."[50]

Arnold wrote to reassure Peggy, now his betrothed: "Let me beg of you not to suffer the rude attacks on me to give you one moment's uneasiness; they can do me no injury. I am treated with the greatest politeness by General Washington and the officers of the Army, who bitterly execrate Mr. Reed and the Council for their villainous attempt to injure me."[51] He hoped to be back at Peggy's side by Friday: "'till then all nature smiles in vain; for you alone, heard, felt, and seen, possess my every thought, fill every sense and pant in every vein."[52] If Peggy was uneasy about these attacks on her intended, it did not deter her. That April Arnold's dear Peggy became his bride.

On April 8, a fine spring morning, Benedict Arnold and Peggy Shippen were married. The ceremony took place in the library of her family home and was conducted by the Episcopal Bishop William White. Arnold's mother Hannah, a devout Protestant, would have shaken her head. Although the bishop was a representative of the Church of England, the church that had driven Quakers, Puritans, and many other Protestant dissenters to cross the Atlantic, his sympathies were with the American cause. The bridegroom was still unable to stand without help and leaned on the arm of his aide, Franks, next to his lovely bride as he took his vows. Throughout the reception that followed he sat with his injured leg resting on a camp-stool.[53] In preparation for the wedding, Arnold scraped together all the funds and credit he could to buy the beautiful country estate of Mount Pleasant, a splendid house and some ninety-six acres on the Schuylkill, near where the Shippens had taken refuge during some of the fighting for Philadelphia. He settled the estate on his dear Peggy and his sons. It was a grand gesture but for the moment he and Peggy moved into a modest house in Philadelphia owned by her father while he rented the magnificent Mount Pleasant estate to the Spanish ambassador to help with his mortgage payments.[54] Hannah and his two younger sons journeyed to Pennsylvania and moved in with Arnold and Peggy. This was especially helpful to Peggy as she was soon pregnant with her first child.

★ ★ ★

Arnold and Washington conferred about the best course of action. Washington had recommended a congressional committee investigate. Arnold preferred a court-martial to clear his name, an expedient he had asked for on other occasions. Other officers, including some of Washington's best men, had looked to courts-martial when charged by Congress with wrongdoing and were invariably cleared. Congress had never been particularly kind to Arnold, especially the outspoken Massachusetts delegation, but he was confident he could rely on a court-martial. His fellow officers would see how wronged he was. They understood the difficulties of dealing with politicians. If honor and reputation were to be preserved, he was confident he could depend on the help and understanding of his brothers in arms to exonerate him. Their verdict would justify the sacrifices he had made and victories he had won for his often ungrateful country.

TWENTY-ONE

The Court-Martial

*. . . I have suffered, in seeing the fair fabric of reputation,
which I have been with so much danger and toil raising
since the present war, undermined by those, whose posterity
(as well as themselves) will feel the blessed effects of my
efforts . . ."*
                     —Benedict Arnold, summation, at Court-Martial[1]

*Great God! Is it possible that, after the bold and perilous
enterprises which this man has undertaken for the service and
defense of his country, the loss of his fortune and the cruel
and lingering pains he has suffered from the wound received
fighting their battles, there can be found among us men so
abandoned to the base and infernal passions of envy and
malice as to persecute him with the most unrelenting fury, and
wish to destroy what alone he had the prospect of saving out of
the dreadful wreck of his health, fortune and life; his character?*
                                   —Silas Deane to Nathanael Greene,
                                                      May 29, 1779[2]

I t was with immense relief that Major General Arnold, leaning heavily on his cane, entered the smoky warmth of Norris's Tavern that frigid morning of 1779, two days before Christmas. With some difficulty he settled himself at the long table before the fire in the improvised courtroom, ready for the start of his much-delayed court-martial.

There he sat, dressed in the buff and blue uniform of his rank, a wounded warrior. But there are worse blows for a proud man than a crippled leg. It had been nearly a year since the Pennsylvania executive council broadcast their charges against him to every state. He had suffered from months of humiliation, frustration, and dishonor, unable to respond. The court-martial was the only way to clear his name. God willing, vindication was at hand.

He had hoped the trial could be held in Philadelphia and spare him the eighty-mile journey to the army's winter headquarters in Morristown, New Jersey. That proved impractical. December was never an auspicious time of year for travel, and he was still crippled and had to go by coach. This year such a journey was especially treacherous. Snow had begun early. There were four snowstorms in November and another seven in December. When he finally reached Morristown it lay under two feet of snow. The condition of the army gathering there was even more miserable than usual. Officers not fortunate enough to have the use of a house slept in tents on the frozen ground. Still they were luckier than the 10,800 ragged and hungry Continental soldiers in nearby Jockey Hollow, frantically building huts to house themselves and their officers before they sickened from the bitter cold. None knew, as the court-martial convened that day, that before their deliberations were done the worst snowstorm of a frigid century would smother the encampment in another four to six feet of snow, marooning them all.

None of the eight charges the Pennsylvania council had levied against him back in February were for cowardice or the questionable surrender of a fort, the usual accusations of an officer's failings. No one would dare accuse the country's best general, its "Hannibal," of cowardice. Instead, he faced accusations alleging that during his service as commandant of Philadelphia he had misused his authority to enrich himself.[3] It was painful that after a lifetime overcoming the humiliation of his childhood, and even after his brilliant military success, his personal honor should be besmirched in this way. Painful almost beyond endurance.

Scanning the faces of the thirteen officers now seating themselves around him to hear his case, Arnold was keenly aware what a disastrous mistake it had been for Washington to select him as commandant of Philadelphia. It may have seemed the perfect post for him while his leg healed, since he could not yet ride a horse let alone take the field. But Washington was certainly aware that for all Arnold's genius as a military commander this political minefield would be treacherous to negotiate. For a proud man like Arnold, and a protégé of Washington, it proved impossible.

He trusted Washington and his fellow officers to protect him from the vicious slurs and ultimate disgrace proposed by the Pennsylvania executive council and his enemies in Congress. He knew now that was naïve. Over and over again Washington had shown him every sign of his high estimation. When Arnold was recuperating with his sister and sons in New Haven, Washington had sent him a magnificent present of a pair of French epaulettes and a sword knot, one of three he had been sent by a French gentleman. His fellow officers shared his resentment of civilians with their demeaning, miserly attitude toward the army that kept them free. Most of the officers were men of property. They were patriotic but sensitive about their personal honor. Yet the importance of honor seemed to escape John Adams and many of his fellow delegates who mocked the army's officers as "Mastiffs, Scrambling for Rank and Pay like Apes for Nuts."[4] Early in the war when Washington had suggested offering a bounty for a year's enlistment, Adams had warned that only "the meanest, idlest, most intemperate and worthless" men would sign away their liberty on such terms.[5] Of course such bounties had become routine to fill the ranks. Washington, writing from Valley Forge, had pleaded with Congress: "We should all be considered . . . as one people, embarked in one cause, in one interest, acting on the same principle and to the same End."[6] The very jealousy of the army's proper "subordination to the supreme Civil Authority," he warned, is a likely means to produce a contrary effect." Unfortunately for Arnold the warning had gone unheeded.

Apart from worries about death or disfigurement from battle or disease in camp the soldiers had the problem of supporting themselves and their families while on duty. Congress had been printing currency with abandon and it was rapidly becoming worthless. By the time Arnold's court-martial convened, a captain's annual pay would buy only a pair of shoes. An ordinary private's pay, when he got it, bought virtually nothing.[7] Many officers had resigned their commissions in disgust. Arnold remained confident the court-martial would exonerate him and preserve his good name and reputation. He was anxious to have his case heard, the sooner the better.

The officers and Washington were, as he had predicted, sympathetic to his plight. But, as it turned out, that had not helped. He had underestimated the Executive Council's determination to punish him and their ability to intimidate Congress and Washington to achieve it. He had also underestimated Washington's need to defer to Congress and the Executive Council. Arnold's frustration grew with the months of delay that prevented him from erasing the very public stain on his reputation and honor. Over and over again during his military service men jealous of his achievements or angry over his brusque behavior toward them had accused him of wrongdoing and belittled his valor as recklessness. But occasional good sense on the part of the authorities and the need for his help on the battlefield had brought investigations to an end, leaving his reputation spotless. This time was different. His enemies were more powerful and his defenders weaker. His use on the battlefield was much diminished. He was expendable.

Arnold's hope for a speedy resolution to clear his name was not to happen. First the Council approached Congress with their charges. Congress appointed a committee to investigate. Arnold testified, but despite repeated requests for evidence to support their charges, the council failed to respond. Ultimately the committee dismissed six of the eight charges.[8] Nevertheless, Reed managed to overturn the report and had four charges sent to a court-martial. Arnold resigned his commission on March 19 but that did not cool the Council's fervor. In April the Pennsylvania Council threatened Congress with secession if it did not insist upon a court-martial for Arnold.[9]

Washington had originally scheduled the trial for May 1.[10] Learning of this date Reed responded in high dudgeon, claiming he needed more time for witnesses to be present, openly warning Washington: "Such is the dependence of the Army upon the transportation of this state [Arnold was accused of using twelve public wagons for private purposes] that should the court-martial treat it as a light and trivial matter, we fear it will not be practicable to draw forth wagons in the future, be the emergency what it may, and it will have very bad consequences."[11] Arnold probably did not know of the threat, or Reed's pretence that the Council asked "nothing of Congress but that he should not continue to command in this state"—he had already resigned his post after all. Washington agreed to postpone the court until July 1, eliciting from Arnold the warning of his own danger, that "a set of artful, unprincipled men in office may represent the most innocent actions and, by raising the public clamor against your Excellency, place you in the same situation I am in . . . I have nothing left but the little reputation I have gained in the Army," he pleaded. "Delay in the present case is worse than death." He reminded Washington that the Council had already had three months to produce their evidence and reckoned they "wish to put it [the court-martial] off until the campaign opens, considering undoubtedly that the service will then prevent the court-martial from sitting, and cause the trial to be postponed until the end of the campaign."[12] And that, of course, was exactly what had happened. Washington was in the embarrassing position of having to postpone the court-martial time after time to conciliate the Pennsylvania Council, and then the campaign season demanded his attention and he could not spare the officers for a trial.

In the meantime Arnold continued to live in Philadelphia awaiting his court-martial. With the well-publicized Council charges against him, he often found himself harassed by local people as a reputed friend to loyalists. That first summer at his post, there were well-placed fears that patriots who fled the city during the British occupation would be eager for vengeance against neighbors who had remained. That didn't happen. Captain Charles Willson Peale, a radical, noted in his diary, "to my surprise, I have not seen or heard of one rude encounter."[13] In July councilors grumbled of "a great unwillingness in the People of the City to give the necessary information against the disaffected."[14] Reed, Peale, and the radicals were disappointed in the public. They were also furious that when Peale presented Arnold with a long list of suspected enemy sympathizers, Arnold refused to arrest them. The Council's animosity and the mob's anger were increasingly aimed at prominent local moderates, chief among them the state's well-known attorney general, pamphleteer, signer of the Declaration of Independence, James Wilson. Wilson became unpopular for defending, successfully, those the Council had accused of treason. Of twenty-three men who stood trial for treason between September 1778 and the following April, only four were found guilty, and even in these cases the juries had asked for leniency against the death penalty.[15] The jury acquittals made the radicals angrier still. Wilson would defend hundreds of suspected loyalists.

During 1779 radical anger against the moderates increasingly turned to organized mob violence. Wilson was a leader of the moderate group, Arnold a supporter. But Arnold would arrive too late to help his friends on October 4, when the crisis came. Fearing an armed confrontation Wilson, Robert Morris, Captain George Campbell, Colonel Stephen Chambers, Peggy's brother-in-law Edward Burd, and thirty other republican moderates barricaded themselves in Wilson's house. To the strains of fifes and drums two hundred of Reed's radical stalwarts armed and supported by the militia, marched from the commons to Wilson's house and surrounded it.[16] The crowd grew by another two hundred as enraged men, some apparently convinced the high prices from a depreciating currency were due to a loyalist plot, joined the march and converged on Wilson's home. When they arrived Captain Campbell went to a third storey window and began shouting down at the mob, waving a pistol. Someone in the crowd fired at him. He shot back hitting a few members of the crowd. Then he was hit. Wilson's other friends began firing from the upstairs windows, at first driving the crowd back. But the mob surged forward, led by men carrying hammers and bars of iron. Suddenly the front door was battered down and the crowd burst in. An exchange of gunfire took place on the stairway. Chambers was shot and killed before the mob was driven from the house and a stack of furniture braced against the door.

Arnold, hearing the commotion, rushed to Wilson's home. Stones were flung at him as he reached the crowd. He had just pulled out his pistols, his back to a wall, when Reed arrived and challenged him: "What are you doing here, General? You have no more voice in the military affairs of this city."

"You've raised a riot, Reed," Arnold responded, "and now you have no power to quell it." At this point Continental soldiers appeared and the violence stopped. The toll was serious. One of Wilson's friends had been bayoneted and six or seven men lay dead, others were badly wounded. Reed's response was to arrest everyone inside and outside the house. Arnold, Wilson, Morris, and their fellow republicans were released once they posted bail, but Reed released the members of his militia mob and got an amnesty for them.

Two days later, as Arnold was returning from meeting with a group of moderates at Grey's Ferry, he was attacked in the street by a violent mob. He drew his pistols to defend himself and threatened to shoot two men who tried to reach him.[17] Angry and embarrassed, he wrote Congress: "A mob of lawless ruffians have attacked me in the street and threaten my life, now I am in my own house, for defending myself when attacked."[18] He appealed for their help. "As there is no protection to be expected from the authority of the state for an honest man, I am under the necessity of requesting Congress to order me a guard of Continental troops." He concluded, "This request I presume will not be denied a man, who has so often fought and bled in defense of his country." Alas it was denied. Arnold was not popular in Congress and Congress was not in a position to preempt the authority of the Pennsylvania government. Arnold was curtly informed that his application "ought to be made to the Executive Authority of the state of Pennsylvania in whose disposition to protect every honest citizen Congress have full confidence."[19] It was humiliating treatment.

Still, now that the court-martial was to convene at last, Arnold believed he would have the wholehearted sympathy of his fellow officers. The charges would be dismissed, his name cleared. The assurance he had written Washington back in May still held. "I have no doubt," he wrote, "of obtaining justice from a court-martial, as every officer in the Army must feel himself injured by the cruel and unprecedented treatment I have met with."[20] Major General Benedict Arnold was ready to defend himself with his usual vigor.

Courts-martial were surprisingly common among the officers of the American army. The Continental Congress repeatedly brought charges against any generals whose efforts had not met with success. In 1777 Congress ordered a court-martial for Major General Philip Schuyler for abandoning Fort Ticonderoga to the British. As his friend, Arnold was surely well aware of Schuyler's plight.

About the same time Congress ordered Schuyler's court-martial, it ordered a court-martial for Major General Arthur St. Clair, previously a British general, on suspicion of disloyalty. Congress had no real evidence against Schuyler or St. Clair, and there had been a long delay in their trials, comparable to Arnold's but worse in that the two men were suspended and unable to prepare any defense because Congress had not formulated any charges. After six months of delay a committee of Congress had to order their colleagues to send Washington their charges. It was another four months before that was done. St. Clair's court-martial took place a full year after the original complaints were made. In the end charges that he had advance notice of British movements and failed to stop them were dismissed, and St. Clair was acquitted with highest honors. The same court tried Schuyler who was also acquitted.

Then there was luckless John Sullivan, another major general, who got similar treatment later that year for failing to charge at Staten Island. Congress ordered Washington to suspend him but Washington needed good officers, and Sullivan saw action at Brandywine and Germantown. Even the renowned Anthony Wayne found himself investigated after a surprise attack on his forces resulted in 150 deaths. Outraged, Wayne demanded a court-martial to clear his name. Sullivan, now exonerated, presided, and Wayne was acquitted with the highest honors. Major General Robert Howe, who was presiding over Arnold's own court-martial, had himself been court-martialed after failing to successfully defend Savannah. In due course Howe too had been acquitted. Washington seems to have selected Howe to preside at Arnold's trial not only for his experience in the dock but because, like Arnold, he had suffered from poor relations with local politicians, in his case those in South Carolina and Georgia. Howe even fought a duel with a man who accused him of not properly defending Charleston.[21]

Many members of the court were known to Arnold, seasoned veterans of the struggle. There was General Henry Knox, for example, a Bostonian now in charge of the army's artillery. The

winter after Arnold and Ethan Allen surprised and captured Fort
Ticonderoga, Knox managed to haul the fort's cannon all the way
to Boston. Knox was a tall, husky man with a booming voice, the
seventh of ten sons. He had little formal education but became a
self-taught expert on artillery. Like Arnold he had needed to work
as a youth. Knox's father had squandered the family fortune, then
abandoned the family when Knox was nine, forcing the boy to
leave school. He found a job in a bookstore and eventually owned
his own bookshop. Arnold's father had a successful shipping business, but when it failed he fell into debt and became a public drunk.
Arnold was removed from boarding school and instead served an
apprenticeship to an apothecary. Knox, as Arnold later would, married the daughter of a loyalist. Then there was William Irvine, now
a general too, originally a surgeon in the British navy. Irvine had
served in the attack on Canada led by Montgomery and Arnold, and
had been taken prisoner in Quebec. He was later exchanged. The
judge advocate for the trial whose responsibility it was to present
the case was General John Lawrence, a twenty-nine-year-old New
York lawyer who had emigrated from the west of England in 1767,
been admitted to the bar in 1772, and three years later joined the
American army.

In many ways the procedure of a court-martial was little different
from that of a civilian court. The jury was comprised of thirteen
officers chosen from different regiments, including a president who
presided, and a vice president. The accused individual could ask that
any particular officer be dismissed. The trial then began with the
judge advocate reading the charges and asking the accused how
he wished to plead. Witnesses could be called as the prosecution's
case was presented and were questioned by the members of the
court and cross-examined. When the prosecution's case was complete the accused was invited to make an opening statement, submit
his evidence, and call his own witnesses. The jury's deliberations
were secret and, except in a capital case, only a simple majority was

needed to find guilt. If the verdict was "guilty," the jury was asked what punishment they recommended.

With everyone settled around the table the court-martial was ready to proceed. Arnold was asked how he pleaded. He replied, "Not Guilty." He would defend himself. The Pennsylvania council then began their presentation with their proceedings from February 3, when they announced their original eight charges against Arnold, a clever way of getting all these on the record, then moved to the four counts Congress had forwarded for the court's consideration.

> *First*: That while in Valley Forge in the Spring of 1778 Arnold had given permission for a ship belonging to people in Philadelphia residing with the enemy and "of disaffected character" to enter an American port without permission from the state or from Washington.

> *Second*: He had the shops and stores of Philadelphia shut on his arrival but made purchases for his own benefit "as is alleged and believed."

> *Third*: Imposing menial offices upon the sons of freemen while on militia duty then claimed he had the power to do so. The charge added that Arnold claimed it the "duty of the militia to obey 'every order of his aids' (not a breach of the laws and constitution) as his . . . without judging of the propriety of them."

> *Fourth*: Appropriating wagons of the state called forth on a special emergency last autumn to transport private property, and that of persons who voluntarily remained with the enemy last winter [stayed in Philadelphia], and were deemed disaffected to the interests and independence of America.[22]

271

Arnold did not deny the allegations of permitting the *Charming Nancy* to enter port, or using public wagons for moving private property, but had reasonable explanations for each of these. The ship's captain, Robert Shewell, he pointed out, had appeared with the militia and done militia duty, and in short was not unfriendly to the American cause. As for the wagons, they were idle and he had offered to pay to have them remove property from a part of New Jersey in imminent danger of falling to the enemy.[23] On the charge of shutting the shops in Philadelphia, his proclamation was in compliance with Washington's instructions and the resolution of Congress "to establish military law in this city [Philadelphia] and suburbs, until the civil authority of the state can resume the government thereof." [24]

Witnesses appeared for the Council and were closely questioned by the court and Arnold. William Matlack, the aggrieved militia soldier, testified to his dismay at the order to fetch a barber. Arnold questioned the witnesses himself and produced various documents. On Matlack's complaint, he explained that in his view the militia on duty take on the character of soldiers and that this policy was supported specifically by laws in several states where militia, when called up, are subjected to the same rules and discipline as the Continental Army. In any event Matlack's complaint involved a very minor incident.[25] There was much discussion about the details of his use of the wagons and the fact that they were ordered to cross over the state line to New Jersey.

The Council hastened to add one of their main grievances, Arnold's moderation toward loyalists. They complained of Arnold's discouragement and neglect to "civil, military and other characters, who have adhered to the cause of their country with an entire different conduct toward those of another character, are too notorious to need proof or illustration."

Not until January 21 did Arnold get to make his opening statement. Despite the number of witnesses to be examined, it was probably the terrible weather that had occasioned the long delay.

Dr. Thacher wrote of the fierce blizzard that struck January 3: "No man could endure its violence many minutes without danger of his life."[26] During the night several of the officer's marquees were ripped and blown down, trapping their occupants. The next morning officers had to be rescued. Soldiers were found in their tents "buried like sheep under the snow."[27] Witnesses who had testified and Council members may have left before the blizzard, but it is likely many if not most of them were marooned in the town, living on reduced rations, clustered in distinctly uncomfortable proximity to their adversaries.

Arnold introduced a series of witnesses and documents. Finally, summing up, he began by submitting testimonials including a letter from Washington dated July 1777, when the commander was worried about Burgoyne's march into New York State and was sending Arnold north to bolster the defense. In it Washington described Arnold as "active, judicious and brave, and an officer in whom the militia will repose great confidence," adding, "I am persuaded his presence and activity will animate the militia greatly, and spur them on to a becoming conduct." Clearly the commander thought highly of his good relations with the militia.

Arnold appealed to his judges and former colleagues:

> Is it probable that after having acquired some little reputation, and after having gained the favourable opinion of those whose favourable opinion it is an honor to gain, I should all at once sink into a course of conduct equally unworthy of the patriot and soldier? No pains have been spared, no artifice has been left untried to persuade the public that this has been the case.[28]

He then went over every charge. He submitted correspondence between the Pennsylvania council, the committee of Congress and himself, including his plea in a letter to John Jay of March 17, 1779, for an immediate decision on the charges against him in which he wrote: "I flatter myself, that every member of that honorable body must have some idea of what I have suffered on this occasion, and that they will relieve me from a situation, the cruelty of which is beyond my power to express." He had resigned his post the next day. Arnold then broke into an emotional account of the toll the Executive Council's vendetta had taken, "the pain and anxiety I have suffered, in seeing the fair fabric of reputation, which I have been with so much danger and toil raising since the present war, undermined by those, whose posterity (as well as themselves) will feel the blessed effects of my efforts, in conjunction with you and others, in rescuing them from a tyranny of the most cruel and debasing nature."[29]

The following day he rested his case with a prayer: "I have looked forward with pleasing anxiety to the present day when, by the judgment of my fellow soldiers, I shall (I doubt not) stand honorably acquitted of all the charges brought against me, and again share with them the glory and danger of this just war."[30] The court adjourned to consider its verdict.

On January 26 everyone returned to Norris's Tavern and the court reconvened. The judge advocate asked Howe to report the decision of the jury. As Arnold held his breath the reply came: The court found him guilty of two charges—that he should not have let a ship in possession of the enemy enter an American port was "irregular," and his use of wagons, although paying for them, was "imprudent and improper" and should not have been made. They dismissed the two other charges. When asked what sentence they recommended, Howe replied that for the two infractions Arnold was to receive a reprimand from Washington. It was a terrible and unexpected blow.

On February 12, 1780, Congress formally approved the verdict but, typically, did not communicate this to Washington for several weeks. On April 6 Washington's letter of reprimand, written as gently as the commander felt comported with the letter of the sentence, was dispatched to his best general:

> Dear Sir:
>
> The Commander-in-Chief would have been much happier on an occasion of bestowing a commendation on an officer who has rendered such distinguished service to his country as Major General Arnold. But in the present case a sense of duty and a regard to candor oblige him to declare that he considers his conduct in his issuance of the permit as peculiarly reprehensible, both in a civil and military view, and in the affair of the wagons as imprudent and improper. As I am with great respect, Dear Sir, your most obedient servant.
>
> G. Washington

He included with the formal reprimand a personal letter, off the record, that he hoped would console Arnold.

> Sir:
>
> Our profession is the purest of all. Even the shadow of a fault tarnishes the luster of our finest achievements. The least indiscretion may rob us of the public favor, so hard to be acquired. I reprimand you for having forgotten that, in proportion as you have rendered yourself formidable to our enemies, you should have been guarded and temperate in your deportment toward your fellow citizens. Exhibit anew those noble qualities, which have placed you on the list of our most valued commanders. I will myself furnish you, as far as it may be in my power, with opportunities for regaining the esteem of your country.
>
> As I am with great respect, Dear Sir, your most obedient servant,
>
> G. Washington[31]

It was all entirely too late. A final humiliation, no matter how tactfully couched. Perhaps if his fellow officers had found him innocent and dismissed the charges confirming his service with the highest honors, he could have gotten past the frustration and dishonor of the past year. But not now. Back in May after Congress had been pressured into agreeing to some four charges against him, and Washington had been pushed into postponing, for what was to be the first of many times, the court-martial to restore his good name, he was contacted by a British commissioner on a peace mission to the Congress.

TWENTY-TWO

Becoming Gustavus Monk

Having made every sacrifice of fortune and blood, and become a cripple in the service of my country, I little expected to meet the ungrateful returns I have received from my country, but as Congress has stamped ingratitude as the current coin, I must take it.

—Arnold to Washington, May 5, 1779

ime and again over the years that followed, Arnold must have thought back to the reasons why he had abandoned the cause for which he had fought and bled, a decision that devastated his reputation at the time and destroyed his honor forever. There were, of course, the increasingly vicious assaults on his reputation and his court-martial with its deeply disappointing results. He was angry and bitter, tired of fighting the enemies on his own side. But there were two particular points during this period pushing him to abandoning the American cause that his shocked contemporaries and most later historians missed in their haste to attribute the meanest motives to him from the beginning, motives transparently contrary to his years of brave and selfless dedication. Of course the ignominy he experienced before he left the cause was only a foretaste of what was to come. Jared Ingersoll, a New Haven attorney and later delegate to Congress, who had converted to the revolutionary side when threatened by the Sons of Liberty, put Arnold's defection down to "personal ambition and pique and an untamed individualism."[1] With the shock of Arnold's betrayal there was a rush by many patriots to conclude, even a need to conclude, that Arnold had always been mercenary, selfish, reckless. Only a deep character flaw could explain his switching sides. No decent man would do it. He was given no credit for his valor before that switch, military brilliance and courage that saved the new states and led to the French alliance, no credit for having continued to serve in the army despite the insulting behavior of Congress. Historian Charles Royster, in his portrait of Americans during the Revolutionary war, claims Arnold insisted from the start on being on top of everything while, after his treason, he writes that "Americans saw more than a criminal in Arnold—they saw a freak. He was not just a deserter or an assassin on a grand scale, he was an aberration in nature."[2] British military historian J. W. Fortescue assesses Arnold's combination of martial skills as "staggering," dubbing him "the most formidable opponent that could be matched against the British in America." Nevertheless Fortescue feels compelled to add that Arnold was "of course shallow, fickle, unprincipled and unstable in character."[3] How such a person could have accomplished amazing military achievements Fortescue doesn't feel the need to explain.

Brushed aside were inconvenient facts. Arnold, unlike most of his fellow officers, continued fighting for the cause despite being hauled repeatedly before congressional committees for malfeasance, despite being passed over for promotion while junior officers were promoted. Other officers had left the service for far less. He remained at Saratoga for the sake of the cause and the men in the ranks when Gates treated him with distain and confined him to his tent during the battle. While Gates never set foot on the battlefield, Arnold dashed into the thick of the fighting without any official position and achieved victory only to see Gates get the credit. He risked his life time after time and suffered grievous and crippling wounds. He was denied the naval commission he hoped would take him from Philadelphia. Even after he resigned his commission as they demanded, he was berated and dishonored by the Pennsylvania executive councilors. When he was attacked in the city streets by their thugs Congress refused to provide a guard for him.

Congress owed Arnold years of salary while he exhausted his own financial resources to pay his men. Yet greed was often cited as his chief motive. But financial problems were not the only, or even the worst, reality pressing on him. He was besieged by enemies in the Pennsylvania executive council and in Congress. Their demeaning attacks were broadcast in the city's gazette and throughout the country. Only the chance to clear his name made it possible to bear these insults. Despite all this he wanted to serve. The same day he resigned his commission in Philadelphia he wrote Washington offering to take a field post in the army as soon as he was fit. On Washington's advice he appealed to Congress to refute the Council's charges rather than demand a court-martial at once. He expected to be exonerated. Then he changed his mind, or at least hedged his bets, as the chance he could clear his name promptly dimmed.

Five days before his wedding John Jay, president of Congress, ordered Washington to summon a court-martial on four of the eight charges. While Congress found no evidence to support several of the charges against him, it caved in to the powerful and vindictive Pennsylvania council. This blow came as his sister Hannah and two youngest sons were arriving to live with the new couple, to be a family. The joys and responsibilities of his new family life made the necessity to retain his honor and position all the more vital.

Congress's decision was a bitter blow. Arnold wrote Washington on April 18 deeply upset: "Your Excellency will doubtless be surprised to find, that Congress have directed a court-martial to try me (among other charges) for some of those of which their committee have acquitted me in the fullest and clearest manner; and though this conduct may be necessary for the public interest, it is hard to reconcile it to the feelings of an individual, who is thereby injured."[4] He understood Congress was eager "to avoid a breach with the State." But he wrote Washington predicting that Reed would "use every artifice to delay the proceedings," and begged "that an early day may be fixed for it as possible" closing with a heartfelt appeal: "When your Excellency considers my sufferings, and the cruel situation I am in, your own humanity and feeling as a soldier will render everything I can say farther on the subject unnecessary." Washington obliged and two days later informed Arnold that he had scheduled the court-martial for May 1, only a short time away.[5]

Four days later, as Arnold feared, Reed demanded Washington postpone the court-martial indefinitely so he could gather evidence. At the same time Reed threatened to deny wagons to the army and warned Congress that Pennsylvania would secede if they didn't press for a court-martial.[6] On April 26 Washington wrote to inform Arnold that the court-martial set for May 1 had been postponed. This was one of Arnold's pivotal moments. He felt sure this would be only the first of many postponements. Washington was his friend and supporter but Washington and Congress felt compelled to accommodate Reed. Washington would, or could do nothing to help.

On May 5 Arnold wrote Washington again, his misery leaping from the text:

> From a knowledge of my public conduct, since I have been in the Army, no man is better qualified to judge whether I have merited the treatment I have received.[7]

If your Excellency thinks me a criminal, for Heaven's sake let me be immediately tried, and if found guilty, executed. I want no favor; I only ask justice. If this is denied me by your Excellency, I have nowhere to seek it but from a candid public; before whom I shall be under the necessity of laying the whole matter. . . . Having made every sacrifice of fortune and blood; and become a cripple in the service of my country, I little expected to meet the ungrateful returns I have received from my countrymen; but as Congress have stamped ingratitude as a current coin, I must take it. . . . Delay in the present case is worse than death.

Washington replied two days later to inform Arnold he had set the trial for June 1 but the campaign season was approaching and assembling the officers required to sit as a jury, as Reed surely knew, was increasingly unlikely. Arnold was delighted with the news though, writing Washington how happy he was to hear of the new date:

As nothing can be more disagreeable than the cruel situation I am in at the present, not only as my character will continue to suffer until I am acquitted by a court-martial, but as it effectually prevents my joining the army, which I wish to do as soon as my wounds will permit; and render my country every service in my power at this critical time; for though I have been ungratefully treated, I do not consider it as from my countrymen in general, but from a set of men, who void of principle, are governed entirely by private interest.[8]

He concluded, "The interest I have in the welfare and happiness of my country, which I have made ever evident when in my power, will I hope always overcome my personal resentment for any injury

I can possibly receive from individuals."[9] Arnold wrote to Congress asking for a copy of its committee report and letters between the committee and the Pennsylvania Council for his use at the court-martial. The chairman of the congressional committee replied the next day that it would not be possible to provide copies of these key documents. Arnold then set out for the army's headquarters at Middlebrook where the trial was to take place only to find it was postponed yet again.

Arnold had seen enough. The court-martial would not convene until late December, another eight months, but it was in early May, when it was postponed for the first time, that he made the initial contact with a British representative. Lieutenant Christopher Hele was on parole in Philadelphia after being arrested by Congress for delivering the Carlisle manifesto and proclamation. Arnold invited him to visit.[10] Hele brought with him a letter written by Colonel Beverly Robinson, commander of the Loyal American Regiment. The same letter had been used to recruit other disenchanted Americans.[11] Its author was a former friend of Washington and owned an estate near West Point with extensive friends and tenants in that area. It was Robinson's house Arnold would use when he became commander of the West Point garrison.

Robinson's letter was artfully designed to appeal to the patriotism of rebels, conceding that their "only object has been the happiness of their country." It never mentions Arnold's grievances against the American cause. The arguments it espouses undoubtedly helped Arnold justify to himself his decision to join the British. These patriotic rebels, Robinson writes, "will not be influenced by motives of private interest to abandon the cause they have espoused." After all, the British government was now offering "everything, which can render the colonies really happy": an American assembly, freedom of commerce "in every part of the globe subject to the British navy," "the blessings of good government," and "they shall be sustained in time of need, by all the power necessary to uphold them, without being themselves exposed to danger or subjected to the expenses that are always inseparable from the conditions of a state."[12] Robinson then reminds his readers of the present alternatives; the needless suffering "without limitation of time," "America a scene of desolation." He asks whether Arnold wants the country to enjoy "peace and all the blessings of her train?" Will you "pursue the shadow of liberty, which escapes your hand, even when in the act of grasping it? And how soon would that very liberty, once obtained, turn to lewdness, if it not be under the safeguard of a great European power? Will you rely upon the guarantee of France?"

Then Robinson slips in the least palatable part of the argument. A peace agreement was not to be "negotiated and agreed upon between us as between two independent powers; it is necessary that a decisive advantage should put Britain in a condition to dictate the terms of reconciliation." But there was no need to worry, he writes, because it is Britain's "interest as well as her policy to make these [conditions] as advantageous to one side as the other." Robinson urges speed to save lives "without unnecessary waste of blood of which we are already as sparing as though it were again our own."[13] This was patently false as British officers had been brutal. He then appealed directly to Arnold as the one man who can bring peace:

> There is no one but General Arnold who can surmount obstacles so great as these. A man of so much courage will never despair of the republic, even when every door to a reconciliation seems sealed. Render then, brave General, this important service to your country. The colonies cannot sustain much longer the unequal strife. Your troops are perishing in misery. They are badly armed, half-naked, and crying for bread. The efforts of Congress are futile against the exhaustion of the people. Your fields are untilled, trade languishes, learning dies. The neglected of a whole generation is an irreparable loss to society. The youth, torn by thousands from their

rustic pursuits or useful employment are mown down by
war. Such as survive have lost the vigor of their prime,
or are maimed in battle.

Clearly this was meant to evoke Arnold's own crippled condition. Again Robinson refers to global trade, "all ruled by a uniform
system that bears on every feature the stamp of liberty." British
constraints on the American shipping trade, one of the main provo-
cations for war although not explicitly stated, will presumably be
eliminated. Robinson sees great glory ahead, a glory designed to
appeal to a merchant seaman like Arnold: "United in equality, we
will rule the universe, we will hold it bound, not by arms and violence, but by the ties of commerce . . . the lightest and most gentle
bonds that human kind can wear."

In June, with the court-martial postponed yet again, this time
because of a British attack on the Hudson River forts, Arnold took
another step toward the British. He sent for Joseph Stansbury, a
Philadelphia china merchant and a known loyalist, to discuss the
political situation. Stansbury opposed independence and armed
resistance but prudently took the oath of allegiance to the patriot
cause. In October 1776, however, passersby heard "God Save the
King" being sung in his house and he was sentenced to house arrest
for a time. Stansbury had welcomed the British when they conquered the city and was appointed a commissioner for selecting and
governing the city watch.[14] He was also a British secret agent and
later became a courier for John André, Clinton's aide and chief of
British intelligence, and an acquaintance of Peggy Shippen.[15] After
his conversation with Arnold, Stansbury left for a secret journey
to New York City to convey the exciting news to John André and
General Clinton.

The British had already approached other leading American
officers and statesmen, including Israel Putnam, John Sullivan, Philip Schuyler, Ethan Allen, Samuel Holden Parsons and

Congress's representatives in Paris, Silas Deane and Benjamin Franklin.[16] Ethan Allen was ready to bring Vermont to the British.[17] A string of trusted American "patriots" were already working for the British. Benjamin Church, the director of the first American army hospital, was a paid informer of Gage in Boston. Metcalf Bowler, the chief justice of Rhode Island and William Heron, a member of the Connecticut assembly, were supporting the British. Edward Fox of Maryland, the clerk in the Continental Congress treasury in Philadelphia, offered to procure information and received payments. William Rankin, colonel of militia in York, Pennsylvania, was an informer. General Charles Lee, an experienced British officer who—like other British officers who fought for the Americans had been unable to get the desired promotion in the British army—had wanted Washington's post, was taken prisoner by the British, and had a secret plan to end the revolution. Arnold alone would suffer the terrible consequence of his betrayal.

Clinton was wary about the contact with Arnold. Writing later to Lord Germain he confessed, "I was not at first sanguine in my idea of General Arnold's consequence, as he was said to be in a sort of disgrace, had been tried before a general court-martial and not likely to be employed, and whatever merit this officer might have had, his situation, such as I understood it then to be, made him less an object of attention."[18] For his secret correspondence with the British Arnold chose the alias Gustavus Monk. The choice is key to his attitude toward his actions. Gustavus Adolphus was a famous seventeenth-century Swedish king, the Lion of the North as he was known, a brilliant military leader who brought his army into the Thirty Years War in support of the Protestant cause. He would die in the struggle. George Monk was a general in Parliament's army during the English civil war of the mid-seventeenth century. After the overthrow of the monarchy, after Oliver Cromwell overthrew Parliament, and during the chaos that followed his death, Monk marched his troops from Scotland to London where he set in motion the events that led to recalling Charles II and restoring the monarchy. He was hailed for returning the country to royal government and elevated to the highest ranks of the nobility.

On Stansbury's arrival in New York he met with the Reverend Jonathan Odell, a priest whose pro-British newspaper articles resulted in his being placed on parole in New Jersey and escaping to New York. Odell took Stansbury to British army headquarters where they met with the new head of British intelligence, Major John André. André had the persona of the consummate gentlemen, a lover of theater, a passable artist—he had drawn a likeness of Margaret Shippen—and popular aide to General Howe. But beneath that glamorous exterior lay the ruthless soldier and now spymaster for General Henry Clinton. André was at General Grey's side when they launched a surprise attack on Anthony Wayne's men in the dead of night, writing later: "We ferreted out their piquets and advanced guards, surprised and put them to death and, coming in upon the camp, rushed on them as they were collecting together and pursued them with a prodigious slaughter."[19] The Americans who fled were caught and butchered. But the veneer of the charming gallant would be the image André took to the grave, admired by contemporaries of both sides.

Stansbury was spirited back to Philadelphia before he was missed while André contacted Clinton, who approved the information he was sending Arnold and gave André the code names John Anderson and Joseph Andrews. Stansbury was to refer to Arnold as A.G. and André as Mr. Andrews.[20] They decided Arnold should remain in place for the time being and provide logistical information about the American army. He was simply to be a high-placed spy. Just a month earlier John André had become Clinton's chief intelligence officer. With his dramatic and inexperienced bent, he now provided a list of helpful suggestions about what information would be useful, but was vague about the reward Arnold might expect. Arnold's "own judgment" André suggested, "will point out the services required," adding:

For fair satisfaction we give the following hints. Counsel [of Congress]. Contents of dispatches from foreign abettors (France). Original dispatches and papers which might be seized and sent to us. Channels through which such dispatches pass, hints for securing them. Number and position of troops, whence and what reinforcements are expected and when. Influencing persons of rank with the same favourable disposition in the several commands in different quarters. Concerting the means of a blow of importance. Fomenting any party which when risen to a height might perhaps easily be drawn into a desire of accommodation rather than submit to an odious yoke [the yoke of France.]. Magazines—where any new are forming. To interest himself in procuring an exchange of prisoners for the honor of America.

After assuring Gustavus Monk that in "the very first instance of receiving the tiding or good offices we expect from him, our liberality will be evinced; that in case any partial but important blow should be struck or aimed, upon the strength of just and pointed information and co-operation, rewards equal at least to what such service can be estimated at will be given." André then suggested not just information but battlefield successes Arnold might facilitate, noting that the "zeal of that able and enterprising gentlemen" might enable them to seize "an obnoxious band of men, to the delivery into our power or enabling us to attack to advantage and by judicious assistance completely to defeat a numerous body," then "would the generosity of the nation exceed even his most sanguine hopes."[21] Of course Arnold had resigned his commission and was not yet fit enough to return to the battlefield. André added that should Arnold's "manifest efforts be foiled and after every zealous attempt flight be at length necessary, the cause for which he suffers will hold itself bound to indemnify him for his losses and receive him with the honors his conduct deserves."[22]

The British were guarded in their attitude toward Arnold. There was always the possibility this was a ploy to penetrate their intelligence network and learn key information. In fact Clinton was unenthusiastic about this American hero wounded and under attack from his own party. Still he was willing to get what he could in the way of information from Arnold. After learning from Stansbury that his proposals were agreeable to Clinton, Arnold wrote to assure the British commander that he "may depend on my exertions and intelligence."[23] But he added: "It will be impossible to co-operate unless there is a mutual confidence." Since he had everything at stake he asked for "some certainty my property here secure and a revenue equivalent to the risk and service done. I cannot promise success. I will deserve it. Inform me what I may expect."[24] The British steadfastly refused to be specific about what reward he might expect.

Arnold and Stansbury would correspond and their letters would be in cipher. This was essential since letters might be intercepted. Each man was to have a copy of Blackstone's *Commentaries on the Laws of England*.[25] Each word in their letters would be represented by three figures, the first the number of the book's page on which the word would be found, the second the number of the line, the third the number of the word in that line. Alternatively they might resort to invisible ink, which would be exposed either by acid or flame. Particular topics were to be expressed in misleading language, for example the health of an old woman.

André also had plans for correspondence with Margaret Arnold that would pass through a mutual friend, Peggy Chew, with invisible ink interleaving prosaic chat about social events and clothing, that Margaret Arnold would read.[26] But André had to be content with Benedict as he was unable to involve either Peggy Chew or Margaret Arnold in this correspondence. Indeed, there is no actual evidence that this plan was ever put in place or that Arnold's wife was aware of his conspiracy.[27] One of Arnold's letters to Stansbury has a postscript with Margaret's compliments, but she had met

Stansbury. André did write one letter directly to Peggy. It referred to materials for clothing he might get for her.[28] Historian Carl Van Doren insists "she could not miss his zeal to be further employed or misunderstand what he meant," and characterizes her response to André "as prim a note as was ever written by a conspirator."[29] Apparently even a "prim" note could not dissuade Van Doren from his insistence that she was involved in the conspiracy. In her note Peggy thanked André for his offer to supply millinery materials but noted that Major Giles "was so obliging as to promise to procure what trifles Mrs. Arnold wanted in the millinery way." In fact, a busy young wife in charge of a household with her sister-in-law and Arnold's two young sons, soon expecting her first child, she seems to have been unaware of how far her husband's discontent had led him.

The risks of betraying the cause were considerable for Arnold. Unless his own efforts helped the British succeed—and at that point in the war it looked like they would win—he stood to lose all his property, while his family would be in considerable danger and forced to flee. His enemies would feel triumphant that their suspicions were vindicated. Even now he could still pull back, provided no evidence of his approach to the enemy became known. In this desperate gamble he was not likely to take his beloved young wife into his confidence. It was far too dangerous for her. He certainly would not ask her advice, priding himself on making his own decisions. Nor would he involve his closest aides, Major Franks and Colonel Varick, who might betray his confidence. He would have to bear the risks alone. It was actually the safest course.

Arnold began to send intelligence about the Continental Army's conditions and plans. He had been asked to seize congressional papers but replied that this was impossible and anyway, "Their contents can be known from a member of Congress." Obviously the British had an active informer in that body and Arnold knew it. When he asked what Clinton's campaign plans were he was rebuffed. André wrote that Clinton "cannot reveal his intentions as to the present campaign nor can he find the necessity of such a discovery or that the want of a proper degree of confidence is to be inferred from his not making it."[30]

The British kept Arnold at arm's length. His secret correspondence with them continued during the summer while he awaited the convening of his court-martial. In June André pointed out that general information was helpful but "the most brilliant and effectual blow finally to complete the overthrow of the present abominable power would be the destruction of the Army," and "This may be effected by a grand stroke or by successive severe blows."[31] He had suggestions: the taking of a considerable seaport and defeating the troops assigned to the defense of the province. Could Arnold obtain command of Carolina? Perhaps he might arrange for British troops to surprise and ambush a large body of troops, or intercept a fleet to or from France. Arnold might see to the burning of barracks or the spiking of all the guns of a fort or field artillery. But for what he labels "a general project," André recommended anything on the west side of the Hudson. Could Monk command one of Washington's advance troops and allow them to be surprised, leaving Washington vulnerable to attack, while at the same time the British could seize the Congress? To affect these, Arnold was instructed to "Join the Army, accept a command, be surprised and be cut off."[32]

All this was a betrayal of his military skills, and terribly risky. And while the British expected so much from him they were always vague about what reward he might expect. In July he sent a request through Stansbury for a financial guarantee, whatever the result of his efforts might be. Along with his request in earnest of his good faith, Arnold sent specifics about the state of Washington's army and campaign plans and information about the French fleet.[33] He then tried to return to the army, but first the court-martial had to take place. Two days after receiving André's letter, he wrote Washington asking that the court-martial be expedited, and informing him that he was able to walk "with ease" and hoped soon to be able to ride. He was ready to rejoin the army.[34] The trial had to come first, however, and with the campaign season underway there would be further postponements. In a letter from Mr. Andrews, André, to Monk that month, Andrews is again vague about financial rewards as he requests a plan of West Point, information about vessels on the Hudson and other very specific questions about American military arrangements and ports.[35] Andrews then suggests Arnold assume a command and arrange a face-to-face meeting: "I am convinced a conversation of a few minutes would satisfy you entirely and I trust would give us equal cause to be pleased." He then urges Arnold to undertake more than spying. "Let us not lose time or contract our views which on our part have become sanguine from the excessive strain of your overtures," André insists, "and which we cannot think you would on your side confine to general intelligence whilst so much greater things may be done and advantages in proportion as much greater can be reaped." But Arnold was not ready to risk so much without more specific assurance of the reward. He might, after all, be abandoned by the British after arranging for an American defeat, or be discovered by them and hanged as a traitor.

It was in October, while still awaiting his trial, that Arnold had rushed to the aid of the Philadelphia moderates, including his brother-in-law barricaded in the home of James Wilson, a well-respected patriot, as they withstood the violent, armed assault from Reed's partisans.

The second and final point in Arnold's decision to adhere to the British cause came when the long-awaited court-martial failed to vindicate him, instead ordering Washington to write him a letter of censure. The final decision was up to Congress. The Pennsylvania council, having gotten their way, suddenly expressed concern for his feelings and asked Congress "to dispense with that part of the sentence which imposes a public censure, and may most affect the feelings of a brave and gallant officer."[36] Although the court-martial had failed to find Arnold guilty of any intentional wrong, Congress insisted that he receive a public censure. Despite Washington's attempt to be as gentle as possible in the formal letter of censure and the personal letter that accompanied it, it was too late. Personal letters did not obscure the humiliation of public disgrace. Arnold's feelings seem to have been in turmoil. Although his efforts focused on helping to bring about a great British victory and gaining the reward for having arranged it, he was still frantically seeking alternatives to avoid following through on the suggested treason.

Even after the court-martial's verdict on January 26 it wasn't until February 12 that Congress approved the court verdict, another blow. Congress then took its time letting Washington know its decision. In the meantime Arnold had no commission and no steady income. This was especially difficult as Peggy's baby was due in March and he was already in debt. Now desperate, Arnold appealed once more to Congress to settle his financial accounts. Congress delegated the matter to a five-member committee which, in due course, declared the task "impracticable with that accuracy and attention which the nature of them demand," and recommended the issue be dealt with by the Board of Treasury. Arnold protested to no effect. Again he tried to get involved in privateering with a navy command, writing Washington on March 6 that the Admiralty was considering him for a command.[37] His surgeons, he added, "are of opinion it will not be prudent for me to take a command in the Army for some time to come." He had proposed a plan to the Admiralty for commanding a naval expedition that would need three or four hundred men from the army to act as marines, if Washington agreed to spare them. Arnold wrote again two weeks later when Washington had not replied. Peggy had given birth to a little son the day before. They named him Edward after her father and grandfather. Arnold reminded Washington of the condition of his wounded leg.[38] "My surgeons flatter me that a voyage to sea and bathing frequently in salt water will be of great service to strengthening my leg and relaxing the muscles, which are greatly contracted and thereby rendering it more useful."

Even as André was pressing him to take a post in the army, Arnold was feverishly exhausting other expedients to use his skills and support his family while still serving his country. The naval expedition would not have helped the British. It certainly could not interfere in a meaningful way with a French fleet.

During this desperate time Arnold, writing his old friend from Connecticut Silas Deane, poured out his grief and despair.[39] "I believe you will be equally surprised with me, when the court-martial having fully acquitted me of the charge of employing public wagons, or defrauding the public, or of injuring or impeding the public service. Yet in their next sentence say, 'As requests from him might operate as commands, I ought to receive a reprimand.' Not for doing wrong, but because I might have done wrong; or rather, because evil might follow the good that I did!" He then mentions his proposal to the Admiralty about leading an expedition. Should that fall through he proposed going to Boston with the intention to take command of a private ship.

Deane was especially sympathetic as he had gotten into a serious and humiliating row with Congress himself while working diligently as their secret diplomat in France.[40] He had been sent as an undercover agent to Paris early in 1776 to obtain French assistance. He managed to recruit various French soldiers including Lafayette on the promise of commissions and, more importantly, obtained essential military equipment for the Continental Army.[41] The equipment was purchased on credit, so Deane had ships carrying the armaments to America return with cargos to help pay for the weapons. Congress was unable to pay. He and the other American agents wrangled with each other, and he became thoroughly exasperated with the machinations of Congress, their representatives, and the French court. Deane wrote Jonathan Williams, a merchant and patriot, a letter whose sentiments echoed Arnold's: "It is too much for men to spend the prime of their lives in vexation and anxiety for nothing but to be found fault with and blamed."[42] While the French praised Deane, William Lee, who had also been in Paris, accused Deane of double-dealing. Shortly afterward, Congress recalled him. Lee also accused Franklin and others, and while Lee was much scorned in European courts as a devious individual, Congress treated him as a credible witness. The delegates embarked on a lengthy and contentious inquiry into Deane's financial arrangements, creating splits between Adams-Lee and friends of Franklin, Morris, and Deane. The miserable episode caused Lafayette to complain, "There are open dissensions in Congress, parties who hate one another as much as the common enemy."[43] Deane had not brought his financial papers with him from France, and had to rely on his reputation. A tie vote in Congress about detaining Deane permitted him to return to Europe in 1780 as a private, and thoroughly embittered, citizen. John Adams had been lobbying for Deane's diplomatic post and was his replacement. Not surprisingly Deane lost confidence in the Revolution.

The day after Arnold wrote Deane of his plans for a naval expedition the Admiralty Board wrote Washington that they had abandoned Arnold's plan. Washington informed Arnold that, in any event, he could not easily spare the men for Arnold's expedition and hoped he would return to the field.[44] If Arnold needed to take a leave of absence first and go to sea for his health, permission would be needed from Congress, although Washington would not object. Then on April 6 Washington sent his required censure to Arnold.

One of the so-called services the British suggested to Arnold was to help them conquer a major port, and asked if he could get the command of Charleston, South Carolina. They had attempted to conquer Charleston in 1776 but the palmetto-log walls of Fort Sullivan absorbed their cannon balls like a sponge while the Americans fired back at the British warships with impressive accuracy. In short, the attempt was a fiasco. In late March 1780 an angry and desperate Arnold sent Clinton key details about Charleston. General Clinton then led a more powerful siege of the city. Congress had suggested to Charleston's leaders that in the emergency they arm their slaves. They flatly refused. General Lincoln and his army planned to abandon the city before it became encircled but the State leaders insisted they remain. In due course the British cut off their line of retreat. With no relief in sight, on May 12 Lincoln and his army of five thousand Continentals and militia surrendered. It was a great British triumph and a serious blow for the Americans but Arnold received no particular benefit. Perhaps General Clinton thought the satisfaction of having been helpful would be all he needed.

There was more bad news as Arnold's other options continued to collapse. On April 27 the Board of Treasury reported that Arnold owed Congress one thousand pounds. He protested to Congress, asked how he might appeal, and when they might hear his appeal. They replied he must "state in writing any objections he may have to the report of the Board of treasury on his accounts."[45] All alternatives to betrayal now seemed exhausted, except for simply retiring from the service in debt and disgrace.

If he were to do the great service he promised the British, Arnold now decided that the ideal command for him, given his infirmities and need to have a strategic location to surrender, was West Point, with its commanding location on the Hudson River. Washington considered it the "Key to the Continent."[46] West Point was the main fortification on the Hudson at its northern point. It stood on a plain that towered over the Hudson at an unusually narrow stretch of the river where the Hudson made two right-angle bends, first west and then north. Ships had to slow down to negotiate the turns, making them especially vulnerable. Congress recognized the strategic importance of this spot, and after years of dithering, sent a young Polish engineer, Thaddeus Kosciuszko, to take charge of strengthening the fortifications there. Kosciuszko spent more than two years completing the task. By the spring of 1778 the Americans had managed to stretch a seventeen-hundred-foot-long iron chain across the river there. The chain itself was impressive. Each of its

1,200 links weighed between 90 and 120 pounds. It was attached to a series of logs that kept it at the right depth to cripple enemy ships attempting passage. Ironically Fort Arnold, named for Arnold, had been built at the end of the West Point plain. West Point's defenses were the latest in military technology. Three concentric circles with batteries of cannon protected the fort at West Point from a land attack. A separate fortification, Fort Putnam, protected Fort Arnold, and was protected itself by a redoubt overlooking it. To the south, West Point was protected by another series of forts protected by another series of redoubts. More redoubts were constructed across the river. The Hudson was regarded by the British as the crucial link between the New England and mid-Atlantic states, and formed the all-important water route to Canada. It was, as the Indians dubbed it, "the Great Warpath." Arnold himself had fought on that warpath time after time.

Arnold now began a campaign to get command of West Point. He met with his old patron, Philip Schuyler, a delegate to Congress from New York, to lay out the reasons why he was the ideal person to command the fortress. He also wrote to all the other delegates in Congress from New York with the same arguments. When he hadn't heard from Schuyler for some time, and afraid some other officer might get the post, on May 25 he sent another letter. He explained that he had only requested a leave of absence for the summer due to his health, thinking it would be a "very inactive campaign and that my services would be of little consequence."[47] The situation turned out quite differently, however, and although still in pain he wished "to render my country every service in my power" and asked Schuyler to speak to Washington on his behalf. Schuyler did meet with Washington recommending Arnold for the command at West Point. An earlier meeting between Washington and Schuyler had been inconclusive, but this time reading Arnold's second letter to Schuyler, Washington seemed prepared to approve Arnold for the post. Schuyler wrote Arnold that Washington spoke of your "abilities," "your sufferings," "the well-earned claims you have on your country." Washington had not yet made all the decisions for the coming campaign but it seemed to Schuyler that Arnold would be given an important command or station in the field.[48]

Arnold's correspondence sending important military information to the British was proving exasperating. Although they benefited there was great risk for him but no benefit. The British were refusing to be specific about what they were prepared to do for him and to date had done nothing, despite the information he had sent them. He wrote on July 7 explaining Washington's plan to wait for the French fleet to arrive at Newport, Rhode Island, before beginning his campaign and providing many particulars about American plans and strength. Having received no answer he wrote again on July 11 asking for a personal conference, clearly annoyed. "A mutual confidence between us is wanting, the persons we have employed have deceived us, or we have been unfortunate in our negotiation, in which on both sides we are deeply interested. If the first, then it is here that our correspondence ought to end. If the latter, a stricter attention and proper regard to the interests of both parties may remedy the misfortune."[49] Since the British had obstinately refused to be specific about payment, Arnold was specific, although cloaking the demands as business dealings, not so far from the truth. "My stock in trade is 10,000 pounds sterling, with near an equal sum of outstanding debts, an equal sum I expect will be put into stock and the profits arising be equally divided." He noted that he had "advanced several sums already, and risked still greater without any profit. It is now become necessary for me to know the risk I run in case of a loss." He asked that the bearer be given one thousand guineas, "on receipt of which I will transmit to you their full value." He supplied a great deal of information about West Point's vulnerabilities and suggested if Clinton set his troops on shore some three miles south of the fort he would find "a good road to bring up heavy cannon."[50] The plans of West Point, however, were to be paid for. No more vague promises.

Sure he would get the command of the fort, he wrote André again the very next day complaining he had received no answer to his previous letter or any verbal communication.[51] He again asked for an appointment. He added that the "mass of the people are heartily tired of the war and wish to be on their former footing." They expect great progress from the current campaign and if the British persevere, "the contest will soon be at an end. . . . The present struggles are like the pangs of a dying man, violent but of a short duration." He repeated his request for the sums he mentioned in his earlier letter. On July 13 André finally replied.[52] He asked for more information about West Point fortifications and that Arnold suggest a plan for taking it that will ward off any suspicion from himself. As for a meeting, perhaps Arnold might visit Elizabethtown or another place near British lines under a flag of truce. The letter never addressed Arnold's request about payment. Clearly the British were playing Arnold for all the information they could get from the high-powered spy but were not willing to provide any reward or even a specific response to his request. His patience was at an end.

On July 15 Arnold had had enough of this game and wrote André that the matter be settled "previous to cooperating."[53] Since he might lose all his American property he asks that Clinton secure his property to him, "valued at ten thousand pounds sterling, to be paid to me or my heirs in case of loss, and as soon as that shall happen. A hundred pounds per annum to be secured to me for life, in lieu of the pay and emoluments I give up, for my services as they shall deserve." He added that if he pointed out how Clinton could "possess himself of West Point, the garrison, stores, etc. twenty thousand pounds sterling I think will be a cheap purchase for an object of so much importance." Arnold insisted that at present one thousand pounds be paid to his "agent," adding, "I expect a full and explicit answer." He planned to leave for the army on July 20. He then wrote Congress reminding them they owed him four years' pay and asking for four months advance to purchase horses and equipment to enable him to take the field, which they did.[54]

The British finally agreed to Arnold's terms. In return for the plans of West Point and assistance in taking it and the surrender of the garrison, he was promised twenty thousand pounds sterling and a general's commission in the British army. André was clear though: Arnold "must not suppose that in case of detection or failure that your efforts being known you would be left a victim, but services done are the terms on which we promise rewards."[55] If Arnold's plans failed he would be rescued, but without the requested funds or military commission. André would meet him personally somewhere near West Point. Arnold set off for the Hudson Highlands.

But the best laid plans were about to go awry. Washington and Arnold met near Stony Point where the commander, busy supervising his army as it crossed the river, informed Arnold with pleasure that he was "to command the left wing, the post of honor." Arnold's shocked reaction was not what Washington expected. Later at headquarters Arnold pleaded with the commander's chief of staff that his leg was not fit enough for him to take the field, all the time pacing up and down on the injured limb. Washington agreed to think further about the assignment but his orders on August 1 confirmed his decision to have Arnold in the field. Peggy, in Philadelphia dining with Robert Morris when she was told of her husband's new assignment, was greatly upset. Did that mean she knew of his plot to surrender West Point? Probably not. A field command was far more strenuous and dangerous than garrison duty and her husband was still not physically sound.[56]

Washington was changing his mind about attacking Manhattan. Clinton was changing his campaign plans as well. Washington had hoped to lure him out of the city but instead he was returning his troops to New York, having failed to trap the French fleet at

Newport. Since Washington was unwilling to attack in that case, he brought his army back across the Hudson, writing Arnold on August 3, "you are to proceed to West Point and take the command of that post and its dependencies."[57] Relieved, Arnold set out riding north to take charge of the "Key to the Continent."

TWENTY-THREE

Treason

J ust when all Arnold's insistence on a face-to-face meeting with
a British officer, and all his efforts to obtain the command of
West Point succeeded, everything unraveled. Perhaps it was
inevitable. A clandestine meeting in a war zone was dangerous, and
while Arnold was brilliant on the battlefield he was a novice at spy
craft and sabotage, and desperate. John André, his British contact, a
flamboyant officer with a taste for the dramatic and keen to make
his reputation, was a novice as well. The stakes were huge: potential
victory in the Revolutionary War, Arnold's coveted honor and reputation, and his wife and children's future secured or all totally lost.
But there were too many possibilities for error. And it all unraveled.

General Clinton had regarded Arnold with suspicion from the first.
But Arnold's information about American plans and strengths had
been helpful, very helpful. Clinton and André had just returned to

New York, having won a great victory capturing Charleston and its defending army. It was time to turn to Arnold's offer. The alternative to capturing West Point with his help was a long, impractical siege and a force of some twenty thousand men.[1] Clinton decided to risk trusting Arnold's good faith to gain possession of it. For his part John André, his chief of intelligence, was jubilant. Clinton had just made the young major his adjutant general. André came from a Huguenot family. His father was a successful trader and merchant, and André, his eldest son, was meant to follow him into the family business. But his father died unexpectedly, leaving his fortune to be equally divided among his five children. As a result André, who was more interested in a military career than a career in business, never had the funds to purchase an important military commission. His charm, dedication, and talent had to serve instead. And they did. "Good fortune follows me," André wrote home in excitement. "The Commander-in-chief has raised me to the first office in the Army, if that of most confidence and least profit is to be styled so."[2] He had not yet received the rank of lieutenant colonel that customarily went with his new post and would mean a raise in pay. When Clinton elevated him previously to deputy adjutant general there were objections to his getting the rank of major, and even when he got it he remained on a captain's pay. Still he had been astonishingly successful. "I am full of gratitude toward the General for so much kindness and impress'd with the greatest zeal to deserve it," he wrote, "but can hardly look back at the steep progress I have made without being giddy."[3]

Arnold's correspondence with the British would become more dangerous once he was based at West Point and serving as its commander. In a busy city like Philadelphia it was easier for loyalists like Stansbury, Arnold's courier, to come and go discreetly. A war zone behind American lines was quite different. Stansbury refused to continue and suggested that André deal directly with the disaffected general. On August 3 Clinton reluctantly agreed to let André meet with Arnold. André could determine whether the man could be trusted. It was exceedingly dangerous to send André behind enemy lines, and Clinton was loath to let his favorite aide and good friend take the risk. A face-to-face meeting pleased Arnold, however, who wasn't sure his messages were getting through to Clinton. Even their direct correspondence with assumed names placed Arnold and André in great peril. If any letters were identified as theirs, how to explain the communication between two officers on opposing sides. A face-to-face meeting was still more incriminating. Yet André was keen to go. If meeting Arnold resulted in the British taking West Point his future would be made. It was risky, but what an opportunity for an ambitious and daring young officer.

Clinton was ready to move on the project. Ten ships of the line under Admiral Sir George Rodney arrived in New York from triumphs in the West Indies. With this reinforcement Clinton prepared to move up the Hudson. To deceive Washington he spread word he was heading for the Chesapeake. Washington had used the tactic to lure Clinton out of New York City so he could attack it. Two could play at that game.

Arnold reached West Point on August 5 to assume command from Robert Howe. He chose for his headquarters the home of Colonel Beverly Robinson, Howe's headquarters. Colonel Robinson was with the British in New York City leading a loyalist regiment and acting as a British spy. It was his skillfully framed letter that had been used to lure Arnold to the British cause. Robinson was one of the state's wealthiest men and his home in the Hudson highlands was a comfortable, rambling structure decorated with costly furniture. It was situated across the river from West Point and about two miles south of it. The site, flanked on two sides by mountains and forests, was quite gloomy, especially as the season wore on. For Arnold's purpose though its location was perfect; out of sight of the garrison troops and conveniently located, should he need to make a quick escape, not that he expected he would need to.

In the meantime Arnold set to work to make West Point vulnerable. He wrote Clinton that the fortress was a "wretchedly executed" post and if Clinton landed his troops three miles below it there was a good road to use for hauling his cannon.[4] The fort's fortifications had been powerful but were allowed to fall into disrepair, and he meant to see that their repair never took place. He also bent his mind to reducing the garrison. A week after his arrival Arnold informed Washington many problems at West Point needed attending to if the fort was to be strengthened.[5] The great chain across the Hudson needed to have new logs fitted. He asked the governor of New York to send teams to haul it out of the river for the purpose.[6] His aim, of course, was to make it easier for a British ship to move easily up the river. Arnold claimed two cannon were defective and he planned to send them off to be repaired.[7] On the premise that supplies were needed for winter he ordered five hundred soldiers off to cut wood. Two hundred others were sent, prior to his arrival, to help guard Fishkill. Arnold's old friend, Colonel John Lamb, the 2nd Artillery commander at West Point, complained that sending so many men to Fishkill was excessive and would prevent needed repairs being made at West Point, weakening the fort's defense. Arnold refused to order the men back.[8] Indeed he wrote Washington that he was sending another fifty men to support the inhabitants of Westchester.[9]

Arnold somehow managed to pass on key information. When he found out Washington planned to attack New York City after tricking the British into sending a large force to Rhode Island, he informed General Clinton who quickly returned to the city.[10] Arnold tried, but failed, to get the names of America's secret agents.[11] Nor was he above helping encourage dissent. After Congress refused to raise the pay for army officers, he wrote General Greene on August 23 urging that "a small committee of a thousand or fifteen hundred men of all ranks" present a petition to Congress.[12] Writing Greene again on September 12 Arnold complained it was "a matter much to be lamented that our Army is permitted to starve in a land of plenty. There is a fault somewhere; it ought to be traced up to its authors and if it were preferred they ought to be capitally punished."[13]

For months Arnold had been convinced the British were going to win the war. They had just taken Charleston and the army defending it, and had overwhelmed a force led by Arnold's nemesis and Washington's would-be replacement, General Horatio Gates at Camden, South Carolina. The good general, Congress's hero of Saratoga, had fled from the battle. Since the British were almost certain to win the war and their offer to the Americans was reasonable, it made sense to end the fighting as quickly as possible and spare everyone the terrible costs. Arnold was not alone in believing that an American victory was now impossible. That summer and fall, notwithstanding the fitful assistance of France, Washington and other patriots were in despair. Washington wrote in May, "Unless a system very different from that which has long prevailed be immediately adopted through the States, our affairs must soon become desperate, beyond the possibility of recovery. . . Indeed, I have almost ceased to hope."[14] Arnold meant to do something major to hasten return to British rule.

Peggy had stayed at home in Philadelphia with her baby when Arnold returned to the army. She and her sister-in-law Hannah shared the family home. Their letters reveal a very caring relationship. Arnold's little son Henry lived with them while Henry's two older brothers were at school in Maryland. The family was not financially well off, Arnold was in debt, but they were comfortable and, in Peggy's case, surrounded by a loving family and old friends. But as Arnold's plans for the betrayal of West Point developed, he decided that his wife and their baby should join him. If his plan succeeded they would be safer with him than in Philadelphia, filled as it was with radical patriots and a Congress that already regarded him with hostility. If his plan failed, Peggy and little Edward would still be safer away from Philadelphia where traitors found guilty of betraying the revolutionary cause had been hanged.

The long overland journey north to West Point was hazardous. Peggy was not strong. She would only be traveling with six-month-old Edward and a nurse. Arnold sent her detailed instructions and advice that covered every stage of the more than 140-mile journey. Peggy was advised to "get out of the Carriage in Crossing all Ferries, and going over all large Bridges to prevent accidents."[15] The little party set out on September 6. The journey north took them six days. Shortly after they left Hannah wrote Peggy: "I address you, my dear Mrs. Arnold, from the regions of gloom and solitude."[16] "If you could conceive how we miss you and the dear little bantling, you would pity us. Harry was inconsolable the whole day you left us, and had, I believe, not less than twenty of the most violent bursts of grief, his little brother Edward seems to be the principal theme of the mournful song." Hannah had received a letter from Benedict, "who, lover-like, is tormenting himself with a thousand fancied disasters which have happened to you and the family, however hope by the day after to-morrow you will be able to remove all his distressing fears." She closed with the prayer that "Heaven guard you safely to him, for in your life and happiness his consists. . . . Sweet repose to you and yours." Peggy and little Edward were expected to stay at West Point for several weeks but by September 27, less than two weeks after her arrival, she and her baby would be on their journey home.

While Peggy was en route to him, Arnold and Clinton were planning the logistics for his meeting with André. Arnold had wanted the meeting within his own lines but Clinton insisted it take place in neutral ground near the Hudson with a British ship close by. He also insisted that André wear his uniform and be accompanied by Colonel Robinson, an experienced intelligence officer. Since Robinson's home was in the area he could claim to be intending to retrieve some of his belongings. The two would go under a flag of truce approved by Clinton and a letter signed "Gustavus." Letters were exchanged and the plan was set. Arnold and André would meet at Dobbs Ferry on September 11 at noon. In preparation for their meeting Arnold wrote to Colonel James Livingston, commander of the regiment at Verplanck's Point and Stony Point, to retreat to West Point if the British ascend the river. André wrote to Colonel Sheldon, trusting "I shall not be detained . . . I shall rather risk that than neglect the business in question, or assume a mysterious character to carry on an innocent affair and, as friends have advised, get to your lines by stealth."[17]

André and Robinson rode on horseback to the north end of Manhattan, across the King's Bridge at Spuyten Duyvil, then boarded an armed sloop, the *Vulture*, which took them upriver to Dobbs Ferry. Clinton had given approval for André to accompany Robinson writing "as you are with him at the forepost, you may as well be of the party." He planned to wait for André's return at the headquarters of General Knyphausen north of New York City, to be the first to get the news [18]

Arnold had gone to the home of Joshua Hett Smith, a loyalist attorney at Haverstraw. The Smith house was closer to their meeting place, and a stage in Peggy's journey to West Point. Arnold informed Washington that he was going to Dobbs Ferry to establish signals in case the British came up the river. At Haverstraw a barge with eight men, innocent of their actual mission, set out to row Arnold the thirteen miles to the meeting place. As they neared a British gun boat the crew spotted them. Having no notion about the planned meeting, the British crew fired on Arnold's barge, sending the bargemen rowing madly back to safety. The shots very nearly hit Arnold. Once on shore Arnold waited nearly nine hours until sunset, when he returned to the Smith house to meet Peggy and their baby. André and Robinson spent the same long afternoon of September 12 next to the blockhouse at Dobbs Ferry, waiting for Arnold before finally returning to the *Vulture* and sailing back to New York.

Although busy planning the next attempt to meet, Arnold couldn't resist writing General Greene the next day gloating over Gates's humiliation at Camden. After the British victory at Charleston Gates had been appointed commander of the southern department. At Camden he led his army in a disastrous battle: "I am happy to find that General Gates's information was so ill founded," Arnold wrote. "It is an unfortunate piece of business to that hero and may possibly blot his escutcheon with indelible infamy."[19] Arnold conceded, tongue-in-cheek, "I may not be right to censure characters at a distance," but added that the event "in no way disappointed my expectations or predictions on frequent occasions, and notwithstanding the suggestions of his friends that he had not retreated to the borders of Virginia, he must have been at a great distance and pretty secure from danger, as he had no advice of the retreat of the Maryland troops for at least four days." Arnold was right, Gates's incompetent and cowardly behavior did finally "blot his escutcheon with indelible infamy." Of course Arnold's own behavior was about to blot out all his own achievements despite his courageous leadership and triumphs.

While their first attempt to meet had failed, neither Arnold nor André were about to give up. Two days after the failed attempt Robinson returned by barge to nearby Tarrytown. Colonel Livingston spotted him and wrote Arnold that while Robinson was "under pretense of a flag" he thought his real purpose was to spy out the area. Should he send men to check.[20] Arnold hastened to warn him not to interfere, it was only a small party close to New York, then began considering safer ways for the meeting with André to take place. He wrote to Colonel Lamb to secure the banks near Dobbs Ferry so he would not be fired on and sent André various alternative plans.[21] If André wanted to try the previous plan again he might travel to the headquarters of either Lieutenant Colonel Jameson, in charge of the lines near Dobbs Ferry, or Major Tallmadge. Both men had been instructed to immediately escort Mr. John Anderson to Arnold. Alternatively Arnold would send a confidant to meet him at Dobbs Ferry on Wednesday, September 20, to conduct him by water to "a place of safety" where Arnold would meet him. André would "need to be disguised, especially if enemy boats were in the area." If André sent no reply, his escort would be waiting for him, according to the last alternative. Arnold then added disguised references to the sums he demanded. He concluded his letter to André/

Anderson, "Meet me if possible. You may rest assured that if there is no danger in passing your lines, you will be perfectly safe where I propose the meeting of which you shall be informed on Wednesday evening if you think it proper to be at Dobbs Ferry."

While Arnold was laying out these plans Washington informed him he would be at King's Ferry and asked Arnold to escort him to Peekskill. Washington then meant to continue on to Hartford, Connecticut, and on his return would meet Arnold at his headquarters at the Robinson house. He asked that Arnold "keep this to yourself as I want to make my journey a secret."[22] Of course Arnold conveyed the information to André. On September 16 Arnold wrote Washington confirming the guard Washington had requested and closing with "sentiments of the most profound respect and esteem, your Excellency's most obedient servant."[23] The "profound respect and esteem" were doubtless genuine but it would be the last letter Arnold would write his patron and friend as an officer in the American army.

The evening before André was to leave for his meeting with Arnold Clinton hosted a farewell dinner for him at the Kip Mansion in New York. There was feasting, drinking, toasts, and hearty singing while a band played the popular favorite, "The Roast Beef of Old England."[24] Clinton proposed a special toast: "A word in addition, gentlemen, if you please. The major leaves the city on duty tonight, which will most likely terminate in making plain John André, Sir John André, for success must crown his efforts."[25] After the dinner Clinton met privately with André and gave him three pieces of advice: not to change his dress as Arnold proposed, not to go within the American lines, and not to carry any communications. These were sound warnings but André would violate all three.

Arnold invited Smith and his wife and nephews, who were on their way to Fishkill, to lunch at the Robinson House where they joined Dr. William Eustis, an army surgeon, Colonels Meigs and Lamb, and others. Arnold reminded his aides Franks and Varick that they were to ride to the Smith house later to meet Washington and his entourage for dinner, then accompany them to Peekskill. Both Franks and Varick were upset Arnold was socializing with Smith, a Tory familiarly referred to as "Snake in the Grass Smith," but Arnold dismissed their complaints. While all were at lunch Arnold got a message from Robinson, then on board the *Vulture,* asking to meet. When Arnold explained to his guests that he was to meet with Robinson, Lamb suggested Washington be shown the request first. After lunch Arnold and Franks crossed the river and rode to the Smith house to meet Washington, Hamilton, and Captains Samuel Shaw and James McHenry for a dinner meeting. The party then got into a barge for the trip to Peekskill. Arnold did inform Washington of Robinson's letter. The commander found the meeting improper for an army officer. Robinson's errand was, or was supposed to be, a civilian affair. Washington spied the *Vulture* close by and fretted over its proximity. All slept peacefully, how-ever, Clinton having missed his opportunity to capture Washington before he left for Hartford. Washington planned to return to West Point five days later, though, and spend Saturday night there.

As Washington wished Arnold wrote Robinson that it would be improper for them to meet. He added that Robinson could confide in Smith who would meet him at Dobbs Ferry or on board the *Vulture* the evening of September 20. He would have a boat and a flag of truce. The letter to Robinson included one to André notifying him that he would be met by boat at Dobbs Ferry on the 20th. Arnold added: "It will be necessary for you to be disguised and if the enemy boats are there, it will favor my plan, as the person is not suspected by them. If I do not hear from you before you may depend upon the persons being punctual at the place above mentioned." Returning to the Smith house Arnold recruited Smith to the venture by telling him that Robinson had additional propositions for Congress. He confided that he personally detested the French alliance, ridiculing the "impropriety and inconsistency of an absolute monarch being the ally of a people contending for freedom, who kept his own subjects in absolute slavery."[26]

Wednesday, September 20 dawned gray and chilly as André set out for his meeting with Arnold. When he got to Dobbs Ferry he discovered that the *Vulture* had moved off and was at Croton, ten miles beyond British lines. Unfortunately that morning Sutherland had spotted a white flag on the eastern shore of the river, and believing Arnold was trying to send a message sent a boat to Dobbs Ferry. As his boat neared the shore the Americans fired on it and the boat speedily returned to the *Vulture*. The British officers on board the *Vulture* followed Clinton's orders to stay near the ferry. Colonel Lamb was suspicious of the ship though and ordered it "shooed off."[27] André managed to get a boat to take him to the *Vulture* and spent the day aboard. About seven o'clock that evening he was put ashore where Robinson and Captain Andrew Sutherland were waiting.

Nothing seemed to go smoothly. Smith's task was to convey André to Arnold. He thought it highly unusual to use a flag of truce at night. He was given a pass for a boat but had trouble finding one. In desperation he approached a local farmer herding his cows, Samuel Cahoon. Cahoon had no boat or oars but agreed to deliver the letter to Arnold. André, on board the *Vulture,* paced hour after hour during the night, eventually going below for fear he would raise suspicions. He wrote to Clinton explaining that Arnold hadn't appeared. "This is the second excursion I have made without an obvious reason, and Colonel Robinson both times of the party. A third would infallibly fix suspicion." André also sent a letter on behalf of Sutherland to Livingston complaining that the previous day his boat, under a flag of truce, had been fired upon. When Arnold was shown the letter he recognized André's handwriting. The next morning, Thursday the 21st, to avert suspicion from the ship's crew, André pretended to be ill. He planned to make another attempt that evening.

Samuel Cahoon appeared at the Robinson house that morning with Smith's letter, explaining that he had not been able to get a boat to meet André. Arnold was furious and tried to find a boat himself. Arnold urged Smith to try again that night. American officers were to be informed he had permission to pass at any time, day or night. Poor Samuel Cahoon informed Smith he was far too tired to try again that evening, and in any case was especially reluctant to go with a flag after dark. Wouldn't morning do? His wife didn't want him to go. His brother Joseph who was to accompany him was also hesitant. Arnold was upset. He gave each of them fifty pounds of flour and threatened them with arrest if they refused to do as he asked. Although he handed them sheepskins to muffle the oars, he assured them it was all perfectly safe.[28]

It was a gloomy, moonless night as the two brothers rowed Smith the three miles to the *Vulture*. The ship's officer heard them approach and in orders laced with curses, insisted they come alongside. Smith climbed up the ship's rope ladder and, explaining his business to the surly officer, asked to see the captain. Unimpressed, the officer was threatening to hang him when a messenger from the captain appeared and ordered Smith below, where he met with Robinson and Sutherland. He showed them his letters and Robinson went to fetch André, who had been sleeping. André appeared wearing a dark blue cloak over his uniform and followed Smith down the ladder to the boat where the nervous Cahoon brothers waited. Rowing against the tide, in the dark they crossed the river. Arnold was hidden in a clump of fir trees waving a lantern to help Smith find him. He brought André to Arnold. Smith somewhat reluctantly returned to the boat, leaving the two men together. In the darkness of an autumn night, under the trees the two conspirators intent on plotting a British victory in the Revolution met face-to-face.

Their meeting in the flickering light of lanterns was the first time the two men had seen each other: the intense, crippled but solidly built soldier, the slim, elegant, and self-assured young British officer. Their conversation didn't begin well. André and Clinton were still trying to manipulate Arnold and André began by offering Arnold £4,000 less than they had agreed upon. Arnold reacted with outrage. As a known loyalist, his grand house and property in New Haven and property in Pennsylvania would immediately be confiscated and he had a family to support. André agreed to urge Clinton to provide the promised sum. Arnold had six documents with him with extensive details of West Point's garrison and defenses, although he had no map. The meeting had started late, and as their discussion over how to attack the fort went on, it began to be light. In the gloom of the forest they didn't notice dawn breaking until Smith came to warn them. André hurried back to the boat but the tide had turned, and the exhausted Cahoon brothers were not willing to row him to the *Vulture*. Arnold decided it was safer for them to ride the six miles to Smith's house while Smith returned the boat. André could spend the day at the house and leave in the evening. On their ride there André was abruptly reminded that he was behind enemy lines when a sentry challenged them. Arnold gave him the password and they were allowed to proceed. As the sun rose the *Vulture* was having its own difficulties. Livingston's troops began firing at her. Arnold and André heard the pounding of the guns from the Smith house and dashed to an upstairs window to see what was happening. After ninety minutes of trading shots, the tide rose and André was dismayed to see the *Vulture* sail down the river, leaving him stranded. Ironically Arnold had lent Lamb the funds to build the artillery post firing at the *Vulture*.[29]

André was anxious to leave as soon as possible. Since the river was bound to be heavily patrolled by boats that evening, Arnold advised Smith and André to cross the river by ferry. Smith would escort André to White Plains. He could then proceed by land. This would mean crossing the so-called neutral territory popular with bandits before getting safely back to British lines. André agreed to hide the papers with details of West Point in his stockings. Since he would be traveling through American lines he also agreed to take off his uniform and put on simple, country dress. He put another cloak over his blue one. Arnold gave André a horse, black with a white star and a Continental brand on its shoulder. They said farewell and André set off into the night. He had broken all three of Clinton's instructions to him. He and Arnold would never see each other again.

TWENTY-FOUR

Bridges Burned

[André] had done his duty with full knowledge of the risk, so could not be dishonored in his death.

—J. W. Fortescue, *A History of the British Army*

"I should as soon have thought West Point had deserted us as he ..."

—*Ordinary Courage: The Revolutionary Adventures of Joseph Plumb Martin*

The heart which is conscious of its own rectitude, cannot contemplate to palliate a step which the world may censure as wrong. I have ever acted from a principle of love to my Country, since the commencement of the present unhappy contest between Great Britain and the Colonies. The same principle of love to my Country actuates my present conduct, however it may appear inconsistent to the world, which very seldom judges right of any man's actions. I have no favor to

314

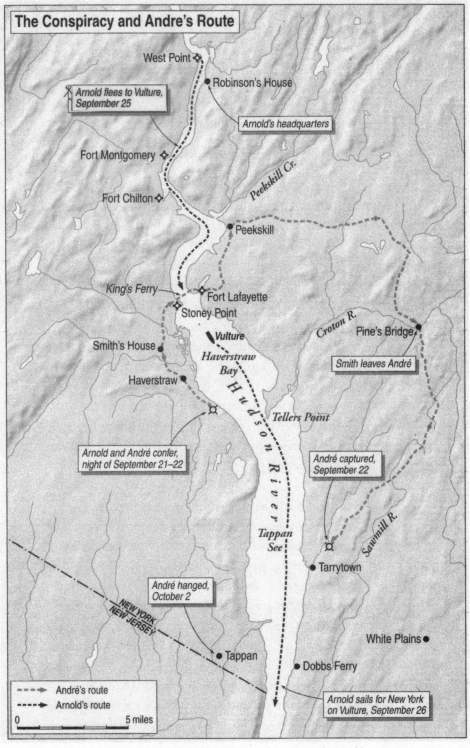

The Conspiracy and Andre's Route

West Point

Robinson's House

Arnold flees to Vulture,
September 25

Arnold's headquarters

Fort Montgomery

Peekskill Cr.

Fort Chilton

Peekskill

King's Ferry

Fort Lafayette

Stoney Point

Croton R.

Pine's Bridge

Vulture

Smith's House

Haverstraw
Bay

Smith leaves André

Haverstraw

Tellers Point

Hudson River

Arnold and André confer,
night of September 21–22

André captured,
September 22

Tappan
See

Sawmill R.

André hanged,
October 2

NEW YORK
NEW JERSEY

Tarrytown

White Plains

Tappan

Dobbs Ferry

Arnold sails for New York
on Vulture, September 26

- - - → André's route
- - - → Arnold's route

0   5 miles

Conspiracy and Escape Routes of Andre and Arnold

ask for myself. I have too often experienced the ingratitude
of my Country to attempt it.

—Benedict Arnold to George Washington,
on board the *Vulture*, September 25, 1780

Arnold's decision to abandon the American cause, driven by injured pride, anger, and the pursuit of honor as he saw it, tragic in itself, spread tragedy to the lives of those about him. When he didn't return from the Smith House that night his aides were concerned. Franks and Varick were suspicious of Smith, and had picked a fight with him when he dined at their headquarters earlier. Arnold was furious with them for insulting a guest, warning them, "if he ask the devil to Dine with him the Gentlemen of his Family should be civil to him."[1] Peggy admitted to Franks and Varick that she also distrusted Smith but pleaded with them to drop the matter, assuring them that her husband would never do anything dishonorable. During her stay at West Point Arnold had his aides take her on various outings, presumably giving him the freedom to continue his plans for the surrender of the fort in privacy.

He was back now at his headquarters awaiting events. Everything seemed to be going according to plan. Smith had returned to report all was well when he left André north of White Plains. Washington and his retinue were to return to West Point on September 25. They arranged that Washington and his senior staff, Hamilton, Knox, the Marquis de Lafayette, and other officers would breakfast with Arnold and Peggy at the Robinson House that morning. When they were nearly at Arnold's headquarters Washington decided to check the state of the redoubts on that side of the river and sent the rest of his men on ahead, joking with the marquis, "I know you young men are all in love with Mrs. Arnold and wish to get where she is as soon as possible."[2] He asked that they tell her not to hold breakfast for him, he would join them shortly.

Off they galloped. Peggy greeted them and went upstairs to feed her baby while Arnold joined the officers chatting amiably as they assembled at the table. Suddenly Colonel Solomon Allen appeared at the door with a letter for him. Arnold read it privately. It was from John Jameson, second in command at North Castle, reporting that a John Anderson had been stopped on his way to New York. He had Arnold's pass and suspicious documents "of a very dangerous tendency" tucked in his stockings with very explicit details about the defenses of West Point as well as information about Washington's council of war held September 6. Jameson added that he was sending John Anderson to Robinson House but would send the papers he had been carrying directly to George Washington.[3] Shocked, Arnold told Allen to tell no one about the contents of the letter, then dashed to the porch and ordered his servant to bring him a horse and to alert his barge crew. He rushed upstairs to tell Peggy he was leaving at once to join the British. The startled young woman fainted. Just as Arnold was placing her gently on her bed a servant of Washington's arrived announcing that the commander would be there momentarily. Arnold sped downstairs asking Franks to fetch Dr. Eustis for Peggy and leaving a message for Washington that he was off to West Point and would be back in an hour. When Arnold got outside and there was no horse waiting for him, he took Allen's horse and rode toward the river.

The morning he and Arnold parted, André accompanied by Smith and his servant rode toward Stony Point about two miles away.[4] They were challenged by a sentry at the ferry, but showing their passes were allowed to continue. Smith was well known to Livingston's officers and chatted with them while they waited for the boat. At King's Ferry Livingston offered Smith supper and inquired about his journey. He declined the meal and agreed to deliver a dispatch to Arnold. They rode on. Eight miles east of the river, near Compound, they were stopped. It was now evening and they were questioned about where they were going in the dark and again Smith showed their passes from Arnold and explained to a suspicious captain their urgent business. They were being sent by Arnold to meet a man at White Plains to get intelligence from the British army. The captain allowed them to pass but warned them that traveling at night was exceedingly dangerous since there were groups of bandits preying on travelers. On his advice they decided to spend the evening at a nearby house and continue their journey in the morning.

Early the next day under a threatening sky the three men continued on their way, stopping for breakfast then getting back on their horses. Fifteen miles north of White Plains Smith told André he could go no further as they were now beyond American lines. He planned to head north to visit relatives before reporting back to Arnold and gave André eight Continental dollars and a map of the area. André offered Smith his gold watch in thanks but Smith declined, and he and his servant headed north toward the Robinson House to inform Arnold all was well. André was left alone to find his way back to British lines.

He picked his way along, stopping to water his horse and sort out his directions as he entered the dangerous "neutral grounds." Five miles from his destination, stopping to consult a map, he was waylaid by Paulding, Williams, and Van Wart, local men on militia duty but also on watch for likely victims to rob. One man was standing lookout while his friends played cards. Spotting the lone rider they quickly blocked the road pointing their muskets at André. The tallest of the three, Paulding, was wearing a red-faced green coat and the cap of a Hessian soldier, the disguise he had used to escape from a British prison camp. Seeing the coat and cap André thought they were loyalists and called out, "Gentlemen, I hope you belong to our party."[5] "What party?" Paulding asked. André replied "the Lower Party." "We do," Paulding said. "Thank God! I am once more among friends," André answered. "I am a British officer." He then showed them his gold watch to prove he was a British gentlemen. That was all they needed to see. Paulding then admitted, "We are Americans." Realizing his mistake André changed his demeanor, chuckling, "God bless my soul, a man must do anything to get along." Paulding asked his name and André answered John Anderson, showing them the pass signed by Arnold. He claimed he was on the general's business and must not be detained. Paulding shot back, "We care not for that," and ordered him to dismount. "Damn Arnold's pass," one of his associates shouted, and demanded his money. When André said he had none they decided to search him.

They led him off into the woods, Paulding assuring André they did not mean to take anything from him but that there were many bad people traveling the road and they had to be sure he wasn't one of them. They ordered him to undress. As he did so he handed each article of clothing to Williams to search. They found and took his gold watch and eight Continental dollars. They had noticed that although he was wearing rustic clothing he had fine, expensive boots and ordered him to take them off. He pulled off one boot and handed it to Williams who found nothing in it. But when he began putting the boot back on one man noticed the bulge in his stocking. They ordered him to take his stocking off and then they discovered the documents hidden there. Paulding, who could read, examined the papers and exclaimed that André was a spy. They found the documents in his other stocking and asked what he would pay them if they let him go. André agreed they could have the horse, his watch, and one hundred guineas. But studying the documents again they decided they ought to take him to the nearest army post. The lowering clouds produced a fine drizzle as the little procession with André, followed by his three armed captors, rode along. André offered them money to take him to Kingsbridge. They debated whether to accept the bribe but turned down his tempting offer, fearing if they took him to British lines they would be arrested.

After various stops for food and drink they delivered André and his documents to Colonel James Jameson at North Castle. Jameson was the second in command there but decided to take action on his own. He rewarded André's captors for their loyalty with a gift of André's watch and horse. Examining the documents André had been carrying, however, Jameson decided they must have been stolen. He ought to have waited for Colonel Tallmadge, Washington's intelligence chief, who was due back shortly before deciding on a course of action. Instead he ordered Colonel Solomon Allen, with an escort of four militia men, to deliver John Anderson to Arnold together with a letter explaining events. He intended, however, to send the documents themselves to George Washington. Jameson also wrote a letter to Washington accompanying the documents. In it he claimed, oddly, that Arnold had wanted all the documents sent to him but that he thought the documents "of a very dangerous tendency" and "thought it proper your Excellency should see them."[6] Of course it was all untrue. Arnold didn't even know of the seizure of the documents let alone give any instructions to Jameson. Jameson's entire behavior was strange.

As soon as Tallmadge returned and saw the documents he recognized Arnold's handwriting and suspected treason. He and Jameson argued over what was to be done. Tallmadge apparently suggested some drastic measure, perhaps arresting Arnold, which Jameson refused. Jameson did agree though to reverse the decision to deliver John Anderson to Arnold. Instead André and his escort were ordered to reverse direction. André was to be taken to South Salem instead, where there was a detachment of dragoons. But Jameson utterly refused to countermand his order for Allen to deliver his letter to Arnold informing him that John Anderson had been arrested and the documents he carried sent to Washington.[7] As soon as Tallmadge set eyes on André, despite André's rough dress and dirty condition, he was convinced he was a military man and a gentleman.

★ ★ ★

Washington arrived at Robinson house just after Arnold's departure. Major Franks greeted him with apologies for Arnold's absence, explaining he had gone to West Point and would be back in an hour and that Mrs. Arnold was feeling ill. Washington took a hasty breakfast and, when Arnold hadn't returned, decided to go to West Point to meet him and inspect the garrison. He took a barge across the river with Lafayette and Knox. Colonel Lamb came down to greet them, surprised at the visit. But when Washington asked where Arnold was, Lamb pointed out he hadn't been at the fort for the past two days. Washington thought this odd but as he was at the fort he decided to inspect the defenses. For the next two hours he examined the fortifications and was thoroughly dismayed by their state of disrepair, the half-empty magazines, broken walls including one wall of Fort Putnam, rusty wheels, crumbling parapets.[8] When he questioned the West Point officers about the sorry state of the defenses he was told there was a serious shortage of manpower to fix the problems and Arnold had added several additional projects for them to undertake.

It was nearly four o'clock that afternoon when Washington crossed the river and returned to Robinson House. He was given a large packet containing the documents taken from André, along with a revised report from Jameson and a letter from André himself disclosing his real identity. When André arrived filthy and exhausted at South Salem, and learned the documents he had carried were to be sent to Washington, he had decided to reveal his true identity. During a walk with Lieutenant King, commander at South Salem, in the garden of the house where he was confined, he confessed he was Major John André, British adjutant general. He asked for pen and paper to write directly to the commander in chief. André explained to Washington that he was writing "to rescue myself from an impression of having assumed a mean character for treacherous purposes or self-interest, a conduct incompatible with the principles that activate me, as well as with my condition in life. . . . The person in your possession is Major John André, Adjutant General of the British Army."[9] André explained that he

321

was to meet someone to get intelligence but was detained and then unable to return to his ship as planned. He had proceeded under a flag of truce and had a pass on his return. "Thus I have the honor to relate, I was betrayed into the vile condition of an enemy in disguise within your posts. . . . I am branded with nothing dishonorable, as no motive could be mine but the service of my King, and as I was involuntary an imposter." In Arnold's letter to General Clinton after arriving in New York he made the same plea. He was sure of André, having proceeded under a flag of truce and a pass "being immediately sent to New York."[10] In André's letter to Washington he mentioned some American officers taken prisoner at Charleston who were engaged "in a conspiracy against us" and might do as an exchange for him.

Trying to take all this in, Washington summoned Knox and Lafayette into a private room to inform them of André's arrest and Arnold's treason. Washington was deeply disturbed: "Arnold has betrayed us. Who can we trust now?" Orders were promptly given to intercept Arnold and bring him back unhurt. Ten ships were ordered to take up positions to protect West Point from any British attack.

Washington's dismay was well placed. There were fears that Arnold's example would prompt further defections. Arnold's Life Guards at West Point left for home.[11] Eight days after Arnold's flight Adjutant General Colonel Alexander Scammell wrote of the shock, "That a man so high on the list of fame should be guilty as Arnold, must be attributed not only to original sin, but actual transgression," but in seeming contradiction he echoed Washington's fear, "We were all astonishment, each peeping at his next neighbor to see if any treason was hanging about him: nay, we even descended to a critical examination of ourselves."[12] British intelligence reporting on the American reaction to Arnold's treason reported that the treason revealed "their distrust of themselves."

Arnold had been on his way down the Hudson to New York for an hour by the time Washington returned to the Robinson House.

When Arnold left Peggy and his assembled breakfast guests behind, he rode directly to the river where he had found his bargemen waiting. He ordered them to row him south, down the Hudson. When they passed Verplanck's Point he spotted the *Vulture*. On Arnold's command the crew rowed toward the British sloop while he frantically waved a white handkerchief tied to his cane in a sign of truce to the British crew on the *Vulture* and to Livingston on shore not to fire on the barge. Once alongside the *Vulture* Arnold climbed aboard and informed Robinson that André had been arrested. He called down to his astonished bargemen, "My lads, I have quitted the rebel Army and joined the standard of his Britannic Majesty." He offered them commissions in the British army if they defected, promising one, Larvey, "to do something more." Larvey called up to him, "No, Sir, one coat is enough for me to wear at one time."[13] Two of his bargemen did agree to the offer. The others were taken prisoner to New York where Clinton gave them parole. Just before the ship sailed off Arnold hurriedly penned a letter to Washington along with one to Peggy and left them at the blockhouse. About three o'clock that afternoon the *Vulture* set sail down the Hudson River to New York, every mile taking Arnold farther from home, family, friends, colleagues, and his place as a hero of the American revolutionary army. His scheme to surrender West Point had been discovered and there was no going back. There could be no retreat.

Had Arnold planned to arrange for the British to capture Washington and his staff? While that was bruited afterward, it seems highly unlikely. When he and André parted there was no certainty when an attack on West Point would take place and Washington had no plan to stay there. The plot would have had to be set for September 25, when Washington was scheduled to return to West Point, for that to have been the scheme. Nevertheless, the plot to permit the West Point fortress to fall to the British would have been a grievous loss for the American army, especially after the recent loss of Charlestown with its defending army.

Arnold's letter to Washington after his flight opened with a plea that however others may, indeed, would see his behavior, he intended only the good of his country:[14]

> The heart which is conscious of its own rectitude, cannot contemplate to palliate a step which the world may censure as wrong. I have ever acted from a principle of love to my Country, since the commencement of the present unhappy contest between Great Britain and the Colonies. The same principal of love to my Country actuates my present conduct, however it may appear inconsistent to the world, which very seldom judges right of any man's actions. I have no favor to ask for myself. I have too often experienced the ingratitude of my Country to attempt it. But from the known humanity of your Excellency, I am induced to ask your protection for Mrs. Arnold from every insult and injury that a mistaken vengeance of my country may expose her to. It ought to fall only on me; she is as good and innocent as an angel, and is incapable of doing wrong. I beg she may be permitted to return to her friends in Philadelphia, or come to me, as she may choose.

He asked that Peggy be permitted to write to him. A letter for Peggy was enclosed in his letter to Washington. Arnold assured Washington that his close aides, Colonel Varick and Major Franks, were also ignorant of his intentions.

Arnold also took responsibility for André's situation, writing Washington that it was at his direction that André had come to him with a flag of truce and returned in disguise. Robinson also wrote to Washington but his letter was a plea for André's innocence and a demand for his freedom. André had gone "with a flag at the request of a General Arnold, on public business with him, and had his permit to return by land to New York," Robinson argued. That being so, he "cannot be detained by you, without the greatest violation of flags, and contrary to the custom and usage of all nations. . . . I must desire you will order him to be set at liberty and allowed to return immediately. Every step Major André took was by the advice and direction of General Arnold, even that of taking a feigned name, and of course he is not liable to censure for it."[15]

Washington's response was to write to his officers up and down the river near West Point to strengthen the fort as quickly as possible and to order Colonel Jameson to take every precaution to prevent André from escaping. André was to be escorted under heavy guard to Robinson House. Contrary to Robinson's plea that André was entitled to immediate release, Washington wrote Jameson, "I would not wish Mr. André to be treated with insult, but he does not appear to stand upon the footing of a common prisoner of war. Therefore he is not entitled to the usual indulgences they receive, and is to be most closely and narrowly watched to insure that André must not escape."[16] Washington also wrote summoning Colonel John Laurens, judge advocate general of the Continental Army who, nine months earlier, had prosecuted Arnold at his court-martial.

Peggy, stunned by Arnold's unexpected and desperate announcement that he was leaving immediately to join the British army, had fainted. When she regained consciousness he was gone. She was wild with fears for her own and her baby's safety, feeling quite rightly abandoned in this remote military post far from friends and family. To her terrified mind no one could be trusted, they were plotting to kill her child. Peggy's guests and Arnold's aides did not yet know of his flight. Varick testified later that Peggy was in "the most alarming distress of mind."[17] He was told "that she had complained that she had no friends, she was left alone, and on your [Franks] telling her that she had many friends (here enumerating yourself, me, and General Arnold)—on your mentioning him, she exclaimed in an agony of grief, *Oh no, he is gone, gone forever.*"

This statement confirmed what were still just suspicions of Franks and Varick that Arnold had fled. Washington had just recently arrived for breakfast and knew nothing of Arnold's flight. Once he and his officers learned the truth, Alexander Hamilton left, trying in vain to catch up with Arnold. As Hamilton explained in a letter to his fiancée Elizabeth, General Schuyler's daughter, "I saw an amiable woman, frantic with distress for the loss of a husband she tenderly loved, a traitor to his country and to his fame, a disgrace to his connections, it was the most affecting scene I ever was witness to."[18] Unable to calm her, Franks sent for Washington. She knew Washington—he had dined at her father's table in Philadelphia, he had freed her brother Edward when he was captured. Yet when Washington appeared she did not recognize him, and flailing in her fright her gown dropped from her shoulder. Washington was embarrassed and quickly left the room.

Later there were claims, apparently started by Aaron Burr, that Peggy knew about Arnold's plot and was instrumental in it, just feigning distress.[19] But those who knew her best and knew her at the time, her family, Arnold's aides, and Washington himself were convinced of her innocence and her very genuine hysteria. Hamilton described Peggy's anguish to his fiancée: "You may imagine that she is not easily to be consoled. Added to her other distresses, she is very apprehensive the resentment of her country will fall upon her (who is only unfortunate) for the guilt of her husband."[20] "Could I forgive Arnold for sacrificing his honor, reputation, and duty," he added, "I could not forgive him for acting a part that must have forfeited the esteem of so fine a woman. . . . At present she almost forgets his crime in his misfortunes, and her horror at the guilt of the traitor, is lost in her love of the man. But a virtuous mind cannot long esteem a base one; and time will make her despise, if it cannot make her hate." When Major Franks learned of the rumor that Peggy was complicit in Arnold's plot he was incensed. Arnold had assigned Franks the responsibility of guarding Peggy while she was at West Point. He insisted on her innocence when questioned later by a friend. As further proof that Arnold would not have confided in her Franks mentioned her delicate state of health:

> Paroxysms of physical indisposition attended by nervous debility, during which she would give utterance to anything and everything on her mind. This was a fact well-known amongst us of the General's family; so much so as to cause us to be scrupulous of what we told her, or said in her hearing. General Arnold was guarded and impenetrable towards all around him, and I should believe her to have been ignorant of his plans, even without my knowledge of this peculiar feature in her constitution; but *with it*, such a strong corroborative proof, I am most solemnly and firmly convinced that General Arnold would never confide his detestable scheme to her. . . . He was moreover, too well aware of her *warm patriotic feelings.* [21]

Washington was deeply sympathetic, and when Peggy regained her composure he gave her the letter Arnold has asked him to deliver and informed her that Arnold was safe. Then the commander did as Arnold had asked and gave Peggy the choice of returning to her father and family in Philadelphia or going to Arnold in New York City. She chose to go home to her family. On September 27, two days after Arnold's flight, Peggy, escorted by Major Franks, left with the nurse and her baby son for the long journey home to Pennsylvania. Had she been complicit in Arnold's plot, or loved him above all else, she would never had elected to return to Philadelphia where the Executive Council radicals and Congress were already hostile to her husband, and where she and her child would be in real danger. But she chose to go home to her family, whatever the danger, rather than to join her husband in the British bastion of New York.

The news of Arnold's defection caused a national furor with wild parades and bonfires that burned him in effigy. His two older sons were taken into the home of Arnold's old friends, Comfort Sage and his wife. Mrs. Sage closed her curtains that his children might not see the horrible image of their father that a raucous crowd carried in parade past their door. The rioting in Norwich where Arnold was born and raised was particularly vicious, the rioters even overturning his father's gravestone. In New Milford, Connecticut, residents carried effigies of Arnold and Satan through the streets as firecrackers were exploded.[22] Later the effigy of Arnold was hanged, cut down, and buried. A similar parade wound through the streets of Philadelphia with effigies of Arnold and Satan, Satan carrying a pitchfork and offering gold. At the end of the parade the effigy of Arnold was burned.

Arnold's defection had an impact on Europeans considering whether to support the American Revolution. John Adams was in the Netherlands trying to get a loan and financing when the Dutch learned about Arnold's treason. Baron van der Capellen informed Adams that Arnold's treason, together with the loss of Charleston and Gates's defeat at Camden, had destroyed Dutch confidence.[23] "Never has the credit of America stood so low." Adams was to inform Congress to "depend upon no money from hence."

The feelings among Arnold's fellow soldiers and officers were intense. General Greene, a friend of Arnold's, learning of his treason, judged: "Since the fall of Lucifer, nothing has equaled the fall of Arnold. His military reputation in Europe and America was flattering in the vanity of the first General of the age. He will now sink as low as he had been high before, and as the devil made war upon heaven after his fall, so I expect Arnold will upon America."[24] He added, "Should he ever fall into our hands, he will be a sweet sacrifice." Rewards were placed on Arnold's head and Washington plotted to have him captured.

When the news reached Hannah of her brother's flight to the British, she was in Philadelphia with Arnold's little son Henry.

Hannah had often been upset at Arnold's long absence in the army and the dangers he faced during the war, but she was also distraught at the war itself and the terrible pain it caused. Yet now writing to a friend from New Haven she referred to the "distressful step" that he had taken.[25] She asked that her bed, which was to have been sent to Arnold, be kept until she sent for it, praying that "if my wretched life is continued, that I shall one day quit this land of strangers and return to that of my birth." Of course Arnold's fine house in New Haven was promptly confiscated as punishment for his treason, and would be sold. "Let me ask the pity of all my friends," Hannah grieved, "there never was a more proper object of it . . . Do write. Forsake me not in my distress, I conjure you, but let me hear at all opportunities." She reported that Arnold's sons, "The little unfortunate boys in Maryland," and young Harry were well, then remembered the tragedy that had struck her friend. "I was so swallowed up in my own distress I had forgot yours, in the loss of your little son! But mourn not for him, my friends, he has escaped the snares and miseries of a wretched, deceitful and sorrowing vale of tears."

When Peggy returned home she wanted nothing more than to remain quietly with her family, especially her father. That was not to be. Indeed Major Franks reported to friends that only the intervention of Joseph Reed, of all people, had saved him and Mrs. Arnold from physical violence.[26] Less than a month after her return the Pennsylvania Executive Council that previously had been so hostile to Arnold, decided she had to leave. On October 27 they announced:

> The Council, taking into consideration the case of Mrs. Margaret Arnold (the wife of Benedict Arnold, an attainted traitor, with the enemy at New York) whose residence in this city has become dangerous to the public safety; and this board being desirous as much as possible, to prevent any correspondence and intercourse being carried on with persons of disaffected character in this State and the enemy at New York, and especially with

the said Benedict Arnold, therefore, Resolved, That the said Margaret Arnold depart this State within fourteen days from the date hereof, and that she do not return again during the continuance of the present war.[27]

Peggy's father was permitted to accompany her most of her way to New York. A day after they left Edward Burd, her brother-in-law, wrote his father, "You have doubtless heard of the unfortunate affair of Mrs. Arnold. We tried every means to prevail on the Council to permit her to stay among us, and not to compel her to go to that infernal villain her husband in New York. The Council seemed for a time to favor our request, but at length have ordered her away."[28] Her forced departure, he wrote, threw the entire family "in the deepest distress." Her father had promised the Council and Peggy had signed, engaging not to write to Arnold or to receive letters without showing them to the Council if they permitted her to stay. This wasn't enough for the Council that had done so much to ruin her husband's life and reputation. "If she could have staid Mr. Shippen would not have wished her ever to be united to him again." "It makes me melancholy," he added, "every time I think of the matter. I cannot bear the idea of her re-union. The sacrifice was an immense one at her being married to him at all. It is much more so to be obliged, against her will, to go to the arms of a man who appears to be so very black."

Four days before Christmas Peggy's father arrived back home after bidding farewell to his favorite child. They would correspond over the years but would see each other again only once. He wrote Peggy's beloved grandfather, "My poor daughter Peggy's unfortunate Connection has given us great grief. She is however safe arrived at New York and well provided for, which is all the Consolation we could expect considering all Circumstances. . . . When will this terrible War with all its Evil have an end?"[29]

★ ★ ★

330

Of all those touched by Arnold's action, John André's tragic execution would be followed by an even more "giddy rise" to the highest pinnacle of public esteem than even he could have imagined. But first came his ordeal, and Smith's. Smith had served as André's escort from the *Vulcan* and guided him through the American lines toward White Plains. He was now seized by Washington's orders and brought to him for questioning. Smith insisted he had done nothing wrong, that everything he did was at the orders of General Arnold. "Sir," Washington retorted, "do you know that Arnold has fled and that Mr. Anderson whom you piloted through our lines, proves to be Major John André, the Adjutant General of the British Army, who is now our prisoner?" Pointing to a tree visible through the window Washington threatened "unless you confess who were your accomplices, I shall suspend you both on that tree."[30] Smith stood his ground. He was a lawyer, and after insisting on his innocence added that as a citizen he was not to be tried by a military court. However, under persistent questioning he explained all he knew of the affair.

A cold autumn rain cast its gloomy chill on André and his escort, as he was taken by horse and then by barge to Robinson House. André arrived at Robinson House not long after Smith and was questioned. Afterward he and Smith were sent under heavy escort to Fort Putnam. The two men were not permitted to speak to each other or even given an opportunity to converse. As they rode André was near the front of the column, Smith near the rear. They crossed the river in two barges, each prisoner in a different boat. Sitting next to Tallmadge on the barge, Tallmadge asked André if he had intended to participate in the attack on West Point. André said he was, and pointed out the spot where the British meant to launch an attack.[31] André asked Tallmadge how he would be regarded by Washington and a military tribunal. Tallmadge, hesitant at first, finally replied with a story. He had a "much-loved class-mate in Yale College," he told André, "by the name of Nathan Hale, who entered the army in 1775."[32] Hale had been disguised as a civilian when he was captured on his return from a mission to Long Island to get information on the British army. "Do you remember the sequel of the story?" Tallmadge asked. Hale had suffered especially cruel treatment. He was summarily hanged the following day without a trial. The night before his execution he was denied the service of a chaplain or even a Bible. He had been allowed to write two letters, one to his brother, another to a friend who he didn't realize had been killed. Allowed to make a last speech, he ended it with the now famous phrase, "I only regret that I have but one life to lose for my country." After his death the British officer in charge destroyed both letters. "But you surely do not consider his case and mine alike?" André asked Tallmadge. "Yes, precisely similar," Tallmadge answered, "and similar will be your fate!"[33]

Hale's brutal treatment was cause of great bitterness among Americans and is important for Washington's determination that André be treated with scrupulously correct treatment, unlike that meted out to Hale. Despite this the British were, and remain, incensed by Washington's treatment of André. Fortescue, author of the classic history of the British army, explains their view that Washington used disguised spies and kidnappers himself, and hoped Clinton would exchange Arnold for André. The British acknowledged the appropriateness of the trial of André but they were convinced the threat to execute him as a spy was "employed chiefly as a means of putting pressure of a peculiarly cruel kind upon Clinton, and it was for this reason and for no other that it was so much resented by the British Army and the British nation."[34]

At Stony Point they were provided with horses for the remaining journey. They reached Tappan, where they were to be incarcerated, at sunset. Word had traveled quickly and as their column drew up in front of the old Dutch church the town green was jammed with residents, with others peering from windows and doorways. Smith wrote, "We were paraded before the church. Many of my *quondam* friends flocked around us, and from them I received the bitterest invectives."[35] Smith was lodged in a cramped spare room in the church while André was provided a bedroom and adjoining living room in the stout stone building that accommodated the Casparus Mabie Tavern. As Washington ordered "[e]very attention was paid him suitable to his rank and character." Both were kept under heavy guard, with guards constantly with each man. The locals hurriedly built two coffins that they carried back and forth past the windows of the rooms where André and Smith were incarcerated.

On September 27 Clinton wrote to Washington. Ignoring André's rustic disguise he pointed out that since André had gone into American-held territory under a flag of truce and had passports for his return he had "no doubt but that your Excellency will immediately direct that this officer has permission to return to my orders at New York."[36] Clinton was an aloof, stiff man but he had warmed to this amiable, elegant young officer, and was thoroughly alarmed at his predicament. Washington was unmoved by Clinton's appeal. Keen to resolve the affair as quickly as possible he ordered André's case to be heard by a board of general officers on September 29. The board was to determine "in the light of which he ought to be considered, and the punishment that ought to be inflicted."[37] It was a distinguished board comprised of six major generals and eight brigadier generals. André was brought into the church where the officers were sitting, wearing the clothes in which he had been captured, and was seated at a small table. Alexander Hamilton, who was a member of the board, described the proceedings and André's comportment to Colonel Laurens:

"When brought before the Board of officers, he met with every indulgence, and was requested to answer no interrogatory which would even embarrass his feelings. He frankly confessed all the facts relating to himself." Indeed, the facts were not controverted, and the Board reported that André ought to be considered as a spy, and agreeably to the law and usages of nations, must suffer death. André met the result with manly firmness. "I foresee my fate," said he; "and though I pretend not to play the hero, or to be indifferent about life, yet I am reconciled to whatever may happen, conscious that misfortune, not guilt, has brought it upon me."[38]

The following day Washington replied to General Clinton's letter reminding him that the circumstances in which André was caught would have justified summary execution.[39] Instead Washington had referred the case to a board of officers, who reported André had made a "free and voluntary confession." André had arrived in the night from an armed sloop for an interview with General Arnold—André did not name his contact—"in a private and secret manner," had changed his dress within the American lines and then passed through the lines in disguise carrying several papers that contained intelligence for the enemy. "It is evident," Washington wrote, "that Major André was employed in the execution of measures very foreign to the objects of flags of truce, and such as they were never meant to authorize or countenance in the most distant degree." In fact, during his examination André had admitted "that it was impossible for him to suppose that he came on shore under the sanction of a flag." André's execution was set for five o'clock in the evening the first of October.

Clinton was distraught and, according to Chief Justice Smith, prepared to hang as many American spies as he held prisoner. He was in tears at a meeting of British officers as he read the letter André had sent him.[40] Instead of sending Washington a threatening letter, he was persuaded to write a more conciliatory one attempting to persuade Washington that the board was not properly informed of all the pertinent facts, adding, "I think it of the highest moment to humanity that your Excellency should be perfectly appraised of the state of this matter before you proceed to put that judgment in execution." A threatening letter would be sent however. Arnold was to write it, and it would be sent with Clinton's.

Washington postponed the execution until October 2 to give Clinton's three emissaries, lieutenant-generals Robertson and Elliot and Chief Justice William Smith, time to plead for André. They arrived accompanied by Colonel Robinson. General Greene met them on behalf of Washington. After a long conference Greene reported to Washington. They had delivered a letter from Arnold to Washington expressing gratitude for Washington's kindness to Peggy, then arguing that André ought not to be considered a spy concluding with an eloquent appeal: "Suffer me to entreat your excellency for your own and the honor of humanity, and the love you have of justice, that you suffer not an unjust sentence to touch the life of Major André."[41] But then Clinton had Arnold write that if Major André "should suffer the severity of their sentence, I shall think myself bound by every tie of duty and honor to retaliate on such unhappy persons of your army, as may fall within my power . . . I have further to observe that forty of the principal inhabitants of South Carolina have justly forfeited their lives . . . [Clinton could not] in justice extend his mercy to them any longer if Major André suffers, which in all probability will open a scene of blood at which humanity will revolt." "If this warning should be disregarded," he concluded, "and he suffer, I call heaven and earth to witness, that your excellency will be justly answerable for the torrent of blood that may be spilt in consequence." Arnold could not have known what prisoners Clinton had in Charleston nor was he in any position to threaten their lives. The letter was obviously written by and for Clinton with Arnold pointing out the threat executing André would produce. Arnold was in no position to dispute it. He was as distraught as Clinton. His plans for ending the war by surrendering West Point had failed; he was now useless to the British as a spy, having been exposed as a traitor. He had compromised the chief of British intelligence, close confidant of General Clinton, a highly regarded and much-loved officer. Arnold was, and must have felt, supremely responsible for André's predicament as well as his own. At any rate, despite persuasions and threats, Clinton's delegation was informed that Washington's opinion had not altered. The three delegates tried once more, arguing that André be permitted to return to New York to no avail. Washington was unmoved.

André was reconciled to his fate but he worried that Clinton would reproach himself what had happened, telling Hamilton, "I would not for the world, leave a sting in his mind that should embitter his future days." When he wrote Clinton thanking him for his kindness he exonerated him of any responsibility for what happened, reminding Clinton that he had gone against his advice.[42] Then he proclaimed, "With all the warmth of my heart, I give you thanks for your Excellency's profuse kindness to me, and I send you the most earnest wishes for your welfare, which a faithful, affectionate, and respectful attendant can frame." He asked Clinton's help for his mother and three sisters, "to whom the value of my commission would be an object."

Believing he was to die on October 1 Andre wrote Washington that morning, pleading to die like a soldier not a spy, by a firing squad, not a gibbet. "I trust that the request I make to your Excellency at this serious period, and which is to soften my last moments, will not be rejected. Sympathy toward a soldier will surely induce your Excellency and a military tribunal to adapt the mode of my death to the feelings of a man of honor. Let me hope, Sir, that if aught in my character impresses you with esteem towards me, if aught in my misfortunes marks me as the victim of policy and not of resentment, I shall experience the operation of those feelings in your breast, by being informed that I am not to die on a gibbet."[43] Based on the verdict of the board however, Washington felt he could not grant this request. The board of inquiry had been split, six for and six against hanging, and General Greene had made the decision for hanging. Hamilton disagreed, writing Elizabeth that he felt this was too hard, that delicate sentiment, virtue, fortitude "pleads for him, but hard-hearted policy calls for a sacrifice. He must die . . . I must inform you that I urged a compliance with André's request to be shot; and I do not think it would have had an ill-effect, but some people are only sensible to motives of policy, and sometimes, from a narrow disposition, mistake it."[44] He then predicted, correctly, "When André's tale comes to be told, and present resentment is over, the refusing him the privilege of choosing the manner of his death will be branded with too much obstinacy."

There was criticism among the British later that Arnold never offered to surrender himself in exchange for André when it was learned that André was captured. But in 1782 a Captain Battersby, who "enjoyed the friendship of military men of the highest social rank," came forward stating that "It was currently reported and believed in the lines, that Arnold himself proposed to Sir Henry that he might be permitted to go out and surrender himself in exchange for André, and that the reply was, 'Your proposal, sir, does you great honor, but if André was my own brother I could not agree to it.'"[45] This assertion was published and never denied by any of the British officers in Clinton's circle. The biographer who offers this evidence rightly points out that the offer would be in keeping with Arnold's temperament, adding, "what was there left for Arnold to live for after his disgrace and the failure of the conspiracy? That he realized his unhappy fate, I do not doubt. Such a sensational death, a voluntary sacrifice of his life to save the life of André, exhibiting alike his courage and his generosity, would not, in his despair, have been altogether repulsive. It would unquestionably have been better for his fame if Sir Henry Clinton had assented to his offer."[46]

André's courtly behavior, his graciousness and manly courage made a very great impression on all his captors. He was to die at noon on October 2. Not hearing any response from Washington about his request to be shot André thought it had been approved. It was a perfect, almost summer-like day. André ate the meal sent him as his others had been, from Washington's table, dressed and chatted with his guards. As the hour for his execution approached Washington ordered the shutters closed so he and his staff were hidden from the view of the large crowd that had gathered on the hill where the execution was to take place. André's escort arrived to the beat of drums. He placed his tricorn on his head and followed the guards. Outside he was flanked by officers and a guard of five hundred dragoons, four abreast. They followed a fife and drum corps and were followed by a black coffin on a horse-drawn wagon. André marched along nodding to the board of officers that had tried him. Dr. Thather witnessed the execution and described the event in his journal: "Melancholy and gloom pervaded all ranks and the scene was affectingly awful. The eyes of the immense multitude were fixed on him who, rising superior to the fears of death, appeared as if conscious of the dignified deportment he displayed. His only hesitancy was when he saw the gallows. "Must I die in this manner?" he asked the captain of the guard. "I am reconciled to my fate but not to the mode."[47] The captain replied, "It is unavoidable, Sir." Other than this, Dr. Thatcher remembered, "not a murmur or a sigh ever escaped him and the civilities and attentions bestowed on him were politely acknowledged."[48] André, as requested, climbed onto the wagon under the gallows, stood in the coffin, removed his hat and put the rope around his neck and covered his eyes with his handkerchief. He was given the opportunity to say final words: "I have nothing more to say gentlemen but this, you all bear me witness that I meet my fate as a brave man." His hands were tied, and at the end he said quietly, "It will be but a momentary pang." At the signal the horses pulled the wagon from under his feet, his body swinging in an arc as the crowd gasped. In 1821 the Duke of York arranged to have André's remains, which had been buried near the gallows, removed and reinterred in Poet's Corner at Westminster Abbey, oddly alongside Britain's literary greats.

Two days after André's execution Congress's Board of War stripped Arnold's name from the list of officers. Deeply alarmed after André's execution, Arnold wrote Washington fearful for the fate of his family.[49] "Necessity compelled me to leave behind me in your camp a wife and offspring that are endeared to me by every sacred tie." "If any violence be offered to them," he warned, "remember I will revenge their wrongs in a deluge of blood." It was rather late to think of his family's danger, and Washington was the unlikeliest person to harm them.

TWENTY-FIVE

Afterword

"They will not give me a chance to die a soldier's death."
—Benedict Arnold, when his offer to serve the British
in war against France was rejected.

A nd what of Benedict Arnold, hero of the American Revolution, now in the British camp? Five days after André's execution Arnold wrote a letter "To the inhabitants of America" in an attempt to explain his behavior and plead for reconciliation with the Mother Country.[1] He refers to loyalists and other Americans suffering under "that class of men who are criminally prolonging the war from sinister views, at the expense of the public interest." He reminded his fellow countrymen how he had fought for the defense of his country and to remedy her grievances, reluctantly agreeing to independence. But now that the country's "worst enemies are in her own bosom," he adds, "I should change my principles, if I conspired with their designs." The people of America, he pointed out, should have been asked whether to accept the latest British proposals "to negotiate under a suspension of arms, for an adjustment of differences." No authority had been given by the American people to conclude the alliance with France, "the Articles of Confederation remain still unsigned."[2] He preferred the offers from Britain to those from France, "the enemy of the Protestant faith . . . fraudulently avowing an affection for the liberties of mankind, while she holds her native sons in subservience and chains. . . . I fought for much less than the parent country is as willing to grant to her colonies, as they can be to receive or enjoy." He prays for the safety of Americans in arms but is ready to devote his life to the reunion of the British Empire to spare his country misery. "As for the critics whose hostility to me originates in their hatred to the principles, by which I am now led to devote my life . . . they may be assured that, conscious of the integrity of my intentions, I shall treat their malice and accusations with contempt and neglect."[3]

Although raising interesting points Arnold's letter failed to still the uproar over his actions or rehabilitate his reputation. On October 20 he followed the letter to his fellow Americans with a "proclamation" to "the officers and soldiers of the Continental Army who have the real interest of their Country at heart, and who are determined to be no longer the tool and dupes of Congress or of France."[4] Arnold wrote that he was authorized by General Clinton to offer them positions in the British army commensurate with those they then held. Certainly there were sufficient reasons for dismay and discontent among the army troops. The following year Washington would have to cope with two serious mutinies. But Arnold's offer was stillborn. The mutineers wanted better treatment in the American army or threatened to go home. They did not threaten to join the British army.

Arnold's hope for reconciliation with Britain was shared by many Americans, at least initially, including the leaders of the Revolution. Independence was not an easy or welcome choice and made slowly. Just days before the battle at Lexington and Concord Benjamin Franklin admitted that he had traveled "almost from one end of the continent to the other, and kept a variety of company, eating, drinking, and conversing with them freely, and *never, the least expression of a wish for a separation, or a hint that such a thing would be advantageous to America.*"[5] John Jay concurred: "It has always been, and still is my opinion and belief, that our country was prompted and impelled to independence by *necessity*, and not by *choice.*" Thomas Jefferson, author of the Declaration of Independence, admitted that even after war began the possibility of separation from Great Britain *"was contemplated with affliction by all."*[6] Jefferson's coauthor John Adams confessed, "there was not a moment during the Revolution when I would not have given everything I possessed for a restoration to the state of things before the contest began, provided we could have had a sufficient security for its continuation."[7] But Britain's efforts at appeasing the colonists came too late and Arnold's plea fell on deaf ears. It was one thing, after all, to deplore the separation, and another to betray the cause of independence.

Arnold had lost the esteem of his countrymen but never really gained that of his new allies. Most British leaders and many of their troops never fully trusted or respected Arnold. His arrival in New York on September 25 was linked to general mourning at John André's fate and the failure of his plot. For the professional soldiers, Arnold's betrayal of his own cause made any benefit they received from his renowned military skill too dearly bought. Johann Döhla, a Hessian soldier, noted in his diary on October 6 that at the evening tattoo General von Knyphausen informed his regiment that Major General Benedict Arnold, "who had deserted from the Americans, had been named a brigadier colonel of an English regiment," adding, "on the other hand, the loss of the brave and good Major John André was lamented."[8] After recording the details of André's capture, trial, and hanging he observed again that André's death "was mourned by the entire army." Hessian Captain Johann Ewald concurred. As the British army settled into its winter quarters on Long Island Ewald wrote, "it seemed as if all courage was gone with Major André's death."[9]

To make amends for the failure of his plot and for André's death Arnold was anxious to prove himself useful to the British cause. Two months after arriving in New York he was given command of a force of 1,600 men serving under General Cornwallis bound for Virginia.[10] Arnold's two major missions for the British army would force him to campaign in the two states that were the greatest test of his new allegiance, George Washington's Virginia and Arnold's own home state of Connecticut.

Some of his new troops were more disgusted at his betrayal of the American cause than happy to have his military expertise. Captain Ewald, who served on Arnold's Virginia campaign, wrote in his journal of his loathing of Arnold, objecting to many of Arnold's military decisions even when they proved successful.[11] His depiction of Arnold's background reeks of class bias. He writes that Arnold having once declared himself bankrupt "in an unlawful way . . . engaged in horse trading in the West Indies," and was "one of the most fiery and zealous of rebels," a description correct only in that Arnold did, among other things, buy and sell horses. But that was bad enough. Horse traders were considered a disreputable lot. Ewald concedes Arnold "could be very polite and agreeable, especially at table, but if one stayed too long in his company, then the apothecary and horse trader showed through the general."[12] Arnold's plot to betray West Point was characterized by Ewald as a "cunning trick on his countrymen" that "brought the good André to grief."[13] He conceded that Arnold's "dishonest undertaking . . . had it succeeded, could have actually turned the war more favorably for England." "Nevertheless," Ewald felt it could not be justified:

for surely self gain alone had guided him, and not remorse for having taken the other side. If he really felt in his conscience that he had done wrong in siding against his mother country, he should have sheathed his sword and served no more, and then made known in writing his opinions with his reasons. This would have gained more proselytes than his shameful enterprise, which every man of honor and fine feelings—whether he be friend or foe of the common cause—must loathe.

In contrast to Ewald's own willingness to pay with his life for England's success, he regards Arnold as "so detestable to me that I had to use every effort not to let him perceive, or even feel, the indignation of my soul."[14] Doubtless others among Arnold's troops, particularly the officers, were sorry to be serving him.

At noon on December 20 Arnold and his troops set sail for Virginia. His instructions were to attack enemy magazines, distribute proclamations to the inhabitants, and arm the well-affected. Colonel Simcoe, leader of the rangers, and Colonel Dundas were privately instructed to take command should Arnold be killed or incapacitated.[15] Their little fleet, on leaving New York, was struck by a fierce gale that scattered their vessels but they managed to rendezvous at Cape Henry in Chesapeake Bay. From there Arnold led his men up the James River, at one point sending Ewald with a group of troops to attack, and if possible, capture American forces seen on the banks. Ewald complained in his journal that he had no time to protest the order fearing if he did Arnold "on his false principles, would hold me for insubordination or cowardice," but adding rather smugly, "I risked nothing. If it had turned out unsuccessfully, the failure would have fallen on him, since the attack took place under his eyes." In fact Ewald and the British soldiers succeeded in driving off the Americans. Arnold then came ashore, praised the bravery of the men, "and expressed heartfelt thanks for my good will" Ewald wrote.[16]

Wherever Arnold and his troops went, his past dogged him. Washington and Thomas Jefferson, then governor of Virginia, put bounties on Arnold's head. Jefferson offered five thousand guineas for his capture.[17] In early January when American militia were sighted, Arnold sent an officer with a white flag asking for their surrender.[18] Ewald writes that the American officer asked whether the English officer had been sent by the traitor Arnold because he "would not and could not give up to a traitor. If he were to get hold of Arnold he would hang him up by the heels, according to the orders of Congress." Arnold's men plundered plantations they passed as they moved swiftly into Virginia. The government of the state was alarmed and ill-prepared. When Clinton captured Charleston in May of 1780 Virginia lost most of its Continental Line along with their commander, Brigadier General William Woodford, who was taken to New York where he died. A month earlier the Virginia government had taken the precaution of moving from Williamsburg to Richmond with their new governor, Thomas Jefferson. But Jefferson felt there was little to fear, and failed to strengthen the state's defenses. Arnold and his men, therefore, met with little opposition.

Ewald describes their army's actions as resembling "those of the freebooters, who sometimes at sea, sometimes ashore, ravaged and laid waste everything."[19] In a series of rapid marches they besieged Richmond. After Jefferson refused the offer to surrender to spare the tobacco warehouses, when the British captured the city they put the warehouses to the torch, the smell of burning tobacco pervading the area. The Virginia assembly fled once again, this time to Charlottesville, where Jefferson took shelter in his home at nearby Monticello. Warned that British cavalry were on the way he sent his family off but stayed behind to collect his papers. The British were already on the streets of Charlottesville when he finally fled, galloping into the woods, just barely escaping.

Despite all the handsome rewards for capturing Arnold and efforts to stop his campaign, he managed to evade them as he and his men moved into their winter camp at Portsmouth. In accordance with Arnold's instructions a large assembly of citizens was convoked and urged to take an oath of allegiance to England. Ewald estimated that the more than four hundred persons present, all over twenty-two years old, "gladly swallowed the oath after they were earnestly assured that the King was firmly resolved to protect them continually as loyal subjects during the war with a strong corps."[20] Further, Arnold promised them that he would "constantly sacrifice his blood and his life for them." But it was that British promise of constant protection that worried would-be loyalists. British armies tended to depart when their campaign objectives demanded, leaving supporters to fend for themselves. On this occasion, Ewald reports, the wealthiest residents were "entertained at the expense of the good King." He added scornfully, "all our pretended loyalist friends whose hearts Arnold thought he had won, were in high spirits." In a private conversation that evening with the "richest resident of the area," Ewald asked him why he didn't raise a battalion for the defense of the neighborhood.[21] It was a conversation that gets to the crux of the problem for the British cause. The loyalist answered:

> I must first see if it is true that your people really intend
> to remain with us. You have already been in this area
> twice. General Leslie gave me the same assurances in the
> past autumn, and where is he now? In Carolina! Who
> knows where you will be this autumn? And should the
> French unite with the Americans, everything would
> certainly be lost to you here. What would we loyally
> disposed subjects have then? Nothing but misfortune
> from the Opposition Party, if you leave us again."[22]

Ewald was disgusted:

> How can you be called friends of the King if you won't
> venture anything for the right cause? Look at your

Opposition Party: they abandon wife, child, house, and home, and let us lay waste to everything. They fight without shoes and clothing with all passion, suffer hunger, and gladly endure all the hardships of war. But you loyalists won't do anything! You only want to be protected, to live in peace in your houses. We are supposed to break our bones for you in place of yours, to accomplish your purpose. We attempt everything, and sacrifice our own blood for your assumed cause.[23]

As if to prove Ewald's point, not long afterward he was shot in the knee.

But the loyalist's fears were justified. American armies began converging in the region and by fall the British would suffer a devastating defeat in Virginia. Before that, however, in June of 1781 Arnold returned to New York. That August Peggy gave birth to their second son who they named James Robertson after the royal governor of New York.

In early September, just days after their baby's birth, Arnold was selected to command an expedition into Connecticut, his home state. This was the most difficult test of his commitment to the British cause and it was to be his last campaign. He was chosen because he was familiar with the area, and under the circumstances could not refuse. His mission was to attack New London and destroy the large quantities of materials stored there. The town and depot were defended by two forts, Fort Trumbull and Fort Griswold. Arnold's men arrived in a fleet of some thirty vessels and managed to capture the lightly defended Fort Trumbull with little loss of life. But the story was very different at Fort Griswold, where the garrison refused to surrender. It was eventually overrun by Arnold's men with a great loss of life, particularly on the patriot side, and has been reckoned one of the most tragic events of the entire war.[24] Most of the prosperous town of New London, not far from Arnold's hometown of Norwich, was burned with widespread devastation, and a massacre took place at the fort. Outraged Americans laid the tragedy for both at Arnold's door.

While Arnold did not order or approve the chaotic killing that occurred when his men overran Fort Griswold—he was on the other side of the river when it occurred—as the commander he might, perhaps ought, to have been able to prevent it.[25] In his report to Clinton afterward Arnold explained that he had been informed there were only twenty or thirty men in Fort Griswold and its residents were on board ships or busy saving their property.[26] Afraid the enemy ships would escape if Fort Griswold were not captured promptly, Arnold ordered his troops to make an immediate attack. They would assault the well-situated fort on three sides. Looking from a vantage point down on the fort after dispatching his orders however, Arnold discovered that the fort was far better defended than he was led to believe and the men who escaped from Fort Trumbull were reinforcing Fort Griswold. He immediately sent instructions to countermand his order to attack, but it was too late.

Before they attacked, as custom demanded the British had sent a flag to offer the garrison the chance to surrender, threatening, Rufus Avery remembered, that "if they had to take the fort by storm they should put martial law in force, that is whom they did not kill with balls should be put to death with sword and bayonet."[27] They sent the demand twice. The garrison commander, Colonel William Ledyard, twice rejected the offer to surrender to spare the garrison, responding: "We shall not surrender let the consequences be what they may." The assault began. The fighting was fierce as British troops and loyalists assaulted under heavy fire. On their fourth attempt they charged with fixed bayonets and were met by the defenders wielding long spears. There were great losses on both sides. The British suffered eighty-five men killed, including two of the officers leading the assault and sixty men wounded, most mortally. Arnold reckoned the American loss "very considerable."[28] Some eighty-eight Americans were found dead and another seventy were taken prisoner. After conquering the fort Arnold's men burned the American ships in the harbor at New London along with the warehouses and wharfs. Unfortunately, as Arnold explained in his report to General Clinton afterward, one of the ships contained a large quantity of powder "unknown to us." It exploded. A change of wind set New London ablaze "notwithstanding every effort to prevent it," and parts of the city were "unfortunately destroyed." He failed to mention however, that other buildings and private homes were methodically set ablaze while he narrowly missed being shot when fired at by a furious woman. Clinton would not have objected to the burning of the homes of rebels. That had been a British practice beginning with the battle at Lexington and Concord. But Clinton was convinced that Arnold "took every precaution in his power to prevent the destruction of the Town, which is a misfortune which gives him much concern." Arnold commended the valor of his men to Clinton.

Details of the attack, albeit third hand, in the memoirs of General Heath, the American officer commanding part of the Continental Army in New York State, are more damning. Heath refers to a letter of General Jonathan Trumbull charging the British soldiers with behaving "in a wanton and barbarous manner."[29] According to Trumbull, when the American commanding officer, Colonel Ledyard, ordered a ceasefire and surrendered by carefully handing his sword, reversed, to the commanding British officer, "the officer immediately plunged it in the Colonel's body, on which several soldiers bayoneted him." At that point an American officer standing near Colonel Ledyard "instantly stabbed the British officer who had stabbed the Colonel, on which the British indiscriminately bayoneted a great number of Americans." Arnold's soldiers, he wrote, then went on a rampage, their weapons piled against walls as they ransacked the fort for booty.

A close reading of the events from American Rufus Avery's firsthand account provides a different scenario, one more in keeping with the military chaos that surrounded the seizure of the fort. The fighting had been fierce and deadly. Hot shot had been poured down on the attackers who then repelled the British bayonet assault with spears. An author highly critical of Arnold writes that Ledyard gave the order to surrender "just as the gate was forced and hundreds of British soldiers mad with anger and pain surged inside."[30] Ledyard walked forward to hand over his sword when someone to the side of him stabbed him with a bayonet.[31] At that point there was chaos. The Americans charged the British who, wild from the vicious fight to enter the fort, struck back with frenzy. A drum roll finally brought the British soldiers to order and the killing stopped.[32]

Reflecting on the British behavior, General Heath offers a military man's more sympathetic rationale for the vicious actions of Arnold's men, which is supported by a military history expert on that era and is worth quoting at length. Heath writes:

> It is not meant to exculpate or to aggravate the conduct of the enemy on this occasion—but two things are to be remembered: first, that in almost all cases the slaughter does but begin when the vanquished give way, and it has been said, that if this was fully considered, troops would never turn their back, if it were possible to face the enemy, secondly, in all attacks by assault, the assailants, between the feelings of danger on the one hand, and resolution to overcome it on the other, have their minds worked up almost to a point of fury and madness, which those who are assailed, from confidence in their works, do not feel; and that consequently when a place is carried, and the assailed submit, the assailants cannot instantaneously curb their fury to reason, and in this interval, many are slain in a way which a cool bystander would call wanton and barbarous, and even the perpetrators themselves when their rage subsided, would condemn; *but while the human passions* remain as they now are, there is scarcely a remedy.[33]

Few Connecticut residents were so understanding, and Arnold's reputation in his home state sank even lower, if that were possible. His two expeditions for the British army, however, were military successes and he managed to survive despite the sharpshooters keen to get a handsome reward for capturing or killing him. The Connecticut campaign would be Arnold's last for the British military.

On October 19, 1781, Cornwallis and his army of some ten thousand men surrendered at Yorktown. It would be the final major battle of the war. Two months later Arnold, Peggy, and their two little sons sailed across the Atlantic into exile in England. He would never see his native land again. General Cornwallis was a fellow passenger. Hannah didn't want to follow them into exile. She would spend her later years living with Arnold's sons Richard and Henry, who she had done so much to raise. Arnold was still hoping in vain that there might be some reconciliation between Britain and America.

Arnold was well treated by the King and government ministers, was presented at Court and received compensation for his losses in America, and the Crown gave him large grants of land in Canada. Peggy was awarded a pension of £500 a year, and each of her children received £100 annually.[34] But Arnold was never able to gain either the military commissions or business success he sought. His lovely young wife, the belle of Philadelphia, remained by his side enduring a painful separation from her home and family. She and Arnold had two more sons and a daughter. All their sons followed their father into the military.

It was a sad exile for Arnold and Peggy, misplaced Americans, relics of an unpopular and unsuccessful war. They were spurned by old friends. Even Silas Deane, Arnold's Connecticut friend living in exile in London refused to meet him publicly, although they continued to meet privately. The Arnolds were hissed at when they attended the theater.[35] Since the liberal party in Britain condemned Arnold's behavior at West Point, he had to rely on only one party for commissions.

Yet flashes of the Arnold pride and temper survived, including one characteristic duel. Arnold learned that Lord Lauderdale had "cast some reflections" on his political character in the House of Lords.[36] Lauderdale, Peggy wrote her father, "is violent in the opposition . . . the only man in the House of Lords who voted against an address of thanks to the King, upon a late proclamation." Attacking the Duke of Richmond on the question of reform in Parliament, Lauderdale was reported to have said that "he did not know any instance of Political Apostacy equal to the Duke of Richmond's, except General Arnold's." Arnold demanded an apology for this attack on his character. Lauderdale then denied having made the statement and gave what Peggy referred to as "a kind of apology." Arnold was not satisfied and drew up one he would accept but his lordship refused to sign. Arrangements were made for a duel.

It was to take place at seven o'clock on a Sunday morning. Peggy wrote, "what I suffered for near a week is not to be described; the suppression of my feelings, lest I should unman the General, almost at last proved too much for me; and for some hours, my reason was despaired of. I was confined to my bed for some days after." Lord Hawke, a friend of Arnold's, was his second, Charles Fox the second for Lauderdale. The men were both to fire at the same time. Arnold fired but missed. Lauderdale refused to fire. Arnold stood calmly urging him to do so. Lauderdale admitted he had "no enmity to General Arnold" but nevertheless refused to apologize and said Arnold might fire again if he chose. This Arnold would not do, nor would he leave the field without either an apology or Lauderdale firing again. A consultation took place. Arnold insisted he would not leave without satisfaction. That being the case, Lauderdale apologized to the satisfaction of Arnold and the seconds. So all ended well. As Peggy wrote, "It has been highly gratifying to find the General's conduct so much applauded, which it has been universally, and particularly by a number of the first characters in the Kingdom, who have called upon him in consequence of it."

In 1787 Arnold and Peggy spent time in St. John's, Canada, where he launched a mercantile business and sailed, as in years past, on his own ship to the West Indies. His sons Richard and Henry joined him and the business flourished for a time. During one of his trips back to England, however, the warehouse in which his goods were stored caught fire and his son Henry, who was sleeping on the premises, was badly burned. While Arnold was away on voyages Peggy spent anxious periods alone among strangers. At one point Arnold was captured in the West Indies by the French and put aboard a French prison ship.[37] He managed to escape at night by climbing down the side of the ship. Using several planks as a raft he was able to reach a small boat and found his way to the English and safety.

In 1787 Peggy arranged to visit her father and family in Philadelphia one more time. While her family was delighted to see her, many of her old friends shunned her and she was saddened by their behavior. She returned to England, especially enjoying spending the summers there. The Arnolds finally moved back to Britain in 1791 and settled in London.

When war broke out between France and Britain in 1798 Arnold wrote to the Duke of York pleading to serve in the military. He laid before the government a plan to capture the Spanish possessions in the West Indies.[38] He desperately wanted to serve in the West Indies, an area he knew well from his seafaring years. The government rejected the plan. Worst still for Arnold, he wasn't wanted. After yet another rejection at the war office he told Peggy, "They will not give me a chance to seek a soldier's death."[39]

He was more melancholy after this rejection. His family remained close and loving, and he devoted much time and effort to securing the future of his sons. His will bequeathed his Canadian property to his older sons, Richard and Henry, left an annuity for

Hannah, with the remainder of the estate, such as it was, going to his "beloved wife and her heirs."[40] Sadly, there were many children, many debts, and only a modest estate. Peggy would have a very difficult time managing and would live in reduced circumstances.[41] But apart from Arnold's family concerns the grave personal disappointments and insults were hard to bear for one so proud. At sixty his strong body grew weak; he was unable to sleep. Since he was deep in debt he worried constantly about the future welfare of his family in England and North America.[42]

Near the end he became delirious. There is a family legend that in one of his clearer intervals as he lay dying he asked for his uniform, the uniform of a Major General of the Continental Army. He was wearing that uniform when he fled from West Point to the *Vulture* and had carefully preserved it. "Bring me, I beg you, the epaulettes and sword-knots which Washington gave me; let me die in my old American uniform, the uniform in which I fought my battles. God forgive me for ever putting on any other." But uniform or not, he was not to get the soldier's death he longed for. At half past six on the morning of June 14, 1801, tormented with despair and regret, Benedict Arnold died.[43]

FINAL THOUGHTS

The details of Benedict Arnold's life have been laid before the reader as I have discovered them. The question remains: What is one to make of the man? Was Arnold a thoroughly evil man, greedy, vainglorious, and self-serving, as his angry contemporaries and later generations have concluded? Certainly, he was ambitious and able, a man on the make, a man in a hurry. He was extraordinarily successful in business and on the battlefield. Never having had actual military experience before the Revolutionary War, he turned out to be a brilliant, bold, and inspiring commander, arguably the best officer on either side. Arnold fought passionately for the cause of independence until his defection late in the war. He was generous to friends but openly scornful and impatient with those less committed or brave. Impatience and bluntness make enemies, and Arnold's enemies were tenacious. As for his politics, Arnold was a moderate, not a radical, a fact that infuriated the radical Pennsylvania Executive Council. They accused Arnold of favoring the enemy because of his unwillingness to arrest the long list of Philadelphians the Council claimed were loyalists.

Some historical understanding is needed here. Arnold was willing, even eager, to die a soldier's death to win independence. Such single-minded dedication to personal honor was a common characteristic of Arnold's time and vocation. Charles Royster reckons that Continental Army officers' self-conscious imitation of European models might make them "doubly touchy because of the officers' difficulty in securing satisfactory recognition as gentlemen in the first place."[1] Royster's insight clearly applies to Arnold, who had been abruptly deprived of a university education and suffered the public humiliation of his father's alcoholism and indebtedness. Later, despite Arnold's superior military achievements, members of Congress passed him over for promotion and, when grudgingly promoting him much later, did not correct his seniority. He was robbed of credit for his role in the victory at Saratoga where he rallied the troops and led the victorious charge, suffering a grievous wound in the process. Instead the honors were bestowed upon his commander, General Horatio Gates, who had remained in his tent as the battle raged, and had banned Arnold from participating. Even Washington had let him down. The commander had promised to have an early court-martial hearing, yet it had been delayed time and again as the Pennsylvania Council won successive postponements. Arnold had asked for a commission in the navy, a command for which his experience suited him perfectly and which would accommodate his lameness. Yet Washington insisted he serve in the field army. Hounded for financial malfeasance by enemies in and out of Congress but unable to defend himself against their charges for months, Arnold endured more than his share of slurs upon his reputation.

Arnold's disgust with the attitude of Congress and of many civilians toward the Continental Army was shared by most of its officers and men. Even Lafayette, who was aware of the army's privations, was shocked when he rejoined Washington in Morristown in 1779 to find "An Army that is reduced to nothing, that wants provisions, that has not one of the necessary means to make war. . . I confess I had no idea of such an extremity."[2] Two years later Lieutenant Colonel Huntington of Connecticut wrote his brother of his disgust "at the rascally stupidity which now prevails in the country at large," demanding, "Why do you not reinforce your army, feed them, clothe and pay them?"[3] He concluded in despair, "I despise my countrymen. I wish I could say I was not born in America."

On the other hand, while the officers' growing professional self-consciousness may have been natural, it did look very sinister to many of their fellow revolutionaries.[4] Delegates feared the rise of another Oliver Cromwell, who would deploy his troops to seize power. Yet while worried about a successful army general, they were quick to punish military failure, levying charges of misconduct against officers who surrendered a fort or suffered a military defeat. To ensure their control, Congress insisted on micromanaging an army they were unable or unwilling to keep decently supplied with food, clothing, shelter, arms, or pay.

Treatment of the army was not the only issue. Many patriots shared Arnold's criticism and doubts about the direction of the war. Charles Royster writes that the reaction to Arnold's treason "revealed that in his crimes, as in his achievements, he shared many attributes with his countrymen."[5] By 1780 when Arnold defected many of his countrymen were dismayed at the direction of the war, fearing it was lost, and also upset at the alliance with their old enemy France. The French alliance seemed to have been of little benefit up till that point while involving many risks.[6] George Mason, a former delegate to the Continental Congress from Virginia, wrote in June 1781 that even those in northern Virginia "well-affected to the French alliance . . . grow uneasy and restless & begin to think that our Allies are spinning out the war, in order to weaken America, as well as Great Britain & thereby leave us, at the End of it, as dependent as possible upon themselves."[7] Carl Van Doren points out that the mood of disenchantment was enhanced by the presence of Britain's Carlisle Commission that year, offering Americans everything they had demanded except independence. All this public disapproval caused great consternation among the country's leaders. Van Doren finds:

> In the prevailing bitterness and suspicion the zealous patriots were intolerant of opposition or dissent. The British peace offers in June and the lingering presence of the peace commissioners in New York till November, made many honest Philadelphians wonder if it would not be wiser for America to return to its old place in the Empire on favourable terms than to go on fighting bloodily for independence—and in the end perhaps fail to win it. Independence was an idea, the Empire a reality. Other Philadelphians honestly dreaded the French alliance, out of doubt as to French motives.[8]

If Arnold had genuine grievances he had other options than treason. He might have followed the example of scores of Washington's officers and simply resigned his commission and returned to civilian life. What made that path more difficult in his case was the insistence of Congress that he still owed them £1,000, a sum that would probably have bankrupted him. His children would suffer the humiliation he had of being the sons of a debtor. Wartime conditions and his absence for several years had taken a toll on his shipping business. He had also spent lavishly to purchase a grand home for his lovely Peggy. In the end he opted for continuing to play a part in the war and to retrieve his honor by offering his services to the British. If all worked out and the British won, as seemed almost certain at the time, he would be applauded for helping end the bloodshed and securing a British victory. He insisted upon an important commission in the British army for his own self-esteem, and financial aid to reimburse him for the certain loss of his American property. In the event he chose the losing side and became a pariah, dishonoring himself and his family. His behavior was dishonorable, his choice was tragic.

The real tragedy is not that we have insufficiently demeaning language to ensure Arnold's actions remain shocking to our own and future generations. It is that a brilliant and heroic man opted to betray the victory he had done so much to achieve in order to retain his personal honor and in the process dishonored his name for eternity. If time cannot bring forgiveness, can it not bring some measure of understanding?

ACKNOWLEDGMENTS

I am happy to have the opportunity to thank all my wonderful family, friends, colleagues, and the history and publishing professionals who have made this long project a pleasure over the many years of work involved. My agent John Taylor Williams and his talented assistant, Katherine Flynn, were enthusiastic about the subject and eagerly helped me develop it. The publishers of Pegasus Books, Claiborne Hancock and Jessica Case, loved the subject and my approach and could not have been more helpful in bringing the book swiftly and expertly into print.

The Washington, D.C. Legal History Roundtable and George Mason University Art and History Department members offered valuable comments on my presentations. I also wish to thank the archivists and librarians who generously offered their expertise and assistance. Thanks go to James Campbell, archivist of the New Haven Colony Historical Society and the New Haven Museum, the archivists of the Historical Society of Pennsylvania, the University of Pittsburg manuscript collections, the Library and Archives of Canada, especially the Quebec branch, the Library of Congress and the George Mason Law School's reference librarians for their crucial help. Research assistants Nicole Kolinski and Scott Harris were wonderfully diligent and creative, juggling work for me with the necessity of graduating from law school. I am indebted to the many fine scholars who have preceded me and uncovered key information on numerous aspects of Arnold's life.

My loving and amazingly patient family and friends have endured many conversations about Arnold when politely inquiring how the book was proceeding. Special thanks go to my dear friend Michael Unger who learned more about the subject than he probably ever really wanted to know. My greatest debt is to my sister Ellen Ghasemi who ploughed into the research with zest, discovered wonderful and colorful material, read and commented on every chapter and made the entire project one of joy.

ENDNOTES

INTRODUCTION

1. J. W. Fortescue, *A History of the British Army*, vol. 3 (London: Macmillan, 1899), p. 410.
2. Jared Sparks, *The Life and Treason of Benedict Arnold* (Boston: Harper, 1835), p. 5.
3. Ibid., p. 8.
4. Charles Royster, *A Revolutionary People at War: The Continental Army and American Character, 1775–1783* (Chapel Hill, N.C.: Univ.of N.C., 1979), p. 290.
5. Ibid., p. 291.
6. I am particularly fortunate in being able to make use of Russell M. Lea's fine collection of revolutionary war correspondence, only published in 2008. See Russell M. Lea, *A Hero and a Spy: The Revolutionary War Correspondence of Benedict Arnold* (Westminster, Md.: Heritage, 2008).
7. Isaac Newton Arnold, *The Life of Benedict Arnold; His Patriotism and His Treason*, (Chicago: Jansen, McClurg & Co., 1880), p. 4.
8. Mary Caroline Crawford, Mrs. John A. Logan, and Everett Titsworth Tomlinson, *Peggy Shippen: The Traitorous Belle of the American Revolution: Brief Historical Accounts of Mrs. Benedict Arnold* (2016); Forrest Bachner, *The Colour of the Times: Margaret Shippen Arnold and the American Revolution—A Novel of Treason* (Gilbertsville, N.Y.: Illume, 2016); Allison Pataki, *The Traitor's Wife: The Woman Behind Benedict Arnold and the Plan to Betray America* (Brentwood, Tenn.: Howard, 2014); Nancy Rubin Stuart, *Defiant Brides: The Untold Story of Two Revolutionary-Era Women and the Radical Men They Married* (Boston: Beacon, 2014);

ENDNOTES

Stephen Case and Mark Jacob, *Treacherous Beauty: Peggy Shippen, The Woman Behind Benedict Arnold's Plot to Betray America* (Guilford, Conn.: Lyons Press, 2012); Bruce Adamson and Tim Shippen, *America's First Conspiracy: The Peggy Shippen and Benedict Arnold Story* (2012); Ann Rinaldi, *Finishing Becca: A Story about Peggy Shippen and Benedict Arnold* (New York: Great Episodes, 2004).

9. Eliot A. Cohen, *Conquered into Liberty* (New York: Free Press, 2011), p. 196.
10. William Blackstone, *Commentaries on the Laws of England*, 4 vols. (1765–1769), 1:395.
11. Ibid., pp. 395, 400.
12. Fortescue, *A History of the British Army*, p. 178.
13. Lewis Burd Walker, "Life of Margaret Shippen, Wife of Benedict Arnold," Letters of Peggy Shippen and Family in *The Pennsylvania Magazine of History and Biography*, vol. xxv, Philadelphia, 1901, p. 156.

ONE: THE PRICE OF HONOR
1. Russell M. Lea, ed., *A Hero and a Spy: The Revolutionary War Correspondence of Benedict Arnold* [hereinafter *Arnold Correspondence*] (Westminster, Md.: Heritage, 2008), p. 283.
2. Isaac Newton Arnold, *The Life of Benedict Arnold* (Chicago, 1880), pp. 204–205.
3. Ibid., p. 212, MSS of F. S. Foster.
4. Ibid., p. 205.
5. Ibid., p. 29
6. Ibid.
7. James Thacher, *The Battles and Generals as Seen by an Army Surgeon*, reprinted in *Eyewitness to the American Revolution* (London: Longmeadow, 1994), p. 75.
8. Ibid., p. 57.
9. Ibid., p. 75.
10. *Arnold Correspondence*, p. 291.
11. Thacher, *Battles and Generals*, p. 67.
12. Ibid., p. 80.
13. Arnold, *Life of Benedict Arnold*, p. 213.
14. Ibid.
15. Andrew Jackson O'Shaughnessy, *The Men Who Lost America: British Leadership, the American Revolution, and the Fate of the Empire* (New Haven, Conn.: Yale Univ. Press, 2013), p. 155.
16. Ibid., p. 155.
17. Ibid., p. 155.
18. Fortescue, *A History of the British Army*, p. 241.

19. *Arnold Correspondence*, p. 291.

20. Ibid., pp. 291–292.

21. James Kirby Martin, *Benedict Arnold: Revolutionary Hero: An American Warrior Reconsidered* (New York: NYU Press, 1997), p. 408.

22. *Arnold Correspondence*, pp. 292–293.

23. Ibid.

24. Ibid., p. 293.

25. Lincoln spent five months recuperating at home. His leg, like Arnold's, never fully healed, and he limped the rest of his life.

26. Arnold, *Life of Benedict Arnold*, p. 213.

27. Hannah had been looking after Arnold's three young sons since his wife died in 1775.

TWO: GREAT EXPECTATIONS

1. Among many essays on the importance of personal honor to George Washington and John Adams see Peter McNamara, ed., *The Noblest Minds: Fame, Honor, and the American Founding* (Lanham, Md.: Rowman & Littlefield, 1999); Lorraine Smith Pangle and Thomas L. Pangle, "George Washington and the Life of Honor" pp. 39–72 and C. Bradley Thompson, "John Adams and the Quest for Fame," pp. 73–96.

2. Hamilton Bullock Tompkins, "Benedict Arnold, First Governor of Rhode Island"; (A paper read before the Newport Historical Society, October 1919), *Bulletin of the Newport Historical Society*, no. 30: 1–18; Like many successful merchants including his great-great-grandson, he had his critics. Samuel Gorton, in his book *Simplicity's Defense* complained that Arnold sold strong drink and ammunition to the Indians, trading with them on the Sabbath, and refused to sell goods to settlers of Warwick unless they agreed to be under the jurisdiction of Massachusetts.

3. James Kirby Martin, *Benedict Arnold, Revolutionary Hero: An American Warrior Reconsidered* (New York, 1997), p. 16.

4. Ibid., p. 17.

5. F. M. Caulkins, *History of Norwich* (Hartford, Conn.: Case, Lockwood & Co., 1866), p. 254.

6. James Thomas Flexner, *The Traitor and the Spy: Benedict Arnold and John André* (Syracuse, N.Y.: Syracuse Univ. Press, 1953; reprinted 2010), p. 3; Martin, *Benedict Arnold*, 253.

7. Martin, *Benedict Arnold*, p. 24.

8. Some books put the date of his birth at January 14, 1741. The difference is a calendar change. The date of January 3 is "old style." Parliament changed the beginning of the year from March 15 to January 1, beginning in 1751.

9. Caulkins, *History of Norwich*, pp. 352–353.

ENDNOTES

10. There was a Dr. David Jewett, surgeon, from Montville who fought in the Revolution but it is unclear whether this is the same Dr. Jewett whose school Benedict attended. See Henry A. Baker, *A History of Montville, Connecticut formerly The North Parish of New London from 1640 to 1896* (Hartford, Conn.: Case, Lockwood & Co., 1896), p. 96.

11. Cited by Martin, *Benedict Arnold*, p. 22.

12. Flexner, *Traitor and Spy*, p. 5.

13. Cogswell was a relation of Benedict's father whose mother was a Cogswell.

14. Boys as young as twelve or thirteen could be admitted to college at this time. See Benjamin Tallmadge, *Memoir of Colonel Benjamin Tallmadge* (New York, 1858; reprinted 1961), p. 6.

15. Flexner, *Traitor and Spy*, p. 6. Flexner adds: "No authentic record from any period of his life shows him torturing the weak—he preferred to cast himself as their protector."

16. See Flexner, *Traitor and Spy*, pp. 4–5; Martin, *Benedict Arnold*, p. 22.

17. Ibid., pp. 4–5.

18. Ibid.

19. Dorothy A. Mays, *Women in Early America: Struggle, Survival and Freedom in a New World*, on diphtheria online at http://library.thinkquest.org.

20. Martin, *Benedict Arnold*, p. 5.

21. In 1771 Dr. Samuel Bard, a prominent American physician, described the course of the disease in "An Enquiry into the Nature, Cause and Cure of the Angina Suffocative, &c.": "On days one through five, children exhibited . . . inflamed eyes, bloated and livid countenance and a few red eruptions on the face . . . the tonsils appeared swollen and inflamed with a few white specks on them, which increased to cover them. . . . A slight fever . . . on days two to three, there was a gradual increase in breathing difficulty and . . . prostration. A dry cough . . . Constant fever became evident . . . as the disease progressed to coma, facial swelling, profuse sweating and increased breathing difficulty, until death occurred on the fourth or fifth day from apparent suffocation.

22. Martin, *Benedict Arnold*, p. 24. Martin dates this letter to August 13, but Lea in his collection of Arnold's correspondence puts it at August 12. See *Arnold Correspondence*, p. 1.

23. Martin, *Benedict Arnold*, p. 24.

24. James Shepherd and Gary Walton, *Shipping in Maritime Trade, and the Economic Development of Colonial North America* (Cambridge, England: Cambridge Univ. Press, 1972), p. 8–9, 86, 88–89 and see appendix 3, Tables 18 and 21.

25. *Arnold Correspondence*, p. 1.

26. *The Public Records of the Colony of Connecticut*, Vol. 1, 1650, pp. 533–34; Vol. 5, October, 1706, p. 5.

27. *The Public Records of the Colony of Connecticut:* Vol. 2, 1676, p. 282; Vol. 2, 1706, p. 5.
28. Caulkins, *History of Norwich*, p. 175.
29. Martin, *Benedict Arnold*, p. 26.

THREE: DESCENT

1. Russell M. Lea, ed., *A Hero and a Spy: The Revolutionary War Correspondence of Benedict Arnold*, (Westminster, Md.: Heritage, 2008); *Arnold Correspondence*; see Hannah Arnold to Benedict Arnold, Norwich, April 17, 1754, p. 2.
2. Francis Manwaring Caulkins, *History of Norwich, Connecticut from Its Settlement in 1660 to January 1845* (Norwich, 1845; repr. Carlisle, Mass., n.d.), p. 178.
3. Dorothy A. Mays, *Women in Early America: Struggle, Survival and Freedom in a New World*, on diphtheria online at http://library.thinkquest. org, page 245.
4. Jeanne Boydston, *Home and Work: Wages, and Ideology of Labor in the Early Republic* (New York: Oxford Univ. Press, 1990), p. 16; Laurel Thatcher Ulrich, *Good Wives: Image and Reality in the Lives of Women in Northern New England, 1650–1750* (New York: Knopf, 1982), p. 182.
5. Elaine Forman Crane, *Ebb Tide in New England: Women, Seaports, and Social Change 1630–1800* (Boston: Northeastern Univ. Press, 1998), pp. 128–130.
6. Kurt Nadelmann, "On the Origin of the Bankruptcy Clause," *American Journal of Legal History*, vol. 1 (July 1957), p. 221.
7. *The Public Records of the Colony of Connecticut*, Vol. 5, May 1711, pp. 223–224.
8. Ibid.
9. Caulkins, *History of Norwich*, p. 180.
10. Ibid., p. 180.
11. *Arnold Correspondence*, p. 3.
12. Caulkins, *History of Norwich*, p. 181.
13. James Thomas Flexner, *The Traitor and the Spy: Benedict Arnold and John André* (Syracuse, N.Y.: Syracuse Univ. Press, 1953; reprinted 2010), p. 9.

FOUR: THE FORTUNES OF WAR

1. Joyce Lee Malcolm, *To Keep and Bear Arms: The Origins of an Anglo-American Right* (Cambridge, Mass.: Harvard Univ. Press, 1994), pp. 139–142.
2. Many authors had asserted that Arnold fled to the army on two occasions before 1757, deserting at one point, possibly in order to reenlist for additional bounty. The confusion was caused by another Benedict Arnold who was from Norwalk, Connecticut, not Norwich, and who was several

times described as a weaver. James Flexner, in *The Traitor and the Spy*, tracks down the mistake. See pp. 7–8; p. 410 n. 2.

3. Fred Anderson, *Crucible of War: The Seven Years' War and the Fate of Empire in British North America, 1754–1763* (New York: Vintage, 2000), p. 151.

4. Rangers used guerrilla-style tactics rather than traditional European massed forces. Rangers would be used by both sides during the American Revolution.

5. Harold Selesky, *War and Society in Colonial Connecticut* (New Haven, Conn.: Yale Univ. Press, 1990), p. 110.

6. Ian K. Steele, *Betrayals: Fort William Henry and the "Massacre"* (New York: Oxford Univ. Press, 1990), p. 124.

7. Selesky, *War and Society*, p. 108.

8. Connecticut Historical Society, vol. 1, p. 236.

9. Anderson, *Crucible of War*, p. 200.

10. Ibid., p. 201.

11. In addition to the 154 men in the Norwich company, there were thirteen men responsible for "the return of the horses." See Connecticut Historical Society, vol. 1, p. 236.

12. Steele, *Betrayals*, p. 110. This was an extraordinary number of mounted men for the militia. The need for haste doubtless occasioned it. Arnold was an excellent rider and the Lathrops had many horses. He is likely to have been one of those on horseback.

13. The letter to the governor of Massachusetts, for example, didn't reach him until August 6. Steele, *Betrayals*, p. 125.

14. Steele, *Betrayals*, pp. 96, 98, 100. Montcalm actually had only about seven thousand men. See William Nester, *The First Global War* (Westport, Conn.: Greenwood, 2000) pp. 53–61. A fort was reckoned to be able to hold off an attack by a force three times as large for several days.

15. Anderson, *Crucible of War*, p. 192.

16. Ibid., p. 192.

17. Steele, *Betrayals*, p. 98.

18. Anderson, *Crucible of War*, p. 192.

19. Ibid., p. 194.

20. Ibid., p. 194.

21. Ibid., p. 194.

22. Ibid., p. 195.

23. Ibid., p. 196.

24. Ibid., p. 197.

25. Ibid., p. 197.

26. Montcalm and his officers did their best to retrieve Indian prisoners. These had been taken to Montreal. Some two hundred were recovered by the end

of August, at an average cost of 130 livres and thirty bottles of brandy each. Perhaps forty were adopted into Indian families and refused to return. About two hundred went missing. Anderson, *Crucible of War*, pp. 198–199.

27. Fred Anderson, *The War that Made America: A Short History of the French and Indian War* (New York: Penguin, 2006), p. 114.

28. Francis Parkman, *Montcalm and Wolfe: France and England in North America*, 2 vols. (Boston: Little, Brown, 1884), vol. 1, pp. 4–5.

29. Ibid.

30. Arnold served only fourteen days. The days varied presumably by how long it took members to fulfill their duties and get home.

31. Steele, *Betrayals*, p. 124.

32. Anderson, *War that Made America*, p. 113.

FIVE: TAKING CHARGE

1. Albert Van Dusen, "The Trade of Revolutionary Connecticut," (doctoral dissertation, Univ. of Pennsylvania), p. 147. See Proquest Publication No. AAT 001640.

2. Gary Walton, "A Quantitative Study of American Colonial Shipping: A Summary," *Journal of Economic History*, vol. 26, no. 4 (December 1966), pp. 595–598.

3. Gaspare Saladino, "The Economic Revolution in Late Eighteenth Century Connecticut" (PhD, Univ. of Wisconsin), pp. 5, 7. Proquest Publication No. AAT 6412747.

4. Saladino, "Quantitative Study," p. 150.

5. James Kirby Martin, *Benedict Arnold: Revolutionary Hero* (New York: NYU Press, 1997), p. 30;. Russell Lea, ed. *Hero and Spy: The Revolutionary War Correspondence of Benedict Arnold* (Westminster, MD) suggests she died of yellow fever. Since yellow fever was a disease more common in tropical areas it seems unlikely this was the cause of her death. On the other hand there was a yellow fever epidemic in Philadelphia in 1762, beginning in August of that year, a season that was unusually hot. On yellow fever see Suzanne M. Shultz, "Epidemics in Colonial Philadelphia from 1699–1799" and "The Risk of Dying" online, p. 27. And see *Arnold Correspondence*, p. 3. Lea writes that she died in 1758, but 1759, as Martin has it, seems the accurate date. Her gravestone states that she died in 1759 although it gives her age as fifty-nine. Still the number may have deteriorated over the years.; Francis Manwaring Caulkins, *History of Norwich, Connecticut: From Its Settlement in 1660, to January 1845* (Carlisle, Mass, 1845), p. 204

6. Francis Manwaring Caulkins, *History of Norwich*, p. 254.

7. James Kirby Martin, *Benedict Arnold, Revolutionary Hero: An American Warrior Reconsidered* (New York, 1997) p. 30.

8. Ibid.

9. Ibid, pp. 30–31.

10. Ian Quimby, *Apprenticeship in Colonial Philadelphia* (New York: Garland, 1985), p. 52.

11. Ruth Wallace Herndon and John E. Murray, *Children Bound to Labor: The Pauper Apprentice System in Early America* (Ithaca, N.Y.: Cornell Univ. Press, 2009), p. 81.

SIX: SMOOTH AND CHOPPY WATERS

1. Isaac Newton Arnold, *The Life of Benedict Arnold* (Chicago, 1880), p. 20; Francis Manwaring Caulkins, *History of Norwich, Connecticut: From Its Settlement in 1660, to January 1845* (Carlisle, Mass, 1845), p. 258.

2. James Kirby Martin, *Benedict Arnold: Revolutionary Hero* (New York: NYU Press, 1997), p. 35.

3. Jim Murphy, *The Real Benedict Arnold,* (New York: Houghton Mifflin Harcourt, 2007), p. 23.

4. Arnold, *Life of Benedict Arnold*, p. 405.

5. Russell M. Lea, ed., *A Hero and A Spy: The Revolutionary War Correspondence of Benedict Arnold* [hereinafter *Arnold Correspondence*] (2006), p. 4.

6. Doneva Shepard, *Doneva Shepard's family, friends and neighbors*, Adam Babcock, webpage.

7. See Lawrence Henry Gipson, *Jared Ingersoll: A Study of American Loyalism in Relation to British Colonial Government* (New Haven, 1920), p. 233 and Benedict Arnold, "Waste Book," MS New Haven Colony Historical Society.

8. Charles Collard Adams, *Middletown Upper Houses: A History of the North Society of Middletown, Connecticut, from 1650 to 1800* (New York: Grafton, 1908).

9. For Sage's Revolutionary War experience see John L. Rockey, *History of New Haven County, Connecticut* (New York: W.W. Preston, 1892), vol. 1., p. 29 ff.

10. Arnold, *Life of Benedict Arnold*, p. 27.

11. Murphy, *Real Benedict Arnold*, p. 25. Martin, who claims Arnold aroused hostility in the old-line residents, sees little significance in his becoming a Mason and notes he did not hold an important position in the lodge. Of course, since he was young and was traveling much of the time this does not seem surprising. See Martin, *Benedict Arnold*, pp. 38–39, 49.

12. Murphy, *Real Benedict Arnold*, p. 27.

13. H. Mansfield, *The Descendants of Richard and Gillian Mansfield Who Settled in New Haven, 1639* (New Haven, Conn.: Mansfield, 1885) p. 24.

14. Arnold, *Life of Benedict Arnold*, p. 27.

15. Murphy, *Real Benedict Arnold*, p. 28.

16. The Molasses Act of 1733 had taxed molasses, sugar, and rum that were imported from non-British colonies like the French West Indies.

17. Samuel Eliot Morison, *The Oxford History of the American People*, vol. 1 (New York: Mentor edit., 1972), p. 252.
18. Ibid., p. 252.
19. John Warner Barber, *History and Antiquities of New Haven (Conn.) From Its Earliest Settlement to the Present Time* (New Haven, Conn.: Punderson & Barber, 1831), p. 49.
20. Murphy, *Real Benedict Arnold*, p. 32.
21. Lawrence Henry Gibson, *American Loyalist: Jared Ingersoll* (New Haven, 1920), p. 204.
22. Peter Boles's last name is sometimes spelled "Bowes" or "Bowles."
23. Many sources describe the Boles affair. I am relying chiefly on Martin, *Benedict Arnold*, pp. 42–45.
24. Martin, *Benedict Arnold*, p. 43.
25. "Arrest Warrant 1766," Sherman Family Collection, 1745–1795, Oversize Item #1, New Haven Colony Historical Society.
26. Martin, *Benedict Arnold*, p. 44.
27. Barber, *History and Antiquities of New Haven*, pp. 49–50.
28. Ibid., p. 50.
29. Martin, *Benedict Arnold*, p. 48.

SEVEN: LOVE, MARRIAGE, DUELS, AND HONOR

1. Willard Sterne Randall, *Benedict Arnold: Patriot and Traitor* (Fort Mill, S.C.: Quill, 1990), p. 63.
2. James Kirby Martin, *Benedict Arnold, Revolutionary Hero: An American Warrior Reconsidered* (New York, 1997), p. 50.
3. Ibid., pp. 50–51.
4. Ibid., p. 51. And see Randall, *Benedict Arnold*, p. 63.
5. Martin, *Benedict Arnold*, p. 51.
6. Ulrich Laurel Thatcher, *Good Wives: Image and Reality in the Lives of Women in Northern New England, 1650-1750* (New York, 1982), p. 37; Elaine Forman Crane, *Ebb Tide in New England: Women, Seaports, and Social Change* (Boston, 1998), pp. 128–130.
7. Randall, *Benedict Arnold*, p. 63.
8. Ibid., pp. 63–64.
9. Jim Murphy, *The Real Benedict Arnold*, (New York, NY, 2007).p. 39. Murphy calculates that £1700 owed in 1767 was equivalent to some $71,700 in 2007.
10. Bruce Mann, *Republic of Debtors* (Cambridge, Mass.: Harvard Univ. Press, 2002), p. 84.
11. Kurt Nadelmann, "On the Origin of the Bankruptcy Clause," *American Journal of Legal History*, vol. 1 (July 1957), p. 224.
12. Murphy, *Real Benedict Arnold*, p. 40. See Lawrence Henry Gipson, *Jared Ingersoll*, p. 232 #2.

13. Russell M. Lea, ed., *A Hero and A Spy: The Revolutionary War Correspondence of Benedict Arnold* [hereinafter *Arnold Correspondence*] (2006), pp. 5–6.

14. Martin, *Benedict Arnold*, p. 52.

15. Ibid., p. 52.

16. Martin, *Benedict Arnold*, p. 52; and Murphy, *Real Benedict Arnold*, p. 36.

17. Isaac Newton Arnold, *The Life of Benedict Arnold: His Patriotism and His Treason* (Chicago, 1880) p. 20; F. M. Caulkins, *History of Norwich* (Norwich, CT, 1845), p. 31.

18. Martin, *Benedict Arnold*, p. 54.

19. See illustrations of the Arnold house in Norwich and Benedict Arnold's house in New Haven.

20. Randall, *Benedict Arnold*, p. 65.

EIGHT: "MY COUNTRY CALLED"

1. "Letter from the Committee of Safety of Massachusetts to the Governor of Connecticut, Massachusetts Archives, vol. 2:370.

2. Henry Steele Commager and Richard B. Morris, eds., *The Spirit of 'Seventy-Six* (New York: Da Capo, 1995; first pub. 1958), p. 90.

3. Circular letter to Massachusetts towns from the Committee of Safety, Massachusetts Provincial Congress, April 20, 1775.

4. Isaac Newton Arnold, *The Life of Benedict Arnold: His Patriotism and His Treason* (Chicago, 1880) p. 20; F. M. Caulkins, *History of Norwich* (Norwich, CT, 1845), p. 34. Proceedings of a Court-Martial for the Trial of Major General Arnold, (New York, 1865).

5. Ibid.

6. Britannus Americanus, Boston, 1766, Charles S. Hyneman and Donald S. Lutz, eds., *American Writing During the Founding Era, 1760–1805*, 2 vols. (Indianapolis, Ind.: Liberty Press, 1983), vol. 1, p. 89.

7. James Kirby Martin, *Benedict Arnold, Revolutionary Hero: An American Warrior Reconsidered* (New York, 1997), pp. 60–61.

8. Russell M. Lea, ed., *A Hero and A Spy: The Revolutionary War Correspondence of Benedict Arnold* [hereinafter *Arnold Correspondence*] (2006), pp. 8–9. Warren would be killed at Bunker Hill and Arnold worked hard to ensure that his young family was financially supported.

9. Commager and Morris, *Spirit of 'Seventy-Six*, p. 90.

10. Arnold, *Life of Benedict Arnold*, p. 36.

11. Commager and Morris, *Spirit of 'Seventy-Six*, p. 90.

12. Arnold, *Life of Benedict Arnold*, p. 37.

13. Ibid., The covenant was written by S.D., Silas Deane.

14. Ibid.

15. John Adams, Second Session of Congress, p. 92, Records of the Continental Congress, second session.
16. *Arnold Correspondence*, p. 15.

NINE: THE RACE TO SEIZE FORTS

1. See among other sources Richard L. Blanco, ed., *The American Revolution, 1775–1783: An Encyclopedia*, 2 vols. (New York: Garland, 1993), 1:20.
2. Blanco, *American Revolution*, vol. 1, pp. 571–572.
3. Eliot A. Cohen, *Conquered into Liberty* (New York, 2011), p. 139.
4. Ibid., p. 136.
5. Ibid.; Fort Ticonderoga, New York, Blanco, *American Revolution*, vol. 1, p. 570.
6. Cohen, *Conquered into Liberty*, p. 138.
7. Ibid.
8. Ibid., p. 141. Cohen describes Easton as "vindictive." His appeal to the War Department after the war claiming to be entitled to a pension was rejected. Papers of the War Department, John Pierce to James Easton, "The Commissioner of Army Accounts rejects Colonel James Easton, October 24, 1785."
9. Cohen, *Conquered into Liberty*, p. 142.
10. Ibid., p. 141.
11. Blanco, *American Revolution*, vol. 1, p. 573.
12. Cohen, *Conquered into Liberty*, p. 141.
13. Peter Force, ed., *American Archives*, Arnold's Report to Massachusetts Committee of Safety, April 30, 1775, vol. 2, p. 748.
14. Cohen, *Conquered into Liberty*, p. 142.
15. Force, *American Archives*, fourth series, vol. 2, p. 557.
16. Ibid., p. 716.
17. Arnold to Massachusetts Committee of Safety, May 29, 1775, *Arnold Correspondence*, p. 22.
18. Joseph Henshaw to Colonel Arnold, May 31, 1775, Hartford, *Arnold Correspondence*, pp. 46–47.
19. Colony of Massachusetts Bay to Col. Arnold, Watertown, June 1, 1775, *Arnold Correspondence*, p. 48.
20. Hannah Arnold to Benedict Arnold, New Haven, June, 1775, *Arnold Correspondence*, pp. 48–49.
21. Isaac Newton Arnold, *The Life of Benedict Arnold: His Patriotism and His Treason* (Chicago, 1880), p. 44.
22. Ibid.
23. Ibid.
24. Arnold to Spooner Committee, Crown Point, June 24, 1755, *Arnold Correspondence*, pp. 57–58.
25. Randall, *Benedict Arnold*, p. 129.

26. Residents of Ticonderoga to Benedict Arnold, Lake Champlain, July 3, 1775, *Arnold Correspondence*, pp. 60–61.

27. Arnold to Continental Congress, Albany, July 1, 1775, *Arnold Correspondence*, p. 66.

TEN: BURIED IN THE PUBLIC CALAMITY

1. Isaac Newton Arnold, *The Life of Benedict Arnold* (Chicago, 1880), p. 48 note.

2. James Kirby Martin, *Benedict Arnold: Revolutionary Hero* (New York, 1997), p. 102.

3. Arnold, *Life of Benedict Arnold*, p. 48 note.

4. Martin, *Benedict Arnold*, p. 104.

5. James Thomas Flexner, *The Traitor and the Spy: Benedict Arnold and John André* (Syracuse, 1953; reprinted 2010), p. 55.

6. Flexner, *Traitor and Spy*, p. 55.

7. Martin, *Benedict Arnold*, p. 102.

8. Ibid.

9. Joyce Lee Malcolm, *Peter's War: A New England Slave Boy and the American Revolution* (New Haven, Conn.: Yale Univ. Press, 2009), p. 85.

10. Barnabas Deane to Silas Deane, June 1, 1775, near Ticonderoga, cited in Arnold, *Benedict Arnold*, p. 45.

11. Martin, *Benedict Arnold*, pp. 98–99.

12. Ron Chernow, *Washington: A Life* (New York: Penguin, 2010), p. 194.

13. Malcolm, *Peter's War*, p. 78.

14. Russell M. Lea, ed., *A Hero and A Spy: The Revolutionary War Correspondence of Benedict Arnold* [hereinafter *Arnold Correspondence*](2006),p. 52–53.

15. Eliot Cohen, *Conquered into Liberty* (New York, 2011),.

16. For earlier accounts of the invasion of Canada through Maine see Arthur S. Lefkowitz, *Benedict Arnold's Army: The 1775 American Invasion of Canada During the Revolutionary War* (El Dorado Hills, Calif.: Savas Beatie, 2007), pp. 23–26.

17. Lefkowitz, *Benedict Arnold's Army*, p. 24.

18. Ibid.

19. Ibid. Note that Martin, *Benedict Arnold*, apparently unaware of Montresor's later admission, writes that Montresor "had moved easily and quickly over the route," p. 107.; Blanco, *American Revolution*, vol. 2, p. 1505.

20. Arnold, *Life of Benedict Arnold*, p. 51.

21. Hal T. Shelton in Blanco, *American Revolution, 1775-1783*, 2 vols. (New York, 1993), vol. 2, p. 1092.

22. Martin, *Benedict Arnold*, pp. 107–108.

23. Roy Chernow, *Washington: A Life* (New York, 2010), p. 210.

24. Lefkowitz, *Benedict Arnold's Army*, on Daniel Morgan, pp. 46–47.

25. Ibid., pp. 47–48.
26. Ibid., p. 49.
27. Ibid.
28. Arnold, *Life of Benedict Arnold*, p. 52.
29. Lefkowitz, *Benedict Arnold's Army*, p. 48.
30. Blanco, *American Revolution*, vol. 2, 1505.
31. Lefkowitz. *Benedict Arnold's Army*, p. 33.
32. *Arnold Correspondence*, p. 68.; and Lefkowitz, *Benedict Arnold's Army*, p. 25.
33. Henry Steele Commager and Richard B. Morris, eds. *The Spirit of 'Seventy-Six"* (New York, n.d.), pp. 153–154.
34. *Arnold Correspondence*, p. 69.
35. Ibid., p. 71.
36. Ibid., p. 74.
37. Ibid.

ELEVEN: HONOR IN A "DIREFUL, HOWLING WILDERNESS"

1. For background on Guy Carleton see George M. Wrong, *Canada and the American Revolution: The Disruption of the First British Empire* (New York: Macmillan, 1935), p. 233ff.
2. Ibid., pp. 229–230.
3. Ibid., p. 230.
4. Not all Canadians were pleased with the Quebec Act settlement. British merchants and immigrants from the thirteen colonies objected and many Canadians were sorry to see the tithe to support the Catholic Church maintained, as well as traditional duties such as the labor duty, the hated corvée. Eliot Cohen, *Conquered into Liberty* (New York, 2011), pp. 133–134.
5. The Quebec Act, 14 Geo. III c. 83. The Northwest Territory comprised the present states of Illinois, Indiana, Michigan, Ohio, and Wisconsin.
6. Cohen, *Conquered into Liberty*, p. 148.
7. Ibid.
8. Ibid., p. 149.
9. Arthur S. Lefkowitz, *Benedict Arnold's Army: The 1775 American Invasion of Canada during the Revolutionary War* (New York, 2008), p. 63.
10. Ibid., p. 63.
11. Russell M. Lea, *A Hero and a Spy: The Revolutionary War Correspondence of Benedict Arnold* [hereinafter *Arnold Correspondence*[(Westminster, MD, 2008), p. 75.
12. Journal of Private Joseph Ware, September 19, 1775, George F. Scheer and Hugh F. Rankin, eds., *Rebels and Redcoats: The American Revolution Through the Eyes of Those Who Fought and Lived It* (New York: Da Capo Press, 1957), p. 117.

13. Isaac Newton Arnold, *The Life of Benedict Arnold* (Chicago, 1880), p. 53.
14. Ware, Journal, p. 117.
15. *Arnold Correspondence*, pp. 75–6.
16. Ibid., p. 78.
17. Ibid.
18. Journal of Private James Melvin, September 19, 1775, Scheer and Rankin, *Rebels and Redcoats*, p. 119.
19. *Arnold Correspondence*, p. 80.
20. Ibid.
21. Ibid., p. 83.
22. Ibid., pp. 83–84.
23. Arnold, *Life of Benedict Arnold*, pp. 65–66.
24. *Arnold Correspondence*, p. 84.
25. Ibid., p. 86.
26. Henry Steele Commager and Richard B. Morris, eds. *The Spirit of 'Seventy-Six"* (New York, n.d.), p. 201.
27. *Arnold Correspondence*, p. 90.
28. Cohen, *Conquered into Liberty*, p. 151.
29. Ibid., p. 152.
30. Ibid., p. 151.
31. Ethan Allen's account, Scheer and Rankin, *Rebels and Redcoats*, p. 114.
32. Ibid.
33. Ibid.
34. Cohen, *Conquered into Liberty*, p. 152. Fortescue judges it "a most discreditable surrender." Fortescue, *A History of the British Army* (London, 1899), vol. 3, p. 54
35. Revolutionary War Archives.
36. Paul David Nelson, *General Sir Guy Carleton, Lord Dorchester* (Madison, N.J.: Fairleigh Dickinson Univ. Press, 2000), p. 64.
37. Ibid.

TWELVE: A FIERCE ATTACK, A WINTER SIEGE

1. For this account of Carleton's adventures getting into Quebec, see Paul David Nelson, General *Sir Guy Carleton: Soldier-Statesman of Early British Canada* (Madison, 2000), p. 74.
2. Nelson, *Sir Guy Carleton*, p. 75.
3. Ibid.
4. Ibid., p. 76.
5. George Washington to Benedict Arnold, Cambridge, Dec. 5, 1775, John Rhodehamel, ed., *George Washington: Writings* (New York: Library of America, 1991), pp. 192–193.

6. Washington to Schuyler, Cambridge, 5 Dec. 1775, Russell M., Lea, ed., *A Hero and a Spy: The Revolutionary War Correspondence of Benedict Arnold* [hereinafter *Arnold Correspondence*](Westminster, MD, Heritage Books, 2006), p. 93.

7. Ibid., p. 94.

8. Ibid.

9. Ibid., p. 95. The following information, unless otherwise noted, is drawn from *Arnold Correspondence*. And see Senter, *Arnold Correspondence*, p. 95. Montgomery had altered the original attack plan of simultaneous attacks on the upper and lower town because deserters might give away the scheme. Arnold to General Wooster, Dec. 31, 1775, *Arnold Correspondence*, p. 98.

10. There was a rumor that deserters had disclosed the American plan to the British. See George MacKinnon, Wrong, *Canada and the American Revolution: The Disruption of the First British Empire* (1935), p. 301.

11. *Arnold Correspondence*, p. 100.

12. Senter writes in his diary that Montgomery was very anxious, "as if anticipating the fatal catastrophe." *Arnold Correspondence*, p. 96. Also see Abner Stocking, "Journal" in Henry Steele Commanger and Richard B. Morris, eds., *The Spirit of 'Seventy-Six* (De Capro Press, New York, 1995; first publ. 1958), p. 204.

13. *Arnold Correspondence*, p. 95.

14. Ibid., pp. 96ff.

15. Ibid., pp. 97–98.

16. The distance from Quebec City to Philadelphia is six hundred miles, as the crow flies.

17. Willard Sterne Randall, *Benedict Arnold: Patriot and Traitor* (New York, 1990), p. 224.

18. Ibid., pp. 224–225.

19. *Arnold Correspondence*, p. 105.

20. Randall, *Benedict Arnold*, p. 225.

21. Bayard Tuckerman, *Life of General Philip Schuyler, 1733–1804* (New York: Dodd, Mead, 1903), p. 118.

22. Nelson, *Sir Guy Carleton*, p. 80.

23. Ibid., pp. 80–81.

24. Tuckerman, *Life of General Schuyler*, pp. 118–119.

25. Randall, *Benedict Arnold*, p. 224.

26. *Arnold Correspondence*, pp. 113–114.

27. Ibid., p. 120.

28. Ibid., p. 121.

29. Ibid., p. 118.

30. Arnold, *Life of Benedict Arnold*, p. 85.

31. Ibid., p. 85.

32. *Arnold Correspondence*, p. 115.
33. Arnold, *Life of Benedict Arnold*, p 85.
34. *Arnold Correspondence*, p. 108.
35. Arnold, *Life of Benedict Arnold*, pp. 87–88.
36. *Arnold Correspondence*, p. 111.
37. Ibid., p. 112.
38. Arnold, *Life of Benedict Arnold*, p. 88.
39. Ibid.
40. *Arnold Correspondence*, p. 124.
41. Arnold, *Life of Benedict Arnold*, p. 94.
42. *Arnold Correspondence*, p. 126.
43. Arnold, *Life of Benedict Arnold*, pp. 90–93.
44. Ibid., p. 92.
45. Ibid., p. 93.
46. Arnold to Gates, Arnold, *Life of Benedict Arnold*, p. 96.
47. Ibid., p. 94.
48. Arnold, *Benedict Arnold*, p. 97.
49. Ibid.

THIRTEEN: DEFENDING THE LAKES

1. Hannah Arnold to Benedict Arnold, August 5, 1776, FO. Vereau 18, no. 3, Quebec Archives.
2. Ibid.
3. Willard Sterne Randall, *Benedict Arnold: Patriot and Traitor* (New York, 1990), p. 260.
4. Ibid., p. 261.
5. Arnold to Gates, July 15, 1776, Russell M. Lea, ed., *A Hero and a Spy: The Revolutionary War Correspondence of Benedict Arnold* [hereinafter *Arnold Correspondence*] (Westminster, MD, Heritage Books, 2006), p. 152.
6. Hannah Arnold to Benedict Arnold, August 28, 1776, MS FO Vereau 17, no. 13, Quebec Archives.
7. Hannah Arnold to Benedict Arnold, September 1, 1776, MS FO Vereau 18, no. 13, Quebec Archives.
8. *Arnold Correspondence*, pp. 150–151.
9. Ibid., p. 151.
10. Ibid., p. 154.
11. Ibid., p. 154.
12. Isaac Newton Arnold, *The Life of Benedict Arnold: His Patriotism and His Treason* (1888), p. 103.
13. Ibid., pp. 103–104.
14. Willard Sterne Randall, *Benedict Arnold: Patriot and Traitor* (New York, 1990), p. 262.

15. Eliot Cohen, *Conquered into Liberty* (New York, 2011), p. 181.
16. Randall, *Benedict Arnold*, p. 262.
17. *Arnold Correspondence*, p. 128.
18. Ibid., p. 129.
19. Ibid., p. 133.
20. Ibid., p. 138.
21. Randall, *Benedict Arnold*, p. 263.
22. Ibid.
23. *Arnold Correspondence*, p. 156.
24. Ibid., p. 155.
25. Arnold, *Life of Benedict Arnold*, p. 107.
26. Valcour Island, *The American Revolution: An Encyclopedia*, Richard Blanco, ed. 2 vols. (Garland, 1993), vol. 2, p. 1687.
27. *Arnold Correspondence*, p. 163.
28. Ibid., p. 164.
29. Ibid., p. 165.
30. Gates to Arnold, Ticonderoga, August 18, 1776, FO Verreau 18, no. 6, Quebec Archives.
31. *Arnold Correspondence*, pp 169–170.
32. Arnold, *Life of Benedict Arnold*, p. 107.
33. Ibid., p. 100.
34. Gates to Arnold, October 3, 1776 MS FO Verreau 18, no 29, Quebec Archives.
35. Randall, *Benedict Arnold*, pp. 291–292.
36. Ibid., p. 292.
37. Ibid., p. 304.
38. *Arnold Correspondence*, pp. 185, 187–189.
39. For the damage to the American fleet see Arnold, *Life of Benedict Arnold*, p. 113–114.

FOURTEEN: DON'T TREAD ON ME

1. Russell M. Lea, *A Hero and a Spy: The Revolutionary War Correspondence of Benedict Arnold* [hereinafter *Arnold Correspondence*[(Westminster, MD, 2008), pp. 186–187.
2. Ibid., p. 196.
3. Ibid., p. 189.
4. Arnold to Gates, Ticonderoga, October 15, 1776 in Isaac Newton Arnold, *The Life of Benedict Arnold* (Chicago, 1880), p. 118, note 1.
5. Striking the ship's flag was a signal of surrender. Arnold to Gates, October 15, 1776, Arnold, *Life of Benedict Arnold*, n. 1, p. 119.
6. William Sterne Randall, *Benedict Arnold: Patriot and Traitor* (New York, 1990), p. 316.
7. *Arnold Correspondence*, p. 203.

8. Ibid., p. 118.
9. Ibid., p. 120.
10. Ibid., p. 117.
11. Ibid., p. 120.
12. J. W. Fortescue, *A History of the British Army* (London, 1899), vol.3, p. 182.
13. New Jersey edition, October 21, 1776 and the *Pennsylvania Gazette*, October 23, 1776; *Arnold Correspondence*, p. 201.
14. Randall, *Benedict Arnold*, p. 323.
15. *Arnold Correspondence*, pp. 218–219.
16. Ibid., p. 219.
17. James Kirby Martin, *Benedict Arnold, Revolutionary Hero: An American Warrior Reconsidered* (New York, 1997), p. 314
18. William Blackstone, *Commentaries on the Laws of England*, 4 vols. (1765–69), vol. I: 395.
19. Blackstone, *Commentaries*, pp. 395, 400.
20. Richard H. Kohn, *Eagle and Sword: The Beginnings of the Military Establishment in America* (New York: Free Press, 1975), p. 4.
21. Max M. Mintz, *The Generals of Saratoga* (New Haven, Conn.: Yale Univ. Press, 1990), p. 122.
22. *Arnold Correspondence*, p. 216; Martin, *Benedict Arnold*, p. 305

FIFTEEN: "BESMIRCHED HONOR"

1. Washington to Arnold, Morristown, March 3, 1777, Russell M. Lea, ed., *A Hero and a Spy: The Revolutionary War Correspondence of Benedict Arnold* [hereinafter *Arnold Correspondence* (Westminster, MD, 2008), pp. 217–218.
2. Ibid., p. 219.
3. Arnold, *Life of Benedict Arnold*, pp. 129–130.
4. Richard M Ketchum, *Saratoga: Turning Point of America's Revolutionary War* (New York, 1997), p. 287.
5. James Lacey and Williamson Murray, *Moment of Battle: Twenty Clashes That Changed the World* (New York: Bantam, 2013), pp. 211–212.
6. *Arnold Correspondence*, p. 221.
7. Randall, *Benedict Arnold*, p. 320.
8. *Arnold Correspondence*, p. 222.
9. John Rhodehamel, ed., *George Washington: Writings* (New York, 1991), p. 270.
10. *Arnold Correspondence*, pp. 203–205.
11. Martin, *Benedict Arnold*, p. 288.
12. Ibid, p. 288.
13. Ibid., pp. 188–189.
14. Ibid., p. 289.

15. Ibid., p. 297.
16. A British officer reported of the stores at Danbury: "We found the greatest magazine the Rebels had ever collected: & full leisure to destroy it—viz. About 4000 bbls of beef & pork; 5000 bbls of flour 100 puncheons of rum; and a vast quantity of rice, coffee, salt, sugar, medicines, tents, clothing, shoes, wagons—harness . . ." *Arnold Correspondence*, p. 230.
17. *Arnold Correspondence*, p. 227.
18. The poor animal was later found to have received wounds from nine balls. Arnold, *Life of Benedict Arnold*, p. 131.
19. *Arnold Correspondence*, p. 228.
20. Ibid., p. 237.
21. Ibid., pp. 237–238.
22. Ibid., p. 238.
23. Ibid., pp. 238–239.
24. Ibid., p. 239.

SIXTEEN: SAVAGE WARFARE
1. Some English towns with tiny populations still had the right to send two members to Parliament, giving the local squire the opportunity to appoint these.
2. J. W. Fortescue, *A History of the British Army* (London, 1899), vol. 3, p. 156. Fortescue claims he gave these speeches in the House of Lords but Burgoyne sat in the House of Commons.
3. Henry Steele Commager and Richard B. Morris, eds. *The Spirit of 'Seventy-Six"* (New York, n.d.), p. 538; James Lacey & Williamson Murray, *Moment of Battle: The Twenty Clashes That Changed the World* (New York, 2013), p. 208 .
4. Commager and Morris, *Spirit of 'Seventy-Six*, p. 538.
5. Fortescue, *A History of the British Army*, vol. 3, pp. 207, 209.
6. Commager and Morris, *Spirit of 'Seventy-Six*, p. 546.
7. Ibid.
8. Cited by Andrew Jackson O'Shaughnessy, *The Men Who Lost America* (New Haven, 2013), pp. 146-147.
9. Commager and Morris, *Spirit of 'Seventy-Six*, p. 548.
10. Joyce Lee Malcolm, *Peter's War: A New England Slave Boy and the American Revolution* (New Haven, 2009), p. 150.
11. Eliot A. Cohen, *Conquered into Liberty* (New York, 2011), p. 201.
12. Ibid.
13. Ibid., p. 202.
14. Ibid.
15. O'Shaughnessy, *Men Who Lost America*, p. 154.
16. Bayard Tuckerman, *The Life of General Philip Schuyler, 1733–1804* (New York, 1903), p. 159.

17. Ibid., pp. 167–168.
18. Arnold to Hancock, Philadelphia, July 11, 1777, Russell M. Lea, ed., *A Hero and a Spy: The Revolutionary War Correspondence of Benedict Arnold* [hereinafter *Arnold Correspondence*](Westminster, MD, 2008), p. 246.
19. Ibid., pp. 245–46.
20. Ibid., p. 246.
21. Ibid., pp. 246–47.
22. Ibid., p. 248.
23. Ibid., pp. 248–49.
24. An account of Burgoyne's reaction to the Indians arriving with two scalps, which describes Jane's hair as black. It might have looked black from blood on it. See Max M. Mintz, *The Generals of Saratoga: John Burgoyne & Horatio Gates* (New Haven, 1990), p. 162.
25. Richard M. Ketchum, *Saratoga: Turning Point of America's Revolutionary War* (New York, 1997), p. 274.
26. There is some confusion about this with some claiming Jane was shot instead.
27. Commager and Morris, *Spirit of 'Seventy-Six*, p. 559.
28. Mintz, *Generals of Saratoga*, p. 162.
29. Ketchum, *Saratoga*, p. 277.
30. *Arnold Correspondence*, p. 247.
31. Ibid., p. 249.
32. Tuckerman, *Life of General Schuyler*, p. 133.
33. Ibid., p. 224.
34. *Arnold Correspondence*, p. 251.
35. Ibid., p. 252.
36. Ibid., p. 253.

SEVENTEEN: DEFENDING NEW YORK, AGAIN

1. Burgoyne to Germain, camp near Saratoga, August 20, 1777, Henry Steele Commager and Richard B. Morris, eds., *The Spirit of 'Seventy-Six* (New York, 1958), pp. 577–578.
2. Ibid., p. 579.
3. Ibid., p. 577.
4. Ibid., p. 578.
5. Ibid., p. 579.
6. Richard M. Ketchum, *Saratoga: Turning Point of America's Revolutionary War* (New York, 1997), p. 370.
7. Ibid., pp. 351, 370.
8. Arnold to Lamb, September 5, 1777, Isaac Q. Leaks, ed., *Memoir of the Life and Times of General John Lamb, an Officer of the Revolution* (Albany, N.Y.: Joel Munsell, 1857), pp. 171–172.

ENDNOTES

9. Andrew Jackson O'Shaughnessy, *The Men Who Lost America: British Leadership, the American Revolution, and the Fate of Empire* (New Haven, 2013), p. 154.

10. James Lacey and Williamson Murray, *Moment of Battle: Twenty Clashes That Changed the World* (New York, 2013), p. 211

11. Ketchum, *Saratoga*, p. 287.

12. Ibid.

13. Ibid., p. 212.

14. *Almons Remembrancer*, August 16, 1777; Commager and Morris, *Spirit of 'Seventy-Six*, p. 569.

15. George F. Scheer and Hugh F. Rankin, eds., *Rebels and Redcoats: The American Revolution Through the Eyes of Those Who Fought and Lived It* (New York, 1957), pp. 263–64.

16. Stark to Gates, Bennington, August 22, 1777, Commager and Morris, *Spirit of 'Seventy-Six*, p. 572.

17. Ibid., p. 573.

18. Ketchum, *Saratoga*, p. 213.

19. Arnold to Gates, Stillwater, September 22, 1777, Commager and Morris, *Spirit of 'Seventy-Six*, pp. 581–582.

20. Ketchum, *Saratoga*, p. 352.

21. Lacey and Murray, *Moment of Battle*, p. 214.

22. Ketchum, *Saratoga*, p. 363. The comment was from Captain Ebenezer Wakefield of Dearborn's light infantry, Mintz, *Generals of Saratoga*, p. 193.

23. Lessing's Field book, vol. 1, p. 52, Arnold, *Life of Benedict Arnold* p. 172.

24. Digby had fought against Arnold at Valcour Island; *Arnold Correspondence*, p. 265.

25. Ketchum, *Saratoga*, p. 363.

26. Churchill papers, *Arnold Correspondence*, p. 266.

27. Ibid., p. 265.

28. Ibid., p. 267.

29. Ibid., p. 268.

30. Ketchum, *Saratoga*, p. 385.

31. *Arnold Correspondence*, pp. 271–272.

32. Ibid.

33. Ibid., pp. 272–273.

EIGHTEEN: THE FATAL BLOW

1. Russell M. Lea, ed., *A Hero and a Spy: The Revolutionary War Correspondence of Benedict Arnold* [hereinafter *Arnold Correspondence*] (Westminster, MD, 2008), p. 280.

2. Ibid., p. 281.

3. Recollections of Captain E. Wakefield, Henry Steele Commager and Richard B. Morris, eds., *The Spirit of 'Seventy-Six* (New York,1983), p. 581.

4. Ibid., p. 594.

5. *Arnold Correspondence*, p. 279–280.

6. Mattoon to Schuyler, Commager and Morris, *Spirit of 'Seventy-Six* (1995), p. 594.

7. Isaac Newton Arnold, *The Life of Benedict Arnold: His Patriotism and His Treason* (1888), p. 201.

8. Ibid., pp. 201–202.

9. Commager and Morris, *Spirit of 'Seventy-Six*, p. 585.

10. Ibid., p. 588.

11. Clinton wrote this from Fort Montgomery, October 8, 1777. J. W. Fortescue, *A History of the British Army* (London, 1899), vol. 3, p. 238.

12. This was a letter of Burgoyne to Germain, October 20, 1777, Commager and Morris, *Spirit of 'Seventy-Six*, p. 599.

13. Ibid., p. 599. Burgoyne had several suggestions for Parliament. British use of Indians to terrorize Americans, their urging of black slaves to rise up, their distrust of loyalists, and abandoning them when they retreated are all reasons for the failure of loyalists to come to their aid, along with a lack of leaders and coordination.

14. *Arnold Correspondence*, p. 278.

15. Arnold, *Benedict Arnold*, p. 197.

16. *Arnold Correspondence*, p. 281.

17. Fortescue, *A History of the British Army*, p. 239–240.

18. Ibid., p. 240.

19. Arnold, *Benedict Arnold*, p. 200.

20. Ibid., p. 205.

21. Ibid., pp. 204–205.

22. Commager and Morris, *Spirit of 'Seventy-Six*, p. 598.

23. Arnold, *Life of Benedict Arnold*, pp. 207–208.

24. Commager and Morris, *Spirit of 'Seventy-Six*, p. 598.

25. Ibid., p. 595.

26. *Arnold Correspondence*, p. 283.

NINETEEN: THE WAGES OF VICTORY

1. William Sterne Randall, *Benedict Arnold: Patriot and Traitor* (New York, 1990), p. 373.

2. Roy Chernow, *Washington: A Life* (New York, 2010), p. 335.

3. Ibid.

4. Ibid., p. 336.

5. John Adams, Autobiography, September. 1775, Henry Steele Commager and Richard B. Morris, eds., *The Spirit of 'Seventy-Six* (New York, 1983), p. 664.

6. Ibid., p. 665.
7. Ibid.
8. Chernow, *Washington* pp. 349–50.
9. J. W. Fortescue, *A History of the British Army*, vol. 3 (London, 1899.), pp. 246–47.
10. Ibid.
11. Commager and Morris, *Spirit of 'Seventy-Six*, p. 693.
12. Ibid., p. 695.
13. Ibid., p. 697.
14. Ibid., p. 691.
15. Ibid., p. 696.
16. Ibid., p. 694.
17. Carl Van Doren, *Secret History of the American Revolution* (New York: Viking, 1941), p. 88.
18. Ibid., p. 97.
19. Ibid.
20. Ibid., pp. 97–98.
21. Journals of the Continental Congress, February 3, 1778.
22. Ibid.
23. Nellie P. Waldenmaier, *Some of the Earliest Oaths of Allegiance to the United States* (privately printed, 1944).
24. Leake, *General John Lamb*, p. 242.
25. Ibid., p. 243.
26. Chief among Washington's critics were the politicians Sam Adams and John Adams, Thomas Mifflin, Richard Henry Lee, and Dr. Benjamin Rush. They were also critical of Silas Deane and Benjamin Franklin's efforts abroad.
27. Randall, *Benedict Arnold*, p. 403.
28. Ibid.
29. Ibid., p. 404.
30. Commager and Morris, *Spirit of 'Seventy-Six*, p. 652.
31. Ibid., pp. 652–53.
32. Ibid., p. 653.
33. Randall, *Benedict Arnold*, p. 405.
34. Ibid., p. 373.
35. *Arnold Correspondence*, p. 294.
36. Ibid., p. 295.

TWENTY: THE EYE OF THE STORM

1. Dave R. Palmer, *George Washington and Benedict Arnold: A Tale of Two Patriots* (Washington, D.C.: Regnery, 2006), p. 290.
2. Russell M. Lea, ed., *A Hero and a Spy: The Revolutionary War Correspondence of Benedict Arnold* [hereinafter *Arnold Correspondence*] (Westminster, MD, Heritage Books, 2006), p. 298.

3. Washington to Henry Laurens, June 2, 1778, in John W. Jackson, *With the British Army in Philadelphia, 1777–1778* (Novato, Calif.: Presidio, 1979), p. 258.
4. Ibid., p. 260. Some of the furniture loaded onto the British ships was thrown overboard to make room for military supplies. p. 259.
5. Ibid., p. 262.
6. Ibid., p. 268–269. André gave his superior, Lord Grey, a portrait of Franklin by Charles Willson Peale that was to remain in the Grey family estate in Britain until 1906, when it was returned to America. It now hangs in the White House.
7. Ibid., pp. 260–266.
8. Carleton E. W. Larson, "The Revolutionary American Jury: A Case Study of the 1778–1779 Philadelphia Treason Trials," *SMU Law Review*, vol. 61, no. 4 (Fall, 2008), pp. 1451–1452.
9. Article I, sec. 9, American Constitution.
10. Article IX of the Pennsylvania Constitution of 1776, explaining that in all prosecutions for criminal offenses, "a man hath a right to be heard by himself and his council, to demand the cause and nature of his accusation, to be confronted with the witnesses, to call for evidence in his favor, and a speedy public trial, by an impartial jury of the country, without the unanimous consent of which jury he cannot be found guilty." It is unclear whether the Council anticipated a jury trial since trials for treason did occur thereafter.
11. Larson, "Revolutionary American Jury," pp. 1451–1452.
12. See Wilbur H. Siebert, *The Loyalists of Pennsylvania* (Columbus: Ohio State University, 1920), p. 56.
13. Ibid., p. 59.
14. *Arnold Correspondence*, p. 302.
15. Journals of the Continental Congress, February 9, 1778 at http://memory.loc.gov/cgi-bin/query
16. The Penns spent the Revolutionary War in England. And see William S. Randall, *Benedict Arnold*, p. 40; Full citation. Arnold, *Life of Benedict Arnold: Patriot and Traitor* (New York, 1990), p. 223.
17. *Arnold Correspondence*, p. 321.
18. William Sterne Randall, *Benedict Arnold: Patriot and Traitor* (New York, 1990), pp. 383-84.
19. Ibid., pp. 384–85.
20. Carl van Doren, *Secret History of the American Revolution* (New York, 1941), p. 184.
21. Randall, *Benedict Arnold*, pp. 387–88.
22. Ibid., pp. 383, 387.
23. Ibid., p. 392.
24. Ibid., p. 387.

25. *Arnold Correspondence*, p. 306.
26. Ibid., p. 303.
27. Ibid., p. 304.
28. Ibid., p. 302.
29. Van Doren, *Secret History*, p. 172.
30. Ibid., p. 414.
31. Richard K. Murdoch, "Benedict Arnold and the Owners of the *Charming Nancy*," *Pennsylvania Magazine of History and Biography*, vol. 84, no. 1, (January, 1960), pp. 22-55.
32. Ibid., p. 177.
33. *Arnold Correspondence*, pp. 310–11.
34. The Council was upset they hadn't countersigned the pass, and some of the materials were hauled to a store in Philadelphia where they were sold and the proceeds shared with Arnold. *Arnold Correspondence*, p. 312.
35. The third charge before the Court-Martial. See next chapter, *Proceedings of a General Court-Martial*.
36. *Arnold Correspondence*, pp. 307–308.
37. Ibid., p. 308.
38. Ibid., pp. 309–310.
39. Ibid., p. 312.
40. Ibid., p. 313.
41. Ibid., pp. 313–314.
42. Ibid., p. 314.
43. Ibid., p. 315.
44. Ibid.
45. Charges against Arnold printed in the *Philadelphia Packet*, February 9, 1779, pp. 317–319.
46. Ibid., p. 319–320.
47. *Arnold Correspondence*, pp. 307–308.
48. Charges against Arnold printed in the *Philadelphia Packet*, February 9, 1779, *Arnold Correspondence*, p. 317–319.
49. Ibid., p. 319.
50. Ibid., p. 319 n. 79.
51. *Arnold Correspondence*, p 316.
52. Ibid., p. 317.
53. Van Doren, *Secret History*, p. 188.
54. *Arnold Correspondence*, p. 324.

TWENTY-ONE: THE COURT-MARTIAL

1. *Proceedings of a General Court-Martial for the Trial of Major General Arnold*, ed. Francis Bailey (New York, 1865 facsimile of orig. edit. of 1780), p. 128.

ENDNOTES

2. Deane to Greene, Willard Sterne Randall, *Benedict Arnold: Patriot and Traitor* (New York, 1990), pp. 469-70.

3. Russell M. Lea, ed., *A Hero and a Spy: The Revolutionary War Correspondence of Benedict Arnold* [hereinafter *Arnold Correspondence*] (Westminster, Maryland, 2008), p. 317.

4. James Kirby Martin and Mark Edward Lender, *A Respectable Army: The Military Origins of the Republic, 1763–1789* (Wheeling, Ill.: Harlan Davidson, 1982), p. 106.

5. Ibid., p. 152.

6. Ibid., p. 106.

7. Joyce Lee Malcolm, *Peter's War: A New England Slave Boy and the American Revolution* (New Haven, 2009), pp. 195-96.

8. Ibid., pp. 320–321.

9. *Arnold Correspondence*, p. 329.

10. Ibid., p. 326.

11. Ibid., p. 327.

12. Ibid., p. 330–331.

13. Carleton E. W. Larson, "The Revolutionary American Jury: A Case Study of the 1778–1779 Philadelphia Treason Trials," *SMU Law Review*, vol. 61, no. 4 (Fall, 2008), p. 1452

14. Ibid.

15. Ibid., p. 1441.

16. *Arnold Correspondence*, pp. 355–356. When later questioned, militiamen cited "the exceeding lenity which has been shown to persons notoriously disaffected to the Independence of the United States" as a reason for this attack. See Larson, "Revolutionary American Jury," p. 1444.

17. Ibid., p. 361.

18. Ibid.

19. Ibid., p. 362.

20. Ibid., pp. 325–6.

21. On Howe see Charles E. Bennett, Donald R. Lennon, *A Quest for Glory: Major General Robert Howe and the American Revolution* (Chapel Hill: Univ. of North Carolina Press, 1991), pp. 122–123.

22. *Proceedings of a General Court-Martial*, pp. 5ff.

23. Ibid., p. 10.

24. Ibid., p. 19.

25. Ibid., p. 114.

26. Malcolm, *Peter's War*, p. 198.

27. Ibid.

28. Ibid., p. 106–107.

29. *Proceedings of Court-Martial*, p. 128.

30. Ibid., p. 144.
31. *Arnold Correspondence*, p. 387.

TWENTY-TWO: BECOMING GUSTAVUS MONK

1. Jared Ingersoll was writing in 1780. See Lawrence Henry Gibson, *Jared Ingersoll: A Study of American Loyalism in Relation to British Colonial Government* (New Haven, 1920), p. 375.
2. Charles Royster, *A Revolutionary People at War: The Continental Army and American Character, 1775–1783* (Chapel Hill: Univ. of North Carolina Press, 1979), pp. 290, 288.
3. J.W. Fortescue, *A History of the British Army*, vol. 3 (London, 1899), p. 410.
4. Arnold to Washington, Philadelphia, April 18, 1778, Russell M., ed., *A Hero and a Spy: The Revolutionary War Correspondence of Benedict Arnold* [hereinafter *Arnold Correspondence*] (Westminster, MD, Heritage Books, 2006), p. 325.
5. Ibid., p. 326.
6. Ibid., p. 329.
7. Ibid., p. 330.
8. Ibid., p. 340.
9. Ibid.
10. Ibid., p. 331.
11. Ibid., pp. 331–33.
12. Ibid., p. 332.
13. Ibid., pp. 332–33.
14. Carl Van Doren, *Secret History of the American Revolution* (New York, 1941), p. 197; John Bakeless, *Turncoats, Traitors & Heroes: Espionage in the American Revolution* (1959), p. 294.
15. André drew a portrait of Peggy Shippen during the British occupation of Philadelphia.
16. Van Doren, *Secret History*, p. vi.
17. Ibid. Van Doren lists other traitors, some who were only identified as traitors when Clinton's papers were discovered.
18. Clinton to Lord Germain, Robert McConnell Hatch, *Major John André: A Gallant in Spy's Clothing* (New York: Houghton Mifflin, 1986), pp. 203–4.
19. Ibid., p. 77.
20. *Arnold Correspondence*, p. 334.
21. Van Doren, *Secret History*, p. 199.
22. Ibid.
23. Van Doren, *Secret History*, p. 205.
24. Ibid., p. 206.
25. *Arnold Correspondence*, p. 343.

26. Carl Van Doren and others have assumed Margaret Arnold was a party to the conspiracy from the start. See Van Doren, *Secret History*, p. 202. Van Doren writes his conclusion that André's "plans for a correspondence with Peggy Arnold make it impossible to doubt that she was perfectly aware of the Conspiracy from the beginning," but then adds, "This letter, apparently so innocent, actually so well devised for its secret purpose, may or may not have been sent, may or may not have reached Peggy Chew and Peggy Arnold. No answer from either of them survives." On this and other highly speculative evidence of Margaret Shippen's involvement in the plot, and contrary to all evidence of contemporaries and her own behavior, Van Doren's book made its reputation. His conclusions have been accepted uncritically by nearly all later authors.

27. Van Doren, *Secret History*, p. 202. Van Doren is so determined to believe Peggy Arnold was involved in the plot that he refers to this failure of André to involve her in correspondence as Peggy having no need to be involved in "a superfluous subplot."

28. Van Doren, *Secret History*, p. 214.

29. Ibid.

30. Ibid., p. 207.

31. *Arnold Correspondence*, p. 348.

32. Ibid., p. 350.

33. Ibid., pp. 350–51.

34. Ibid., p. 351.

35. Ibid., p. 353.

36. Isaac Newton Arnold, *The Life of Benedict Arnold; His Patriotism and His Treason* (Chicago, 1880), p. 266.

37. *Arnold Correspondence*, p. 383.

38. Ibid., p. 384.

39. Ibid., p. 385.

40. For Deane's activities see Robert H. Patton, *Patriot Pirates: The Privateer War for Freedom and Fortune in the American Revolution* (New York: Vintage, 2008), p. 50 ff.

41. Deane managed to obtain the French cannon that helped defeat Burgoyne at Saratoga. See Patton, *Patriot Pirates*, pp. 186, 188.

42. Ibid., p. 190.

43. Ibid., p. 191–92.

44. *Arnold Correspondence*, pp. 385–86.

45. Ibid., p. 387.

46. Ibid., p. 394.

47. Ibid., p. 391.

48. Ibid., pp. 391–92.

49. Ibid., pp. 398–99.

50. Hatch, *Major John André*, p. 205.
51. *Arnold Correspondence*, pp. 399–400.
52. Ibid., p. 401.
53. Ibid., p. 402.
54. Ibid., p. 402.
55. Ibid., p. 403.
56. Ibid., pp. 406–7.
57. Ibid., p. 408.

TWENTY-THREE: TREASON
1. J. W. Fortescue, *A History of the British Army*, vol. 3 (London, 1899), p. 335.
2. Robert McConnell Hatch, *Major John André: A Gallant in Spy's Clothing* (Boston, 1986), pp. 214–15.
3. Ibid.
4. Ibid., p. 205.
5. *Arnold Correspondence*, pp. 416–17.
6. Ibid., p. 423.
7. Ibid., p. 435.
8. Ibid., pp. 422–23.
9. Ibid., p. 435.
10. Ibid., p. 424.
11. Ibid., p. 420.
12. Ibid., p. 424.
13. Ibid., p. 437.
14. Arnold, *Life of Benedict Arnold*, p. 273.
15. Lewis Burd Walker, "Life of Margaret Shippen, Wife of Benedict Arnold," *The Pennsylvania Magazine of History and Biography*, vol. xxv, 1901, p. 44.
16. Ibid., pp. 42–48.
17. *Arnold Correspondence*, p. 430.
18. Hatch, *Major John André*, p. 217.
19. *Arnold Correspondence*, p. 437.
20. Ibid., p. 438.
21. Ibid., pp. 441–42.
22. Ibid., p. 442.
23. Ibid., p. 444.
24. Ibid., p. 451.
25. Ibid.
26. Ibid., p. 449.
27. Ibid., p. 453.
28. Ibid., p. 458.
29. Ibid., p. 471.

TWENTY-FOUR: BRIDGES BURNED

1. Lewis Burd Walker, "Life of Margaret Shippen, Wife of Benedict Arnold," *The Pennsylvania Magazine of History and Biography*, vol. xxv (1901), p. 146.

2. Washington to Lafayette. September 25, 1780, Russell M. Lea, ed., *A Hero and a Spy: The Revolutionary War Correspondence of Benedict Arnold* (Westminster, MD, 2006), p. 493.

3. Ibid., p. 493.

4. Ibid., p. 473ff. Lea, the editor, is very familiar with the area.

5. Ibid., p. 480.

6. Robert McConnell Hatch, *Major John André: A Gallant in Spy's Clothing* (Boston, 1986), pp. 4–5. Jameson also wrote Washington later that he had mentioned his intention of writing Arnold of André's capture to Tallmadge and other field officers, "all of whom were clearly of opinion that it would be right, until I should hear from your Excellency." Again this was not true. *Arnold Correspondence*, p. 515.

7. Hatch, *Major John André*, p. 5.

8. *Arnold Correspondence*, p. 495.

9. Ibid., p. 488–89.

10. Ibid., p. 513.

11. Willard Sterne Randall, *Benedict Arnold: Patriot and Traitor* (New York, 1990), p. 564.

12. Charles Royster, *A Revolutionary People at War: The Continental Army and American Character, 1775-1783* (Chapel Hill, 1979), p. 291.

13. *Arnold Correspondence*, p. 495.

14. Ibid., p. 500.

15. Ibid.

16. Ibid., p. 502.

17. Walker, "Life of Margaret Shippen," p. 151.

18. Hamilton to Elizabeth Schuyler, September 25, 1780, Arnold, *Life of Benedict Arnold*, p. 301.

19. Carl Van Doren, *Secret History of the American Revolution* (New York, 1941) claims Peggy was instrumental in Arnold's betrayal and most scholars have accepted his evidence. However re-examining his claims and taking account of Peggy's behavior before and especially after Arnold's flight it is clear she did not know of his plan.

20. Hamilton to Ms. Schuyler, September 25, 1780, Isaac Newton Arnold, *The Life of Benedict Arnold* (Chicago, 1880), p. 302.

21. Ibid., p. 319.

22. Royster, *A Revolutionary People at War*, pp. 292–293.

23. David McCullough, *John Adams* (New York: Simon & Schuster, 2001), pp. 250–51.

24. Ibid., p. 512.
25. Arnold, *Life of Benedict Arnold*, pp. 303–304.
26. Richard K. Murdoch, "Benedict Arnold and the *Charming Nancy*," Pennsylvania Magazine of History and Biography, vol. 84, no. 1 (January 1960) p. 53, no. 96.
27. Walker, "Life of Margaret Shippen," p. 160.
28. Ibid., pp. 160–61.
29. Ibid., p. 162.
30. *Arnold Correspondence*, p. 505.
31. Hatch, *Major John André*, p. 254 and see *Arnold Correspondence*, p. 517.
32. Arnold, *Life of Benedict Arnold*, p. 305.
33. Ibid., p. 305.
34. J. W. Fortescue, *A History of the British Army*, vol. 3 (London, 1899), p. 336.
35. Hatch, *Major John André*, p. 255.
36. *Arnold Correspondence*, p. 514.
37. Arnold, *Life of Benedict Arnold*, p. 306.
38. Ibid., pp. 306–7.
39. Ibid., p. 307.
40. Randall, *Benedict Arnold*, p. 567.
41. Arnold, *Life of Benedict Arnold*, p. 308.
42. *Arnold Correspondence*, p. 526.
43. Arnold, *Life of Benedict Arnold*, p. 309.
44. Ibid., pp. 309–10.
45. Ibid., pp. 311–12.
46. Ibid., pp. 312–13.
47. *Arnold Correspondence*, p. 542.
48. Ibid., pp. 542–43.
49. Ibid., pp. 543–44.

TWENTY-FIVE: AFTERWARD
1. Arnold to Inhabitants of America, October 7, 1780, Russell M. Lea, ed., *A Hero and a Spy: The Revolutionary War Correspondence of Benedict Arnold* [hereinafter *Arnold Correspondence*] (Westminster, MD, 2008), pp. 544–46.
2. The Articles of Confederation were not ratified until 1781.
3. Hessian captain Johann Ewald, who fought under Arnold and thoroughly disliked him, wrote in his diary that Arnold's letter to Americans met with ridicule for its inclusion of arguments he had never used before: that Congress represented 'the tyranny of the usurpers in the revolted provinces' and that the promises of the British Commission of 1778 were better than the insidious offers of France." Captain Johann Ewald, *Diary of the American*

War: A Hessian Journal, trans. and ed. Joseph P. Tustin (New Haven, Conn.: Yale Univ. Press, 1979), p. 426 n. 36.

4. *Arnold Correspondence*, pp. 563–65.

5. Emphasis in the source. Lewis Burd Walker, "Life of Margaret Shippen, Wife of Benedict Arnold," *The Pennsylvania Magazine of History and Biography*, vol. xxiv, No. 4 (1900), p. 428.

6. Ibid., p. 424.

7. Isaac Newton Arnold, *The Life of Benedict Arnold* (Chicago, 1880), p. 340.

8. Johann Conrad Döhla, *A Hessian Diary of the American Revolution*, trans. & ed., Bruce E. Burgoyne (Norman: Univ. of Oklahoma Pres, 1990), pp. 138–39.

9. Ewald, *Diary*, p. 251.

10. Ibid., p. 258; an estimated 2,200 men served under Arnold.

11. Ibid., pp. xxiii, 260–61.

12. Ibid., p. 296.

13. Ibid., pp. 294–95. The bankruptcy law of Connecticut Arnold used was recent and lawful, and as his behavior demonstrated his moderation, irked the real zealots such as those on the Pennsylvania Executive Council.

14. Ibid., pp. 295–96.

15. Ibid., p. 420 n. 2.

16. Ibid., p. 260.

17. Arnold, *Life of Benedict Arnold*, pp. 347–48.

18. Ibid., pp. 260–61.

19. Ewald, *Diary*, p. 269.

20. Ibid., p. 286.

21. Ibid.

22. Ibid., p. 286.

23. Ibid., pp. 286–87.

24. Arnold, *Life of Benedict Arnold*, p. 348.

25. Ibid., p. 352.

26. Arnold, *Life of Benedict Arnold*, pp. 349–50.

27. "The Narrative of Rufus Avery," in Rev. N. H. Burnham, *The Battle of Groton Heights: A Story of the Storming of Fort Griswold* (New London, Conn., 1899), p. 23.

28. Ibid., p. 351.

29. Memoirs of Major General William Heath, September 10, 1781, Commager and Morris, *Spirit of 'Seventy-Six*, pp. 730–31.

30. Eric D. Lehman, *Homegrown Terror: Benedict Arnold and the Burning of New London* (Middletown, Conn.: Wesleyan Univ. Press, 2014), p. 154.

31. No one saw the stabbing but a long footnote on page 23 of the 1903 edition of Burnham's book explains that Ledyard's clothing showed he was stabbed from the side, not the front and not many times afterward as the popular story asserts.

32. Lehman, *Homegrown Terror*, p. 156.
33. Arnold, *Life of Benedict Arnold*, p. 354. On the behavior of attacking troops see Gunther Rothenberg, Chapter 6, "The Age of Napoleon," in Michael Howard, et. al., eds., *The Laws of War: Constraints on Warfare in the Western World* (New Haven, Conn.: Yale Univ. Press, 1994), pp. 92–94.
34. Ibid., p. 363.
35. Willard Sterne Randall, *Benedict Arnold: Patriot, Traitor* (New York, 1990), p. 594.
36. Walker, "Life of Margaret Shippen," pp. 460–62.
37. Arnold, *Life of Benedict Arnold*, p. 387.
38. Ibid., pp. 388–89.
39. Ibid., p. 391.
40. "The Last Will and Testament of Benedict Arnold", Letters and Papers of Lewis Walker, Box 3, Folder 23, Burd-Shippen Family Papers, 1891–1898. DAR 1966.01, Darlington Collection, Univ. of Pittsburgh.
41. "The Last Will and Testament of Margaret Arnold", Letters and Papers of Lewis Walker, Box 3, Folder 23, Burd-Shippen Family Papers, 1891–1898, DAR 1966.01, Darlington Collection, Univ. of Pittsburgh.
42. The information about Arnold's final illness comes from Isaac Arnold, who had copies of the family letters describing his last illness. Arnold, *Life of Benedict Arnold*, pp. 393–395.
43. Ibid., p. 395. It is uncertain what the source of this tradition is as the author writes "Tradition says."

FINAL THOUGHTS

1. Charles Royster, *A Revolutionary People at War: The Continental Army and American Character, 1775–1788* (Chapel Hill, 1979), p. 288.
2. Richard M. Ketchum, *Victory at Yorktown: The Campaign that Won the Revolution* (New York: Henry Holt, 2004), p. 10.
3. Ibid., p. 11.
4. Royster, *A Revolutionary People at War*, p. 288.
5. Ibid., p. 288.
6. Ketchum cites Loyalist William Smith Jr. in New York, who wrote of a French alliance, "I dread France—She will be guided only by motives of Interest. No Promises will bind her—She will perceive it more advantageous to her Ambition to foment animosities than hastily to plunge into a War—She will deceive both Parties that her ends may be achieved at our Expense." Ketchum, pp. 9–10.
7. Ibid., pp. 155–156.
8. Carl van Doren, *Secret History of the American Revolution* (New York, 1941). p. 181.

INDEX

A

Abercrombie, James, 32
Acland, Major John Dyke, 4, 221
Active, 253
Adams, John
  Board of War and, 184
  Boston Massacre and, 66
  challenges for, 328, 341
  Continental Congress and, 81, 294
  on French alliance, 229
  honor and, 263
  promotions and, xix, 174
Adams, Sam, 72, 172
Adolphus, Gustavus, 285
Albany, 2–9, 31–39, 97–99, 184–200,
  208–209, 220–226
Allen, Enos, 58
Allen, Ethan, 84–85, 110, 125–126,
  270, 284–285
Allen, Joseph, 85
Allen, Mary, 85
Allen, Colonel Solomon, 317, 320
Amherst, General Jeffrey, 88, 109
Anderson, Fred, 37
Anderson, John, 286, 308–309, 317–
  320, 331. *See also* André, Major
  John

André, Major John
  arrest of, 319–322
  code name for, 286, 308–309,
    317–320, 331
  courier for, 284
  death of, 337–338, 342
  escape route of, 315, 317–320
  execution of, xvii, 331, 337–338,
    342
  fate of, 331–339, 341–343
  as soldier, 128, 243
  as spy, 284–293, 301–325
  treason and, 301–313, 320–322
Andrews, Joseph, 286, 291. *And see*
  Major John André
Aquidneck Island, 168, 171
Armstrong, Major John, 2, 216, 225
Arnold, Benedict
  anti-French feelings of, 28–32,
    38–40, 50–51
  apprenticeship of, xvi, xviii, 27–31,
    34, 40–46
  arrest of, 57–59, 267
  betrayal by, xii
  birth of, 14
  business career of, 20–25, 41–44,
    46–68, 106, 135–136, 181

INDEX

campaigns of, xvi, 74–96, 108–115, 119–124, 131–166, 169

charges against, 270–274

childhood of, xvi, 14–18

code name of, 285–300

Continental Army and, xix, 183, 245, 254, 289

Continental Congress and, 93–98, 102–110, 139, 239–240, 268

corresponding with British, 285–303, 358

courier for, 284, 302

court martial against, xi, xvi, xix, 11, 75, 150–155, 167, 260–285, 290–292, 325, 356

death of, 353

defection of, xiv–xviii, 278, 304, 322–323, 328–329, 355–359

duels and, 67–69, 89, 154, 256, 351–352

enemies of, xvi–xix, 4, 9, 16, 67–68, 88–91, 94, 101, 110, 138–139, 145, 150–153, 167–171, 175, 179, 184, 192–194, 204–205, 264–265, 277–279, 289, 355–357

escape route of, 315, 322–323

exile of, xvii, 350–353

expectations of, 11–22

father of, xvi, xviii, 11–28, 42–49, 59, 356

first wife of, 53, 60–64, 67–70, 98–100

flight of, xi, xvii, xx, 316–317, 321–330, 342–344

freemasonry membership of, 52

George Washington and, xiv–xx, xvi, 8–9, 105–115, 120–122, 131–132, 138–143, 168–198, 204, 218, 235, 240–276, 280–285, 292–299, 304–310, 316–328, 338, 340, 344, 356–357

as governor, 240–258

Henry Clinton and, 285–288, 294, 309, 311–313, 347–348

as hero, xii–xvi, 1–3, 9, 166–169, 175–180, 218, 245, 323, 339, 355–356, 359

honor and, xii, xviii, 1–12, 21, 74–83, 355–359

Horatio Gates and, 144, 150–158, 168–169

injuries of, xv, 1–4, 10, 134–135, 223–226

marriages of, 60–64, 258–259

memorial to, xx

mother of, 13–27, 43, 53, 259

navy plans of, 250–253, 256, 292, 356

Pennsylvania Executive Council and, xix, 240, 243–259, 262–266, 271–274, 279–282, 327–330, 355–356

Philip Schuyler and, xvi, 9, 97–99, 102, 152–153, 157, 167, 171, 240, 296–297

plot of, 291, 295–301, 307–317, 321–335, 341–342, 351–353

as politician, 240–258

promotions and, 7–8, 138–140, 173–183, 236, 278, 356

reprimanding, 274–275

resignation of, 177–178, 184, 192–194, 265, 274, 279, 287, 358

rumors about, 67–69

schooling for, xvi, xviii, 16–22

second wife of, xi–xvii, 258–259, 267, 284–292, 299, 305–307, 316–317, 323–330, 335, 346, 350–353, 358

self-defense of, 272–274

serving country, 74–96, 108–115, 119–124, 131–166, 181–183

shipping business and, 20–25, 41–44, 47–59, 62–68, 100, 148–149, 192, 358 sister of, 9, 17–18, 23, 43–45, 49–51, 63, 67, 95, 99–100, 136, 146–151, 167–170, 238, 259, 279, 305–306, 328–329, 350, 353

sons of, 62, 69, 100, 169, 239, 246–248, 259, 279, 289, 292, 305–306, 328–329, 346, 350–353

treason and, xi–xiii, xvii, 166, 245, 266, 301–313, 320–321

wilderness expeditions and, xvi, 108–115, 119–124, 131–139, 169

Arnold, Benedict (father), xvi, xviii, 11–28, 42–49

Arnold, Edward Shippen (son), 247–248, 292, 305–306

Arnold, Governor Benedict (great-grandfather), 12, 247

Arnold, Hannah (sister)

  annuity for, 352–353

  correspondence with, 95, 99, 136, 146–150

  court martial and, 279

  exile of Benedict and, 350

  family of, 9, 17–18, 43–45

  flight of Benedict and, 328–329

  French suitor of, 50–51

  rumors and, 67

  shipping business and, 63, 100–101, 148, 238

  sons of Benedict and, 169, 259, 279, 305–306, 328–329, 350, 352–353

Arnold, Hannah Waterman (mother), 13–27, 43, 53, 259

Arnold, Henry (son), 62, 100, 305, 328, 350, 352–353

Arnold, Isaac Newton, xiv, 1, 202

Arnold, James Robertson, 346

Arnold, Margaret Mansfield (first wife), 53, 60–64, 67–70, 98–100

Arnold, Margaret Shippen "Peggy." See also Shippen, Margaret

  courtship of, 250–257

early years of, 246–249

exile of Benedict and, 350–353

family of, 246–249

flight of Benedict and, 316–317, 323–325, 327–330

George Washington and, 316–317, 335

managing household, 289, 350–353, 358

marriage of, 258–259

meeting Benedict Arnold, 249

rumors about, 299, 325–327

sons of, 289, 292, 305–307, 346

treason and, xi–xv

understanding, xi–xvii

Arnold, Oliver, 12–14, 48

Arnold, Richard (son), 62, 100, 350, 352–353

Austin, Polly, 70

Avery, Rufus, 347–348

B

Babcock, Adam, 50, 69–70

Babcock, Dr. Joshua, 50

Balcarras, Earl, 223

Baldwin, Colonel Jeduthan, 209

Battersby, Captain, 337

Baum, Colonel Friedrich, 206–208

Bedel, Colonel Timothy, 142

Beebe, Dr. Lewis, 153

Bemis Heights, 1–4, 10, 202, 209–210

Bennington, 86, 204–208

Berkshire Mountains, 83

Betsy, 92–93

Bigelow, Major Timothy, 111

Blackstone, William, xviii, 172, 288

Blakeslee, Titley, 57

Board of War, 173, 183–184, 235–237, 256, 338

Boileau, Nicholas, vii

Boles, Peter, 56–58

Boston Massacre, 66, 70–71, 77, 173

Bouchette, Captain Jean Baptiste, 130
Bowler, Metcalf, 285
Bradstreet, John, 103
Brandywine, 235, 269
Brant, Chief Joseph, 199
Brant, Molly, 199
Bray, Asa, 2, 225
Breed's Hill, 103–104
Breymann, Colonel, 224
Breymann Redoubt, 223–224
British army
  challenges of, 32
  corresponding with, 285–303, 358
  defection to, xiv–xviii, 278, 304, 322–323, 328–329, 355–359
  serving with, xii, xx, 80, 103–104, 108, 125–126
  support for, 53–54, 117, 142
  surrender of, 6, 226–227, 232–235, 350
  vulnerability of, 2
  West Point plot and, 295–301, 307–317, 331–332, 341–342
Brooks, Lieutenant Colonel John, 218, 223
Brown, Dr. James, 5
Brown, John
  as agent, 82
  as enemy of Arnold, 94, 101, 110, 138–139, 150–151, 167–168, 171, 175, 184, 192–194
  Fort Ticonderoga and, 87–91, 94–97, 151
  secret journeys of, 118, 125–126
Brown University, 168
Bunker Hill, 103, 206
Burd, Edward "Neddy," 247, 267, 330
Burgoyne, General John
  correspondence with, 163, 212–213
  New York and, 184–197, 219–220, 235, 256, 273

  reinforcements against, 235
  rescuing, xx, 2, 6
Burke, Edmund, 230
Burr, Aaron, 111, 326
Butterfield, Major John, 142

C
Cahoon, Joseph, 312
Cahoon, Samuel, 311–312
Cambridge, 74, 79–81, 94–96, 102–113, 119, 132, 206
Campbell, Captain George, 267
Campbell, John, Lord Loudoun, 31–33
Canterbury, 16–17, 22, 30
Cape Diamond, 133
Carleton, General Sir Guy, 111, 116–117, 130, 160
Carlisle Commission, 230–232, 282, 358
Carlton, 160–161, 163
Carroll, Charles, 141
Carroll, Reverend John, 141
Casparus Mabie Tavern, 333
Catamount Tavern, 86
Cedars, The, 142, 144
Chambers, Colonel Stephen, 267
Charles I, King of England, 77, 171
Charles II, King of England, 231, 286
Charles River, 80, 103
Charming Nancy, 252, 272
Chase, Samuel, 141
Chatham, William Pitt Lord, 32, 231
Chaudiere River, 108, 120
Cheeseman, Captain Jacob, 136
Chestnut Neck, 253
Chew, Peggy, 288
Christie, General Gabriel, 33
Church, Dr. Benjamin, 105, 285
Cilley, Colonel Joseph, 221
Clarke, Sir Francis, 219, 223
Clarkson, Matthew, 204

Clinton, General Henry
  Benedict Arnold and, 285–288, 294,
    309, 311–313, 347–348
  capturing Charleston, 335, 344
  correspondence with, 212–213,
    219–220, 230–232, 284–286,
    322–323, 335–337, 340
  New York and, 6, 212–213
  report to, 347–348
  West Point and, 298–299
Coercive Acts, 230
Cogswell, Reverend James, 16, 22
Cohen, Eliot, xvii, 126
Colburn, Captain Oliver, 114
College of New Jersey, 247
College of Rhode Island, 168
Concord, 72–78, 86, 93, 104, 118, 341,
  348
Congress, 160–165
Connecticut River, 85
Conspiracy, 288–289, 301–325, 337
Continental Army/Continentals
  Benedict Arnold and, xix, 183, 245,
    254, 289
  formation of, xix–xx
  intelligence about, 289, 348
  militia and, 200, 210, 254, 272, 295
  officers of, xiii, 109, 183, 237, 245,
    325, 340, 348, 356
  training, 237
  troops of, 4, 221, 229
Continental Congress
  court martial and, 291
  Fort Ticonderoga and, 94–98
  George Washington and, 81
  Intolerable Acts and, 71
  John Adams and, 81
  promotions by, 139, 173–174, 190
  Quebec Act and, 118
  ratifying treaties, 227–235
  role of, xix, 102–110, 173–174,
    227–240, 357

seeking help from, 268
supporters in, 207–208
Convention, 253
Conway, Thomas, 173, 236–238
"Conway Cabal," 238
Cornwallis, General Charles, 342,
  350
Court martial, xi, xvi, xix, 11, 75,
  150–155, 167, 260–285, 290–292,
  325, 356
Cromwell, Oliver, xiv, xvi, 171, 245,
  285, 357
Croskie, Captain, 68–69

D
Dacres, Lieutenant James, 166
Dalrymple, Sir John, 231
Danbury, 181
Dartmouth, William, Lord, 88, 128,
  131
de Champlain, Samuel, 129
de Vaudreuil, Marquis, 31, 38
Dead River, 120, 122
Deane, Barnabas, 104
Deane, Silas, 104–105, 110, 261, 285,
  293–295, 350
Dearborn, Captain Henry, 1, 5, 210–
  211, 219, 221, 224–225
DeBlois, Elizabeth "Betsy," 170,
  238–239, 249
Declaration of Independence, 11, 52,
  187, 241–242, 249, 266, 341
Declaratory Act, 65
Defection, xiv–xviii, 278, 304, 322–
  323, 328–329, 355–359
Delancey, Captain James, 39
Delaware River, 169, 191, 208, 246, 252
d'Estaing, Charles Henri Hector,
  Comte, 231
Dickinson, John, 243
Digby, Lieutenant William, 6, 165,
  223–224

Dobbs Ferry, 306–311
Döhla, Johann, 341
"Don't Tread on Me" flag, 162, 164–165
Dryden, John, 49
Duels, 67–69, 89, 111, 154, 256, 269, 351–352
Dundas, Colonel Thomas, 343

E
Easton, Colonel James
  as commander, 87
  as enemy of Arnold, 94, 101, 138–139
  Fort Ticonderoga and, 87, 89, 94, 97
Egg Harbor, 253, 257
Elliot, Lieutenant-General George, 334
English Bill of Rights, 54, 66, 171–172
Enos, Lieutenant Colonel Roger, 111, 122, 132, 141, 152
Enterprise, 156
Eustis, Dr. William, 309, 317
Ewald, Captain Johann, vii, 342–346

F
Fell, 130–131
Foot Guards, 72, 75, 78–79, 169. *See also* Militia
Forsey, Hannah, 24
Fort Anne, 210
Fort Arnold, 296
Fort Bull, 32
Fort Carillon, 36, 87
Fort Chambly, 126–127, 153–154
Fort Crown Point
  attack on, 80–82, 87–88, 156, 160–165
  capture of, 165, 184
  governorship of, 92

successes at, 92, 95, 101, 104, 107–110
Fort Dayton, 201
Fort Edward, 33–39, 194–197, 205–206, 210
Fort Frontenac, 103
Fort Griswold, 346–347
Fort Oswego, 31, 186
Fort Putnam, 296, 321, 331
Fort Saint Jean, 119
Fort St. Johns, 92–93, 100, 125–133, 145, 156
Fort Schuyler, 196
Fort Stanwix, xvi, 196–205, 220
Fort Sullivan, 294
Fort Ticonderoga
  abandoning, 184, 268–270
  attack on, 80–82, 87–88
  capture of, xvi, 32, 80–97, 99–103, 106–110, 184, 197–200
  governorship of, 92
  holding, 203
  journey to, 165–169
  retaking, 210–213
  successes at, 92, 95, 107
  surrender of, 191–192, 198
Fort Trumbull, 163, 346–347
Fort Washington, 168–169
Fort Western, 120–121
Fort William Henry, 31–35, 38–39, 85, 189, 228
Fortescue, J. W., xii, xix, 166, 222, 229, 278, 314, 332
Fortune, 50–51, 56
Foster, Captain Jedediah, 142–144
Fox, Charles, 351
Fox, Edward, 285
Franklin, Benjamin, 52, 137, 141, 150, 243, 285, 294, 341
Franks, Major David Solebury, 246, 254, 259, 289, 309–310, 316–317, 321–329

Fraser, Brigadier General Simon, 191, 195–196, 210–212, 221–224
Freeman, Isaac, 210
Freeman's Farm, 3, 210–211
Freemasonry, 52
French and Indian War, 4, 19, 29–44, 49–53, 76, 80, 85, 103, 108
Fuller, Asa, 24

G
Gage, General Thomas, 71–74, 88, 108, 117–120, 142, 186, 285
Gansevoort, Colonel Peter, 199
Gatchell, John, 108
Gates, General Horatio
  battles and, xv, xx, 2–7
  Benedict Arnold and, 144, 150–158, 168–169
  Board of War and, 173
  correspondence with, 144, 166–169
  defeat of, 305–308, 328
  honors for, 2–7, 10, 222–225, 235–238, 279, 356
  Lake Champlain and, 179–180
  Philip Schuyler and, 152, 157, 180, 190, 197–198
  reports to, 150–158
  role of, 109, 176, 190–192
  supporters of, 198–225
General McDougall, 238
George I, King of England, 48
George III, King of England, 71, 76–77, 100, 187, 228
Germain, Lord George, 185–186, 202–204, 211, 230, 285
Germantown, 235–236, 269
Giles, Major, 289
Glover, John, 151, 208, 210, 212, 223
Graves, Vice Admiral Samuel, 119
Great Carrying Place, 120–121
Great Warpath, 88–89, 92–93, 107–108, 296

Green Mountain Boys, 83, 84, 86, 91, 94, 104, 207
Greene, Major Christopher, 111, 122
Greene, General Nathanael, 177, 261, 304, 307, 328, 335–336
Grey, General Charles, 286

H
Haldimand, Major General Frederick, 88
Hale, Nathan, 331–332
Hamilton, Alexander, xv, 111, 237, 310, 316, 326, 333, 336
Hancock, John, 52, 72, 139, 154, 192–193, 214
Hand's Cove, 90
Hawke, Edward Lord, 351
Hawley, Captain David, 160
Hay, Udney, 209
Hazen, Colonel Moses, 153–155, 167
Heath, General William, 348–349
Hele, Lieutenant Christopher, 282
Hendricks, Captain William, 111–112
Henry, John Joseph, 112, 123
Henry, Patrick, 235
Herkimer, Brigadier General Nicholas, 199–201
Heron, William, 285
Hessians, 2, 160, 169, 186, 189, 197, 318, 341–342
Hide, Justice Richard, 24
Hingham, 9, 12
Hinman, Colonel Benjamin, 94–96
Hobby, Remington, 108
Honor
  denigrating, xviii, 7–10, 175–184
  dire events and, 116–128
  duels and, 61–73
  price of, xii, 1–10, 356–359
  public calamity and, 99–115
  quest for, xviii, 1–12, 21
  serving country and, 74–83

Howard, Maria, 118
Howe, Major General Robert
    correspondence with, 203
    court martial and, 269, 274
    duel and, 269
    mission of, 80, 186–187, 192
    New York and, 213, 219–220
    West Point and, 303
Hudson River
    advances along, 3, 32, 142, 205,
       208, 213, 284, 322–323
    command posts on, 183–186, 194,
       209–210, 295–306
    crossing, 205, 209–210
    escape route along, 315
    intelligence about, 290–291
    jurisdiction over, 85
    map of, 217, 315
    West Point and, 295–301, 322–323
Huguenot, 302
Huntington, Lieutenant Colonel
    Jedediah, 357

I
Île aux Noix, 126–127
Import duties, 51, 53–56, 59, 61, 65,
    76–77
Indians
    Boston Massacre and, 70–71
    forces of, xx, 115, 119, 127–128,
       142–143, 159, 186, 206, 210–211
    French and Indian War, 4, 19,
       29–44, 49–53, 76, 80, 85, 103, 108
    Huron Indians, 194–196
    massacre by, 194–201
    meeting with, 124
    Mohegan Indians, 13–15, 23
Inflexible, 156, 160–161
Ingersoll, Jared, 55–58, 64, 67, 85, 278
Intolerable Acts, 71–72, 76, 118
Irvine, William, 270
Isle La Motte, 125

J
James River, 343
Jameson, John, 308, 317, 320–321, 325
Jay, John, 52, 257, 273, 279, 341
Jefferson, Thomas, 341, 344
Jersey, 164
Jewett, Dr., 15
Jockey Hollow, 262
Johnstone, George, 233
Jones, David, 195
Jones, John Paul, 52
Jonson, Ben, 49

K
Kennebec River, 108, 114–115, 120
Kennebec Valley, 114
King, Absolom, 13–14
King, Lieutenant Joshua, 321
Knox, Colonel Henry, 170, 177, 234,
    242, 269–270, 316, 321–322
Knox, Lucy, 170
Knyphausen, General Wilhelm von,
    307, 341
Kosciuszko, Thaddeus, 209, 295

L
La Chine, Quebec, 153
La Chute River, 32–33
La Corne, St. Luc, 189, 196
Lafayette, Major General Marquis
    de, xix, 293–294, 316, 321–322,
    356–357
Lake Champlain
    attacks at, 30–32, 92–95, 155–157
    location of, 87–88, 147, 155
    map of, 147
    militia at, 131
    protecting, 142–144, 150
    successes at, xvi, 93, 95–97, 107,
       175, 179–180, 185–186, 250
Lake George, 30–33, 87–88, 150, 155,
    205

INDEX

Lake Ontario, 30–31, 186, 197
Lamb, John, 169, 170, 205, 234, 304
Lamb, Roger, 6
Larvey, Corporal James, 323
Lathrop, Daniel, 26–27
Lathrop, Jerusha, 27
Lathrop, Joshua, 26
Latimer, Colonel Jonathan, 216
Lauderdale, James Maitland, Lord, 351
Laurens, Henry, 8, 54, 232, 234
Laurens, John, 228, 325
Lea, Russell M., xiv
Learned, General Ebenezer, 200, 208, 210, 212, 216, 219–222
Ledyard, Colonel William, 347–349
Lee, Charles, 109, 140, 155, 285
Lee, Richard Henry, 176, 180, 236
Lee, William, 293–294
Lexington, 72–78, 86, 93, 118, 341, 348
Libel, 67, 184
Liberty, 92–93, 156–157
Lincoln, General Benjamin, 5, 8, 176, 206–207, 210, 213, 295
Livingston, Colonel James, 133, 306
Livingston, Major Henry Brockholst, 204, 214
Livingston, Robert, 128
Locke, John, 49
Lord, Reverend Benjamin, 14
Louis XVI, King of France, 227–228
Louisbourg, 32
Loyal Convert, 160

M
MacPherson, Captain John, 136
Mansfield, Margaret, 53, 60, 100. *See also* Arnold, Margaret Mansfield
Mansfield, Samuel, 52–53, 61, 100, 170
Maria, 160

Marshall, Colonel Thomas, 214
Martin, James Kirby, xiv
Martin, Joseph Plumb, 314
Mason, George, 357
Massachusetts Bay Colony, 12, 71
Massachusetts Charter, 71, 77–78
Massachusetts Committee of Safety, 74–75, 91, 93
Matlack, Timothy, 243, 254–258, 272
Mattoon, Ebenezer, 224
Maxwell, Brigadier General William, 179–180
McCrea, Jane, 194–196, 199
McDougall, General Alexander, 182, 238
McHenry, Captain James, 310
McNeil, Mrs. Sarah, 195
Mease, James, 252
Meigs, Major Return Jonathan, 111, 137, 309
Mifflin, Thomas, 235
Militia
    Canadian militia, 31, 119, 126–127, 131, 135, 140
    citizen militia, xviii, 66–67, 71–74, 80–81, 106, 119, 171
    Connecticut militia, xix, 2, 9, 14, 28–41, 51, 78, 85, 181–182, 207–213, 225
    Continental Army and, 200, 210, 254, 272, 295
    Fairfax militia, 106, 112
    Maine militia, 114
    Minutemen and, 71–72
    mob of, 267
    New England militia, 33, 198
    New Hampshire militia, 114
    New Haven militia, 72, 75, 78–79, 169
    New York militia, 39, 203, 208, 221
    Norwich militia, 30–34

405

raising, 103, 168–176
training, 254–256
Minutemen, 71–72
Mississippi River, 30
Mohawk River, 186, 196–197, 208–209
Mohawk Valley, 30, 184, 196, 238
Mohegan Indians, 13–15, 23
Monk, George, 231, 285
Monk, Gustavus, 277, 285–300. *See also* Arnold, Benedict
Monroe, James, 52
Montcalm, Major-General Louis-Joseph, 31–39
Montgomery, Brigadier General Richard, 109, 117, 125–145, 153–156, 168, 199, 270
Montreal
attack on, 126–130
command of, 141–145
possession of, 31, 107–109, 130–135
supplies taken from, 152–154, 175–176, 258
Montresor, Colonel John, 108–109, 115
Morgan, Daniel, 111, 169
Morris, Robert, 243, 267, 299
Mott, Captain Edward, 84
Mount Pleasant, 259
Mount Vernon, 236
Munro, Lieutenant Colonel George, 35–36
Mutiny Act, 172

N
Natanis, Chief, 124
Neilson, John, 209
New Hampshire Grants, 85
New Haven
business career in, 46–62, 106, 135–136, 181
family in, 95, 99–101, 149–150, 169–170, 180–181, 263, 312–313

house in, 100, 312–313, 329
militia in, 72, 75, 78–79, 169
recuperating in, 9, 226, 263
return to, 99–101, 105–106, 180–181, 226, 239, 263
rumors in, 66–67
schooling in, 16, 89
New York, 161, 163–164
New York, defending, 1–10, 184–200, 202–229
Newburyport, 114–115
Newport, 21, 168, 297, 300
Nixon, John, 210, 219
Norridgewock Falls, 121
Norris's Tavern, 262, 274
North, Frederick Lord, 229
North Castle, 317, 320
Norwich
family in, 13–26, 41–43, 59, 69
hometown of, 13–26, 41–45, 216, 346–347
militia in, 30–34
plague in, 17–18
return to, 21–22, 49–50
rioting in, 328

O
Odell, Reverend Jonathan, 286
Ohio Valley, 30, 33
Oliver, Lieutenant Governor Andrew, 81
Olmsted, Gideon, 253
Oriskany, 199–200
Oswald, Eleazer, 169
Otis, James, 52

P
Palmer, Dave R., xiv
Parsons, Colonel Samuel, 80, 86–87, 284
Paterson, John, 210, 214
Paulding, John, 318–319

Peale, Charles Willson, 266

Peekskill, 183, 205, 309–310

Peggy, 100

Pennsylvania Executive Council, xix, 240, 243–259, 262–266, 271–274, 279–282, 327–330, 355–356

Pennsylvania Packet, 257–258

Philadelphia, 161

Philbrick, Nathaniel, xiv

Pitt, William Lord Chatham, 32, 231

Point Levi, 124

Pointe-aux-Trembles, 130

Polly, 181

Poor, Colonel Enoch, 152–154, 208–212, 221

Potts, Dr. Jonathan Potts, 5

Pownall, Governor Thomas, 35

Prescott, General Richard, 126–127

Princeton, 169, 190

Princeton University, 247

Pringle, Lieutenant Thomas, 156, 160

Prior, Matthew, 49

Providence, 163–164

Putnam, General Israel, 79–80, 284

Q

Quebec Act, 71, 117–118

Quebec City
  attack on, 2, 105–109, 116, 125, 131–141, 223, 270
  complaints about, 151–152
  defending, 31–32, 38
  expedition to, 3, 100, 105–111, 120–123, 151–155, 169–170, 183
  location of, 129–130
  possession of, 141–144
  success at, 128, 175
  voyages to, 50, 63

R

Randall, Willard Sterne, xiv

Rankin, William, 285

Rawdon, Francis Edward Lord, 248

Redman, John, 2, 223

Reed, Joseph, 232, 243–245, 257–259, 265–267, 280–281, 291, 329

Revenge, 156–157

Revere, Paul, 52, 66, 173

Revolutionary War
  conspiracy during, 288–289, 301–325, 312
  fate of, 206–209
  support for, 328
  views on, xii, xiv–xx, 1–3, 10, 278, 294, 328, 339–341

Rhinebeck, 137

Richelieu River, 92, 125, 155

Ridgefield, 181–182

Riedesel, General Friedrich von, 210

Riots, 266–267, 328

Robertson, Lieutenant-General James, 334, 346

Robinson, Colonel Beverly, 282–284, 303–312, 316–318, 321–325, 335

Rodney, Admiral Sir George, 303

Rogers' Rangers, 206

Ross, Captain, 113

Royal Gazette, 258

Royal Savage, 125, 156, 159–161, 184

Royster, Charles, xiv, 278, 356–357

Rush, Benjamin, 17, 243

S

Sabatis, 124

Sage, Comfort, 9, 51, 67, 226, 238, 328

St. Anne, 142

St. Charles River, 129

St. Clair, Arthur, 179–180, 184, 191–192, 198, 213, 269

St. George's Key, 66

St. Lawrence River, 105, 120–130, 142, 155, 186, 192

St. Leger, Lieutenant Colonel Barry, 186–187, 192, 197–201, 220
St. Paul's Church, 137
St. Roch's, 139
Salem, 71, 320–321
Sally, 64
Saratoga
   battle of, xii, xv–xx, 1–8, 217, 305
   concerns about, 202–203, 210
   hero of, xii, xiv–xvi, 1–3
   map of, 217
   victory at, 226–229, 235–237, 279, 356
Saratoga memorial, xx
Sault-au-Matelot, 134
Scammell, Adjutant General Colonel Alexander, xi, 322
Schuyler, Elizabeth, 326
Schuyler, Hon Yost, 201
Schuyler, General Philip
   Benedict Arnold and, xvi, 9, 97–99, 102, 152–153, 157, 167, 171, 240, 296–297
   British proposition and, 284
   Continental Congress and, 102–111
   correspondence with, 124, 127, 141, 144–145, 166, 214–215, 224
   court martial against, 184, 268–269
   Horatio Gates and, 152, 157, 180, 190, 197–198
   replacing, 180, 191, 197–199
   wilderness expeditions and, 109–115, 119, 124
Schuylkill River, 247, 259
Scott, Major John, 154
Sears, Isaac, 54
Secret agents, 284, 304. *See also* Spies
Secret History of the American Revolution, xv
Senter, Dr. Isaac, 122, 134–135

Shafer, John, 123
Shaw, Major Samuel, 234–235, 310
Sherburne, Major, 142–143
Sherman, Roger, 57
Shetucket River, 13
Shewell, Robert, 252, 272
Shippen, Edward, 246
Shippen, Hannah, 246
Shippen, Judge Edward, 247
Shippen, Margaret "Peggy," xi–xvii, 246–250, 258–259. *See also* Arnold, Margaret Shippen
Shirley, William, 31
Silliman, General Gold Selleck, 181–182
Simcoe, Colonel John Graves, 343
Skene, Major Philip, 90, 92, 205
Skenesborough, 92, 205
Skowhegan Falls, 120
Slander, 152, 184, 197, 258
Smith, Joshua Hett, 307, 309–318, 331–333
Smith, Captain Matthew, 111
Smith, Solomon, 28
Smith, Chief Justice William, 334
Smith, Widow, 15
Smugglers, 53–57, 70
Sons of Liberty, 54, 66, 70, 278
South Salem, 320–321
Sparks, Jared, xiii, 166
Spies, xvii, 125, 131, 284–299, 301–325, 332–336
Spooner, Walter, 96
Spooner Committee, 96–97, 101
Spuyten Duyvil, 307
Stamp Act, 54–55, 58, 65, 76
Stansbury, Joseph, 187–190, 284–290, 302
Stark, John, 177, 206–207
Stark, Molly, 207
Stillwater, 204, 209
Stockbridge, 83

Stocking, Abner, 115, 119, 122–123, 133
Stony Point, 299, 306, 317, 332
Sugar Act, 54
Sugar Tax, 53–54
Sullivan, General John, 145, 153–154, 177, 269, 284
Sutherland, Andrew, 311
Swallow, 119

T
Tallmadge, Major Benjamin, 308, 320, 331–332
Tarrytown, 308
Taxes, 51, 53–56, 59, 61, 65, 76–77
Taylor, Daniel, 219
Tea Act, 70
Thacher, Dr. James, 4–5, 273, 338
Thames River, 13
Thomas, General John, 142–145
Thompson, Benjamin, 114
Thunderer, 156, 161
Ticonderoga, xvi. *See also* Fort Ticonderoga
Ticonic Falls, 120
Tories, 105–106, 182, 197, 220, 310
Townshend Act, 65, 70
Trade restrictions, 51, 53–59, 61, 65, 76–77
Trap, Ede, 24
Treason, xi–xiii, xvii, 166, 245, 266, 301–325
Treaties, 227–235
Trenton, 169, 177, 190, 248, 256
Trois-Rivières, 130
Trumbull, 163
Trumbull, General Jonathan, 348
Tryon, William, 181, 189
Tyburn, 127

U
Uncas, Chief Benjamin, 23
University of Pennsylvania, 247

V
Valcour Island, 147, 158–163, 166
Valencia de Alcántara, 186
Valley Forge, 8, 234, 237–239, 242, 248, 252, 264, 271
Van der Capellen, Baron Godert, 328
Van Doren, Carl, xv, 252, 289, 357–358
Van Rensselaer, Catherine, 103
Van Schaick Island, 208
Van Vechten, Lieutenant Tobias, 195
Van Wart, Isaac, 318
Varick, Lieutenant Colonel Richard, 166, 204, 208, 289, 309, 316, 324–326
Vassall, John, 105–106
Verplanck's Point, 306, 323
Vulcan, 331
Vulture, 307, 310–313, 316, 323, 353

W
Walker, Lewis Burd, xiii
Walpole, Horace, 231
Warner, Seth, 92, 206–207
Warpath, 88–89, 92–93, 107–108, 296
Warren, Dr. Joseph, 77, 82
Washington, 161, 163–164
Washington, George
    Benedict Arnold and, xiv–xx, xvi, 8–9, 105–115, 120–122, 131–132, 138–143, 168–198, 204, 218, 235, 240–276, 280–285, 292–299, 304–310, 316–328, 338, 340, 344, 356–357
    bribes offered to, 231
    Continental Congress and, 7–8, 81, 232
    correspondence with, 153–155, 232–233, 237–238, 333–338
    criticism against, 235–237
    crossing Delaware River, 169, 191, 208

freemasonry membership of, 52
mutinies and, 340
role of, 30, 96–97, 151–152, 234–236
treaties and, 228–229
Valley Forge and, 8, 234, 237–239, 248, 264
Waterbury, General David, 162–164, 179
Waterman, Jr., Ebenezer, 13, 24
Wayne, Anthony, 269, 286
Webb, General Daniel, 33–36, 39
Wentworth, Lemuel, 24
West, William, 252
West Point plot, 291, 295–301, 307–317, 321–335, 341–342, 351–353
Westminster Abbey, 338
White, Bishop William, 259
Wigglesworth, Colonel Edward, 162–163
Wilderness expeditions, xvi, 108–115, 119–124, 131–139, 169
Wilkinson, Major James, 7, 145, 209, 213, 219, 237

Willett, Lieutenant Colonel Marinus, 199
Williams, Jonathan, 293, 318–319
Williams, Roger, 12
Wilson, James, xix, 243, 266–267, 291
Windward Islands, 256
Winship, Elizabeth, 24
Wise, John, 57
Wolfe, General James, 116, 129
Woodford, Brigadier General William, 344
Woodworth, Widow, 15
Wooster, Colonel David, 58, 78, 135–137, 140–142, 181
Wynkoop, Captain Jacob, 150–151, 157

Y
Yale, Elihu, 48
Yale College, 16, 26, 46–49, 53, 89, 331
Yale University, xviii
Yantic River, 13